VOICING IDENTITY

MW00813411

Cultural Appropriation and Indigenous Issues

Edited by John Borrows and Kent McNeil

Written by leading Indigenous and non-Indigenous scholars, *Voicing Identity* examines the issue of cultural appropriation in the contexts of researching, writing, and teaching about Indigenous peoples. This book grapples with the questions of who is qualified to engage in these activities and how this can be done appropriately and respectfully.

The authors address these questions from their individual perspectives and experiences, often revealing their personal struggles and their ongoing attempts to resolve them. There is diversity in perspectives and approaches, but also a common goal: to conduct research and teach in respectful ways that enhance understanding of Indigenous histories, cultures, and rights, and promote reconciliation between Indigenous and non-Indigenous peoples.

Bringing together contributors with diverse backgrounds and unique experiences, *Voicing Identity* will be of interest to students and scholars studying Indigenous issues as well as anyone seeking to engage in the work of making Canada a model for just relations between the original peoples and newcomers.

JOHN BORROWS is a professor of law and Canada Research Chair in Indigenous Law at the University of Victoria Law School.

KENT MCNEIL is an emeritus distinguished research professor at Osgoode Hall Law School at York University.

Voicing Identity

Cultural Appropriation and
Indigenous Issues

EDITED BY JOHN BORROWS AND KENT MCNEIL

UNIVERSITY OF TORONTO PRESS
Toronto Buffalo London

© University of Toronto Press 2022
Toronto Buffalo London
utorontopress.com
Printed in Canada

ISBN 978-1-4875-4467-6 (cloth)   ISBN 978-1-4875-4469-0 (EPUB)
ISBN 978-1-4875-4468-3 (paper)   ISBN 978-1-4875-4470-6 (PDF)

Library and Archives Canada Cataloguing in Publication

Title: Voicing identity : cultural appropriation and Indigenous issues / edited
   by John Borrows and Kent McNeil.
Names: Borrows, John, 1963– editor. | McNeil, Kent, 1945– editor.
Description: Includes index.
Identifiers: Canadiana (print) 20220389195 | Canadiana (ebook) 2022038939X |
   ISBN 9781487544683 (softcover) | ISBN 9781487544676 (hardcover) |
   ISBN 9781487544690 (EPUB) | ISBN 9781487544706 (PDF)
Subjects: LCSH: Indigenous peoples – Research – Moral and ethical aspects –
   Canada. | LCSH: Indigenous peoples – History – Research – Moral and
   ethical aspects – Canada. | LCSH: Indigenous peoples – Study and teaching –
   Moral and ethical aspects – Canada. | LCSH: Indigenous peoples – History –
   Study and teaching – Moral and ethical aspects – Canada. | LCSH: Cultural
   appropriation – Canada. | LCSH: Canada – Ethnic relations.
Classification: LCC E76.7 .V65 2022 | DDC 971.004/970072 – dc23

We wish to acknowledge the land on which the University of Toronto Press
operates. This land is the traditional territory of the Wendat, the Anishnaabeg, the
Haudenosaunee, the Métis, and the Mississaugas of the Credit First Nation.

University of Toronto Press acknowledges the financial support of the Government
of Canada, the Canada Council for the Arts, and the Ontario Arts Council, an
agency of the Government of Ontario, for its publishing activities.

Canada Council   Conseil des Arts
for the Arts   du Canada

ONTARIO ARTS COUNCIL
CONSEIL DES ARTS DE L'ONTARIO
an Ontario government agency
un organisme du gouvernement de l'Ontario

Funded by the   Financé par le
Government   gouvernement
of Canada   du Canada

Canadä

MIX
Paper from
responsible sources
FSC® C016245

Contents

VOICING IDENTITY

Cultural Appropriation and Indigenous Issues

Introduction

JOHN BORROWS AND KENT MCNEIL

Issues of Indigenous voice and cultural appropriation permeate many aspects of North American life. Museums often acquired Indigenous artefacts and artworks without permission and without regard to their cultural and spiritual significance. Other egregious examples of appropriation can be seen in the naming of sports teams and mascots and in the tourism industry. The clothing and arts worlds are also rife with inappropriate use of Indigenous images. But where is the line between appropriation and legitimate use? When physical objects and art that have makers are involved, there may be disagreement over how and where to draw this line, but most people would probably agree that such a line does exist. But where knowledge, traditions, and cultural practices are concerned, this is not so clear.[1] Are some matters so much a part of a culture that they can only be studied, expressed, or participated in by persons who have an intimate, living connection with that culture?

This last question is of particular concern to the academics who have contributed to this book. We all research and write about Indigenous issues, but only half of us are Indigenous. Are there limits on what non-Indigenous scholars can research, write about, and teach? Are there subjects that Indigenous academics cannot examine within and beyond their communities because of their identities, legal obligations, and social location? If so, what are those limits and who gets to determine them? The chapters in this book grapple with these issues and attempt to address them from a variety of angles and perspectives.

John Borrows

Nigig indoodem. I am Otter Clan. Neyaashiinigmiing indoonjibaa, W̱SÁNEĆ akiing indaa. I am from the Chippewas of the Nawash First Nation and I currently live in W̱SÁNEĆ territory on southern Vancouver Island. Kegedonce nindizhinikaaz Anishinaabemong. My Anishinaabe name is Kegedonce.

Kegedonce was also the name of my third great-grandfather and it means orator or speaker. In the Anishinaabemowin double vowel system, the name is written as Giigidons. "Giigido" means "he or she speaks."[2] The final morpheme "ns" makes giigido diminutive;[3] it signals a person who speaks for others in reference to a governance role in our community. As ogimaa,[4] or chief, my third great-grandfather's duty was not to speak for himself but for those for whom he was responsible.[5] He was to faithfully report what was said during governance councils in future meetings. Kegedonce was both free and limited in what he could say.[6] His own voice was respected and encouraged, but he also had to follow the group's consensus as expressed in those councils. This example illustrates that Indigenous voice and its relationship to broader communities is something the Anishinaabe have long considered.[7] It is part of how we are constituted as a people.

I have recently written about the revitalization of Anishinaabe constitutional responsibilities as guides for our relationships in a book entitled *Law's Indigenous Ethics*.[8] I suggested that Anishinaabe constitutional practices should help us address questions (among others) related to the appropriation of Indigenous land, law, and education. Anishinaabe Law aims to make decisions rooted in love, truth, bravery, humility, wisdom, honesty, and respect. These are the Anishinaabe nizhiwaaswo-gikoomisinan gimishomisinan kikinoomagewinan or seven grandmother/grandfather teachings. They are important guides in sharing our ideas. Honouring Elders by practicing law in a relational context can help us address issues of Indigenous voice and appropriation in ways which advance Indigenous Peoples' own laws.

In particular, Indigenous Laws often highlight the importance of forming councils to make judgments informed by a variety of viewpoints. Potlatches, feasts, circles, clan assemblies, and confederacies are some of the ways Indigenous Peoples make decisions. Judgment is perspectival and requires different angles of vision to see questions and their potential answers more clearly. For example, Anishinaabe creation stories place councils between clans at their centre, as the animals determined how to bring life-giving soil to the earth's surface. Moreover, Anishinaabe political meetings, called zagaswaa'idiwin, place shared breath through pipe ceremonies at their heart.

Drawing inspiration from Indigenous legal frameworks, we created this book, in part, as an exercise in gathering voices to help more clearly identify issues related to Indigenous voice and cultural appropriation. It is like a council, gathering to discuss what might be done to both protect Indigenous knowledge, people, and communities while enhancing freedom for all, including Indigenous Peoples. As in any council, we might not agree with what is said. At the same time, each contribution more clearly illustrates what is at stake and ways to address the problem before us.

In addition to Indigenous legal frameworks guiding our questions related to voice and appropriation, this book also considers power imbalances created by racism, colonialism, sexism, and homophobia. I hope this might encourage the further development of trauma-informed perspectives on this issue, which should be required in the application of all laws.[9] This includes the Charter of Rights and Freedoms, which contains civil liberties such as freedom of speech, thought, opinion, and conscience. Unfortunately, Indigenous people have often been denied these rights, as individuals and groups.[10] This signals the need for applying these rights in relational context that is responsive to imbalances of power and privilege. Since no right is absolute, proportionality, relationality, and constraint must help us process different views related to Indigenous voice and appropriation.

Kent McNeil

I attended the University of Saskatchewan in the 1960s, earning a BA in history. Despite having studied Canadian history, I do not recall learning anything, apart from the "Riel Rebellions" as they were then called, about the histories and cultures of Indigenous Peoples on the Prairies where I grew up. My family on my father's side homesteaded in Treaty 2 territory in southeastern Saskatchewan in the 1880s, believing their title to the farm came solely from a grant by the Canadian government, whereas it really originated in agreements the government entered into with the Indigenous Peoples of the territory. There was no awareness that the government had acted as an intermediary, as required by the Royal Proclamation of 1763,[11] and that my family's right to live and farm there was actually a Treaty Right that came with obligations to respect the rights of the Indigenous parties.[12]

Fortunately, after I left university non-Indigenous historians such as Jim Miller, Sarah Carter, and Jean Friesen began to introduce their students to very different understandings of Prairie history that take appropriate account of the Indigenous Peoples and their prominent place in that history. Indigenous scholars such as Anthony Hall, Blair Stonechild, and Paul Chartrand joined the ranks of academia and enriched their students' minds with deeper appreciation of Indigenous history and cultures. Professor Stonechild has recently revealed that, when he was a student at McGill University in the early 1970s, he found himself "educating professors about Indian Rights, as they knew virtually nothing about Indian Treaties, the Royal Proclamation of 1763, or Aboriginal Rights."[13] The research and teaching of Indigenous and non-Indigenous professors alike have thus been providing students and the broader public with more accurate knowledge of this country's history and the many contributions the Indigenous Peoples have made.[14] I think it not only appropriate for our shared history to continue to be unearthed and taught by researchers from these different backgrounds – it is an academic responsibility.[15]

With this broader background motivating my work, the immediate inspiration for this collection came from an experience I had in relation to the publication by UBC Press of my recent book, *Flawed Precedent: The* St. Catherine's *Case and Aboriginal Title*. The *St. Catherine's* case,[16] decided by the Judicial Committee of the Privy Council in London in 1888, was the governing precedent on Indigenous land rights in Canada right up until 1973 when the Supreme Court of Canada finally began to question it in *Calder et al. v Attorney-General of British Columbia*.[17] In addition to constitutional division-of-powers issues, the *St. Catherine's* case involved the nature of the land rights of the Anishinaabe People in northwestern Ontario prior to their entry into Treaty 3 in 1873. A major problem with the case was that this matter was considered and ruled upon without any involvement of the Anishinaabe themselves. They weren't parties to the action and no Anishinaabe were called as witnesses, despite the fact that Treaty 3 had been entered into just twelve years before the case went to trial in Toronto and many of the Anishinaabe who had participated in the negotiations would still have been alive. It is unlikely they even knew the trial was taking place or imagined what its impact would be. Nor were other witnesses called to present evidence on Anishinaabe culture, political organization, laws, and relationship to the land. The Privy Council's decision was thus made in a factual vacuum,[18] and yet it became the leading judicial precedent on the nature of Indigenous land rights for almost a century, not only for the Anishinaabe but for other Indigenous Peoples in Canada as well.

When it came to designing the cover for *Flawed Precedent*, I proposed an image that would represent Anishinaabe culture at the time of Treaty 3. In the collections of the Royal Ontario Museum (ROM), I was fortunate to locate a beaded knife sheath that, according to the Museum, had been obtained at the time of the Treaty by artist Frederick Arthur Verner, who was present at the negotiations. But when I suggested using an image of this beautiful knife sheath on the cover, I was told by UBC Press that they couldn't do so because this would amount to "cultural appropriation." Instead, they first proposed cross-sections of logs, presumably because the defendant in the case was a lumber company. After I vetoed that, they suggested an abstract design consisting of criss-crossing lines that seemed to bear no relation whatsoever to book's contents. I protested, as the Press's suggestions for the cover would do just what the *St. Catherine's* case had done and that I was arguing against, namely, exclude the Anishinaabe People and their culture and traditions from discussions of their rights. To its credit, the Press was persuaded by this argument and agreed to include an image of the knife sheath on the cover.

This experience got me thinking more about cultural appropriation. I understood that using images from Indigenous cultures for personal or commercial gain without attribution or compensation amounts to wrongful appropriation, and that these are not the only kinds of inappropriate cultural taking.[19] But what if the intention is to recognize and celebrate Indigenous cultures, while providing appropriate acknowledgment to the extent possible? In the case of the knife sheath, the maker is unknown, and I relied on ROM's opinion regarding its provenance, as I explained in a caption accompanying a complete image of the sheath on page vi of the book. What more could be done?

My experience with the book cover was just one of the motivations for the workshop that led to this collection of essays. Another was a lengthy conversation I had with a colleague over the place of academics in researching, writing, and teaching about Indigenous cultures and legal orders. This colleague felt that some Indigenous academics think it is inappropriate for non-Indigenous academics to venture into this realm, partly because they lack the experience of being Indigenous and so are not in a position to address these matters. This presents a dilemma for non-Indigenous academics, a damned-if-you-do, damned-if-you-don't scenario. On the one hand, if we venture too far into Indigenous cultures and ways of thinking, we can be accused of overstepping appropriate bounds and possibly of cultural appropriation. On the other, if we shy away from these matters, we might be told we are failing to take Indigenous understandings and perspectives into account.[20] Non-Indigenous academics are left wondering whether there is a line we should not cross, and if so where it is located. There is a danger that some will play it safe by not addressing these matters at all or only addressing them superficially because they are afraid of crossing that invisible line or getting Indigenous understandings wrong.

John and Kent

Where legal education is concerned, Call to Action 28 of the 2015 *Final Report of the Truth and Reconciliation Commission of Canada* provides:

> We call upon law schools in Canada to require all law students to take a course in Aboriginal people and the law, which includes the history and legacy of residential schools, the *United Nations Declaration on the Rights of Indigenous Peoples*, Treaties and Aboriginal rights, Indigenous law, and Aboriginal-Crown relations. This will require skills-based training in intercultural competency, conflict resolution, human rights, and anti-racism.[21]

Most of these topics should be within the competence of non-Indigenous academics, as they involve history, Indigenous-settler relations, and international law. But Indigenous Law is also included. If this area is off-limits for non-Indigenous law teachers, the burden of teaching such courses could fall disproportionately on Indigenous academics, who all too often already face impossible demands and unreasonable workloads. Surely, responsibility for introducing students to Indigenous Law should not fall solely on the shoulders of Indigenous professors but should be a shared responsibility that other professors bear as well.

Motivated by these considerations, we thought it would be timely to plan a book and prepare for its publication by convening a workshop where a small group of academics could get together to discuss these issues in an informal setting. Professor McNeil's visitor's position as the Law Foundation of Saskatchewan H. Robert Arscott Chair at the College of Law in Saskatoon provided us with an opportunity to do so. Professor Borrows worked alongside Professor McNeil in planning, inviting speakers, and chairing the workshop. The project was generously supported by Dean Martin Phillipson and financed by the Law Foundation of Saskatchewan, for whose assistance we are very grateful. Dean Phillipson remarked that, as these are issues all of us who research and teach in this area confront and struggle with, a workshop addressing them directly would be a very useful endeavour. The workshop was entitled "Indigenous Voice, Cultural Appropriation, and the Place of Non-Indigenous Academics," and a small number of academics from across Canada were invited to attend. We aimed to include as equal a balance as possible between Indigenous and non-Indigenous scholars and between junior and senior professors. The hope was that this would generate a stimulating exchange where the participants could talk freely about their experiences and views on the interrelated topics of the workshop and learn from one another. The workshop that was convened in Saskatoon early in October 2019 resulted in the open and respectful discussion we had hoped for, even exceeding our expectations. A tally of interest afterwards indicated that everyone thought a book collection of essays based on the workshop would be a worthwhile enterprise.

We told the participants that we hoped their contributions would be more personal and experiential than academic. While academic discussion and analysis were not discouraged, we were more interested in learning about issues they may have faced, how they dealt with them, what they learned, and so on. We wanted to hear their personal views and perspectives. Readers will discover as they read the essays in this book that the contributors took our instructions to heart. Some authors share intimate experiences, feelings, and thoughts. Many of them confessed to us that they found their essay much more difficult to write that a typical academic piece. The personal aspect of the exercise took them outside their comfort zones and made them feel vulnerable. The non-Indigenous participants in particular were not used to writing for public consumption in this way. We are extremely grateful to all of them for taking these risks and being willing to share their personal experiences. We hope their openness will assist others in dealing with these challenging issues.

As expected, one aspect of Indigenous voice and cultural appropriation that became apparent during and after the workshop is that non-Indigenous academics are not the only scholars who face these issues. There are many different Indigenous nations and cultures. The Royal Commission on Aboriginal Peoples expressed the view that, in Canada, there are between fifty and eighty "Aboriginal nations" having the right of self-determination, each consisting of "a sizable body of Aboriginal people with a shared sense of national identity that constitutes the predominant population in a certain territory or collection of territories."[22] The shared sense of identity, the Commission said, "comprises such elements as a common history, language, culture, traditions, political consciousness, laws, governmental structures, spirituality, ancestry, homeland or adherence to a particular treaty."[23] Examples they gave of "historical nations" are "the Huron, the Mohawk, the Nisga'a, the Haida, and the Métis of Red River, among others."[24] Does a Mohawk academic from Akwesasne have any more authority to research and teach about Haida traditions and law, one might ask, than a non-Indigenous academic who grew up on the West Coast? Does being Indigenous provide the Mohawk scholar with special insight into Haida culture and worldview that a non-Indigenous scholar can never acquire?

Two recent examples of the kinds of problems Indigenous people may face in this regard can be provided, one from the United States and one from Canada. Our discussion of the American example relies on David Bernstein's description of the controversy around Aaron Carapella's *Map of Our Tribal Nations: Our Own Names and Original Places*, released in 2012.[25] Carapella, who is Cherokee, was frustrated by the lack of maps depicting Indigenous homelands prior to European colonialism. Starting at age nineteen, he spent fourteen years conducting library research, visiting reservations, and talking with tribal leaders and Elders in order to produce a map of historical tribal territories that sought to use the original names for the 584 tribes he located on the map.[26] He did his best to make it as accurate as he could in the circumstances. "I'm really trying to be as fair as possible and not upset any tribe," he said. "Of course, there are always differences of opinion as far as which tribe had which territory. I apologize in advance for any inaccuracies, and I hope people will bring them to my attention."[27] The map provoked a storm of criticism. Some critics claimed that he got the tribal names or their spelling wrong. Others questioned the appropriateness of using maps that draw on "Western ideas of nationhood or territory" and are "deeply connected to a non-Indigenous set of values."[28] More relevant to our current discussion, some people challenged Carapella's authority to produce a map representing territories of tribes other than his own. Bernstein concludes:

Intending to make a map "to instill pride in Native people," Carapella's creation had instead thrust him into the morass of Indian identity politics. The controversy over Carapella's map is – at its heart – a disagreement over how Native people should narrate their past. The conflict centers on how much to privilege culturally specific ways of understanding the world in Indians' stories about themselves and their relationship with the nation-state.[29]

The recent Canadian example comes from the world of entertainment. Cikwes (Connie LeGrande), a Cree songwriter and performer, utilizes Inuit throat singing in her music. When she received a nomination for a folk music award at the Indigenous Music Awards held in Winnipeg on 17 May 2019, a number of Inuit performers accused her of cultural appropriation and said they would boycott the awards ceremony as a result. One of the Inuit throat singers, who goes by the name Riit, explained: "Just because you're part of another Indigenous group, it doesn't give you the right to take traditions from other groups."[30] This is an important point. While this example goes beyond the situation of academic research, writing, and teaching, it does show that Indigenous people are not immune to accusations of cultural appropriation.

Regarding research and teaching by non-Indigenous academics, the more appropriate question may be not what is their *place*, but rather what are their *responsibilities*. In treaty areas of Canada, the Indigenous Peoples remind us that we are all treaty people. The right of non-Indigenous peoples to reside in these areas comes from the treaties. But with rights come responsibilities. One responsibility non-Indigenous academics have is to educate their students and other Canadians on their obligations under the treaties. The Indigenous parties have always insisted that the treaties do not involve *surrender* of their lands and governmental authority, but rather a *sharing* of lands, resources, and jurisdiction with the newcomers.[31] Non-Indigenous Canadians therefore have an obligation to respect this ongoing treaty relationship. In other parts of the country where treaties have not been entered into, academics also have a responsibility to explain why, and to educate Canadians on the rights of the Indigenous Peoples, both as perceived by the Canadian state and as understood by Indigenous Peoples themselves.

One way scholars can provide respectful, direct support for Indigenous Peoples is by entering into partnerships and conducting research in cooperation with them that is driven by their needs and priorities. Good examples are described in a recent book coedited by one of the contributors to this collection, Keith Thor Carlson, entitled *Towards a New Ethnohistory: Community-Engaged Scholarship Among the People of the River.*[32] In the right circumstances, we think it is appropriate for non-Indigenous people, including academics, to work with Indigenous Peoples as allies.[33] Because Indigenous people today make up only about 5 per cent of the Canadian population, their political clout, especially in elections, is limited. During the protests in February 2020 over police treatment and arrests of Wet'suwet'en People who oppose construction of the Coastal GasLink Pipeline through their territory, many non-Indigenous Canadians joined in solidarity with Indigenous people across the country.[34] The media, and hence the public and governments, took notice. Public awareness was also raised by support from allies of the Lakota/Dakota of Standing Rock, who oppose the Dakota Access Pipeline, and by the many Americans of all races who believe that "Black Lives Matter." Let's face it – Indigenous people did not create colonialism and racism, so they should not bear the burden of undoing them and creating more respectful and just relations. If anything, non-Indigenous Canadians are the ones who should shoulder the bulk of the responsibility for this vital work.

The Chapters

No overview or summary of the chapters in this book can do justice to their diversity and richness. They range across a number of common themes, including who is authorized to engage in research and teach about Indigenous societies and cultures, and under what circumstances; how this can be done respectfully in ways that support Indigenous self-determination and revitalization; and what role scholars can play in ensuring that Indigenous cultures, histories, and laws are accorded their appropriate place in Canada. Although the contributors come from various Indigenous and non-Indigenous backgrounds and have different points of view, they share a common commitment to dismantle the legacy of colonialism. They have written about their personal experiences and recounted stories in ways rarely encountered in academic work. For this, we are extremely grateful.

Sarah Morales starts by locating herself in relation to her work, as is expected of Indigenous scholars. She describes where she is from, both geographically in Coast Salish territory on Vancouver Island and in relation to her community and family. She emphasizes the need for researchers working with Indigenous Peoples to develop relationships that lead to trust and create obligations. Her own study of Hul'qumi'num Law has deepened her connections with individuals and community and her understanding of the accompanying responsibilities. Her moving descriptions of her experiences reveal the complexities and challenges this work can involve, as well as the benefits, both for the community and in terms of her own personal and intellectual development. As she attests, "this is not work for the faint of heart," but "it is a labour of love." It involves establishing good relations and abiding by three fundamental Indigenous legal principles: humility, reciprocity, and trust. It is work that Elders have encouraged her to share and in which others who are accountable to Indigenous communities can participate. Sarah acknowledges there may be wrong turns along the way, but she is optimistic that stumbling blocks can be overcome and that we can move forward on this exciting journey together.

Keith Thor Carlson describes himself as a settler Canadian of Swedish cultural heritage. He grew up in Powell River, a pulp-and-paper company town in the territory of the Tla'amin People in British Columbia. He has spent his academic career as a historian working with the Stó:lō Coast Salish people of the lower Fraser River watershed. He is highly respected both by the Indigenous people with whom he partners and by the academic community. But that isn't what his chapter is about. Instead, it tells a profoundly personal story about his family and a tragedy involving his adopted Indigenous brother, Kerry. This is not a story that can be summarized in this Introduction – it must be read in its entirety for its impact to be felt. We are very grateful to Keith for being willing share his personal experiences of how colonialism and racism have impacted him and his family. His story reveals how these deep wounds in the fabric of Canadian society affect us all, Indigenous and non-Indigenous alike, and yet he expresses hope that "together we can develop and share the knowledge, creativity, and vocabulary necessary to dismantle settler colonialism and build something new in its place."

Aimée Craft's chapter addresses the issue of the line between support and celebration of Indigenous cultures and exploitation of them. As an Anishinaabe-Métis woman from Treaty 1 territory in Manitoba, she surveys the Indigenous art in her office and the clothes she wears, wondering whether she has the requisite permission to display them. In so doing, she acknowledges that cultural appropriation is not necessarily limited to taking of Indigenous things by non-Indigenous people. It is an ethical issue that "engages reciprocity and the development and maintenance of relationships." It also depends on how things are acquired, what they are used for, and whether proper respect has been paid and protocols followed. One needs to be aware that there are often spiritual and cultural dimensions to Indigenous art that may limit its use, requiring deference to Indigenous legal orders. The ethics involved are similar to the ethics that should guide research: both are "dependent on the building of relationships, mutual consent and reciprocity."

Hadley Friedland contrasts her atheist upbringing with the spirit-imbued worldview of her Cree partner, who wonders how white people can believe the Earth isn't alive. Having lived in a Cree community in Alberta since adolescence, Hadley has come to appreciate the depth of cultural difference between Indigenous and Euro-Canadian beliefs. She expresses appreciation for the many times she has been corrected by Cree Elders and relations – for example, for ignoring a dream. But the challenge is trying to appreciate divergent worldviews without being judgmental, without trying to determine right and wrong, true and false. For her, this requires a willingness to admit what we don't know and may never know – to leave space for "genuine unknowing." In researching and teaching about Indigenous Law, as Hadley does, this means putting aside preconceived notions and opening oneself to possibilities that do not fit comfortably within one's accustomed understanding of reality. Acknowledging that we are all whole human beings with intrinsic value, yet understanding that being human also entails being tentative and not knowing, "allows for not just cognitive, but relational and empathetic learning."

Lindsay Borrows poses the question of how the foundational Indigenous legal principle of respect can lead us to take a wide variety of voices into account, enriching our own understanding and helping in the quest for justice. In Lindsay's Anishinaabe culture, mino-audjiwaewin or manaaji'idiwin (respect) is one of the Seven Grandparent teachings. Manaaji'idiwin, a relational and reciprocal teaching, means "to go easy on someone." The actions or opinions of others may cause us to be angry, frustrated, or upset. These emotions are natural and should not be suppressed or ignored but, instead of allowing them to have negative impacts on ourselves and others, we can use them as instruments for positive change. We can work cognitively to challenge our negativity bias and cultivate our capacity to act respectfully, which in turn can improve relations and encourage others to listen. Relating the principle of respect to Indigenous Law that is often sourced in stories, Lindsay observes that a variety of voices can result in different interpretations, enriching our understanding. This does not mean we should avoid critique, but rather that we should engage in debate with civility and manaaji'idiwin.

Felix Hoehn addresses the issue of cultural appropriation from the perspective of a non-Indigenous legal academic whose work is aimed at attempting to redress injustices created by colonialism. He contends that cultural appropriation should be viewed through the lens of sovereignty rather than property. His chapter then discusses four questions that could be asked by any non-Indigenous academic whose work involves Indigenous legal issues: "(1) Should *non-Indigenous* persons become scholars of Aboriginal law? (2) Should I always identify myself as non-Indigenous to be clear that I speak with a non-Indigenous voice? (3) Are there limits to the teaching roles appropriate for non-Indigenous scholars of Aboriginal law? (4) As a non-Indigenous scholar of Aboriginal law, to what extent should I be expected to participate in ceremonies or practices that are part of Indigenous cultures?" In seeking personal answers to these questions, Felix shares thoughtful insights for others to consider as they ask themselves how non-Indigenous academics can assist in making Canada a nation where Indigenous sovereignty is acknowledged and just relations achieved.

Karen Drake and A. Christian Airhart also take on the issue of whether non-Indigenous professors should teach Indigenous Law, by which they mean the law of Indigenous Peoples rather than Canadian law as it relates to Indigenous Peoples, which is usually termed Aboriginal law. Since the Truth and Reconciliation Commission of Canada recommended in their 2015 Report that law schools make it mandatory for students to take at least one course on the history and rights of Indigenous Peoples that includes Indigenous Law, many law faculties have implemented that call to action. But should the burden of teaching Indigenous Law be borne solely by Indigenous faculty members? What qualifications are necessary to teach Indigenous Law, and how can competence to teach it be acquired and by whom? In addressing these questions, Karen and Christian consider various theories that can be utilized in searching for answers, such as liberalism, critical theory, postmodernism, and Indigenous constitutionalism. Narrowing their analysis to Anishinaabe constitutionalism, they conclude that within that theory it is acceptable for non-Indigenous professors to teach Anishinaabe Law if they do the requisite intellectual, emotional, physical, and spiritual work. They point out that, for Indigenous Law not to be marginalized in a single course, it should be integrated into the law school curriculum more generally. For that to happen, non-Indigenous professors need to learn and teach Indigenous Law.

Michael Asch relies on his extensive experience as an anthropologist in addressing the issue of how non-Indigenous academics can research and write about Indigenous Peoples without being guilty of cultural appropriation. For him, abiding by the consent requirements codified in the 2018 Tri-Council Policy Statement: Ethical Conduct for Research Involving Humans is a start, but not enough. In addition, academics should try to build relationships with the Indigenous Peoples they work with that are similar to treaty relationships, as he envisages them. Michael explains how formative experiences from his youth, including the silencing impact of McCarthyism in the United States in the 1950s and the Civil Rights Movement in the 1960s, influenced his views on the issue of voice. Undergraduate studies under Professor Sol Tax taught him that it is possible for academic anthropologists to "marry politics and scholarship with integrity" and to work to promote Indigenous Peoples' "right to survive and to thrive as peoples." Real-life experience working with Indigenous people came when he moved with his wife Margaret to Wrigley in the Northwest Territories to conduct research with the Dene. Michael's description of that time provides insight into what consent can mean in a cross-cultural environment and how mutually respectful, caring relationships can be developed. Drawing on that experience, he suggests that treating Indigenous teachings as processes enmeshed in the fabric of a way of life rather than as objects is one way to avoid cultural appropriation. While we may never have a full understanding of what we are taught, we still have an obligation to communicate in the best way we can what we have been given to share with others.

John Borrows's chapter argues that Indigenous Peoples should be wary of using Canadian legal frameworks when contesting cultural appropriation. They should use their own legal traditions. The Supreme Court of Canada has defined Indigenous culture in a very narrow way. In the process, it has marginalized Indigenous Peoples' self-determination. Through two examples, this chapter contends that those who use the state's frameworks when addressing cultural appropriation might themselves generate injustice, unfairness, and discrimination in the process. This is ironic, given that these efforts aim to overturn these very harms. This is why this chapter suggests turning away from the state and towards Indigenous Peoples' own laws when challenging cultural appropriation. Proportionality, fairness, reasonableness, and protection must be seen through a lens of Indigenous normativity to revitalize Indigenous people's abilities to determine what is appropriate and inappropriate within their societies.

Robert Hamilton situates himself as a settler from New Brunswick where he grew up and where his European roots go back generations. He explains how his decision to focus his legal scholarship on Aboriginal and Treaty Rights arose from personal observations of instances of racism and suppression of Indigenous Peoples' legitimate efforts to continue earning a living from the forests and the sea. His own work is directed, not at Indigenous Peoples, but at the dominant society "to clear the ground so the varied exercises of Indigenous resistance, revitalization, and resurgence can take hold, free from undue constraint." He sees his role as a non-Indigenous legal academic as being to identify and critique aspects of Canadian law that perpetuate exploitation and maintain unjust relations, preventing Indigenous Peoples from exercising their right of self-determination. He makes a crucial distinction between acceptable scholarship that assesses the costs and benefits for Indigenous Peoples of resource development projects such as pipelines, and scholarship that supports a legal regime that would allow these projects to proceed without Indigenous consent. In sum, "non-Indigenous lawyers and legal academics working in this field should focus on how the Canadian legal system can, to the greatest extent possible, stop denying Indigenous freedom." Moreover, non-Indigenous scholars need to listen to Indigenous people with open minds and be willing to see familiar things differently, while accepting the diversity of viewpoints and opinions among and within Indigenous nations.

Joshua Ben David Nichols focuses on the issue of Indigenous voice. He starts by unpacking the meaning of "Aboriginal perspective," a term that Canadian courts employ without definition and in contrast to the common law perspective. However, for judges the common law occupies a privileged position, not only because it is "law," but also because the only Aboriginal perspectives taken into account by the courts are those that are cognizable by the common law. Moreover, Joshua points out that, just as there is no one Canadian perspective, there is no single Aboriginal perspective; rather, there are a multiplicity of perspectives. Because Aboriginal perspective depends on who is speaking and in what context, it cannot be defined. Instead, it involves self-determination, requiring us to "make room for the deep pluralism and strange multiplicities that give living meaning to perspectives and speech within and between the constitutional traditions of peoples."

kQwa'st'not and Hannah Askew discuss ways in which environmental organizations can interact respectfully with Indigenous Peoples, learning from them and the relations they have with the physical world and other forms of life. Hannah is the Executive Director of the Sierra Club BC and kQwa'st'not (Charlene George) is from the Coast Salish~NuuChaNulth t'souke community on Vancouver Island. They are working together "to help facilitate cross-cultural organizational transformation for Sierra Club BC," a process they describe as "difficult and uncomfortable." Historically, the Sierra Club has tended to disregard the presence of Indigenous Peoples, for example by viewing parts of their territories as "wilderness." Altering this mindset "requires hard work, an open mind, humility, and willingness to change." A major part of this work involves club members learning about local Indigenous environmental practices and laws that govern their relationships with the land. In this chapter, kQwa'st'not and Hannah speak in their own separate voices, alternating back and forth as they describe their efforts to bring transformative change to one environmental organization. By sharing their personal stories and experiences, they hope to provide useful insights for others undertaking similar work in other organizations.

Hamar Foster starts by referring to the controversy over Robert Bringhurst's trilogy on Haida oral literature, which involved all three themes of this collection – Indigenous voice, cultural appropriation, and the place of non-Indigenous academics. He moves on from there to discuss a different controversy, one in which he was personally involved, namely the decision in 2017 by the Benchers to disassociate the Law Society of British Columbia from Justice Matthew Baillie Begbie and remove his statue from the foyer of the Society's offices. Begbie had presided over the trials of six Tsilhqot'in warriors in 1864 that resulted in the execution of five of them for murder. Hamar delves into the history of these trials and other aspects of Begbie's life as a judge in a way the Benchers, in their superficial examination of the events, did not. Entering the current controversy over removal of monuments honouring historical figures who contributed to colonialism and participated in the mistreatment of Indigenous Peoples, Hamar argues that it is essential to get the history right and not rush to judgment without careful investigation of the people and events in question.

Emma Feltes is doing research on the Constitutional Express, the Vancouver-to-Ottawa chartered-train journey organized by the Union of British Columbia Indian Chiefs in 1980 to oppose patriation of the Canadian Constitution without Indigenous consent. Emma was prompted to undertake this research by her friend and mentor, the late Arthur Manuel, who wanted the stories of those involved to be told. This work has brought her face-to-face with one of the central themes of this book: How do non-Indigenous academics, especially anthropologists such as herself, engage in research pertaining to Indigenous Peoples in respectful ways that avoid appropriation and do not perpetuate settler-dominant relationships? Emma's chapter is about her attempt to situate herself in this uncertain space as she conducts her research on the Constitutional Express. In navigating these murky waters, she is guided by suggestions she received from Gwitchin Elder Mildred Poplar, advising her to "get it right the first time," ask herself "whose original thought" it is, and "never give credit to one person – the politics are the people in their communities." Structuring her chapter around this advice, Emma addresses questions that any non-Indigenous person engaging in this kind of research needs to face.

Sa'ke'j Henderson recounts his early life as a student in Oklahoma and the indignities he and other "split-head" Indians had to endure in an education system that he describes as "cognitive imperialism or government-sponsored ethnocide or cultural genocide." As their political awareness grew, they began to organize and fight back against this forced assimilation. Energized on the summer intertribal powwow trail, they sought renewal of their "Indigenous knowledge systems, languages, and performance laws or ceremonies." In university, they targeted appropriation of Indian names, costumes, and symbols for mascots and sports teams. Sa'ke'j chose to confront the injustices he experienced and observed by going to law school in order to "understand justice by learning the oppressor's laws." As is well known, he has spent a lifetime doing this work. In this chapter, he describes some of the successes he and others of his generation have achieved, but also expresses frustration with the legal roadblocks they continue to encounter. He is nonetheless hopeful that "a better trans-systemic future is still waiting for the next generations of split-headed scholars, lawyers and activists to envision and create a better United States, Canada, and world."

This collection is not intended to provide definitive answers to questions of Indigenous voice, cultural appropriation, and the place of non-Indigenous academics. Instead, it is aimed at stimulating thought and discussion that may be of assistance to scholars who care deeply about these issues and who want to research, write, and teach in ways that foster better understanding and respectful relations between Indigenous Peoples and non-Indigenous peoples.

NOTES

1 See, for example, Michael F. Brown, *Who Owns Native Culture?* (Cambridge MA: Harvard University Press, 2003).

2 The word giigido is found in *The Ojibwe People's Dictionary* online: <https://ojibwe .lib.umn.edu/main-entry/giigido-vai>.

3 Examples of the 'ns' final morpheme in Anishinaabemowin are found online: <https://ojibwe.lib.umn.edu/word-part/ns-final>.

4 Meanings attached to ogimaa are found online: <https://ojibwe.lib.umn.edu/search ?utf8=%E2%9C%93&q=ogimaa&commit=Search&type=ojibwe>.

5 Interview with Basil Johnston. Ogimaa is related to the word *agindaussoowin*, which means to count. Johnston told me that a leader counts his or her followers because he knows who they are. But see an alternative meaning published by Anton Truer, who writes:

> The Ojibwe word for leadership – *ogimaawiwin* – literally means "to be esteemed" or "to be held to high principle". It comes from the morphene *ogi*, meaning high, found in other Ojibwe words such as *ogichidaa* (warrior), *ogidakumig* (on top of the earth) and *ogidaaki* (hilltop).

Anton Treuer, *The Assassination of Hole in the Day* (St. Paul: Borealis Books, 2011) at 14.

6 For more sustained reflection on freedom and its limits in Anishinaabe Law, see John Borrows, *Freedom and Indigenous Constitutionalism* (Toronto: University of Toronto Press, 2016) at 3–18.

7 In the present day, Anishinaabe Law is being revitalized to address how we can continue to own our relationships with others, called dibenindizowin (freedom) and mino-bimaadiziwin (good life) in our communities. *Ibid.*

8 John Borrows, *Law's Indigenous Ethics* (Toronto: University of Toronto Press, 2019).

9 Myrna McCallum, *The Trauma Informed Lawyer Podcast*, online: <https://podcasts.apple.com/ca/podcast/the-trauma-informed-lawyer-hosted-by-myrna-mccallum/id1514824294>.

10 John Borrows, "Unextinguished: Rights and the Indian Act" (2016) 67 University of New Brunswick Law Journal 1.

11 Reprinted in RSC 1985, App. II, No. 1. See *Guerin v The Queen*, [1984] 2 SCR 335 at 383.

12 On treaties as the source of settlers' rights and obligations, see Michael Asch, *On Being Here to Stay: Treaties and Aboriginal Rights in Canada* (Toronto: University of Toronto Press, 2014).

13 Blair Stonechild, *The Knowledge Seeker: Embracing Indigenous Spirituality* (Regina: University of Regina Press, 2016), 17.

14 For guidance from a prominent Indigenous scholar on how this should be done, see Donald L Fixico, "Ethics in Writing American Indian History" in Devon A. Mihesuah, ed, *Native Americans and Academics: Researching and Writing about American Indians* (Lincoln: University of Nebraska Press, 1998), 84.

15 In its Final Report, the Truth and Reconciliation Commission included several Calls to Action under the heading "Education for reconciliation." Among other things, it instructed governments and educators to "[m]ake age-appropriate curriculum on residential schools, Treaties, and Aboriginal peoples' historical and contemporary contributions to Canada a mandatory education requirement for Kindergarten to Grade Twelve students" and to "[p]rovide the necessary funding to post-secondary institutions to educate teachers on how to integrate Indigenous knowledge and teaching methods into classrooms." See *Truth and Reconciliation*

Commission of Canada: Calls to Action (Winnipeg: Truth and Reconciliation Commission of Canada, 2015), Nos. 62–5.

16 *St. Catherine's Milling and Lumber Company v The Queen* (1888) 14 App. Cas. 46 (PC).

17. [1973] SCR 313.

18 The trial Judge, Chancellor Boyd, attempted to fill this void with erroneous and racist assumptions about Anishinaabe society that had no basis in evidence: see *St. Catharine's Milling and Lumber Company v The Queen* (1885) 10 OR 196 (Ont. Ch.); Kent McNeil, *Flawed Precedent: The* St. Catherine's *Case and Aboriginal Title* (Vancouver: UBC Press, 2019), ch 4.

19 E.g., see Amanda Pask, "Cultural Appropriation and the Law: An Analysis of the Legal Regimes Concerning Culture" (1994) 8 Intellectual Property Journal 51; Rebecca Tsosie, "Reclaiming Native Stories: An Essay on Cultural Appropriation and Cultural Rights" (2002) 34:1 Ariz St LJ 299; Mathias Seims, "The Law and Ethics of 'Cultural Appropriation'" (2019) 15:4 International Journal of Law in Context 408.

20 A well-known novelist, Wallace Stegner, whose stories and non-fiction works are set in the American West and the Cypress Hills region of Canada, has been rightly accused of making Indigenous Peoples disappear from the landscape when settlers arrived: see Elizabeth Cook-Lynn, *Why I Can't Read Wallace Stegner and Other Essays: A Tribal Voice* (Madison: University of Wisconsin Press, 1996), ch. 5. Stegner was writing in an earlier era when the myth of the "disappearing Indian" still exerted influence: see Keith Thor Carlson's and Sa'ke'j Henderson's chapters in this volume. For more recent novels set in the same region on both sides of the Medicine Line (the forty-ninth parallel) in which Indigenous Peoples are prominent, see Guy Vanderhaeghe, *The Englishman's Boy* (Toronto: McClelland & Stewart, 1996) and *The Last Crossing* (Toronto: McClelland & Stewart, 2002).

21 Vol. 1, *Summary: Honouring the Truth, Reconciling for the Future* (Toronto: Lorimer, 2015), 323 [*Truth and Reconciliation Report*].

22 *Report of the Royal Commission on Aboriginal Peoples*, Vol. 2, *Restructuring the Relationship* (Ottawa: Supply and Services Canada, 1996), Part 1 at 178, 181.

23 *Ibid* at 178.

24 *Ibid.*

25 See David Bernstein, *How the West Was Drawn: Mapping, Indians, and the Construction of the Trans-Mississippi West* (Lincoln: University of Nebraska Press, 2018), 1–3.

26 Cindy Yurth, "Putting Them on the Map: Native Cartographer Offers a Different Picture of America," *Navajo Times* (17 January 2013) online: <https://navajotimes .com/news/2013/0113/011713map.php>.

27 Quoted *ibid.*

28 Bernstein, *supra* note 25 at 2.

29 *Ibid* at 2–3.

30 Quoted in Brad Wheeler, "Throat Singers Decry Cultural Appropriation at Indigenous Music Awards," *Globe and Mail* (4 May 2019) online: <https://www.theglobeandmail.com/arts/music/article-inuit-performers-decry-cultural-appropriation-in-upcoming-indigenous/>.

31 E.g., see Harold Cardinal & Walter Hilderbrandt, *Treaty Elders of Saskatchewan: Our Dream Is That Our Peoples Will One Day Be Clearly Recognized as Nations* (Calgary: University of Calgary Press, 2000); Aimée Craft, *Breathing Life into the Stone Fort Treaty: An Anishinabe Understanding of Treaty One* (Saskatoon: Purich Publishing, 2013).

32 Winnipeg: University of Manitoba Press, 2018.

33 In her iconic 1964 song, "Now That the Buffalo's Gone," Buffy Sainte-Marie welcomed allies in the fight to retain Indigenous lands.

34 See Martin Lukacs, "The Long Road to This Winter of Protests," *The Tyee* (27 March 2020) online: <https://thetyee.ca/Analysis/2020/03/27/The-Long-Road-This-Winter-Protests/>.

1 *Su-taxwiye*: Keeping My Name Clean

SARAH MORALES

A Naming Ceremony

One of the fundamental principles of an Indigenous research methodology is the necessity for the researcher to locate oneself in relation to one's work.[1] The notion of relationality requires that you know about me before you can begin to understand my research and writing. As Indigenous scholars, we write about ourselves and position ourselves at the outset of our work because the only thing we can write about with authority is our own experiences.[2] Locating yourself is an important way to gain trust in a community, whether it be an Indigenous community or a community of readers. This practice was confirmed and taught to me by own family and community when I first began my study of Coast Salish Law, in particular the legal tradition of the Hul'qumi'num'-speaking Peoples of Vancouver Island.

Eenthu Su-taxwiye tun'I tsun 'utl' Tl'ulp'a'lus.[3] As I previously stated, I am Coast Salish and a member of the Cowichan Tribes. My father is Robert Morales. His mother, my grandmother, was Della James. She was an Indigenous woman from the Cowichan community on southern Vancouver Island. His father, my grandfather, was Bernabe Morales. He was an Indigenous man from the Sinaloa region of Mexico. My mother is Brenda Morales. Although non-Indigenous, she has lived in the Cowichan community for the past thirty years. Her mother, my grandmother, was Francis Joyce Aldcroft (née Ellis). Her family has roots in Scotland and England. Her father was William Glen Aldcroft. His family has roots in Maine, USA. It is custom in the Coast Salish world to introduce yourself in this manner as it provides for opportunities for people to connect with you and reflect on their obligations to you and vice versa.

You may presume that because I am a scholar who researchers, writes, and works with Coast Salish communities and legal traditions, I would privilege my Cowichan heritage. However, this is not the case. In fact, it was through examining the Hul'qumi'num legal tradition that I gained a greater appreciation for "all my relations." What I have come to appreciate is that ancestry alone is not sufficient to define what I am discussing. Through my work, I have reached an understanding that politics and law takes one beyond ancestry in defining community and in defining one's own relationship with community. Similar to the classification by the United States Supreme Court in *Morton v Mancari*,[4] the Hul'qumi'num Mustimuhw (Hul'qumi'num People) are more than just a racial grouping – they are a sovereign entity whose lives and activities have been governed by the Canadian government in a unique fashion. This history and resulting relationship, be it positive or negative, has influenced our legal tradition and politics. As a result, when I define myself as a Hul'qumi'num Mustimuhw, I am encompassing something much greater than what is recorded in the Cowichan membership records in the offices of Indigenous Services Canada. I am defining myself by our own laws and politics. I am acknowledging and respecting "all my relations."

The Hul'qumi'num politics of identity was illustrated to me at the outset of my research on the Hul'qumi'num legal tradition. One rainy evening, in the fall of 2008, my father and I went to visit my great uncle Angus Smith. As the Elder of our family, it was appropriate that I speak with him first about the work that I was about to engage in and seek his advice on how to do this work in a good way. Furthermore, he was a respected Elder in the Cowichan community and had often spoken on the need to focus on our own laws. I had envisioned him playing an integral role in my project and knew that his support would be vital to the success of my work.

After I had discussed my desire to research and examine Hul'qumi'num Law, a conversation ensued about how to do that work in a good way. Because of the nature of the work that I wanted to conduct and the research questions that I wanted to ask, it became apparent that there was a need for leaders, Elders, and community members to be able to relate to me. Although I had grown up in the Cowichan community, my great uncle explained that receiving a traditional name would enable people to determine who I was as a Hul'qumi'num Mustimuhw. It would help people see their connections and obligations to me, and also help them understand my obligations and responsibilities to them.

That evening, it was decided that I would be named early the next year with my father. My great uncle was quite pleased because he had been wanting to name my father for some time. Our naming ceremony was a beautiful experience. Before the ceremony, I had the opportunity to hear our family teachings and genealogy from my great uncle as he prepared us for the event to follow. I had the opportunity to be fully engulfed in the customary laws and processes surrounding the giving of a name.[5] I was witness to issues and conflicts that can occur over the passing down of these significant ancestral markers.[6] Finally, in the ceremony itself I had the opportunity to stand beside my father and have my family walk beside us as our names were announced and witnessed by our community.

At the luncheon following the ceremony, Luschiim (Arvid Charlie), one of our hired speakers,[7] stood up and explained to us that we were now expected to live up to the standing of our ancestors, and that we were never to shame our name. As I have engaged in this work over the past decade, I have carried this teaching with me. I have found that holding my name has strengthened my own sense of personal and community identity. It serves as a way to build connections among my community, my research, and myself.

More importantly, it has helped to keep me accountable. One of the teachings I have received is that keeping my name clean requires me to use it – to bring it out in public settings. When I bring out my name in a public setting, I am also bringing out my ancestors and all my relations who carry my ancestral name. As such, I act with care. I choose my words wisely. I draw on the teachings of our snuw'uyulh (this is the word my Elders have expressed to me as most closely resembling the word "law," but it has many translations in English including "our way of life" or "living a good life"). I know that if I bring shame to my name, I am also bringing shame to all those to whom I am connected through my name. It is a great responsibility and one that I am privileged to carry.

The Importance of Connecting

Some of the pivotal questions raised in this collection of essays concern the manner in which we teach and learn Indigenous Law, and who should teach, research, and write about these different legal orders. From my experience of working, researching, and practising Hul'qumi'num Law, I have to come to realize that an object or thing is not as important as one's relationship to it.[8] What I mean by this is that our ontology is developed through a continuous process of building, maintaining, and evaluating the relationships that surround us. "All my relations" is an expression I heard often growing up. Whenever I was present at a community event or meeting, the speaker would always start by acknowledging "all my relations." Although I felt as though I understood what the speaker was trying to achieve by acknowledging "all my relations," it wasn't until I started to critically engage with Hul'qumi'num Law that I began to see how that one simple phrase shapes the entire ontology and epistemology of my community. The way we view the world and our reality within it is based upon our relationships to our ancestors, the people, and the land around us – all our relations. As such, in order to understand and think critically about the questions raised above, each of us needs to engage in a process of building, maintaining, and evaluating our relationships to the people and places from which these legal orders arise.

Through my work with the Hul'qumi'num legal tradition I have come to rec- ognize that relationships are fluid and constantly evolving. Within our own laws and legal processes, rarely, if ever, are our relationships defined simply in the dichotomous terms of Indigenous/non-Indigenous, member/non-member, status/non-status, or on-reserve/off-reserve. I have seen this illustrated in Hul'qumi'num property law where there are practices that provide norms and standards for the access rights of kin to family or community-owned locales, and the development of protocols that allow for non-kin to access community and family-owned resources sites in certain circumstances.[9] I have also heard this discussed by community members and Elders working to develop child and family wellness laws within the Coast Salish world. In determining the extent of their jurisdiction over children and families, they often draw on per- sonal experiences and family anecdotes to ensure that no child with community roots[10] is left behind. In both these examples, what is apparent is the underlying principle in the Hul'qumi'num legal tradition that there is a strength and utility that flows from being connected – connected to family, community, ancestors, and territory.

Recognizing this strength, legal processes within the Island Hul'qumi'num communities create space and opportunities for individuals to be brought into the community and into our kin networks. Island Hul'qumi'num oral traditions about the First Ancestors demonstrate some of the basic legal principles that people use to express their relationship to the land and each other.[11] The family group descended bilaterally from these legendary ancestors is called hwunut- saluwum in the Hul'qumi'num' language.[12] It is not a lineage group, moiety, or clan, distinguishing Island Hul'qumi'num (and Coast Salish) social organiza- tion from that of other Indigenous Nations, such as the neighbouring north- ern Northwest Coast Peoples. Rather, membership in a hwunutsaluwum tends to be flexible over time, emerging less from rigid social ordering and more from the *actual practice* of ordered kin relations. Hence, Island Hul'qumi'num Peoples can affiliate with a broad range of people who live in different areas throughout the Coast Salish world. Personal choice and life circumstance link others beyond the "core" descent group of individuals within the hwunutsalu- wum. Through practised affiliation, a group can include in-laws or even visitors who claim membership through distant ancestors. However, merely claiming affiliation is not sufficient; rather, to validate legal claims within a potentially extensive network of kin, people have traditionally feasted and Potlatched, and continue bestowing Indigenous names or ritual privileges and prerogatives.[13] By connecting to a descendant group of the First Ancestors a person has oppor- tunities to access the rights and cultural teachings associated with that group.

As you can see from the examples above, belonging and the rights associated with belonging, such as access to knowledge, are fluid and capable of change over time. There is no strict dichotomy between "insider" and "outsider." Through the development of relationships, oftentimes recognized through customary practices, individuals have the ability to redefine their connection to people and place in the Coast Salish world. These connections serve to benefit not only the individual, but the community as a whole. With the introduction of new kin relations comes the possibility of access to new hunting, fishing, and gathering sites. It also has the potential to increase access to family-specific teachings and customary practices. Furthermore, it can have the effect of strengthening or renewing relationships between large communities of Island Hul'qumi'num Peoples.

In my own example, I illustrated how my naming ceremony redefined the ways in which my community relates to me. It also redefined my kinship relations in the Cowichan community. My immediate family on my father's side is very small. When he and I received our traditional names in January of 2009, there were only a handful of us at our family meetings and standing as witnesses for the work. However, since that day, my family has grown. I now make it a point to introduce myself by my traditional name whenever I'm speaking or presenting in public. As I have done this, I have had relatives come up to me and introduce themselves as my aunties and uncles. I have had people come up to me and explain their connection to my family. I have found that my traditional name acts as a bridge to a greater family – one that far exceeds the numbers of my more immediate family.

In this work of revitalizing and teaching Indigenous Law, in particular Hul'qumi'num Law, it seems apparent that these same principles of kinship and sharing would apply to all of us engaged in this work. Our families and communities acknowledge the strength of being connected and of forming connections. They have developed practices, reflected in our First Ancestor stories, to build and maintain relationships with others: for example, customary marriages, naming ceremonies, and adoption practices. Our ability to relate to each other and the world around us is vital to the continuance of who we are as Hul'qumi'num Mustimuhw. As the world has expanded around us, so too have our relations. We have not lived in isolation to those around us; rather, we have formed relationships with one another, welcoming them into our families, communities, and territories.[14]

This important work provides another opportunity for our communities to expand their kinship networks, not just with the scholars or researchers interested in this subject area, but also with students, judges, lawyers, and other practitioners in the legal system. These are reciprocal relationships, which means that, in order to do this work in a good way, all parties involved in the process, Indigenous and non-Indigenous, community members and non-community members, etc., must be able to relate to one another and determine their obligations to one another. It is only through this type of transparency that accountability will be achieved and work will be done in a good way.

The Task at Hand

This is an exciting time for those of us engaging with Indigenous Laws and legal traditions. There has been an increasing awareness of Indigenous legal traditions, spurred in part by the work of Indigenous and non-Indigenous academics researching in this field of law[15] and by the final report of the Truth and Reconciliation Commission of Canada, which speaks to the importance of recognizing, teaching, and operationalizing Indigenous legal traditions in many of their calls to action.[16] But it is not just a matter of awareness – Indigenous legal traditions and the right of self-determination are being recognized formally by the Canadian state. On 28 November 2019 the Province of British Columbia passed Bill 41 or the *Declaration on the Rights of Indigenous Peoples Act.*[17] This legislation implements the *United Nations Declaration on the Rights of Indigenous People* (UNDRIP) as provincial law. With its twenty-four preambular paragraphs and forty-six operative articles, UNDRIP is anchored in the complementary human rights of equality and self-determination. Implementing it effectively necessarily means giving space to Indigenous Peoples to develop and implement their own laws and legal institutions. Furthermore, on 1 January 2020, the *Act Respecting First Nations, Inuit and Métis Children, Youth and Families* came into force and effect. This legislation states that one of its main purposes is to "affirm the inherent right of self-government, which includes jurisdiction in relation to child and family services,"[18] and affirms that the right is recognized by Section 35 of the *Constitution Act, 1982* and "includes jurisdiction in relation to child and family services, including legislative authority in relation to those services and authority to administer and enforce laws made under that legislative authority."[19] Recently, on 21 June 2021, the *United Nations Declaration on the Rights of Indigenous Peoples Act*[20] received Royal Assent and came into force. This Act provides a roadmap for the Government of Canada and Indigenous Peoples to work together to implement the UN *Declaration* based on reconciliation and cooperative relations. As a result, Indigenous Peoples, communities, and groups all across Canada are currently engaged in the hard work of drawing out, revitalizing, and redefining for themselves the laws that will apply to communities.

As one can imagine, and I can personally attest, this is not work for the faint of heart; however, it is a labour of love. Canadian laws and legal institutions have inflicted and continue to inflict great harm on our communities. At times, this makes it almost an impossible task to take the time and devote the resources needed to engage in this transformative work. Furthermore, our communities' vision is obstructed with tears – tears shed for our young ones removed from our homes and communities, tears shed for our youth lost to the opioid crises, tears shed for our murdered and missing grandmothers, mothers, aunties, and daughters, and tears shed for the once bright futures of our kin now dimmed by the criminal justice system – and we cannot see our laws embedded in our landscapes and oral traditions. But our laws are there, quietly and majestically surrounding us, waiting for renewal. These are the laws that will bring health and healing to our communities.

The need for this type of work and recognition raises important questions about how to do it in a good way,[21] such as questions around where this type of research and learning should take place, and who is best equipped and has permission to do it. Questions also arise regarding the proper resources or sources to be relied upon when doing this type of work. The list goes on and on. As a Coast Salish scholar, teaching in Coast Salish territory at a Canadian law school on the subjects of Coast Salish Law and languages, Coast Salish involuntary obligations, and Coast Salish land-based learning, I can tell you that these are questions that have weighed heavily on my mind, and even more heavily on my heart. At first my inability to reconcile the answers within my own understanding caused me a lot of turmoil, but I have come to understand that these are not questions for me to answer – Indigenous communities, like my own, will answer these for themselves. Accordingly, depending on the community, location, time, and circumstances, judges, lawyers, students, researchers, consultants, etc. may receive different instructions as to how to do this work in a good way.

The Importance of Accountability

As I understand it, connecting is about establishing good relations, and within the framework of good relations, as defined by specific Indigenous legal orders, we can come to understand the principles that must govern our work. I would like to share a few of the teachings shared with me and my own personal experiences which have helped me establish a framework for working with my own community and other Coast Salish communities. This framework is built around three principles – humility, reciprocity, and trust – each of which is vital to remaining respectful and accountable in the work I am currently engaged in.

Humility

The principle of humility has been conveyed and shown to me many times since I began exploring and engaging with the Hul'qumi'num legal tradition. In one of my first interviews with Cowichan Elder Luschiim (Arvid Charlie), I had asked a specific question about Hul'qumi'num Law, our snuw'uyulh. In a firm but gentle way, he corrected me in the way that I was approaching our legal tradition. "We are almost putting the cart ahead of the horse when it comes to snuw'uyulh … The teachings start at a very early age. So you understand the values of snuw'uyulh at an early childhood, and it gets deeper and broader as you're putting on age."[22] I understood this teaching as a lesson in the importance of learning *how* to learn, or how to approach law in the Coast Salish world, and not just focusing on the answer to a research question. This teaching was reaffirmed by my husband's uncle, Joe Norris, who shared his experiences of learning the teachings of snuw'uyulh with me:

> It's really important to look at our teachings today. Looking back, when my grandmother was talking to me about a child being conceived, and in the fourth month, God puts the soul into the baby. When you're carrying a child, that's when it starts to kick, so that's when the teachings begin – you start talking to the child the mother was carrying. So she said I was very alert when I was born because I recognized their voices. When my grandfather spoke to me, I knew who he was. So that's the teachings. It goes all the way back to that time. All the way back to that era and how our Elders taught. So you always knew who you were and walked with dignity ... It's taken me sixty-seven years to really come full circle in the teachings that were given to me. So it's not overnight. It takes time.[23]

These Elders have helped me to recognize that learning and understanding Hul'qumi'num Law is a process. While I undoubtedly would refer to them as "experts" in the Hul'qumi'num legal field, they themselves acknowledge that they still have a lot to learn about Hul'qumi'num Laws. This has helped me to remain humble and cautious in my approach to this work. It reminds me that I am still a "baby" learner with a lot more knowledge to gain, but also reminds me that I am not expected to know all the answers.

This principle of humility has proved invaluable in the community-based work that I am currently engaged in. Recently I was speaking at a community forum on child and family wellness. As those of us who work and research in this field know, this is a topic that literally pulls at the heartstrings of our community members in very tangible and concrete ways. Accordingly, these meetings are often places where frustrations bubble to the surface and emotions are tough to contain. After the evening ended, my cousin, a current Cowichan band councillor, came over to me and expressed the importance of humility in enabling us to do this hard work because it illustrates to our people that we are here to listen, learn, and help.

Humility also ensures that we remain teachable and open to the teachers, whoever they may be, in our communities. Community meetings and focus groups have been invaluable sites of learning. The knowledge and teachings that have been shared in those spaces have deepened my understanding of Hul'qumi'num Law in ways that have benefitted both my research and my personal life. I have been taught important legal principles by all cross-sections of my community, some in the most humbling of circumstances.

This serves as a reminder that the true "experts" in our field of study reside in our communities, and sometimes our role may simply be to amplify their voices.

Reciprocity

As an Indigenous scholar who researches and works in my community, my work – at its core – *emanates* from my home.[24] This means that the issues I and others in this field of study, write, teach, and advocate about on a systemic level are also issues we face in our daily lives, which grind down, threaten, and take the lives of our loved ones. The research we undertake demands and creates life-long obligations and responsibilities far beyond the university. In our university roles we teach, write, serve on committees, and go to meetings. But at home, because of our kinship connections, the work has no bounds.[25]

Snuw'uyulh is the basis for giving, sharing, and supporting relatives in the Coast Salish world.[26] Furthermore, it is the foundation for reciprocity with non-relatives in the Coast Salish world. As alluded to above, kinship is indispensable to the Hul'qumi'num Mustimuhw. Strong kinship ties brought both security and protection to the Coast Salish people. As such, a Hul'qumi'num person could fulfil their kinship obligations to family members by sharing and providing physical, emotional, and spiritual support.[27]

What does it mean to share and provide physical, emotional, and spiritual support in the work of researching and teaching Indigenous Laws and legal orders? As one can imagine, the responsibilities could be vast and all-encompassing, especially for those of us with deep roots and close ties to communities. And that is as it should be. In a history mired with unlawful takings and unjust enrichments, reciprocity for the teachings shared and educational opportunities granted should take whatever form the community deems to be most beneficial. Furthermore, this reciprocity needs to take place both at an individual and a community level because relationships are being fostered and maintained in both spaces.

I will share a small example of what this could look like, based on an experience I had in early 2020. One afternoon I went to the Elders' luncheon to invite our Elders to a community event we were holding in relation to our child and family wellness legislation project. I introduced myself, connecting myself to my family, the project, and the work I do at the university. After providing the information about the event, I offered to stay and answer any questions the Elders might have about the project. Soon after I ended my remarks, a few hands shot up and I made my way around the room to answer questions. However, it soon became apparent that my Elders did not require further information about the project but rather were interested in seeking legal advice about a number of personal concerns. One couple seemed significantly distraught.

They expressed to me that they had not received their social assistance cheque and were worried about where they would get their next meal. They asked me if I could call the ministry office for them and find out what was going on. Seeing their distress, I offered to help as best as I could. After two hours, numerous phone calls, the drafting of a letter and providing them with some general instructions, I left feeling anxious and hopeful that the issue had been resolved. I spent the remainder of the afternoon running errands for the event. Minutes before the band office closed, I returned to drop off some items, and to my surprise my Elders were waiting for me in the reception area. They expressed to me that although the issue had been resolved, they would not receive their cheque for a couple of days and they were hungry. Fortunately, one of my errands that afternoon had been to pick up gift cards from a local restaurant to serve as door prizes. I quickly dug through my bag and gave them a handful to help them out for the next few days. Appreciative, they gave me a hug and went on their way.

I share this story to help illustrate my previous observation that our families and our communities are in need. And although I firmly believe that revitalizing and living according to our own laws and legal orders will go a long way towards meeting those needs, oftentimes there are more pressing and immediate concerns that require attention. Accordingly, doing this work in a good way means that sometimes we will be asked to step in and help address those more immediate concerns. As a result, our learning will take place while wiping noses, changing diapers, soothing tears, serving food, helping Elders, cutting meat, gathering medicines, driving to and from community meetings, attending funerals, and standing up for our relations any way we are asked and able to.[28]

Trust

The principle of trust is intertwined with the teachings of humility and reciprocity. Being trustworthy is highly valued within Hul'qumi'num communities.[29] This is reflected in the Coast Salish practice of calling witnesses. Penelakut Elder Florence James described the process to me in the following terms:

> So when you call a witness and you pay them to be there, you have invited them and that is going to be your witness. Witness all the work and they are going to help you, to stand by you and say this is the way it was said.
>
> And if anything comes up from it, you call your witnesses back. They are going to stand up and say this is what happened. This is the way it was done. That is why you have a witness in the house. They help you to know and stand up and say this is how I seen it.[30]

Trust comes into play in two aspects of this process. First, an individual needs to be trustworthy in order to be called as a witness. Second, witnesses also help to foster trust within the community. The process helps to affirm to community members that proper protocols are being followed and that individuals have rights to the gifts bestowed upon them.

As academics, researchers, and practitioners engaged in this work, there are witnesses all around us. Witnesses who are aware of our connection to the communities we work with and learn from. Witnesses who are holding us accountable to our obligations. Witnesses who will stand up and support us and witnesses who may stand up and speak against us if we do not do this work in a good way. Just as trust can be fostered through good relations and reciprocal actions, trust can also be broken through the opposite.

Although the responsibilities associated with this work are great, I have been encouraged by my Elders to share their teachings and my own limited understanding of our Laws and legal tradition with others. In one of my last conversations with my great uncle Angus he spoke these words to me:

> When I'm sitting here all by myself, I often wonder who is going to carry all this work for us – to make things right. You've got a name and you're the one that's going to do this kind of work ... Somebody's got to be there to help her. Help our people with this kind of work because we need it.[31]

My Elders have a great desire to encourage younger generations to seek in-depth understandings of our snuw'uyulh. They want them to learn from the Elders in our communities; however, they also recognize that this is a vital and vast work that will take the help of others as well. In closing one of our research gatherings, late Stz'uminus Elder Willie Seymour spoke these words to me:

> I thank you for your commitment – for your commitment to traditional teachings and academics. You know, I always say, we have the tools in each hand. We can take the academics and the holistic ways and use them together like nobody else can.[32]

As the statements by my Elders illustrate, these communities are trusting us with their teachings. They are trusting us with their families. They are trusting us with their future generations.

As I stated above, this is an exciting time for those of us engaging with Indigenous Laws and legal traditions. It is also an exciting time for Indigenous Peoples. The future holds promise that their laws will be stood up alongside the common law and the civil law in the Canadian legal system. It holds promise that their children and future generations will be governed according to their own legal standards and dispute resolution processes. But as stated by my Elders, they cannot do this work alone. It will take the hard work of many, accountable to Indigenous Peoples, to bring about this change. Inevitably this journey will entail wrong turns and stumbling blocks. At times we may need to retrace our steps or find our way back to each other. But that is to be expected. Our relationships are not static, and renewal brings with it opportunities for growth and positive change. I am grateful to be included on this journey and look forward to our paths crossing along the way.

NOTES

1   Kathy Absolon & Cam Willnett, "Putting Ourselves Forward: Location in Aboriginal Research" in Leslie Brown & Susan Strega, eds, *Research as Resistance: Critical, Indigenous & Anti-Oppressive Approaches* (Toronto: Canadian Scholars Press, 2005) 97 at 97.

2   *Ibid.*

3   My name is *Su-taxwiye*. I am from Cowichan Bay.

4   [1974] 417 US 535 at 554.

5   Preparing for the naming ceremony took months. During family meetings, the significance and processes surrounding the naming were explained in great detail. I was given duties to fulfill, such as hiring dancers and lady singers, attending singing practices, feeding those we had hired and paying them, gathering items for the giveaway, etc. For more details surrounding naming ceremonies, see Hul'qumi'num Treaty Group & University of Victoria, "*Nuheylhum*: Naming Ceremony" DVD (Ladysmith, BC: Hul'qumi'num Treaty Group, 2008). This DVD describes each of the stages of a naming ceremony: (1) *Stl'eshun*/Invitation; (2) *Sts'ewulhtun Shqwaluwun*/Contribute Money; (3) *Hwiineemstum*/Call Witnesses; (4) *Sts'uyulh*/Acknowledgment; (5) *Tus 'u tthu*/Begin the Work; (6) *Nuw'els Shulmuhwtsus*/Rattlers Ceremony; (7) *'Imush tthu Neetum*/Named Go Around; (8) *Tthu Hun'tsew Sne*/A Name is Reborn; and (9) *Snuw'uyulhs tthu syuwen'*/Ancestors' Teachings.

6   See Sarah Morales, *Snuw'uyulh: Fostering an Understanding of the Hul'qumi'num Legal Tradition* (PhD diss., University of Victoria Faculty of Law, 2014) [unpublished] [Morales, *Snuw'uyulh*]. Ancestral names and the ability to pass on ancestral names is a kinship right. The name originally selected for my father was one of my great uncle Angus's names. He had received two Hul'qumi'num names – one from his own father and one while he was working as a babysitter for a new initiate. In order to thank him for his work done that winter dance season, the family of the new dancer had passed on to him an ancestral name. The name originally chosen for my father was the name that my great uncle had been gifted. However, because the name did not come from his kinship line, some individuals in the community challenged his ability to pass it on to my

father. Although my great uncle had met with the family members, from whom the name was given, and received their permission to pass it on, resistance was still voiced by community members. As a result, my great uncle decided not to give that name to my father and, instead, would pass down his other name to him. His second Hul'qumi'num name came from his father's side of the family, to which my immediate family has no ancestral connection (as he and my grandmother were half-siblings on my great-grandmother's side). As a result, when my great uncle stood before the community and passed down his name, he also took my father "as his own" – customarily adopting him in order to pass down this inherited right. Although my great uncle was upset about the discord surrounding the original name he wanted to pass down to my father, he did not want to bring bad feelings to the naming ceremony and so he decided not to challenge the objecting community members. Instead, he quietly voiced his frustration with our family and announced that he would not give his permission for his name to be given to anyone else. Brian Thom, a family friend and professor of anthropology at the University of Victoria, explained to me that my great uncle's decision not to permit the passing down of that ancestral name ever again was virtually destroying it and that it was in keeping with the old Potlatching practices.

7 A speaker is an individual who is hired to represent another individual or group of individuals at a cultural event ("work"). Because of the training they receive in language, family histories, cultural protocols, etc., they are considered "experts" and are relied upon to ensure that the "work" is carried out according to cultural protocols and no mistakes are made. Interview with Robert Morales (16 February 2011).

8 See generally, Morales, *Snuw'uyulh*, *supra* note 6.

9 See Brian Thom, *Coast Salish Sense of Place: Dwelling, Meaning, Power, Property and Territory in the Coast Salish World* (PhD diss., McGill University Department of Anthropology, 2005) [unpublished] [Thom, *Sense of Place*].

10 Often described as having one Cowichan grandparent, or ancestral rights that connect them to Cowichan customary laws, practices or territory.

11 See Thom, *Senses of Place*, *supra* note 9; See Morales, *Snuw'uyulh*, *supra* note 6.

12 Sarah Robinson, *Spirit Dancing among the Salish Indians* (PhD diss., University of Chicago Department of Anthropology, 1963) [unpublished] at 27.

13 Sarah Morales & Brian Thom, "The Principle of Sharing and the Shadow of Canadian Property Law" in Angela Cameron, Sari Graben, & Val Napoleon, eds, *Creating Indigenous Property: Power, Rights, and Relationships* (Toronto: University of Toronto Press, 2020), 120.

14 This is not to suggest that some of these Indigenous/settler relationships have not been forced upon Indigenous communities, nor does it suggest that all relationships have been beneficial to Indigenous Peoples. Rather, it simply acknowledges that in some instances Indigenous Peoples, like the Hul'qumi'num

Mustimuhw, have used agency and followed their own legal principles in forming and maintaining relationships.

15 See generally John Borrows, "Outsider Education: Indigenous Law and Land-Based Learning" (2016) 33:1 Windsor YB Access Just 1 [Borrows, "Outsider Education"] (which speaks to some of the work of these scholars). See also the writings of Val Napoleon, Hadley Friedland, Jeffrey Hewitt, Lindsay Borrows, Aaron Mills, Robert Clifford, Karen Drake, Aimée Craft, Andrée Boisselle, Jeremy Webber, Hannah Askew, Kerry Sloan, and Nancy Sandy.

16 See Truth and Reconciliation Commission of Canada, *Truth and Reconciliation Commission of Canada: Calls to Action* (Winnipeg: Truth and Reconciliation Commission of Canada, 2015), Calls to Action 27, 28, 42, and 50.

17 *Declaration on the Rights of Indigenous Peoples Act*, SBC 2019, c 44.

18 *An Act Respecting First Nations, Inuit and Métis Children, Youth and Families*, SC 2019, c 24, s 8(a).

19 *Ibid* at s 18(1).

20 *United Nations Declaration on the Rights of Indigenous Peoples Act*, SC 2021, c 14.

21 See generally John Borrows, "Outsider Education," *supra* note 15; Sarah Morales, "Locating Oneself in One's Research: Learning and Engaging with Law in the Coast Salish World" (2018) 30 CJWL 144.

22 Interview with Arvid Charlie (23 June 2010).

23 Interview with Joe Norris (16 June 2010).

24 Philip Deloria, "Commentary on 'Working from Home in American Indian History'" (2009) 33 American Indian Quarterly 545 at 545.

25 Conversation with Hadley Friedland (29 October 2020).

26 Morales, *Snuw'uyulh*, *supra* note 6 at 233.

27 *Ibid*.

28 Conversation with Hadley Friedland (29 October 2020).

29 Morales, *Snuw'uyulh*, *supra* note 6 at 236.

30 Interview with Florence James (19 July 2010).

31 Interview with Angus Smith (8 November 2009).

32 Interview with Willie Seymour (16 June 2010).

2 At the Corner of Hawks and Powell: Settler Colonialism, Indigenous People, and the Conundrum of Double Permanence

KEITH THOR CARLSON

I was a graduate student at the University of Victoria in 1988 working towards my Masters of Arts degree when on October 5 my sister interrupted my class to tell me that my brother Kerry had died. He had been speeding the wrong way down Powell Street in Vancouver, a one-way road that intersects with Hawks Avenue, with the police in pursuit. He had died instantly. He hadn't suffered.

Kerry might not have suffered in his final moments, but he did face challenges throughout his short eighteen years of life. His story, though distinct and his own, is also in many ways representative of the larger tragic story of Indigenous people's historic and ongoing struggle with Canadian settler colonialism. And, as a non-Indigenous person – a settler Canadian who benefits from the displacement of Indigenous people from their lands and resources, and who carries the advantages of white privilege wherever I go – I am part of Kerry's story. But the influence goes in both directions. Kerry's story also profoundly shapes my own, and, I believe, speaks to the wider story of non-Indigenous Canadians. For despite anything an earlier generation may once have thought, wished, or tried to do, Indigenous people and settler Canadians are both here to stay; this is the conundrum of double permanence.

The permanence of both Indigenous people and settlers is a conundrum because neither Canada's economic and political systems, nor our national narratives, are set up to deal with this truism. Rather, as a settler colonial state, the Dominion of Canada was premised on the convenient assumption that Indigenous people would either die off or be assimilated. Nineteenth and early twentieth century politicians determined that, as a "vanishing people," Indigenous long-term interests need not be a priority.[1] As such, Canadian federalism was never set up to acknowledge or accommodate distinct spheres of Indigenous governance and authority – despite Aboriginal and Treaty Rights being recognized in our common law traditions and more recently enshrined in our Constitution. It is little wonder, therefore, that many Canadians continue to be surprised and frustrated when Indigenous people rightly demand that certain economic developments or political initiatives not occur without their informed consent. An even greater wonder, it seems to me, is that Indigenous people continue to show patience for settler colonial society and continue to seek, as well as offer, peaceful ways to build genuine reconciliation. Through my scholarship, I aspire to contribute to this process.

My brother and I grew up in a town that was named after Dr. Israel Wood Powell and my brother died on a street in Vancouver that was named for that same man – the first Superintendent of Indian Affairs in British Columbia. While Powell was personally more sympathetic to Indigenous people than most of his contemporaries, he was also the overseer of federal assimilation policies on Canada's Pacific coast. Under Powell's leadership, the process of alienating Indigenous people from their lands and restricting them to Indian reserves was standardized and systematized. My hometown of Powell River emerged instantly in 1912 in the middle of Tla'amin Coast Salish territory, where no more than a handful of white people (almost all transient loggers or British remittance men) had been living previously. The Powell River Company selected the location because of the Powell Lake watershed's hydro-electric potential. The electric turbines produced such huge amounts of power that the Powell River Company became, and remained for more than half a century, the world's largest pulp and paper mill. But in damming the river and building their mill, the Powell River Company destroyed ancient salmon foodways and displaced the Tla'amin people living in the settlement of Tees'kwat.[2]

My story, and my brother's story, are intrinsically linked to sites associated with Dr. Powell and to settler colonialism. And as Indigenous scholar Thomas King says, "the truth about stories is that that's all we are."[3] In deciding what to share and what to hold back, we are not only expressing our identity, we are also shaping our relationship with others. King says "you have to be careful with the stories you tell. And you have to watch out for stories that you are told."[4] In the subsequent print version of his Massey lectures King decided to add a chapter titled "Personal Stories," where he shared tragic stories that were not present in his original oral tellings, including an account of his friends' struggle with their adopted daughter's Fetal Alcohol Spectrum Disorder.[5]

Like King, I too have wrestled over the course of my life and career with how much of my story, my brother's story, and my family's story to share in print – to make a part of my public statements of positionality. Perhaps, it's my Swedish cultural heritage (the most emotion my paternal grandfather ever showed me was a firm handshake, yet I knew that he loved me dearly and I had a close and lovingly supportive relationship with him). I have never been comfortable displaying my emotions. Sharing makes me feel vulnerable. But as my wife Teresa (who is most definitely neither Swedish in ethnicity nor character) says, sharing, even if it makes you feel vulnerable, is the way to build understanding. Right now, I think the world needs more understanding, and so I'm making myself vulnerable and I'm sharing. Additionally, in the past I've never wanted to discuss the Indigeneity of my adopted brother to avoid the perception I was using him and his story to legitimate and validate my work as an academic historian who has made a career studying and publishing about Indigenous Peoples' history. This is the first time I've shared this story in print.

On my brother's tombstone my parents arranged for the words "Your path was difficult, our love walked with you." I was only four years old when Kerry came into our lives, but I remember vividly the trip my parents, my little sister Stormy, and I took from our home in Powell River to Vancouver on a hot July day in 1970 to pick him up. We went into a big office building where my little sister and I were ushered into a small waiting room and each offered a lollypop while Mom and Dad followed a woman down the hall. What seemed like forever finally ended when my parents came back into the room and Mom was holding in her arms my new twenty-one-day-old little brother. He was beautiful.

The ride home took the typical eight hours (two ferries and a lot of winding highway to travel a mere 100 km as the crow flies). I got to hold Kerry on my lap for part of the way. There were no seatbelts or baby seats in our lives back then.

A few years later, when I asked my parents questions for a school project on "family and community," Dad explained to me that he and Mom had decided to adopt my brother because they felt that the world was getting too heavily populated and so they should restrict themselves to just two biological children. Mom explained that by adopting Kerry we were helping a mother who had been unable to keep and raise a child of her own. As per the rules and policies of the BC provincial government at the time, my parents were provided with no background information about Kerry's mother.[6] But, my mom explained to me, as she and Dad were finalizing the paperwork on the day we picked Kerry up, the social worker took her aside and told her that Kerry's birth mother was "part Native" and that "she had been having a pretty rough time." That was all I have ever learned about my brother's biological family.

There was, and remains, a lot to unpack in that sentence about my little brother. Today there is a robust and growing body of scholarship examining and debating the meaning of Indigenous identity and the assumptions (both affirmative and redemptive, as well as exploitative and colonial) behind what it means to be "part" anything. Likewise, the extent to which either ancestry, blood quantum, and DNA, on the one hand, or community affiliation and recognition, on the other, are the better arbitrators of "authenticity" in Indigeneity also remains the subject of much discussion.[7] But back in 1970, from my perspective, Kerry was simply my little brother. We shared a bedroom and we shared our toys. Mostly we shared time together. As we grew up, he did all the things that little brothers do to annoy their big brothers, and I know I did things that annoyed him too.

Seven months after we adopted Kerry our family grew again. I came home from pre-school one afternoon and there was a girl sitting in our kitchen with my mom. To protect her privacy, and her birth family's, I won't reveal her real name. I'll just call her Sharon. Sharon was from the nearby Sliammon (Tla'amin) First Nation. Mom explained that Sharon was going to live with us for a while; that Sharon and I were now foster brother and sister. I didn't know what "foster" meant, and it would be two decades before I would learn about the federal-provincial constitutional disputes over Indigenous child welfare funding in the 1960s and 1970s that had facilitated the tragic assimilative policies associated with removing Indigenous children from their mothers and communities and placing them with non-Indigenous settler families (what came to be known as "the '60s Scoop").[8] All I knew then was that I had an additional sister and I was thrilled. Sharon was five or six years older than me and from my perspective was incredibly smart and strong. She shared a bedroom with Stormy. She gave me piggy back rides, she taught me what hockey is, and when I started kindergarten in September of 1971 we walked to and from school together.

By the time she came to live with us Sharon had been betrayed and hurt many times. As I came to understand it, her mother had left her when she was seven or eight. After that she had been living with members of her extended family. But something had gone wrong. Sharon explained to me that there was a scary man who lived in that house. Sometimes Sharon went back to spend a weekend with her relatives on the reserve, but on those days the scary man wasn't supposed to be there. I remember one time when we drove the ten kilometres north of town to drop Sharon off, that a big, scary looking, angry man was standing on the porch shouting at a woman. My mom stopped the car, and she and Sharon spoke in quiet voices which I couldn't make out from the back seat. I just remember my mom turning the car around and driving us all back to our house. Then Mom sent me and my little sister outside while she and Sharon sat at the kitchen table and drank tea, and talked. Sharon stayed with us for over two years before she returned again to live on the reserve. This time, I think, she went to live with her birth father. Sadly, years later I heard that while under his care she experienced additional hurt and trauma.

I remember walking home from school with Sharon one day, and she was crying – softly without sound, but with tears. I asked her what happened. She said a girl in her class had called her a "wagon burner." When I asked her why the girl had said that, Sharon didn't answer me. She just kept crying. I was confused. I thought she was referring to wagons like the little red wagon that Sharon and I used to pull Kerry and Stormy around in; Sharon and I also used it as a sort of go-cart to ride down the hill located farther up our street. Made of metal, that wagon couldn't burn even if someone tried to set it on fire, that much I knew. And besides, Sharon never set things on fire.

At that time I wasn't yet aware of the way early Hollywood portrayals of Indigenous people burning the covered wagons of hardy, white, westward-moving pioneers had reinforced the notion of First Nations as wild and heartless savages who perpetrated acts of cruelty on innocent white settlers. And

Hollywood was merely tapping into an even older literary tradition. Historically, such images depicted in fiction and newspaper accounts had served to justify in settler colonial minds both violence and the taking of lands from Indigenous people through duplicity.[9] Such images have served to justify resisting Indigenous efforts to secure recognition of their rights in Canadian courts and the activation of their rights in Canadian legislation and public action.[10]

At the dinner table that night Dad told Sharon that she should stand up to the girl who had called her a wagon burner, and maybe even punch her antagonist if she didn't apologize. Dad said the girl was a racist. When I asked what that meant, he said something to the effect that a racist was someone who didn't like other people just because of the colour of their skin; a person who said and did things with the purpose of hurting. The words seared into my heart, and my memory of that conversation still stings me today. I remember thinking at the time of how one of my own classmates had earlier that week told a joke with a racist slur that hurt the feelings of the twin sisters who had recently joined my class after their family had fled Uganda's dictator Idi Amin. As I listened to my father, I felt ashamed that I had not said anything to support the girls (indeed, I had laughed along with other of my classmates). But, even with that new self-awareness and recognition, I was still a long way from coming to understand the way racism was in fact more than just an intentionally hurtful word or purposeful action designed to denigrate people with darker complexions.

As a child I came to appreciate that racism shaped people's behaviours. My family had a close relationship with Eva Mosely – an elderly woman who was a member of Powell River's first Black family. We visited Eva regularly and I remember fondly listening to her stories about how her grandparents had escaped from California during the American Civil War and been welcomed to British Columbia by Governor James Douglas – a man with African ancestry whose wife was Cree/Métis. In BC Eva's family found new opportunities, but they also found racism. They eventually ended up in Powell River, but the mill refused to hire her father, telling him point blank that "they did not employ Negros." In her grade twelve year, despite earning the highest grades in graduating class, the principal denied Eva the scholarship that was annually awarded the summa cum laude to enable them to attend university. And when Eva met and fell in love with a white man, she and her fiancé were told by both the United Church minister and then the Anglican priest that they were sorry, but they just couldn't let the couple be married in their churches. Eva and her partner Jack instead lived "common law" in a house just outside the city limits (and despite all this they later donated land to the school board so the expanding municipality would have property to build a new elementary school).

Similarly, one of my closest friends all through high school was South Asian, born in Fiji. His name was Ron. Ron used humour to deflect racist slurs. Sometimes, however, that strategy didn't work. I remember vividly a night at the recreation centre when a gang of older thugs called Ron a "Paki." When he tried to laugh it off, they just got more aggressive and jumped us. Both my friend and I got beat up that night. But that wasn't entirely new for either of us. Ron was literally assaulted out of the blue at least half a dozen times during our high school years by racists while Ron and I were walking down the hallways of our school, or when he and I were swimming at the local beach. These boys called him racist slurs and then started shoving and punching him until Ron fought back. Sometimes, when I'm back in Powell River visiting, I bump into those guys. They act like they don't remember me or the altercations. I wonder if their consciences bother them. I wonder if they realize the extent of the emotional hurt they caused Ron beyond the physical hurt they inflicted. We've had several high school reunions, but Ron has never returned to Powell River to attend, and he and I have lost touch over the years.

Not all the violence in Powell River was racially motivated. A lot of it was ethnic- or class-based. Our home town was divided into class-based neighbourhoods. And these were often further subdivided into discernable ethnic enclaves. Cranberry (where I lived) and Wildwood were working-class neighbourhoods consisting mostly of descendants of Italian and Irish immigrants with a smattering of Ukrainian, Scandinavian, and working-class Scottish and English families. Westview was where the professional families lived – especially south Westview. Doctors, lawyers, accountants, teachers, RCMP officers, senior administrators and managers from the pulp mill, government office administrators, and small business owners made up the majority of the people in the mosaic of the Westview neighbourhood. Each of these communities were physically separated by slowly shrinking undeveloped forest lands. If you were from Cranberry or Wildwood you resented Westview. But most of the physical violence and emotional bullying took place within, not across, these communities.

I got badly beat up in my math class in grade eight by a boy who was one or two years older than me (I guess he had failed math one or twice already). He punched me in the head from behind as I was sitting at my desk. Then he kicked me after I fell onto the ground. He was white and so was I. But we both came from working-class families, and in our working-class neighbourhood violence was a regular part of life. I think he just needed a target and I was available. The torment was repeated several times over the coming months whenever the teacher decided to leave the classroom and go have a smoke in the staffroom. I was thirteen, tall, skinny, and insecure. I started telling my mom I was sick so could stay home from school on days when my math class was scheduled for third period because I knew on those days the teacher would inevitably go and smoke cigarettes in the staffroom (his addiction wouldn't let him go three classes straight without a smoke break). When I finally told my mom why I was afraid to go to school, she told me to talk to the teacher and the

Vice Principal. When I did, they suggested that I try to make friends with the bully. They never held the bully accountable. And they rejected my idea that the teacher be required to stay in the classroom for the duration of the class time.

These accounts and experiences were part of my story growing up, but I'm embarrassed to say that it was not until after I met my wife that I began to recognize the true breadth and depth of racism and cruelty in British Columbia. Teresa had originally come to Canada from the Philippines at the age of six with her widowed mother to escape martial law under the dictatorship of Ferdinand Marcos. Nothing in my childhood experiences compare to the stories she's told me describing how she was picked on and bullied from the moment she first set foot in a Nanaimo elementary school. The story of her first winter jacket in particular impacted me deeply. Coming from a tropical country Teresa had never experienced cold, let alone a Canadian winter. Her mother saved for months to be able to buy a cheap orange coat from the Zellers department store. Teresa wore it proudly to school, but within just a few minutes of class starting, the boy who sat behind her used a Jiffy marker to pen the word "chink" in bold black letters across her back. Unable to wash the ink away and unable to afford another coat, my six-year-old future wife had no choice but to wear the jacket with the racial slur for the rest of the winter season. The boy was never held accountable, but what still bothers me more is that nobody in the class, including the teacher, offered to help buy Teresa a new coat.

And still, despite these proxy glimpses into racism, I can honestly say it was not until I accepted a position as historical research coordinator for the Stó:lō Tribal Council in 1992 that I began to appreciate the ways in which the concept of "whiteness" created white privilege (unearned advantages), which in turn sustained the structures of systemic racism that continue to characterize many aspects of Canadian institutions and society.[11]

A few minutes after Dad had suggested that Sharon confront her antagonist, Mom provided her perspective. She said fighting wouldn't solve anything and would only make things worse for my sister. "Just ignore the girl. *She* is the one with problems." That was Mom's stock advice for almost all situations involving interpersonal conflicts. As a white woman Mom had never experienced racism, but growing up she had experienced prejudice and bigotry of other kinds, and some of these experiences were scarring. In the hyper-class-conscious company town where she was born and raised (where a person's position in the mill hierarchy determined which house on which street their family lived), she and her widowed mother had years earlier been required by the Powell River Company to leave their home after my grandfather had died. Mom, an only child who was eleven at the time, henceforth lived with my grandmother in poverty in a small house outside the company town in the neighbourhood of Cranberry where their only income came from taking in boarders (several of whom were drunk and abusive) and selling chicken eggs and garden produce.

Several of the children whom my mom had regarded as friends when her father was alive shunned her after she became poor. The rejection clearly had a profound impact on my mother. This was a story she told me several times as I was growing up. And during my own youth, Mom made it a priority to inculcate in her children behaviours and manners that she felt would indicate to others that we had transcended working-class poverty.[12]

In the end, I think Sharon listened to Mom, not Dad. At least, I don't remember hearing about Sharon getting into a fist fight with the girl who called her a wagon burner. But I do remember that Sharon was disappointed when a couple of months later she hosted a party to celebrate her birthday. She was turning twelve I think (maybe eleven) and wanted to have a dance for her birthday. Mom baked and decorated a cake and sent out invitations to all the kids in Sharon's class at our local school, as well as to her friends and relatives who lived out of town on the Tla'amin First Nation reserve. All her friends from Tla'amin showed up. Only one boy from her school class came. All the other neighbourhood kids stayed away. Mom was angry, ostensibly because none of them had let her or Sharon know they weren't coming. "They were probably really busy and couldn't make it," I remember her telling Sharon, though we all were pretty sure that wasn't the real reason. The next day, over breakfast and before our chores, Dad told Sharon to try and not let it bother her. He said something to the effect of, "It's their loss. Your true friends showed up, and you have family who love you." Sharon's friends played records and danced, and they ate a lot of cake and ice-cream. I watched these big kids doing all these cool dance moves, but I didn't dance myself. I was too young and too shy. I do remember feeling really good, though, when one of Sharon's friends from Tla'amin came over and sat beside me and talked to me, telling me that he didn't want to dance either.

When Sharon returned to live full-time with her birth father a year or so later, my mom gave her a recipe card with my mom's name, our address, and our phone number. Over the following years Mom occasionally got phone calls from Sharon. Once, I remember the phone waking us up late at night. Sharon was in the neighbouring province of Alberta. She was at a party and she was drinking. She just wanted to say hi, she said. Another time, she called to talk to Mom in the middle of a Saturday afternoon. Sharon was still in Alberta. Her boyfriend had left her, and she thought she might come home to Powell River – to Tla'amin. She wanted to know if Mom thought that was a good idea. Mom said it was. She told Sharon that it would be a chance for her to go back to school and get her grade twelve diploma.

I'm not certain, but I don't think Sharon ever came back to finish school. At least, I never saw her again. But Mom did. Sharon apparently dropped by our house once or twice when she was in town visiting her birth family, but those visits were incredibly brief and Sharon didn't even stay long enough to accept Mom's invitation to come into the house for tea. She just rolled down the window of the car she was in and spoke in the driveway. But the phone calls did continue off and on over the years, getting less and less frequent as time when by. One call, however, stands out in my memory. I wasn't home when it came, as I was already in Victoria attending university. But my dad phoned to tell me about it afterwards. It had been from a doctor in Alberta who had found the old recipe card with my mom's contact information in Sharon's purse. He was calling to say that Sharon had tried to commit suicide. A gun was involved. She was going to live, but she needed help. I believe Mom and Dad sent some money, and then helped coordinate with social workers and medical staff.

About twenty years later my dad took a phone call from a man in Vancouver. At the time I was working as a faculty member in the history department at the University of Saskatchewan. My research focus was on the history of the Coast Salish of British Columbia and Washington State. The man who called Dad explained that he was Sharon's partner, and that they had been together for several years. He was calling with the sad news that Sharon had been sick for quite a while and had recently died. The man said he had found the old recipe card in Sharon's purse. The paper was tattered, faded, and torn, but at some point, Sharon had had it laminated. Dad explained to me that the man had said that Sharon had spoken fondly of the time she had spent living with us. The man added that Sharon had told him that she had wanted to become a teacher like my mom (before she married my dad, Mom had taught in Catholic Day Schools in Port Hardy, Whitehorse, Grand Prairie, and Kamloops where the classes consisted of a mix of Indigenous and settler youth). But I guess life, and the systemic oppression that Indigenous people face, had gotten in the way of Sharon's dream. Sadly, when news came of Sharon's death, my mother was suffering from dementia and was not able to understand the message my father tried to relate to her.[13]

My brother Kerry's life involved struggles too, especially as he got older. He had a gentle heart and a creative mind, but he was impulsive and appeared unable to understand consequences. His primary school report cards said he was bright and got along well with other children. Then, when my brother was ten years old, a new family moved into our neighbourhood, with a boy who was Kerry's age. This boy was charismatic – a "born leader." He was also manipulative and mean. He soon had a clique of followers, and he got them to do things that hurt others. My brother seemed to be under a spell.

In grade six, Kerry's class went on a weekend camping trip. On the morning of the second day there was a knock on our front door. The teacher was standing there with Kerry. Kerry and two other boys had been sent home from camp, and the teacher was explaining to my mom that Kerry would be suspended from school for two weeks. At the camp, Kerry and the other eleven-year-old boys had been caught smoking marijuana and drinking beer. They had repeatedly shouted profanity at the teacher and chaperones. They had started fist fights with other boys. They had used bug repellent to spray obscenities onto the inside walls of the cabins, and then lit the spray on fire so the words were permanently burned into the walls. One of the cabins had caught fire and was only just extinguished before the other children's possessions had been burned up. The teacher explained that children could have died.

My dad, a four-year navy veteran who spent the rest of his life working in the hyper-masculine field of construction, thought more discipline was what was needed. Mom was devastated, but her response was to shower my brother in love. Love fixed things, Mom had repeatedly explained as we were growing up. The school principal arranged for Kerry to see a psychiatrist once a month, and Mom arranged for all of us to go to family counselling with a social worker. Mom tried hard. We all did, including Kerry, but trouble seemed to stalk Kerry.

By grade eight Kerry had been picked up several times by the RCMP for shoplifting. He skipped school regularly and failed almost all of his classes. He smoked and sold pot; he drank excessively on weekends after sneaking out of the house; and he stole money from me, my sister, and my parents. There was a suicide letter, and at least one failed suicide attempt. The drugs kept getting harder. He spent a night in the hospital having his stomach pumped after taking pills he had stolen from a cabinet in the doctor's office during a routine check-up. He dropped out of school, and my dad used his connections in the construction world to get Kerry jobs with various roofing companies and contractors. But Kerry inevitably failed to show up for work on time, and when he did show up he was often hungover. He stole from the cash registers when the bosses weren't looking. He got fired, repeatedly.

It was the year Kerry should have entered grade nine that I left Powell River to attend university in Victoria. Kerry and I stayed in touch. I wrote him letters (he didn't write back), but he did occasionally talk with me on the phone. Twice, Mom provided Kerry with ferry and bus tickets to travel down to Victoria so we could spend a few days together. On occasions like that, when it was just the two of us, we could talk. He would confide in me, and I would confide in him. He didn't know why he stole, he explained. He did drugs because it was fun. He meant it when he told Mom that he was sorry, and he meant it when he said he wouldn't do whatever-it-was-that-he-had-done again. But inevitably, his friends would call and the promises were forgotten; partying was the priority. To party, one needed money, and one needed time, and Kerry took these two things whenever he could from whomever he could.

It was September of 1988 when my dad and Kerry worked out a plan for what Dad called a "another fresh start." I was still in Victoria at the time, recently married and in the first term of my MA program, researching the history of the decolonization in the Philippines. Dad had always been of the opinion, and I shared it, that the challenges facing Kerry were mostly associated with the friends he kept, and in particular, the same boy who had joined Kerry's grade-four class so many years earlier, who continued to coax Kerry into "doing things." Through his work contacts, Dad arranged a labourer's job for Kerry on the yard crew of a hotel in Lake Louise. Two days before the job was scheduled to start, Kerry climbed onto an early morning bus headed to Vancouver. He would have a four hour wait in Vancouver before his scheduled connection took him on the bus ride to Lake Louise – just enough time, Dad said, for Kerry to get a haircut and grab a lunch.

But, Kerry didn't go for lunch and he didn't get a haircut. Instead he went to the "No. 5 Orange" – an exotic dancer club on the edge of Gastown in Vancouver's skid row district near the infamous corner of Hastings Avenue and Main Street. I guess he stayed there all afternoon and into the evening. The next day when the coroner spoke to my father, he said Kerry had such a cocktail of drugs and alcohol in his system that it was amazing that he could walk, let alone ride a motorbike. Alcohol, pot, hash, crack, and if memory serves, speed.

I rushed home from university after learning of Kerry's death and remember my dad telling me that the bartender told the coroner that Kerry had been at the pub all day watching the dancers, drinking, and occasionally "stepping outside" with the guys he was with. Whether my brother knew these guys before he arrived at the club, or whether he just connected with them once he got there, I don't know. What I do know is that Kerry somehow acquired the keys to one of the guy's motorbike and took it for a spin. The owner later told the police that Kerry had stolen it. The bartender said it looked like the guy had given Kerry the keys – that maybe Kerry was supposed to go out and "do the guy a favour."

Whatever the backstory, Kerry started driving the motorbike around Gastown around midnight. The Vancouver Harbour Police spotted him speeding and swerving near the statue celebrating "Gassy" Jack Deighton (a pioneer Vancouver saloon owner, bootlegger, and steamboat man, who also happened to be a pedophile who took a twelve-year-old Squamish First Nation girl for his wife) and they gave chase. Kerry sped the bike at between 90 and 120 km per hour, and headed the wrong way down Powell Street – a one-way street. The police followed with their lights flashing and siren blaring. According to the coroner, when Kerry got to the intersection of Hawks Ave and Powell Street he drove directly into a concrete barricade, flipped over the handlebars, and was thrown against a brick wall. When my father arrived in Vancouver to identify my brother's body, the coroner told him that Kerry had died instantly. He had been wearing a helmet, but when he hit the wall at that speed, and on that angle, his brain was severed from his spinal cord.

Roughly two hours before Kerry died, back in Powell River, as my Mom and Dad were watching the late-night news on TV, something hit the living room window. Dad got up to look on the porch and there he found a dead sharp-shinned hawk.[14] It had flown into the window and broken its neck – it too had died instantly.

Years earlier the psychiatrist who had worked with Kerry had told my parents that they thought my brother's behaviour was likely linked to his birth mother probably having drunk alcohol while pregnant – what today is called Fetal Alcohol Spectrum Disorder. The symptoms included trouble adapting to changing circumstances, impulsive behaviour, a compromised ability to weigh consequences, complications staying on task, problems conceptualizing time and keeping to schedules, and difficulty planning or working towards a goal.[15]

The family counsellor, meanwhile, had earlier given our parents a different diagnosis. Back when Kerry first started getting into trouble with the police, she had said that she thought Kerry's problems stemmed from my mother having shown him excessive love, affection, and forgiveness, and insufficient discipline. She had, to use a phrase that was common in the 1970s and '80s, "spoiled him." Either way, according to the both the social worker and the psychiatrist, the fault for my brother's "problems" – and by extension the responsibility for his death in a high-speed police chase – could ultimately be traced back to one, or both, of Kerry's mothers.

Blaming mothers for the actions of their sons has a long and troubling history that is intimately linked to patriarchy and colonialism. It's part of a larger societal practice of blaming women generally for the behaviour of men. Women who are the victims of rape have too often been told and made to feel that it was their fault for leading the attacker on – for being in the wrong place at the wrong time, for wearing the wrong clothes, for dancing provocatively – for simply being female.

Women have been, and are still today, blamed for shaping men's behaviour and character, regardless of whether they treat men well or poorly. In my family history, blaming mothers for their son's failings has a long history. Similar to the way both my brother's birth and adoptive mothers were blamed by medical professionals and social workers (and certain friends and relatives) for my brother's unwelcome behaviour, my great-grandmother had been blamed for her son's (my maternal grandfather's) lack of manliness during the First World War. My maternal grandfather Sgt. William Vint Wightman's official Canadian military records show him as having been diagnosed with "shell shock" in 1916 after he had been physically injured, partially buried alive, and left for three days in no-man's-land during the Battle of the Somme.[16] He "recovered" and continued to serve for the remainder of the war. He later died of lung cancer in 1944, following more than two decades of illness and suffering resulting from his having also been repeatedly exposed to poison gas in the trenches of Flanders. Family oral histories describe how he additionally endured vivid nightmares and anxiety in the years following his military service. The official *Canadian Medical History of the Great War* described shell shock "as a variety of conditions ranging from cowardice to maniacal insanity." In fact, military medical practitioners at the time determined that shell shock was not caused by exploding shells, but rather by mothers who had excessively pampered and feminized their sons: "'Shell-shock' is a manifestation of childishness and femininity. Against such there is no remedy."[17]

I've always felt a special closeness and affinity to my grandfather Bill even though he died long before I was born. I've likewise often wondered how his mother, my great-grandmother, dealt with the fact that she lost one of her sons (Hurbert) to a German bullet and had two of her other boys (my grandfather Bill and his brother Brice) return home with damaged psyches and carrying the stigma of "childishness and femininity," implicitly due to her poor skills as a mother.[18]

In settler colonial states like Canada, a host of rationales have been deployed in attempts to dismiss Indigenous mothers as unfit to raise their children. Nearly all of these can be boiled down to definitions of *what* Indigenous mothers are in terms of their relationship to settler colonialism, rather than *who* they are as people. That is to say, Indigenous mothers have long represented to the Canadian and American governments the source of future opposition to settler colonial control. As women, Indigenous mothers give birth to children with Aboriginal Rights. Unassimilated Indigenous children are reminders that the settler colonial process of displacing Indigenous people from their ancestral lands, alienating them from their resources, and assimilating them into Canadian societies so that settler society can have unfettered access to those lands and resources remains unfinished and incomplete – an ongoing process.

The children of Indigenous mothers inherit a perspective that decentres and disrupts American and Canadian national myths by challenging the idea that North America's colonial histories ended in 1776 and 1867 respectively. Moreover, they expose the self-serving interests of those who fought for responsible government and then falsely declared victory while simultaneously working to deny Indigenous people the ability to participate in federal elections until the 1960s – by which time Indigenous populations had declined so greatly in relation to settler communities that they no longer posed a political threat.[19]

The children of Indigenous mothers inherit world views that challenge the idea that Indigenous people are best understood as minor characters *in* the early chapters of the unfolding story of nation states, and instead situate Canada and the United States as *things* (events, ideas, and structures) that occur *within* the unfolding of multiple Indigenous histories. The children of Indigenous mothers inherit memories across generations that through their retelling expose the betrayals behind broken treaty promises, reveal the consequences of unfulfilled common law protections, and highlight the hollowness of constitutionally protected rights that though listed remain undefined and non-operationalized.

Indigenous people have not been colonized and displaced from their land because of their race or ethnicity (though alleged racial inferiority and assumed cultural simplicity have often been used to justify the actions).

Rather these things have been done to them because Indigenous people were (and remain) "in the way." It was while working with the Stó:lō in the early 1990s that I first heard Ernie Crey (who would later become Chief of the Cheam First Nation) explain that "Aboriginal rights and title are not based on race. We could be white, or we could be purple, and we'd still have Aboriginal rights to our ancestral land and resources. We have these rights because we were here first."

Kerry's ancestors were here first, long before any of my own. It is that presence that causes problems for settlers. Initially Indigenous people were "a problem" for settlers because they impeded access to land and resources. Later, once they no longer posed a military threat, settlers reclassified them as people 'with problems' because they struggled to live within settler colonial society. The assumed solution to the *Indian problem* was to remove them from their land and place them on reserves. The assumed solution for *Indians with problems* was to remove them from their reserves and from their mothers so they could be assimilated. Indian residential schools, the '60s Scoop, and the ongoing crisis of Missing and Murdered Indigenous Women and Girls all send a clear message to Indigenous women that Canadian society considers them unfit mothers, unfit daughters, and unfit spouses, unworthy of the respect and protections accorded to white settler men and women.

After Kerry died, Mom went into a deep depression. Losing the gift child that had been entrusted to her to love and raise made her feel like a failure. For nearly three months she hardly spoke to anyone and spent many days just lying in bed. Then one morning just days before Christmas 1988, she came downstairs and walked into the kitchen and greeted us with a smile and a cheerful "good morning." I remember we all commented that she looked great, and that we were happy to see her smile. Without prompting, she explained that during the night Kerry had appeared to her, standing at the foot of her bed. "It was real," she asserted; "it wasn't a dream." She went on to explain that Kerry had looked relaxed and content. Mom said my brother had told her that he wasn't suffering anymore; he was in heaven. He had been suffering earlier, but then Mom's mom (my Grandma Marie) had come to him and taken him by the hand, and brought him from purgatory into heaven.[20]

I didn't know what to make of Mom's story. I still don't. I don't know if I believe what she believed, but I've tried. Over the course of my life I've found that, regardless of how hard I try, belief and non-belief both tend to be somewhat situational. It is easier for me to believe in what my childhood catechism teacher referred to as "the communion of saints" when I am in a church celebrating mass (it's also easier to believe this when I'm in a longhouse attending a Coast Salish winter dance); it is easier for me to believe in the physical reality of sasquatch when I am out in the mountains and forests with one of my Coast Salish friends sharing stories around a campfire and watching the moon rise above the trees; and it is easier for me to believe that all people are inherently kind and generous on those occasions when I witness selfless acts by others.

Not believing can also be situational. I know it's easier for many of my non-Indigenous friends to *not* believe that settler colonialism is an ongoing system of oppression when they are not informed about Indigenous history, have not spent time talking with and learning from Indigenous people, have not become educated about the constitutional protections (recognized by the Supreme Court in numerous decisions) of Aboriginal Rights, and have not taken the time to recognize and acknowledge the invisibility of their white privilege.[21]

As a university professor (since 2001) I have had many privileges, such as being largely free to choose the research projects that interest me. Since 1992, when I started working for, and with, the Stó:lō ("People of the River") Coast Salish people of the lower Fraser River watershed, my scholarship has been driven by questions and conversations that have emerged from within communities.[22]

To this day I remain deeply intrigued by, and respectful of, the way the Coast Salish people attribute active agency to ancestral spirits in their lives and in the unfolding of their history, as well as in the revelation of historical knowledge.[23] With my Indigenous research partners, we integrate ceremony and ritual into our research methodologies. I remain as interested in Indigenous historical consciousness (what people think about the past and how they come to know and re-interpret that past over time) as I am in settler history.[24]

. Sitting in a prominent place on the shelf in my living room is the hawk that flew into my parents' window the night my brother Kerry died. My father arranged for a taxidermist to preserve it. Hawks are one of several raptor birds that in Coast Salish cosmology are understood to be messengers. Hawks, like owls, bring messages from the spirit world that help guide people and encourage them to be reflective and cautious so as to enable them to better steer clear from danger. Seeing a hawk swoop past your car as you travel, for example, is widely recognized as an invitation to slow down and assess one's direction and speed.

That hawk reminds me of my brother and his death at the corner of Hawks and Powell. Some roads (like Powell Street in Vancouver) are designed only to permit traffic to travel one way – efforts to challenge that direction are dangerous and potentially deadly. Powell Street honours Canada's settler colonial past and reminds us that it is still with us. Other roads (like Hawks Avenue in Vancouver) are two-way streets. In my mind, Hawks Avenue represents the possibilities and potential of nascent reconciliation in Canada. Importantly, Hawks Avenue does not run parallel to Powell Street. As my brother tragically discovered on the night he was being chased by the police, Hawks runs perpendicular to Powell. Hawks Avenue neither requires people to travel in a single direction, nor does it prevent them from turning around, if after a while they determine that they have been travelling in the wrong direction or have travelled past their desired destination.

In her will, Mom requested that she and Kerry be buried together. Located in Coast Salish territory are not only the graves of my brother's Indigenous birth ancestors, but also those of his adoptive mother and father, all four of his adoptive grandparents, and two of his adoptive great-grandparents. I often reflect upon the fact that all of these bodies have returned to earth and literally become part of the ancestral territory of the Coast Salish people.

In the traditions taught to me by Coast Salish Knowledge Keepers Andy Commodore, Wes Sam, Tilly Gutierrez, Nancy Philips, and Bill Pat-Charlie, my own ancestors' spirits are believed to remain active in the places they frequented during their lives, as well as in those places where their bodies are interred. According to these Elders, my ancestors are able to communicate with the ancestors of the Indigenous people of this territory. According to both my mother's epistemology and that of my Indigenous friends and colleagues, there exist ways to enable dialogue and to build cross-cultural understanding that go beyond face-to-face meetings and government-sponsored reconciliation initiatives. In their traditions, the heavy lifting of building reconciliation may well be being done by the deceased – who in turn are believed to inform the living in ways the living do not always fully appreciate.

Today, as a society, I believe we are at a juncture not unlike Powell Street and its intersection with Hawks Avenue. As settlers we have been following the one-way path of Powell Street for too long (and dragging Indigenous people along with us). The single-minded and unidirectional thrust of settler colonialism harms Indigenous people, while it violates our own settler legal traditions, ethical sensibilities, and moral codes. Many Indigenous people have tried to resist this movement, as have a growing number of Canada's non-Indigenous population, but driving against the flow of settler colonialism is inevitably fraught with dangers.

So how do we turn? When I consider my extended family, I see the conundrum. Both my parents were explicitly anti-racist, but their working-class struggles rendered them blind to their white privilege. They were sympathetic to Indigenous people and tried to be empathetic, but were inevitably patronizing in their application of allyship and support. Likewise, my wife Teresa is perhaps an exemplar of the more recent immigrants of colour who are not directly implicated in the historical actions of displacing Indigenous people, but who are nonetheless beneficiaries of the ongoing structures of settler colonialism despite suffering from racism themselves alongside Indigenous people. Across generations settler Canadians have lived lives that have created stories that link them to the land and give their presence here meaning. These stories are authentic and legitimate. But they have been composed and recited in ways that have for too long worked to eclipse Indigenous people's own much deeper stories and allodial connections to the land. Settlers' personal stories have for too long been informed by, and integrated into, the larger nation state's narrative that incorrectly and self-servingly depicted Indigenous people as inevitably, eventually, disappearing. They are not. We are all here to stay.

Working together, I believe we can develop and share the knowledge, creativity, and vocabulary necessary to dismantle settler colonialism and build something new in its place – to transform the conundrum of double permanence into shared opportunity with mutual advantages.

ACKNOWLEDGMENTS

I am grateful to the friends, colleagues, and family members who provided thoughtful comments and suggestions on an earlier draft of this essay. In particular, Alessandro Tarsia, Colin Osmond, John Lutz, Teresa Carlson, Stormy Carlson, William Carlson, and Ben Carlson.

NOTES

1 See Brian W. Dippie's classic work, *The Vanishing American: White Attitudes and U.S. Indian Policy* (Middletown, CN: Wesleyan University Press, 1982). For the Canadian context, a good place to start is Daniel Francis's *The Imaginary Indian: The Image of the Indian in Canadian Culture* (Vancouver: Arsenal Pulp Press, 1992).

2 For an account of the displacement of the Tla'amin People from Tees'kwat, see my PhD student Colin Osmond's recently completed dissertation "Paycheques and Paper Promises: Economics, Family Life, and Canadian Settler Colonialism in Two Indigenous Communities" (PhD diss., University of Saskatchewan, 2020). The colonization of Tees'kwat mirrored a process that had earlier occurred repeatedly, with minor derivations, all across British Columbia – and was one that I worked with Stó:lō people to document in the Fraser River region: Keith Thor Carlson, *The Power of Place, the Problem of Time: Aboriginal Collective Identity and Historical Consciousness in the Cauldron of Colonialism* (Toronto: University of Toronto Press, 2010). See also Keith Thor Carlson, "Toward an Indigenous Historiography: Events, Migrations, and the Formation of 'Post-Contact' Coast Salish Collective Identities" in Bruce Granville Miller, ed, *"Be of Good Mind": Essays on the Coast Salish* (Vancouver: UBC Press, 2007), 138 [Carlson, "Toward an Indigenous Historiography"].

3 Thomas King, *The Truth about Stories: A Native Narrative* (Toronto: Anansi Press, 2003), 2.

4 *Ibid* at 10.

5 *Ibid* at 155–67.

6 It was only on 1 January 2020, that *An Act Respecting First Nations, Inuit and Métis Children, Youth and Families*, SC 2019, c 24 (Bill C-92), came into effect which

recognized Indigenous communities' inherent jurisdiction over children in their communities.

7 For examples of some of the best scholarship on this subject, see Chris Andersen, *"Metis": Race, Recognition, and the Struggle for Indigenous Peoplehood* (Vancouver: UBC Press, 2015); Kim Tallbear, *Native American DNA: Tribal Belonging and the False Promise of Genetic Science* (Minneapolis: University of Minnesota Press, 2013); Adam Gaudry, "Becoming Indigenous: The Rise of Eastern Metis in Canada" (25 October 2015), online: *The Conversation* <https://theconversation.com/becoming-indigenous-the-rise-of-eastern-metis-in-canada-80794>.

8 See Ernie Crey & Suzanne Fournier, *Stolen From Our Embrace: The Abduction of First Nations Children and the Restoration of Aboriginal Communities* (Vancouver: Douglas & McIntyre Press, 1998); Allyson Stevenson, *Intimate Integration: A Study of Aboriginal Transracial Adoption in Saskatchewan, 1944–1984* (PhD diss., Department of History, University of Saskatchewan, 2015); Raven Sinclair, "Identity Lost and Found: Lessons from The Sixties Scoop" (2007) 3:1 First Peoples Child & Family Review 66. For insights into the cause and expression of the constitutional contestations between the federal and BC governments in the 1950s and early 1960s over funding, programing, and citizenship for First Nations people, see Byron Plant, "The Politics of Indian Administration: A Post-Revisionist History of Interstate Relations in Mid-twentieth Century British Columbia" (PhD diss., University of Saskatchewan, 2009).

9 In Canada, the best example of scholarship exploring the myths of aggressive Indigenous male masculinity and dangerously lascivious Indigenous female femininity are Sarah Carter's *Capturing Women: The Manipulation of Cultural Imagery in Canada's Prairie West* (Montreal: McGill-Queen's University Press, 1997) and her more recent book, *The Importance of Being Monogamous: Marriage and Nation Building in Western Canada to 1915* (Edmonton: University of Alberta Press, 2008). For critical assessments of the Hollywood manipulation and use of images of Indigenous people, see Jacqueline Kilpatrick, *Celluloid Indians: Native Americans and Film* (Lincoln: University of Nebraska Press, 1999); R. Philip Loy, *Westerns and American Culture* (Jefferson, NC: McFarland & Co., 2001); Edward Bushcombe, *Injuns! Native Americans in the Movies* (Chicago: University of Chicago Press, 2006).

10 In my hometown of Powell River, the Tla'amin People only recently secured a treaty with the federal and provincial governments of Canada and British Columbia in 2016. By then most of their territory and resources had been altered and/or alienated through industrial and urban developments.

11 I first became aware of the idea of whiteness and white privilege when reading Veronika Strong-Boag et al, eds, *Rethinking Canada: The Promise of Women's History* (Oxford: Oxford University Press, 1986). For additional scholarship on this subject see Louise Keating, "Interrogating 'Whiteness,' (De)Constructing 'Race'" in Maryemma Graham, Sharon Pineault-Burke & Marianna White Davis,

eds, *Teaching African American Literature* (New York: Routledge, 1998); Noel
Ignatiev, *How the Irish Became White* (New York: Routledge, 2008); Thomas
K. Nakayama & Robert L. Krizek, "Whiteness: A Strategic Rhetoric" (1995) 81
Quarterly Journal of Speech 291; Zeus Leonardo, "The Souls of White Folk:
Critical Pedagogy, Whiteness Studies, and Globalization Discourse" (2002)
5:1 Race Ethnicity and Education 29; Eric Arnesen, "Whiteness and the Historian's
Imagination" (2001) 60 International Labor and Working-Class History 3.

12 Mom insisted, for example, we set the table and used our eating utensils "properly";
she made us take the laundry back in off the clothes line and "do it again" if we
failed to hang the clothes on the line in proper order of pants followed by shirts
followed by socks followed by underwear, explaining "I don't want the neighbours
thinking we just put our clothes out all higgly piggly"; she did not tolerate swearing
or foul language of any kind, etc.

13 In the spring of 2019, after being diagnosed with terminal cancer, and with my
mother in a care home with advanced dementia, my father asked me to assist him in
setting up a scholarship in my mother's name at the local Powell River high school.
He endowed the scholarship with $20,000 so that it could provide $2,000 annually
for ten years to "a female First Nation student heading into higher education."

14 *Accipter straitus* – a bird that does not normally fly at night in the dark.

15 Mayo Clinic, "Fetal Alcohol Syndrome," online: https://www.mayoclinic.org
/diseases-conditions/fetal-alcohol-syndrome/symptoms-causes/syc-20352901.

16 Several months later, top officials in the Canadian military declared that field
physicians, medics, and standard field officers could no longer use the diagnosis
of shell shock to describe men whose minds and emotions had been destroyed by
industrial conflict and by their witnessing of, and participation in, the slaughter
of other human beings. "In no circumstances whatever," the order ran, "will the
expression 'shell-shock' be made use of verbally or be recorded in any regimental
or other casualty report, or in any hospital or other medical document except in
cases so classified by the order of the officer commanding the special hospital for
such cases." Once the term was prohibited, the top brass could boast to Canadians
that soldiers were no longer being diagnosed with the condition (as though shell
shock no longer existed).

17 Sir Andrew MacPhail, *The History of the Canadian Forces in the Great War: The
Medical Services* (Ottawa: F.A. Acland Publishing, 1925), 170.

18 My great-uncle Herbert Wightman was a sniper who was killed by a German
sniper only a few short days after arriving on the front. My great-uncle Brice
Wightman served in the North Irish Medical Corp and was awarded the Croix de
Guerre by the French government. Like my grandfather Bill, great-uncle Brice was
diagnosed with shell shock during the war and struggled with post-traumatic stress
for the remainder of his life.

19 In the United States the Fifteenth Amendment of 1870 granted all US citizens the
right to vote, but it was not until the passage of the 1924 *Snyder Act* (a.k.a. *Indian*

Citizenship Act) that Indigenous people could, in theory, exercise that right. In practice, individual states continued to block Indigenous people from exercising the franchise for decades. It was not until the 1960s that the last state removed the conditions that prevented Indigenous people from exercising their right to vote. In Canada, it was not until the 1960s that First Nations secured the right to vote in federal elections.

20 Mom was a Roman Catholic who had a crucifix on her bedroom wall and who prayed the rosary at home, even though at the time of Kerry's death she had not attended mass more than half a dozen times over the previous two decades. She had, in fact, originally been raised in the United Church and only made the denominational shift after she started working as a nineteen-year-old teacher in remote Catholic Indian day schools. Her German mother, Anna Marie Kammer, had been born and raised Catholic but had changed her last name to Cameron to better avoid anti-German racism during the Great War, and then shifted to Protestantism when she married my Northern Irish grandfather. Mom had first clashed with the priest when (as Mom prepared to adopt Kerry) he told her that artificial birth control was a sin. Her fissure with the Church hierarchy (but not her faith) came when the same priest told her that her mother (who had died six months before Kerry was adopted) would not get into heaven because she had abandoned the true faith when she converted from Catholicism to Protestantism after marrying my Northern Irish grandfather.

21 It is a unique feature of privilege that it is generally only invisible to those who carry it. White privilege is only invisible to whites, male privilege is only invisible to men, class privilege is only invisible to the wealthy, etc., and as a result those with privilege also carry comfort. To those outside the various bubbles these comfort-providing privileges are clear and apparent, and, thanks to this, settler colonialism and racism are sustained without critique from those who benefit from them for as long as their privileges remain invisible.

22 I have sought to co-create projects, and then work with Indigenous community representatives and members to determine how best to balance the emotional and intellectual labour and responsibility we will share as we collaborate to co-execute the project, co-analyse and co-interpret the evidence, and co-mobilize and co-translate the results into language and formats that will achieve the goals that the community and I have together identified as priorities. My scholarly activities exist on a spectrum of shared responsibility and authority that adapts to the shifting needs, priorities, and capacities of my Indigenous partners. Sometimes my partners invite me to do much of the research and analysis on my own (especially on expert witness reports where we need to demonstrate to a judge that my analysis was without prejudice). On other occasions, I am less centrally involved and play a role more akin to that of support personnel. More typically, "the work" of designing, researching, analysing, interpreting, and communicating are shared, thus rendering the research outcomes products of numerous and

sustained conversations. In our collaborative, community-engaged scholarship, my Indigenous partners and I aspire to contribute to the critical process of documenting and interpreting the history of settler colonialism, but we situate it, not as a single-minded, unidirectional process that has unfolded *on* Indigenous people, but rather as a system of colonial displacement and control that has been unfolding *within* the history of Indigenous people. Thus situated, its continuance need not be seen as inevitable.

23 See, for example, Keith Thor Carlson, "Orality About Literacy: The 'Black and White' of Salish History" in Keith Thor Carlson, Kristina Fagan, & Natalia Khanenko-Friesen, eds, *Orality and Literacy: Reflections across Disciplines* (Toronto: University of Toronto Press, 2011) 43; Keith Thor Carlson, "Aboriginal Diplomacy: Queen Victoria Comes to Canada, and Coyote Goes to London" in J. Marshall Beier, ed, *Indigenous Diplomacies* (New York: Paulgrave MacMillan, 2009), 155; Keith Thor Carlson, "Born Again of the People: Luis Taruc and Peasant Ideology in Philippine Revolutionary Politics" (2008) 41:82 Histoire Sociale/Social History 417; Keith Thor Carlson, "Rethinking Dialogue and History: The King's Promise and the 1906 Aboriginal Delegation to London" (2005) 16:2 Native Studies Review 1.

24 See, for example, Carlson, "Toward an Indigenous Historiography," *supra* note 2; Keith Thor Carlson, "Reflections on Indigenous History and Memory: Reconstructing and Reconsidering Contact" in John Lutz, ed, *Myth and Memory: Stories of Indigenous-European Contact* (Vancouver: UBC Press, 2007), 46; Keith Thor Carlson, "The Indians and the Crown: Aboriginal Memories of Royal Promises in Pacific Canada" in Colin MacMillan Coates, ed, *Majesty in Canada: Essays on the Role of Royalty* (Toronto: Dundurn Press, 2005), 68; Keith Thor Carlson with Naxaxalhts'i (Albert McHalsie), "Indigenous Memoryscapes: Stó:lō History from Stone and Fire" in Sarah De Nardi et al, eds, *The Routledge Handbook of Memory and Place* (London: Routledge, 2020), 138; Keith Thor Carlson, "'Don't Destroy the Writing': Time- and Space-based Communication and the Colonial Strategy of Mimicry in Nineteenth Century Salish-Missionary Relations on Canada's Pacific Coast" in Tony Ballantyne & Lachlan Paterson, eds, *Indigenous Textual Cultures, the Politics of Difference and the Dynamism of Practice* (Durham: Duke University Press, 2020), 101.

3 Look at Your "Pantses": The Art of Wearing and Representing Indigenous Culture as Performative Relationship

AIMÉE CRAFT

Looking in the Window-Mirror

As I sit in my office and ponder this question of cultural appropriation, I can't help but look down at my beautiful new Manitobah Mukluks – the "gatherer" style, limited edition, with the Bethany Yellowtail stylized Crow (Apsaalooke) & Northern Cheyenne design – and my Voilà leggings designed by Manitoban Métis artist Andréanne Dandeneau, adorned with her father David's Spirit Bear print. I'm wearing my favourite logo t-shirt with a woodlands-inspired design and simple statement – "Water is Life" – designed by Anishinaabekwe Danielle Morrison. My gaze then focuses on my wrist and the beautiful smoke-tanned moose-hide beaded cuff created by Cree artist Cookie Simpson. My hand then rises to touch my musk ox bone earrings designed by Gwich'in/Métis/Scandinavian artist Naomi Bourque, which are, by the way, really "badass" as my friend Caleb puts it. I then look at the art on my walls: Métis artist Christi Belcourt's print *Offerings to Save the World*, Linus Woods's (Dakota/Ojibway) *She Dances Everywhere* (an original painting commissioned for my first book). On my desk there's Shain Jackson's Coast Salish-inspired inlay of mother-of-pearl in cedar. Next to it is KC Adams's (Cree/Anishinaabe/British) traditionally constructed clay vessel. As I look at this beauty surrounding me, my ears are hearing Kinnie Starr (Mohawk/Dutch/German/Irish) singing softly in the background, "who will save our waters? Save them for our great-granddaughters? Save them for our great-granddaughters' sons?" (also badass).

I stand up to look in the full-length window of my office and to observe my reflection. The night sky provides the dark background for me to look at all of this and wonder, "Am I appropriating?" Jonathan Hart defines cultural appropriation as "members of one culture tak[ing] the cultural practices of another as if their own, or as if the right of possession should not be questioned or contested."[1] Richard Rogers defines it as "the use of one culture's symbols, artifacts, genres, rituals, or technologies by members of another culture – regardless of intent, ethics, function, or outcome."[2]

What is that fine line between the celebration and support of Indigenous art and its exploitative use for other means by other cultures or "outsiders"? I'm careful to think about what using a term like "outsider" means in an Indigenous context because each of us is an outsider, in some way. In my case, I am not part of most of the nations that are represented in the tableau I just painted for you. These brilliant artists come from other territories and other nations, each with their own cultural and artistic inspiration. I am not comfortable with pan-Indigenous claims over art or culture, which is often defaulted to for convenience.

I also wonder if there are different expectations regarding cultural appropriation relating to people of settler origin (see, for example, the widely discussed debate about *who gets to wear beaded earrings*)[3] and the questions that arise *between* Indigenous people and those of mixed Indigenous and settler ancestry. What is the degree of relationship required to meet the expectations of reasonable consent to sit with another person's (or culture's) Indigenous art? And what if their art and culture benefits you, financially or otherwise? How much does your use of their art need to benefit them? What are acceptable relationships of reciprocity in the context of academic and artistic collaborations? Each question leads me down the path of another sub-question and the list grows, like the swollen belly of an expectant mother. But when and how will the answers finally come?

In many ways, there are no singular answers to these questions about cultural appropriation. Western legal constructs fall short of providing us with clear legal responses to questions of Indigenous cultural appropriation and intellectual property. As Rosemary Coombe argues, "simplistic reductions of Native concerns to trademark or copyright considerations and the assertion of intellectual property rights fail to reflect important dimensions of Native aspirations and impose colonial juridical categories on postcolonial struggles in a fashion that reenacts the cultural violence of colonization."[4] Anishinaabe artist Aylan Couchie expressed the view that "the appropriation of Indigenous stories, ways of being, and artworks is simply an extension of colonialism and settlers' assertion of rights over the property of Indigenous people. The history of colonizing Indigenous identity through images, film and narratives has played its part in placing Indigenous perspectives at a subordinate level. It's this hegemonic system, filled with stereotypes and suppression, that continues to thrive within institutions. It erects barriers for Indigenous voices."[5]

As I continue to look in the window-mirror, I wonder if the work of continuously asking these questions is *exactly the work we need to do* to interrogate the ongoing challenge of accommodating the tensions between collective culture, individual artistic expression, and the gift of art to our relatives. We must continue to question what it takes to be in a relationship of reciprocity when we think of employing Indigenous art forms to support the dissemination of knowledge either by, with, for, or about Indigenous people.

Possessing the Relationship

I admittedly struggle with the idea of explaining or interrogating cultural appropriation (or misappropriation)[6] from an Indigenous perspective because the premise of cultural appropriation is some form of possessory right over either a material object or a cultural expression. In Western terms, cultural appropriation can relate to culture or identity (often intertwining concepts) and their unauthorized use by another culture or identity.

Questioning the issue of cultural appropriation requires that we tackle questions of influence, tradition, and collective heritage. It draws attention to the idea of balance and the desired outcome of mino-bimaadiziwin (collective wellness) and asks who will benefit from this use through potential direct and indirect outcomes, including financial and reputational ones. This consequently requires a contextualized approach to each situation in which the potential for cultural appropriation might arise. It becomes less a technical question than an ethical one, which engages reciprocity and the development and maintenance of relationships.

Many of us would agree that mixed forms of media help communicate ideas and that an artistic interpretation of a complex concept can help make it more accessible. And sometimes we think of art as a way to draw people into a conversation. Indigenous art forms are particularly powerful methods of communication, and Indigenous methodologies in art will sometimes incorporate ceremonial aspects. Moreover, Indigenous art's aesthetic value cannot be underestimated.

This is where I think the core issue of good relationships needs to be examined. If including Indigenous cultural imagery and art stands to benefit the user, either through increased financial gain or by bringing attention and notoriety to what is being produced (whether it be events, paintings, books, songs, etc.), the ethics of engagement with culture and the question of misappropriation need to be confronted. This includes tackling the dimensions of power, gender, and socio-economic status as starting points. It requires attention to all dimensions of the relationship, not only those elements that help positively build a relationship for the purpose of obtaining what the user might want, but also requires accepting the relationality as a whole and acknowledging that there may ultimately be no relationship and no desired outcome achieved. That is a risk for the investment of time put into the development of a relationship.

To better illustrate these ideas, think of the context of a book written by a non-Indigenous author who wants a visual representation of an idea. They should intend to pay an artist for the work they will do to bring their core ideas to life and respect the artistic process and the artist's vision. They should credit them appropriately and compensate them appropriately for their work. And is that even enough?

For anyone (whether Indigenous or non-Indigenous) working with an Indigenous artist, or if you are proposing to collaborate or co-create with an Indigenous artist, you must collectively generate an artistic expression in a way that is mutually beneficial and non-exploitative, based on ongoing consent. Also, think about the ethics around what type of art is engaged (both medium and cultural style). For example, I would never put Coast Salish art on the cover of my book about Treaty 1 in Manitoba. It would be a misrepresentation of the content of the book, and likely offensive to the Indigenous artist, who might see their art's use as a commodification and means to sell a book, rather than a way to illustrate ideas through their work. Art in context matters.

In 2017, the Canada Council for the Arts issued a policy statement entitled Supporting Indigenous Art in the Spirit of Cultural Self-Determination and Opposing Appropriation,[7] which affirmed the following:

> The Canada Council believes that an approach that respects First Nations, Inuit and Métis artistic expression, cultural protocols, Indigenous rights and Indigenous worldviews is a fundamental part of the processes of conciliation and reconciliation in this country. We understand this to mean that the customary and contemporary cultural and artistic practices of Indigenous peoples must remain in the control of Indigenous peoples and communities.

The Canada Council policy adopts the principles of the United Nations Declaration on the Rights of Indigenous Peoples (UNDRIP),[8] Articles 11 and 31, which confirm Indigenous cultural self-determination and the obligations of States to recognize and protect the exercise of those rights:

Article 11

1   Indigenous peoples have the right to practice and revitalize their cultural traditions and customs. This includes the right to maintain, protect and develop the past, present and future manifestations of their cultures, such as archaeological and historical sites, artefacts, designs, ceremonies, technologies and visual and performing arts and literature.

Article 31

1   Indigenous peoples have the right to maintain, control, protect and develop their cultural heritage, traditional knowledge and traditional cultural expressions, as well as the manifestations of their sciences, technologies and cultures, including human and genetic resources, seeds, medicines, knowledge of the properties of fauna and flora, oral traditions, literatures,

designs, sports and traditional games and visual and performing arts. They also have the right to maintain, control, protect and develop their intellectual property over such cultural heritage, traditional knowledge, and traditional cultural expressions.

2   In conjunction with indigenous [sic] peoples, States shall take effective measures to recognize and protect the exercise of these rights.

For many Indigenous Peoples around the world, certain forms of art that are representative of their cultures are not a consumable possession; they are deeply embedded in cultural and spiritual practices. In some cases, this art deeply engages with systems of governance and kinship. Therefore the appropriation of these forms of art, even with "good intentions," requires ethical consideration that extends beyond what systems of international and domestic law can provide. An Indigenous ethic and deference to Indigenous legal orders is needed to begin to understand the complexities of systems of relational reciprocity and respect.

This Art Is Culture, Language, Spirit, Law!

An engaged ethic around cultural appropriation requires us to think of Indigenous art as a situs of story and law. For example, many Indigenous women (many of whom I call friends) continue to explore Indigenous beadwork and its normative implications, both past and present (I'm thinking here of Elaine Alexie, Dawnis Kennedy, Cathy Mattes, Christi Belcourt, Sherry Farrell-Racette, KC Adams, and many others). What might seem to the naked eye as a "pretty design" is actually deeply imbued with the living values and legal orders of their Indigenous Nations. This is not something we should cavalierly appropriate, given the undocumented spiritual and cultural consequences that might be attached to the use of this imagery.

I think also of a logo that I had asked Danielle Morrison to design – a representation of the Nibi Declaration[9] and the values and teachings it contains. What Danielle had accomplished through her logo was evident in the moments that Elder Allan White spent interpreting the logo for me, as seen through his eyes. According to him, all of the elements of Anishinaabe nibi inaakonigewin (Water Law) were reflected back to him: a powerful testament to the importance of correlating art and message. This was also an important reminder that when art is attached to Indigenous languages it can take on a different meaning. For example, what was represented in the logo was linked to the concept of gakina gegoo, a term in Anishinaabemowin that means everything or the connection between all things.[10] This demonstrates that concepts are neither singular nor static, but rather living and inter-connected. In this case, the artist's design was able to give life to the language and represent a concept that is too abstract to be communicated effectively in English.

On the Ethics of Giving and Receiving

The foundations of appropriate cultural collaboration (as opposed to cultural appropriation or misappropriation) are relationships of respect and reciprocity. In hearing these words, some of you may think of the concepts that provide foundations for Indigenous treaty making. In many respects they are equivalent in nature because they develop a relationship in which the parties agree to work together. In Anishinaabemowin, this idea is referred to as aagooiidiwin.

The deeper meaning of aagooiidiwin in the Treaty context is that what was being offered at the time of forging the treaty relationship was on top of what we already had: adding to something already there. What the Treaty built upon was the foundation or the framework of Indigenous Laws and governance that was already in place for the Anishinaabe: "the principles and foundations of who we are as Anishinaabe." This includes territorial and cultural sovereignty.[11]

As explained to me by Elder Harry Bone, aagooiidiwin is an important legal principle that derives from inaakonigewin and compels the bringing together of things with the purpose of building relationships. "Aagooiidiwin is that we agree to work together."[12] It is a building of relationship or "bringing people together."[13]

In many cases, research ethics will require the development of a research agreement – an agreement on how to work together. In developing ethical relationships, we can be guided by the principles of ethical research in the Tri-Council Policy Statement, Chapter 9: Research Involving the First Nations, Inuit and Métis Peoples of Canada (TCPS2),[14] which details the ethical criteria for engaging with Indigenous Peoples and research. I note, however, that although Chapter 9 promotes research involving Indigenous Peoples premised on respectful relationships and generally acknowledges that "building reciprocal, trusting relationships will take time," it still generally characterizes Indigenous people as research subjects or participants rather than self-determining actors within the research. These principles of ethical research also continue to foster the impersonal in the research relationship between the researcher and the researched. The researcher is asked to sacrifice personal relationships for the "objectivity" and "rigour" of scientific research. This need for objective distance also allows for some impersonal and exploitative research relationships to be validated by Western ethical standards, while in breach of Indigenous research values that include holistic relationships built over time that are meant to last for lifetimes. However, the TCPS2 acknowledges that it will need to evolve as a living document over time and with more knowledge about how Indigenous research can be conducted ethically.[15]

Efforts to shift research from Indigenous people *being* researched to *leading* the research (from conceptualization to data collection and analysis) have created some dramatic shifts in how the ethical dimensions of research are approached. With respect to research data, most Indigenous research ethics now rely on the concept of OCAP® (ownership, control, access, and possession) developed in the context of health research in the 1990s.[16] These ethical standards align with the key phrase: *no research about us without us*. Indigenous research ethics have required researchers who are engaging communities in research to demonstrate direct involvement in research design, ownership of research data, continuing consent, and net positive benefit to the community. In addition, some of the ethical requirements of research proposals are reviewed by Indigenous research boards who have enacted their own ethical codes. For example, the Health Information Research Governance Committee[17] (HIRGC, created by the Assembly of Manitoba Chiefs in the mid-1990s) developed the Nanaandawewigamig Traditional Code of Ethics[18] with the support of the First Nations Health and Social Secretariat of Manitoba (FNHSSM) research team. It reflects the values of Elders and knowledge keepers throughout the Manitoba region and represents Anishinaabe, Cree, Dakota, Dene, and Oji-Cree teachings. This Traditional Code of Ethics is governed by the HIRGC at FNHSSM, which in 2013 broadened its mandate to holistic health research that includes the health of Mother Earth and all the gifts of the Creator, the social determinants of health, and the impacts of colonization and ongoing colonialism, racism, and oppression.

As I think of the ethics relating to questions of cultural appropriation, the Nanaandawewigamig Traditional Code of Ethics is an excellent guidepost for considering any aagooiidiwin or agreement to work together. It requires daily renewal of gratitude. It requires us to seek things that will benefit everyone. It is grounded in the principle of respect: "to feel or show honour or esteem for someone or something; consider the well-being of, or to treat someone or something with deference or courtesy."[19] Most of the Traditional Code of Ethics is committed to understanding how to demonstrate respect. The Code ends with this: "Listen to and follow the guidance given to your heart. Expect guidance to come in many forms – in prayer, in dreams, in times of quiet solitude and in the words and deeds of wise elders and friends." This last principle illustrates how the answer to questions of cultural appropriation must be evaluated contextually. The other requirements, those of building consent on relationships of respect and reciprocity, go hand in hand with the idea of an engaged ethic. In my research, I refer to Indigenous community ethics first (the protocols and ethics of good relationships within the community and nation), then to the Nanaandawewigaming Traditional Code of Ethics (reproduced below), the regional ethics board (the Health Information Research Governance Committee), and lastly the Institutional Research Ethics Review Board at the University (which is a requirement, regardless of having obtained community ethics approval(s) – see Article 9.9 of TCPS2). In this way I align the ethical standard with the bar set by the Indigenous research partners themselves, and which always begins from the place of respectful relationships.

Reflection on the Wall

As I sit back in my chair with this list of questions about cultural appropriation that my counting fingers can't accommodate, I take a breath. And then my phone pings – it's a message from Danielle, and she wants to chat about an important Indigenous justice initiative that she's helping to advance. And that's it – the sky outside seems less dark – I realize that these works of art that are on me and around me are emblems of my relations and relationships. I have visited Andréanne's studio and know her family well; I eagerly anticipate Naomi's new jewellery and earth-sourced materials and send her encouraging words of support; and I've collaborated with Linus on the design of my book cover and my drum (and I often help him sell his art). Shain's piece was gifted to me when we spoke on a panel together while I have been planning with Christi to paint a mural in our law school. KC and I have made clay vessels together and collaborated on video and performance pieces that show the relationship between water (nibi) and clay (washuske).[20] Kinnie's music figures prominently in the Decolonizing Water videos that our research group has created, and she is a collaborative partner on the project.

I look all around me again, including at the window-mirror, and see that this art that surrounds me and sits with me is rooted in my relationships. Our slow and deeply profound collective and individual Indigenous resistance is what has kept Indigenous art at the forefront of our cultural resurgence.[21] Displaying it is a celebration, a resistance of sorts, against the Canadian colonial imperative of assimilation and the presumption that Indigenous people should be assimilated "as speedily as they are fit to change."[22] However, we must take seriously the possibility that use of Indigenous art may become another form of attempted assimilation, acculturation, or erasure. For example, appropriating Indigenous art and culture into a mainstream in ways that are non-relational causes them to become devalued and risks further entrenching the colonial possessory relationship.

As I continue to look around my space, I think about what is NOT there: copies of my books, gifts that were given to me and that I have regifted, the many t-shirts and items of clothing I have given to guests in my classroom or to my cherished collaborators. And it makes me appreciate what I have gifted as much as what I have been gifted. Each of those reciprocal acts of giving are anchored in the relationships with the artists and the pieces themselves (each represents a memory, an exchange, a collaboration, a deep respect).

In many ways, the ethics of cultural appropriation are similar to the ethics of research in that they are dependent on the building of relationships, mutual consent, and reciprocity. Both the ethics of research and cultural appropriation require a vulnerability, a non-assumptive disposition, deep respect, and a generosity of spirit – all of which mean you may not ultimately get the outcome you originally were seeking by engaging in the relationship. It requires being open to receiving much more, while potentially feeling in a moment that it is far less, and that all of that is good.

NOTES

Pantses is the pluralised form of pant in Cree – you Cree speakers, you know what I mean, eh?

1 Jonathan Hart, "Translating and Resisting Empire: Cultural Appropriation and Postcolonial Studies" in Bruce Ziff & Pratima V. Rao, eds, *Borrowed Power: Essays on Cultural Appropriation* (New Brunswick, NJ: Rutgers University Press, 1997), 138.

2 Richard A. Rogers, "From Cultural Exchange to Transculturation: A Review and Reconceptualization of Cultural Appropriation" (2006) 16:4 Communication Theory 474 at 475.

3 See this string of four messages on Quora to which there is a wide diversity of responses, online: <https://www.quora.com/Is-it-cultural-appropriation-offensive -for-me-a-non-indigenous-person-to-wear-earrings-with-a-dreamcatcher-on -them-My-sister-bought-me-some-as-a-gift-and-Im-not-sure-if-I-should-wear -them>.

4 Rosemary J. Coombe, "The Properties of Culture and the Politics of Possessing Identity: Native Claims in the Cultural Appropriation Controversy" (1993) 6:2 Can JL & Jur 249 at 272.

5 Aylan Couchie, "Returning Our Voices to Us" (16 May 2017), online: *Policy Options Politiques* <https://policyoptions.irpp.org/fr/magazines/mai-2017 /returning-voices-us/>.

6 Misappropriation further emphasizes the inappropriate and non-consensual nature of the use of the culture and of the appropriative act(s).

7 Online: <https://canadacouncil.ca/about/governance/corporate-policies>.

8 *United Nations Declaration on the Rights of Indigenous Peoples* (UNDRIP) (13 September 2007), 61/295 at art 18, online: *UNDRIP* <https://www.un.org /development/desa/indigenouspeoples/wp-content/uploads/sites/19/2018/11 /UNDRIP_E_web.pdf>.

9 Online: <http://decolonizingwater.ca/grand-council-treaty-3-nibi-declaration/>. The *Nibi Declaration* is a reflection of the sacred teachings of water held by Treaty 3 knowledge keepers/Gitiizii m-inaanik to be shared with communities

and those outside of the Treaty 3 Nation. It speaks to the sacred relationship and responsibilities that the Anishinaabe have to water, water beings, and the lakes and rivers around them. The *Nibi Declaration* will help to ensure that any future policy decision, or any potential development project that impacts water, respects the collective understanding of Treaty 3 Anishinaabe Nibi Inaakonigewin.

10 Online: <https://ojibwe.lib.umn.edu/main-entry/gakina-gegoo-pron-indf>.

11 Aimée Craft, "Neither Infringement nor Justification – the SCC's Mistaken Approach to Reconciliation" in Karen Drake & Brenda L Gunn, eds, *Renewing Relationships: Indigenous Peoples and Canada* (Saskatoon: University of Saskatchewan Native Law Centre, 2019), 59.

12 Interview with Elder Harry Bone, July 2013, Craft research archive.

13 Interview with Elder Harry Bone, May 2017, Craft research archive.

14 Online: <https://ethics.gc.ca/eng/policy-politique_tcps2-eptc2_2018.html>.

15 Online: <https://ethics.gc.ca/eng/tcps2-eptc2_2018_chapter9-chapitre9.html>.

16 "Understanding the First Nations Principles of OCAP™: Our Road Map to Information Governance" (22 July 2014), online: First Nation Information Governance Centre <https://www.youtube.com/watch?v=y32aUFVfCM0>. OCAP᾿ is a registered trademark of the First Nations Information Governance Centre (FNIGC), online: <https://fnigc.ca/ocap-training/>.

17 Online: <https://www.fnhssm.com>.

18 Online: <https://d5d8ad59-8391-4802-9f0a-f5f5d600d7e9.filesusr.com/ugd/ce86f2_2d584aac57894fb2b140c4d9100f0ca9.pdf>.

19 Online: <https://d5d8ad59-8391-4802-9f0a-f5f5d600d7e9.filesusr.com/ugd/ce86f2_2d584aac57894fb2b140c4d9100f0ca9.pdf>.

20 "Clay and Water, Artist KC Adams" (23 March 2018), online: Decolonizing Water <https://vimeo.com/261561860>.

21 Here I think of KC Adams's work on reviving traditional practices of clay pottery in particular.

22 Sir John A. MacDonald, in Sessional Papers, vol. 20b, Session of the 6th Parliament of the Dominion of Canada, 1887, 37.

4 Indigenous Legal Traditions, De-sacralization, Re-sacralization and the Space for Not-Knowing

HADLEY FRIEDLAND

1. Where Is Your G-d? Where Is Your Heaven?

I want to start by telling you a story about myself when I was six years old. I was raised a secular Jew, an atheist – not an agnostic mind you – a strict atheist. My parents were rejecting shadows from Judaism and Catholicism that I never saw and had never known. My mother had grown up an army brat, the only constant in her many moves the harshness and shame in the successive Catholic schools she attended. My father had grown up in Brooklyn, with a father who came home from serving in World War II shattered by his own wartime experiences in Japan and reeling from the horrors of the Holocaust, with no idea how to raise two Jewish sons under such a shadow, in such a world. He forced my father and uncle to attend Hebrew school, then mocked their lessons, angry at G-d and everyone else, dissolving himself in increasing amounts of alcohol and rage. For both my parents, I imagine choosing atheism as young adults must have felt like freedom, like a peace after lifetimes of intractable conflict, and it was this peace they likely wanted to pass on to their children by raising us atheist.

To me, as a child, there was simply no divine. There was no mystery that science could not eventually solve or explain, and I was taught that organized religion was an "opiate for the masses,"[1] a crutch for the weak. But I was also raised in a small Alberta town in the 1980s where Christianity was a massive social fact – a given, and moral expectation. This led to many interesting interactions and altercations, but I will tell you about one today.

This was an era where the Lord's Prayer was still recited at the beginning of every school day, and I was always visibly excused. At recess one day, a group of girls in my class surrounded me and began interrogating me about whether I believed in G-d, and when I scoffed that I did not, as I had been taught, they began shoving me with the weary chant I heard far too often in my childhood: "You're going to hell, you're going to hell." Which is what their parents had taught them. Never one to go down without swinging, I locked eyes with the ringleader, a little girl with blonde ringlets named Stacey (how loved she must have been, the time and care it would have taken to make those ringlets every day), and scoffed – "Where is your G-d? Where is your heaven?"

Now recall we were both six and in Piaget's literal concrete operational stage of cognitive development, however precocious we might have been. Abstract concepts were not yet in our repertoire for reason.[2] Stacey's sidekicks ceased their shoving, and Stacey answered with disdain, "In the sky stupid. G-d lives in the sky, and heaven is in the clouds." To which I jeered, "You're stupid. The sky is made up of gases, and so are clouds. If G-d tried to stand on a cloud, he would fall through. Heaven can't be in the sky." To which she replied, "Yes it can," and I retorted with the witty rejoinder, "No it can't." And then, suddenly, one of the other little girls began to sob. I had convinced her there was no G-d. We were, after all, all six years old.

2. How Can White People Believe the Earth Is Not Alive?

Here is another story about myself: Fast forward a few decades, and I am driving in a vehicle with the man who is the father of my children and whom I had been in a relationship with for over ten years.

One day we are driving past a particular mountain range and talking about mining in the area, when suddenly my partner, who is Cree, says, frustrated, "This is what I don't understand – how can white people believe the earth isn't alive. It's obvious." He then proceeded to give me several examples of why this was patently obvious to him, some of which came from his experience working in the mining industry. I had emotionally matured (at least a little bit) since grade one. My cognitive development had matured to the point that I could think through an abstract concept I could not see (as I am sure, so too has Stacey's). However, I had never, until that moment, even turned my mind to the question of whether the earth itself were alive or not.

Differences in our worldviews were nothing new. Our respective abstract reasoning had always drawn on distinctly different unseeable concepts and premises. In every space where I was raised with no divine as a child, my partner was raised being taught and shown that every living thing was "inspirited"[3] and every part of creation was a living thing. To him, the sacred and spiritual were a common-sense part of everyday life. The exemplar of how this infused our parenting styles was our reactions to our daughter being stung by a bee while we were out in the bush. I reached for the first aid kit, and he found a medicinal plant that could be used to draw out the venom, gave tobacco for it, and prayed for her, just as quickly and matter-of-factly. For me, spiritual traditions, from Catholicism and Judaism to Cree worldviews of the inspirited nature of plants, animals, and the earth, all feel equally a bit like a foreign language, something behind a veil. I understand they exist, I hear, and even love, the cadence of the speech, but I don't feel confident in my understanding, and my attempts to speak or engage often feel clumsy and unnatural. In fact, I desperately wanted my children to be raised having a sense of the spiritual I had missed as a child, but I have never been able to create or connect to it in the way my partner can, so I always valued his bringing an unequivocal spiritual certainty into their lives and mine.

Yet there is always more to learn. I had never thought about the spiritual premises that underlie beliefs about the nature of the earth. In the moment, I was struck by the miracle of always learning about and from the ones you love – there is a fresh miracle in realizing that you can know someone for years, even live with them, have children together, build a life, and never actually have had a discussion about whether or not the earth is alive. I also felt a deep sorrow. I imagined what it was to believe so firmly about the nature of the earth and our relationship with it, and to be surrounded by so many people who did not see it this way – people who had the power to make decisions that profoundly impacted the earth, often in terrible ways. And sorrow that I did not even know how to answer his question. I could not tell him how white people could think such a thing.

I was determined to be honest and respectful within an important relationship, and I was filled with an inward curiosity – did I believe the earth was alive? Why did the earth being alive never cross my mind? A flood of memories about school classes, where I saw pictures of cross sections of the earth and memorized the names of the layers, and somehow, implicitly, saw it as a dead thing – an object, not a subject with agency and life. I thought of the biological features I had somewhere learned that were integral to being alive – to life itself, which the earth did not have. And I remembered being taught the hierarchies of living things, that rocks and plants were not sentient, that animals had smaller brains than humans, mammals were smarter than birds, reptiles, and amphibians, and that humans had the largest brains and were the most advanced of all mammals. I had never once been taught that they, or we, were inspirited. I realized these beliefs about the nature of life had been imprinted on my brain from a young age, as real, and ultimately as unprovable, as any religious belief. And so, all I said was, "I don't know." And we drove on.

3. De-sacralization, Re-sacralization and the Space for Not-Knowing

I tell you these stories because I am often reminded of each when we start to engage with the ceremonial, spiritual, or sacred aspects of Indigenous legal traditions. What do we do when we are presented with assertions of the invisible, the infinite, the intrinsic, the inviolable,[4] that we cannot understand or that go beyond our worldview? How do we engage in reasoned dialogue when we have been taught, by authority figures we trust, that the other party's premises are fundamentally unreasonable or even false?[5]

This is a collection of reflections on Indigenous voice, respecting others' voices, cultural appropriation, and the place of non-Indigenous academics. I join as a non-Indigenous academic who writes, almost exclusively, and mostly accidentally, about Indigenous Law. I also join as a white woman who spends the majority of her time in a small Cree community. I first came to live here as a lonely adolescent, longing for family and belonging, young enough to both receive care and be taught. I distinctly remember the first time I was scolded for ignoring a dream. I have lived for decades in this rich web of relations, as a youth, then adult, mother, aunty, partner, and friend, and I am grateful to still be corrected regularly. As more and more Elders pass on over the years, I realize what a gift it was to spend so much time around them that I could take their presence for granted. A silver lining of living in relation to the coronavirus pandemic is being able to spend more time in our home here, working and teaching online without much need to be in the city. There is nowhere else I feel I belong more than here. Among other gifts, there has been a cognitive or intellectual relief in being able to listen to loved ones grapple with this new (to our generation) crisis from a familiar and shared set of premises that, while not precluding disagreement, frames and grounds conversations and responses.

There is no question that differing premises or worldviews, both historically and presently, due to immense power imbalances, lead to impasses where certain reasoning is never engaged with as reason. Judgments are reached – in political arenas, court cases, and everyday decisions – that proceed without engaging with essential aspects of someone else's thought, from simply failing to give it due weight, to deep misunderstandings, outright ridicule, moral censure, or complete dismissal.[6] As Pierrot Ross-Tremblay demonstrates in his work, this also occurs within Indigenous communities, where there are good-hearted people who believe the way out of unfathomable social suffering is to internalize the de-sacralization, to forget, to reject, to embrace a colonial belief system and way of life.[7] There is internal, as well as external oblivion. As he argues:

> At some point, we stop seeing the value of spirits and dreams. This process of de-sacralization leads to abandonment – of our land, of ourselves. As cultural oblivion progresses, we do things that are against our beliefs, transgressions, which leads to predictable suffering, including the idea that we are nothing, we do not exist, no history prior to the reserve.[8]

This is important because it is not so simple as to posit a divide between Indigenous and non-Indigenous individuals and polities at this point in time, because, as Ross-Tremblay indicates, at present, the divide may also exist within Indigenous communities.

Darcy Lindberg points out that one of the biggest barriers for people to engage deeply with Indigenous legal traditions is not what people don't know, but what they think they do.[9] Almost always, when talking about Indigenous Law, someone feels confident to assert certain premises as truth or to definitively rule out possibilities. There does not seem to be space left for genuine unknowing, where we consider the very real possibility we are missing something – that our received knowledge does not encompass all there is.

This lack of awareness of unknowing is not just about Indigenous Laws – this is the received knowledge, that soaks in from day-to-day life, school, textbooks, the media, and now social media. It doesn't just fill the space for engaging with and reasoning through Indigenous Laws, but also in reasoning through the immense and relentless social suffering too many Indigenous people and communities experience today. For example, when we look at the statistics on the steadily rising rates of child apprehensions, incarceration, or terrible victimizations, I ask – what is happening here? Why? It is not unusual to hear back, not openly derogatory arguments about an intrinsic propensity or deficit anymore, but rather a calm, emotionless diagnosis of "intergenerational trauma" to explain and contain these painful realities.[10] It is unusual to hear anything about the inviolable sacredness or intrinsic worth of each child or the collective loss of a unique individual with infinite value.[11]

Returning to Ross-Tremblay's work, I have watched some of my beloved Cree nieces and nephews struggle in and for their lives over the last two decades, and I see they do not believe in their own deep value or the value of their cultural inheritance. Professionals often do not appear to see this value when we reach out, desperate to find help for our relations. Time and time again I feel my words fall flat, and I can almost see the wall of statistics that blind professionals to their uniqueness and colour, the statistics that make an immediate crisis virtually inevitable to them. We talk to each other as if in a foreign language, as if behind a veil. I have come to the point where I think what we need, in the imperfect and messy present, is to stop trying to persuade one another,[12] but to be able to find a way to hold one another and be together in a space of not-knowing. We can rationalize anything as long as we are convinced we are capable of knowing all. Re-sacralization is not necessarily the de-secularization of public places – it is the reclaiming of the inspiritedness and the sacredness of ourselves, of each other, of the other, of us all.

4. Conditions for Teaching and Learning Not-Knowing

What conditions encourage or inhibit respect, compassion, and insight into the strengths and suffering of others or ourselves? What conditions are conducive to developing the "deep ethical empathy" for the other that Emmanuel Levinas argues is necessary in order to overcome oppression and inhumanity?[13]

The question this leads me to is this: when we are teaching and when we are learning, what are the conditions for staying with a space of not-knowing? How can we sit in the discomfort rather than rush to the familiar or the new in a way that does not merely mimic genuine belief but also does not cause us to dismiss that belief implicitly or explicitly or abandon our own? In a way that would not seek to erase and replace and would not push our beliefs onto someone else? In the university context, we are used to imparting knowledge, but how do we impart this equally important not-knowing?

My two stories are instructive – the conditions were very different, even beyond age and cognitive development. In the first, however relatively safe the classroom was to hold different beliefs, only one was normalized and manifested. And outside the classroom, there was no safety at all – the tools we had as children, the only tools we had been given, were moralistic and fundamentalist. We believed we had received complete knowledge, and we believed it was all or nothing. Again, we were six, but these features are present in a fair number of adult settings. In the second, the dominant ethos was relationship, love, and respect. There was still confrontation, and even anger, but it was a mutually respectful, and thus safe, environment. There was room for correction and reflection, but our identities, values, or sense of belonging were not put at risk. It was okay to be together in our otherness, to not know it all.

As Indigenous Laws are increasingly taught in law schools, if we stay at the level of curriculum development, of course content, we can develop and debate different ways of teaching and learning Indigenous Laws or who should teach them. We can build relationships and resources to responsibly learn and teach substantive Indigenous Laws. We can initiate innovative curricular reforms that ignite new ideas and inspire a new generation of lawyers and future leaders. We can teach in the classroom, and we can teach on and with the land, in collaboration with communities.[14] However, having now participated in several different types of pedagogy, as a student and as a professor, I am always struck that the common feedback – the most meaningful, life-changing aspect for students, regardless of the other details – is the explicit acknowledgment they are whole human beings. It's an invitation to bring their whole self to the table – intellectual, emotional, physical, and spiritual – space to be fully human, to be tentative, to be wrong, and to not know. This allows for not just cognitive, but relational and empathetic learning.[15] Perhaps not-knowing is less frightening when we are more secure in our own intrinsic, infinite, and inviolable value, in our own place in a living, inspirited, sacred world.

a native man looks me in the eyes as he refuses to hold my hand during a round
dance. his pupils are like bullets and i wonder what kind of pain he's been through
to not want me in this world with him any longer. i wince a little because the earth

hasn't held all of me for quite some time now and i am lonely in a way that doesn't hurt anymore.

you see, a round dance is a ceremony for both grief and love and each body joined by the flesh is encircled by the spirits of the ancestors who've already left this world.

...

and even though i know i am too queer to be sacred anymore, i dance that broken circle dance because i am still waiting for hands that want to hold mine too.

Billy-Ray Belcourt[16]

NOTES

1 Karl Marx, "Introduction to a Contribution to the Critique of Hegel's Philosophy of Right" in *Collected Works*, Vol. 3 (New York: International Publishers, 1976). The actual quote (translated) is: "Religion is the sigh of the oppressed creature, the heart of a heartless world, and the soul of soulless conditions. It is the *opium* of the people." Online: <https://www.marxists.org/archive/marx/works/1843/critique-hpr/intro.htm>.

2 French psychologist Jean Piaget posited four stages of cognitive development in children. While the concrete operational stage represents a major turning point for children, it is still not a stage where they can reason with abstract concepts. For a simple summary of Piaget's theory of cognitive development, see: Saul McLeod, "Jean Piaget's Theory and Stages of Cognitive Development" (updated 2018), online: *Simply Psychology* <https://www.simplypsychology.org/piaget.html>.

3 For a discussion of how both humans and non-human beings are all seen as being "inspirited," as "within some Nêhiwaw [Cree] worldviews everything in creation is animated by some form of ahcâhk [spirit]," see Darcy Lindberg, "Non-human Equality and Nêhiyaw Food Sovereignty" (5 September 2020) online (blog): *Indigenous Law Association at McGill* <https://indigenous-law-association-at-mcgill.com/2020/09/05/non-human-equality-and-nehiyaw-food-sovereignty/#_ftn2>.

4 Daniel Shapiro defines the sacred as "that which we perceive to be imbued with divine significance," stating we "revere the divine in whatever we view as imbued with infinite, intrinsic and inviolable significance." Daniel Shapiro, *Negotiating the Nonnegotiable: How to Resolve Your Most Emotionally Charged Conflicts* (New York: Penguin Books, 2017) at 98.

5 Shapiro, *ibid*, suggests practical ways to approach this question at a general level at 97–118.

6 See, for example, *Ktunaxa Nation v British Columbia (Forests, Lands and Natural Resource Operations)*, 2017 SCC 54.

7 Pierrot Ross-Tremblay, *Thou Shalt Forget: Indigenous Sovereignty, Resistance and the Production of Cultural Oblivion in Canada* (London: University of London Press, 2019).

8 Pierrot Ross-Tremblay, "The Test of Truth: First Peoples, Canada and the Journey to Reconciliation" at the University of Victoria Symposium: "Rethinking the Relationship between Spirituality and Reconciliation," 9 March 2018.

9 Darcy Lindberg, "Miyo Nêhiyâwiwin (Beautiful Creeness) Ceremonial Aesthetics and Nêhiyaw Legal Pedagogy" (2018) 16/17 Indigenous LJ 51 at 52 [Lindberg, "Beautiful Creeness"].

10 Compare with Mohawk scholar Audra Simpson, arguing that naming and deconstructing people's painful current realities as political and resulting from injustice, rather than as individual and resulting from pathology, is essential for Indigenous resurgence: see Audra Simpson, "What Comes Next? Political Afterlives of the Truth and Reconciliation Commission" (public lecture, University of Alberta, 2017), online: <https://www.youtube.com/watch?v=JUycRXCpetY>. I have discussed concerns with how "intergenerational trauma" is being used at greater length elsewhere: see Hadley Friedland, "Navigating Narratives of Despair: Making Space for the Reasonable Cree Person in the Canadian Justice System" (2016) 67 UNBLJ 269.

11 Compare Lindberg, "Beautiful Creeness," *supra* note 9, who argues "that beauty is essential." He asserts that "law can be beautiful. It can even be imaginative and seem fantastical. Within this beauty lie the precepts of order and rule of law that are found in the common law" (at 53). Note that the interim report of the National Inquiry into Missing and Murdered Indigenous Women and Girls is titled "Our Women and Girls are Sacred" (National Inquiry into MMIWG, 2018), and poses the direct question: "We must learn how the lives of Indigenous women and girls have come to be so devalued." See executive summary online: <https://www.mmiwg-ffada.ca/wp-content/uploads/2018/05/MMIWG-Executive-Summary-ENG.pdf>. Similarly, the Australian Report of the Northern Territory Board of Inquiry into the Protection of Aboriginal Children from Sexual Abuse in 2007 was entitled: *Ampe Akelyernemane Meke Mekarle "Little Children Are Sacred,"* with the explanation that "in our Law children are very sacred because they carry the two spring wells of water from our country within them." Online: <https://humanrights.gov.au/sites/default/files/57.4%20%E2%80%9CLittle%20Children%20are%20Sacred%E2%80%9D%20report.pdf>.

12 Except, perhaps in and through the ceremonial aesthetics Lindberg discusses as part of Nêhiyaw legal pedagogy in "Beautiful Creeness," *supra* note 9.

13 Levinas argues the unavoidable violence of law necessitates that we develop deep ethical empathy for the "other" – an "infinite responsibility of each, for each, before each" – if we are to overcome oppression and inhumanity. The "other" is they who we can never know completely. Emmanuel Levinas, *Basic Philosophical Writings,* Adriann T. Peperzak, Simon Critchley & Robert Bernasconi, eds (Bloomingdale: Indiana University Press, 1996), at 23.

14 See, for example, John Borrows, "Heroes, Tricksters, Monsters and Caretakers: Indigenous Law and Legal Education" (2016) 61:4 McGill LJ 795, and John

Borrows, "Outsider Education: Indigenous Law and Land-based Learning" (2016) 33:1 Windsor YB Access Just 1.

15 Shalene Jobin has articulated an Indigenous learning framework which highlights the importance of cognitive, relational, empathetic, and applied learning. See Shalene Jobin & Avery Letendre, *Indigenous Scholar Summary Report* (Edmonton, Alberta: Public Services Commission, Government of Alberta, 2017) at 18–19 [unpublished, on file with author]. The summary report was the result of bringing together Indigenous scholars from Alberta and Saskatchewan to develop an Indigenous Learning Framework to guide the training journey of government employees around Indigenous Peoples. Co-facilitated by Dr. Shalene Jobin and Dr. Marvin Washington, the Indigenous scholars involved in developing the Indigenous Learning Framework include Dr. Chris Andersen, Dr. Tracy Bear, Brian Calliou, Norma Dunning, Elmer Ghostkeeper, Kirsten Lindquist, Dr. Shalene Jobin, Dr. Verna St. Denis, Dr. Cora Voyageur, and Jennifer Ward.

16 Excerpts from Billy-Ray Belcourt, "Sacred" in *This Wound Is a World* (Calgary: Frontenac House Poetry, 2017), at 17.

5 Mino-audjiwaewin: Choosing Respect, Even in Times of Conflict

LINDSAY BORROWS

Introduction

Recently I was on the phone with a friend from college. During those years of study, we shared an energetic house together with six other official roommates and many unofficial ones. We laughed as we reminisced. Though we are now separated by geography (including an international border), our call brought back fun memories and bridged the distance. She too recently had her first baby and is navigating motherhood while working full-time for an environmental non-profit doing conservation policy work. She confided in me the challenge she is having in her work right now. She is non-Indigenous. Her work requires her to liaise with funders on behalf of local communities in her region of work (where she does not live) and explain the importance of financing Indigenous-led conservation initiatives to the primarily white philanthropists. "I know I'm not best positioned to do this work," she said to me. "I'm trying to work myself out of a job." I asked her to explain. She said that her policy and communications work would be more powerful, rooted, and decolonizing if it came from an Indigenous person instead of herself. Her response was not new to me. I work with many allies who question their positioning and set the same ultimate goal of moving on so their work can continue under the care of Indigenous individuals and communities. I find this to be a truly admirable response. I agree that this could be the right move in many instances. I also detect a sense of fragility sometimes in this message: "it is not my role to speak about this." I worry about what it would mean for non-Indigenous people to move over so entirely that they exit the conversation or pass up their own learning and sharing opportunities. It is all too common for institutions to say, "we don't have the right relationships to speak to this, so we will be silent." I've worked for some of these. The silence then becomes simply that, silence. It is not filled with finding the right ways to amplify Indigenous perspectives.

I believe nuance is required in making decisions around who should speak to what. Sometimes we listen. Sometimes we talk. How do we know what is best in every instance? We cannot. As someone with perfectionist tendencies, I find relief in knowing perfection is not actually reality. The well-known shame researcher, Dr. Brené Brown, says daring leadership requires us to acknowledge that "I'm not here to be right, I'm here to get it right."[1] While there is no unfailing mathematical formula to calculate how we can best be in relationship with one another around difficult issues, there are guiding principles. We need to stumble, even in the face of public scrutiny. Sometimes we will back away too far, and other times we will be too centred. My friend and former Anishinaabe language teacher, Dennis Pebaamibines Jones, posed the question to his students: "Who are these culture cops anyways?" He was referring to the people internally in our Anishinaabe communities who position themselves as the keepers of the "pure" Anishinaabe way of being. They police others, often by using lateral violence or emotionally destructive tactics, and put others down instead of lifting them up with their insights and correction. These are the very people who are often against prison systems, with constructive and transformative "reform the police" messages on their social media accounts. Yet, their own actions are relegating people in our own communities, let alone outside allies, to a position where we might as well be locked behind bars, unable to speak up, learn, and try again. We need to do better at learning gently in community.

Just before the COVID-19 pandemic hit in the spring of 2020 and took centre stage in our worldwide conversations, the media where I live in British Columbia had been diligently reporting news from the Coastal GasLink Pipeline dispute. The dispute was over whether or not to allow a pipeline through Wet'suwet'en traditional territories. Like any community, the Wet'suwet'en are not homogeneous and their citizens and leadership took various positions on the pipeline matter. Wet'suwet'en Law was circulating in common conversation throughout British Columbia for the first time in my adult life.[2] As a student of Indigenous Laws, it was exciting for me to witness people waking up to these ideas. It was also very heavy, as it was a challenging process, primarily for the Wet'suwet'en, but also for others. Just as it takes years to learn Canadian common or civil law, it takes years to learn Indigenous legal traditions. They are complex. It was interesting to see how, after reading news articles and following select social media accounts, some people talked as if they understood Wet'suwet'en governance, instead of admitting it was a concept they had only just learned existed and that people and communities are complex, even Indigenous ones. It was not as simple as hereditary Chiefs versus elected Chiefs versus Coastal GasLink. In response to the dispute, there were youths bravely occupying the legislature in Victoria, stating their solidarity with the hereditary Chiefs.[3] They were in the presence of police, also trying their best to maintain harmony and uphold their understanding of the rule of law.[4] An important international human rights organization made statements, with the limited information they had.[5] An injunction decision discussed the place of Indigenous Law.[6] I flew to the northern town of Smithers, BC (Wet'suwet'en territory), in February 2020 for some other work, at the same time the government officials arrived to enter negotiations with some of the Wet'suwet'en leaders. The Hudson Bay Lodge was full of finely dressed people getting ready for their meetings, with news crews busy outside. It was a big deal, and many people from various angles of the dispute were rightfully angry, tired, and upset. A hallmark of this period that I'm interested in exploring more broadly is the way different people and communities informally "police" the when, where, and how of who can speak up in solidarity. This brings me to the central question addressed in this chapter: how can respect, a foundational legal principle across many Indigenous legal traditions,[7] help us in our quest for justice as we listen to and learn from a wide variety of people?

A Scenario from Normal Daily Life

Throughout our day we might find ourselves frustrated, angry, or upset. For example, imagine you are driving to a morning appointment and someone from a side street pulls onto the road in front of you. You slam on your brakes and your bag falls off the seat, spilling its contents onto the car floor. You honk loudly at their dangerous manoeuvre. They apologetically make eye contact with you in their rear-view mirror, and you mouth curse words at them, eyebrows furrowed. The driver then proceeds to drive 10 km below the speed limit. You arrive irritated and late for your appointment. You get home after your appointment and see your next-door neighbour out in their driveway. She starts complaining to you about the wood smoke from the neighbours on the other side of the street, again. You are friends with the other neighbours and know their financial situation is strained. They can't afford to switch heat sources. You've tried to explain this to the complaining neighbour before, but it obviously didn't have any effect. You don't say anything as you listen, all the while fuming inside at their insensitivity. You go back into your house to find that your toddler spilled juice all over the couch. Your husband has bags under his eyes and his hair is disheveled. He apologizes. "Why don't you pay more attention?" you say sharply, followed by an agitated sigh. You look at your watch. It is not yet 10:30 am, and you have yet to go to work.

Your morning experiences could understandably be seen as one frustration after the next. However, there are also many implicit gifts in your story that go uncelebrated. You had a car to drive, helping you get your errands done more easily. Your meeting went ahead despite your late arrival. You have your health, a home, a spouse, a job, and a child. Despite all of this, if you're anything like me, the reality is you feel frustrated by what has happened, and the last thing you would want is for someone to come along and point out to you that you don't have it so bad after all.

When you interacted with each person throughout your morning, you made choices about *how* to act. Choosing to respond in a spirit of respect, even in these menial daily scenarios, can be deeply challenging. It is even more difficult when our understanding of fundamental rights or liberties are being challenged, often due to deep systemic injustices. We live in a time when respect is often missing from interpersonal relations as well as from civic engagement. It is easy to see examples by visiting various social media platforms or news sites, watching television, hearing conversations in our workplaces, or even in our own homes.[8] This lack of respect can be a barrier to democracy as people become afraid to show up for conversations, or when they do participate it is not in a spirit of learning or progress; instead, it is defensive and reactionary. They show up as a warrior, ready to defend their own views at all costs, using whatever language they want.[9] This chapter considers *what* respect is and *why* it's important, *what* often prevents us from acting with respect in our interactions with others, and *how* to cultivate more meaningful practices of respect.

Mino-audjiwaewin, Manaaji'idiwin and Respect: What Does It Really Mean?

I am Anishinaabe, and a citizen of the Chippewas of Nawash First Nation.[10] Our community is located about a three-hour drive north of Toronto, on the shores of Georgian Bay. For the past ten years, I've been learning Anishinaabemowin, the language of my family from the Great Lakes Region.[11] In Anishinaabemowin, we might say each moment described in the above scenario is an opportunity to practice mino-audjiwaewin[12] or manaaji'idiwin.[13] Respect. This is one of our Seven Grandparent teachings.[14] These teachings are guiding principles that we strive to follow and cultivate in order to live Mino-Bimaadiziwin, a good life.[15]

It is easy to say that the dangerous driver, the complaining neighbour, or the careless spouse did not deserve to be treated with mino-audjiwaewin or manaaji'idiwin (respect). Depending on who you are, it is perhaps even easier yet to say that during the pipeline disputes, the RCMP, the Coast GasLink representatives, or the Indigenous youths occupying the legislature were not deserving of respectful treatment. Their various actions were perceived as harms by some. Yet, respect is multifaceted. It is marked by how we *act* towards others, and how we *feel* towards others. When we do not feel a sense of honour, admiration, or respect towards another because we do not hold what they've done in high esteem, we can still choose to act respectfully, civilly, or politely towards them because they are human. What happens if we believe the following: "If the driver (or neighbour or spouse) had behaved differently, then I would not have cursed/yelled/fumed/harrumphed"? This kind of thinking shifts responsibility for our behaviour to others. It disempowers us from taking responsibility over our own actions. It makes us think that our own disrespectful acts are someone else's fault.

I want to be very clear that I am not above disrespectful behaviour myself at times. We all have Trickster in us, myself included. I am also not suggesting that we must never feel anger, frustration, or negative emotions. Emotions of all kinds are a wild, beautiful, and messy fact of life. They should not be ignored or suppressed.[16] What I am interested in is the research that shows the negative impacts that unhealthy *responses* to these emotions can have on ourselves, our relationships and, by extension, our communities.[17] There are many injustices in the world today. It is healthy that these injustices make us angry, frustrated, upset, irate, etc.[18] These feelings can move us to action and to work towards change and greater goodness. We hear of people experiencing burnout (or maybe have experienced this ourselves) in the many important movements working towards positive change. They then give up, lash out at others, or carry a burden of shame or frustration when things don't go as they had planned. Why? One of the reasons is because our collective spaces are often void of respect. This cripples us from sustaining important conversations. Our good relations suffer as a result.

Anishinaabemowin contains lessons about the importance of intentional embodied behavior. Anishinaabemowin is a language dominated by verbs.[19] I've written elsewhere that one of our words for blueberry pie is chigayatewemitigozhiminibaashkiminisaganibiitoosijiganizhegwaabikiniganibakwezhigan.[20] This means "old time-French person-exploding blueberries-blueberry sauce-layered between thing-bend over and put it in the oven-bread." If you get into each of these words even further, there is yet more nuance. For example, the word Wemitigozhi means a French person. "We" is a waving motion. "Mitig" is a stick. French people are the stick-wavers because when the early French missionaries arrived they brought their crosses with them. The Anishinaabe word for blueberry pie is not an object; it's more of an embodied recipe describing how it comes into being. As we consider mino-audjiwaewin, manaaji'idiwin, or respect in this chapter, I hope to convey that we are analysing a practice more than a concept.

If we take off the "win" at the end of these two words for respect (mino-audjiwaewin, manaaji'idiwin), they become verbs.[21] Respect is not a thing to be objectified or placed on a shelf. It must have life and movement breathed into it by our own bodies and hearts. Respect is about how we treat people, regardless of how our own actions are received. In his work, *Justice as Translation*, James Boyd White writes:

Another danger, very widely realized in our own world, is that talk about concepts tends to nominalize, and hence to reify, everything. The verb, the adverb, the adjective all give way to the noun. The effect is to create a universe of imagined intellectual objects arranged in quantitative or spatial relations to each other but without the principle of life that is found in the active verb. Imagine a language that emphasized the verb instead of the noun and copula; our thought would be full of a sense of movement, life, and change, of actors engaged in action.[22]

One of my formative teachers was the late Anishinaabe Elder Basil Johnston, who lived down the road from my grandparents' and auntie's house.[23] He was an avid linguist who wrote a book called *Anishinaubae Thesaurus*, where he recorded thousands of words and their meanings. In this book he used two words to represent respect: first, mino-audjiwaewin, meaning "honour, respect, revere, esteem," and second, kizhae-aendjigaewin, meaning "to esteem."[24] I will focus on mino-audjiwaewin. Its meaning is worth considering to enhance our understanding of what Anishinaabemowin might signal about respect. I am not fluent, but as an eager student of the language I find meaning in analysing information available on the linguistic components of these words.

In his *Thesaurus*, Basil Johnston explores the prefix of mino-audjiwaewin. He writes:

– **mino-audj; mino-audji** (honour, respect, esteem, regard, revere, admire, have a high opinion for, venerate, worship, pay homage to)
– **w'mino-audji-aun w'kittisseemun** (he/she honours his/her parents)
– **w'mino-audji-aun manitoun** (he/she venerates the deities).[25]

Then in the glossary section at the back of the *Thesaurus*, he makes a note on the second part of the word mino-audjiwaewin:

– **waewaewin**: refers to sound, call, utterance, speech; to the nature, volume, source, tone, pitch, and character of sound, call, utterance, speech.[26]

We might synthesize this to mean that respect is about putting out sounds into the world that convey honour, esteem, and regard for others (including ourselves and the non-human world).[27]

Another translation of respect in Anishinaabemowin is manaaji'idiwin. On the Seven Generations website, language speakers have recorded the following definition of manaaji'idiwin:[28]

– **Manaaji**: to go easy on someone
– **Idi**: in a reciprocal way
– **Win**: a way it is done

The website states that Respect is "To go easy on one another and all of Creation."

Legal scholar John Borrows writes that "respect in Anishinaabemowin is manaaji'idiwin, which literally means 'to go easy on someone.' Respect is an enduring principle of Anishinaabe law. It is frequently referred to, along with friendship and respect, in our treaty relationships. Respect is relational – the morpheme idi in the word manaaji'idiwin makes this fact clear."[29] Borrows goes on to explain that the way governments and churches treated residential school students and their families was not in the spirit of "going easy on one another." It was quite the opposite. The *Indian Act* is another example of how the government has not gone easy on Indigenous Peoples. There are countless examples of lack of respect between Indigenous Peoples and non-Indigenous peoples. Some are more structural, and others are more personal or individual in nature. He then gives some examples of how respect can be conveyed, such as by listening.

Manaaji'idiwin makes me think of gentleness, warmth, empathy, and an ethos of caretaking that we can embody in our actions towards others as we practice this important Grandparent teaching. How then do we move from an intellectual understanding of what mino-audjiwaewin and manaaji'idiwin means, to truly practice/live with it?

Barriers to Respect: Entrenched Systems, Negativity Bias, "Despair-Muscles" and Emotional Safety

One particular summer while I was living at my grandparents' and aunt's house, I spent a few hours a week with my friend and colleague Hannah Askew, learning from the late Elder Basil Johnston as we sat in chairs on the porch of his cottage. We talked about many subjects, but as Hannah and I were law students at the time, he thoughtfully shared teachings relevant to our studies. He spoke highly of Rupert Ross's writings on the criminal justice system (he proudly acted as an official reviewer of one of Ross's books at some point in time).[30] Basil told us that he believed that when someone has done something wrong, they most need to be reminded of their capacity for goodness. He believed the criminal justice system should be set up around this truth, that when we are vulnerable and have done something wrong, we need help, not just punishment.[31] We continue to require respectful engagement even at our lowest moments.

In contrast to this focus on respect for people in their vulnerable times or moments of mistakes, the Canadian legal system generally puts an accused in front of a judge to hear from a lawyer about how terribly they've acted.[32] It is important to note that there can be troubling differences in how people are treated by the justice system because of their backgrounds or their places of privilege in society.[33] These differences unfortunately can affect how respect operates in court or other decision-making tribunals. Those who have been treated with respect ("gone easy on") throughout their life might find it easier in some ways to be civil towards others because there aren't layers of trauma to work through.[34] I want to be clear. I am absolutely not asking those who have been harmed to forgive. I am suggesting we all consider the potential benefits the practice of respect might bring to our own liberation and well-being.[35] When you're not well or if you need time to process the harm you are suffering, or if the paths before you make it nearly impossible to go easy on someone, that is okay. I think manaaji'idiwin, going easy on one another, includes going easy on ourselves when we fall short of our ideals.

The media and Canadian courts can be places of overly negative story-telling. Important research has been done on our predisposition to focus on the negative over the positive.[36] Behavioural psychology calls this the negativity bias.[37] You might recognize it in yourself. Maybe your supervisor told you ten good things in your review, and one area that needs improvement. When you walk away you ruminate on the critique (even though it was delivered in a "compliment sandwich," the good, the suggested improvement, followed up by the good). This focus on the negative serves a purpose. It can help us learn and improve if we integrate the feedback effectively. Our negativity bias, however, only serves us to a certain point. If we don't integrate it holistically into an expansive view of the situation, it can skew our vision too far towards doom and gloom. Our stories about the state of the world could become imbalanced. When we are called into conversation with one another around important issues, one response might be to see respect as a disposable luxury that must give way to our important and pressing causes.

In a conversation between journalist Krista Tippett and author Ross Gay, they discussed the different focus "muscles" we can develop.[38] Each day over the course of one year, Gay had written an essay on something that delighted him. Then he collected his favourite reflections on delight and published a book called *The Book of Delights: Essays*.[39] In the interview, he talked about how he had developed a "delight-muscle" as he engaged in this practice. It became a reflex to see pleasant things in the world around him. Krista Tippett made the point that journalism has a "despair-muscle."[40] It focuses on the negative stories or news of the world, which is an inadequate representation of the situation. They observed that this affects our collective mental health and negatively impacts the ways we choose to move through the world. As we become more aware of our negativity bias, we can more effectively challenge negative self-talk,[41] practice mindfulness,[42] restructure our cognitive pathways,[43] and build our delight-muscles by savouring the positive that we experience each day.

As we cognitively work to challenge our negativity bias, we may simultaneously cultivate our capacity for acting respectfully (going easy on others) in moments of frustration, anger, or harm. For example, when a driver cuts you off on the road, you might instead recognize how lucky you were not to get in an accident. You might breathe a sigh of relief that you are safe, and they are too. You might even shine a positive light on them by inventing a backstory. Maybe they were focused on helping a family member who is in desperate need, leading to their distracted moment. When a police officer arrests an Indigenous grandma for peacefully defending her lands, we might speak out loudly against the action and systems that allow for that, while recognizing that the officer is deserving of our respectful actions, even if our feelings do not match. When we are self-aware and grounded in different cultural teachings of respect, we have an opportunity to "go more easily" on ourselves and others.

I am not suggesting that we suppress our feelings or be inauthentic when dealing with others. What I am proposing takes some work. At the same time, I am saying that our experiences may be richer than we realize. We may be overlooking other dimensions of our relationships. Acting respectfully gives these other parts of ourselves a chance to be felt and expressed in more holistic ways.

Treating people disrespectfully by silencing them, cutting them off, or calling them out harshly, are all ways to reinforce the story that the person in question is bad or not worthy of joining in because of who they are or what they've done. This is what the current prison system does very well. It silences and cuts people out of society, and it disproportionately affects Indigenous people. In January 2020 a report was published stating that over 30 per cent of federal inmates are Indigenous.[44] We are robbing people of their human dignity when we harshly dismiss them. While there are important differences between cutting people out of conversations because we disagree with their views or their cultural backgrounds and putting people into prisons, I'm nonetheless struck by some of the similarities. By silencing others, we are also robbing ourselves of awareness of our own complexities. This practice is not emotionally safe. Emotional safety occurs when people feel appreciated, valued, worthwhile, and trusted.[45] It also develops when we cultivate these qualities in ourselves. Safety needs to accompany vulnerability in order to provide us with useful learning moments, instead of crippling moments of critique.[46] Imagine the possibilities for what we might accomplish if we felt comfortable around each other, instead of feeling like we are under attack. What would it be like if we saw ourselves as interconnected with one another?[47] With open and clear communication, when mistakes are made reparations could happen quickly. Fortunately, according to licensed marriage and family therapist and YouTube therapy blogger, Emma McAdam, 95 per cent of the effort to create this emotional safety can be done by focusing on ourselves; it's not actually about others needing to change.[48] We are responsible for what we put into the world and the boundaries that we set. McAdam points out that the opposite of emotional safety is judgment, blame, attacking, and closed emotions or anger. We could say, "I felt vulnerable when you pulled out in front of me on the road like that," instead of "you're a terrible driver and you shouldn't be allowed on the road ever again." When we use "I" instead of "you" language, the listener can understand our feelings, and they might be more likely to listen rather than react in defence. Personal attacks are not characterized by a practice of respect.

Author and activist Adrienne Maree Brown writes that transformative justice is built on our ability to forgive and believe in people's ability to change.[49] She makes the point that if we can't model this forgiveness between ourselves as individuals, then of course we can't change our systems for the better. I am aware of the critiques of forgiveness, and the potential dangers of not holding others to proper account or of enabling some to act with impunity.[50] I am not advocating pardon without consequences when circumstances warrant chastisement, liability, or retribution. At the same, I agree with Brown when she observes:

> I'm wondering if those of us with an intention of transforming the world have a common understanding of the kind of justice we want to practice, now and in the future. What we do now is find out someone or some group has done (or may have done) something out of alignment with our values ... We then tear that person or group to shreds in a way that affirms our values ... But I also wonder: is this what we're here for? To cultivate a fear-based adherence to reductive common values? What can this lead to in an imperfect world full of sloppy complex humans? Is it possible we will call each other out until there's no one left beside us? ... But if we want to create a world in which conflict and trauma aren't the center of our collective existence, we have to practice something new, ask different questions, access again our curiosity about each other as a species.[51]

Brown's words provide further insight into this section's focus on negativity bias, building "delight-muscles," and practising emotional safety. We can't continually be negative with each other if we want to transform the world for the better. Tearing people down is not building what we want to see. When our ends are not congruent with the means we use to achieve them, we are not being the change we want to see in the world. As Gandhi so aptly encouraged, "We but mirror the world. All the tendencies present in the outer world are to be found in the world of our body. If we could change ourselves, the tendencies in the world would also change ... We need not wait to see what others do."[52] When we respectfully engage with others, we help to create emotionally safe environments which helps reveal to us when our negativity biases are not serving us well.

Feasting Respect

I worked as a lawyer and researcher at the University of Victoria Faculty of Law's Indigenous Law Research Unit (ILRU).[53] Much of our work applies a methodology created by Drs. Val Napoleon and Hadley Friedland that looks to narratives/stories as intellectual tools for law-making and teaching.[54] Through community partnerships representing a wide variety of Indigenous legal traditions, we start by looking to a community's legal tradition's narratives to draw out preliminary understandings of their legal rights and obligations, legal processes, legal responses, practices of enforcement/teaching, authoritative decision makers, and general underlying principles related to a particular legal research question. In order to complete a report, we spend several years working with a community and look to thirty to fifty–plus stories to inform the legal analysis.[55]

This model has an important role, but it should not be universalized and applied in all places.[56] With the caveat that there is danger in looking only to a single story,[57] there is great value in finding the richness within particular stories. I would like to explore the teachings of mino-audjiwaewin that come from one Anishinaabe narrative, "Beaver Gives a Feast," as recorded by anthropologist Frank Speck during his work with the Timiskaming and Temagami First Nations.[58] It is interesting to note that Speck was an early twentieth century, non-Indigenous anthropologist. We have many conversations in our work about both the limitations and value of working with these English language, non-Indigenous, anthropologist-translated versions of stories.[59] I am bringing Speck's recording into this chapter, recognizing that there is something important to learn from his work.

Beaver Gives a Feast

In this story there is a village of animals, whose Chief is Beaver. On special occasions, Beaver Chief would host a big feast by building a wigwam and inviting everyone to come in and eat with him. During one particular feast, Beaver had cut his grease supply into cakes which he passed around from animal to animal. Every time he got to an animal and went to hand them a cake, Beaver would pass wind: boogidi. And every time Beaver Chief passed wind, Otter would burst out laughing. Otter was known to be foolish and did not think about offending Beaver Chief. The other animals told Otter not to laugh because it was disrespectful of the Chief.

One day Beaver sent the message that a feast will be held and that everyone should be invited. The other animals told Otter, "You must not come, you always laugh and show disrespect to our Chief. If you only could keep quiet like the rest of us it would be all right, but you had better stay home."

So everyone attends the feast except Otter. When the feast is held, Beaver notices that Otter is missing. "Where is Otter?" he asks. The animals make up an excuse. Beaver Chief replies, "That's too bad he isn't here. I find him very funny!"

We see from this simple story how complex enacting respect can be. The facts of the story show that Otter was cut out of the group because others did not agree with his actions. He was silenced or, in a way, his comments and participation were "canceled"[60] because they believed he was disrespectful. To the surprise of the other animals, Beaver was not actually offended by Otter's laughter every time he passed gas. Beaver thought this brought humour and lightness to their feasts that perhaps was otherwise missing. Beaver's comment suggests that he actually enjoyed being around laughing Otter.

At ILRU, when we talk about stories in community settings, it always amazes me how many interpretations and lessons are drawn from them, depending on who is part of the conversation. I do not see diversity of interpretation as a threat, but as a testament to the richness of our stories, minds, capacities, and conversations. In the Supreme Court of Canada, for example, the judges frequently decide differently from one another (these are called majority and minority decisions). I offer one interpretation of Beaver Gives a Feast as it relates to mino-audjiwaewin.

We might decide that Otter was in fact being disrespectful in his laughter at Beaver Chief's gas. However, his intentions may have been respectful because he was "foolish" and didn't know any better than to react to the farts (which we know are a fact of life but also a source of humour and potential embarrassment).[61] The animals may have been onto something helpful by trying to show Otter the potential for disrespect that his laughter was showing their Chief. However, they implemented a disproportionate response by completely cutting Otter out of the feast. Their actions could be interpreted as dealing out disrespect to disrespect. It would be wonderful to bring this story into conversation with others and ask one another: how might the animals each have shown more respect to one another?[62] Using this story as a jumping off point, we might think about the current events we are part of, or we observe, and discuss with one another how we might be able to practice respectful relations. Respect can be hollow if we don't do the work of continually defining its meaning and attempting to apply it in practice.

Mino-audjiwaewin and the Sources of Law

When I was in my early twenties and doing my undergraduate degree, I attended the Annual Dartmouth College Powwow in New Hampshire. It occurs each spring, and sees the gathering of Indigenous dancers, singers, and drummers from across North America. I had been working on learning to jingle dance at the time, and this would be my first powwow as a jingle dancer. I had spent countless hours working on my regalia (as did my mom, who is not Anishinaabe), learning the stories and steps of the dance, meeting with other jingle dancers, and practising. I was excited to participate in this healing dance. I was also nervous. I was without my family at this particular powwow. People were from many different tribal backgrounds and had incredible regalia. I felt small, but also wanted to participate in this important cultural event.

The powwow came and it was beautiful. There was so much power in the drumming, dancing, ceremony, food, and visiting. On the second day of the powwow, I was getting tired. I took a seat at a chair off to the side of the circle. There were many people around. Another young student with a group of other students around him came up to me. He sternly told me not to sit there. I didn't know what he meant at first, but I quickly realized I had sat at his group's drum. I knew their teaching was that only men could sit around that drum. I got up, embarrassed and in tears. I had no one to go to. For the rest of the event (and I would soon find out, for the rest of our time as students), none of them would look at me or talk to me. Author Louise Erdrich was also at the powwow jingle dancing and spending time with a family member and friends. At one point she came up to me and complimented my footwork and regalia, saying something like, "You're the girl with the gold jingles" because my cones were gold instead of the traditional silver. She also gave out little deer pins to all the jingle dancers as a gift. Her kindness was a refuge. There were also many other warm remarks and wonderful experiences at the powwow. Yet the experience with the students and the drum was a shadow over the event. My negativity bias was strong.

A few years after the incident, I brought it up with my supervisor Dr. Val Napoleon at ILRU while we were in a workshop together preparing for some upcoming community engagements. I was worried about going into a community for our work and accidentally violating a protocol, such as I did when sitting at that drum when I was female and not a part of their group. The sting of that experience was still with me. I told Val the story and she immediately said, "They should not have treated you that way." I had never truly questioned the way they responded to my action. Napoleon has written about the lack of civility she has witnessed in the social and political life of some Indigenous communities. Of course, she and we know that this is not an issue unique to Indigenous communities, but sometimes we can be our own worst enemies.[63]

I have been on countless projects where I've seen my co-workers who are from a particular Nation barred from accessing resources from their own great-grandparents or other relatives. The guardians of these resources make my (often young and female) co-workers feel disempowered to learn the teachings of their ancestors. I have also been witness to lateral violence in my own community and others. This stings. Napoleon writes:

> As with all societies, disagreement and conflict is simply the ongoing and neces-
> sary consequence of human beings living together. However, when for whatever
> reason, conflict is not effectively or legitimately managed through legal and politi-
> cal orders and their corresponding practices of civility, it can become polarizing

and caustic. When this happens, conflict corrodes and pervades the social fabric of community life from the political to the personal, thereby undermining citizenries' abilities to civilly manage their collective life.[64]

Napoleon makes the distinction that when she talks about civility, she doesn't mean politeness, but rather "disagreeing with respect and about the preservation of reciprocal kinship, community, societal, and intersocietal relationships."[65] It is in no way about shying away from critique but focuses instead on having "intelligent and respectful public debate." Our own Indigenous legal traditions can teach us about how to cultivate respect in our efforts towards democratic engagement, such as in *Beaver Gives a Feast*.

Legal theorists have written about the sources of law. In *Canada's Indigenous Constitution*, John Borrows writes about five particular sources. Deliberative law is law that is made when people come together in conversation (councils, meetings).[66] Sacred law comes from a higher power (Creator, Treaties, Ceremony, etc.).[67] Positivistic law flows from an individual who is collectively recognized as an authority, so what they say is taken as law.[68] Customary law flows from habitual practices created over time.[69] Natural law flows from the earth itself as we look to plants, animals, rocks, water, etc. to learn and reason by way of analogy from them.[70]

These young students from my university who told me sternly not to sit at the drum, and then cut me out of their existence by refusing to engage with me afterwards, may have been following several of these sources of law. They might have seen it as a sacred teaching that their drum should not have a woman there, and I violated this practice. They might have talked with each other about how to respond to me, and all agreed that I shouldn't be talked to after this as my "punishment." Maybe they had a positivist leader in their life who gave them that teaching about the drum, and they believed they were enacting that teaching with me the best they knew how. I don't fully know what their reasoning was, but I did learn many lessons, for good and ill.

When we make decisions about how to treat others, we can look to these different sources of law and attempt to reason our way through them and make good decisions about how to respond/act. It is important, however, to remember that our decision-making processes are made and interpreted by imperfect humans. Therefore, we would benefit from keeping in mind the Seven Grandparent principles of respect, humility, patience, love, courage, wisdom, and truth when making decisions. We should look beyond these principles too, to the many intellectual and spiritual resources across the many traditions of the world, some of which we are part of, and others we can learn from and admire from an outsider position.[71]

Conclusion

In the context of different people and communities informally directing when, where, why, how, and who can speak in solidarity with Indigenous Peoples and issues, this chapter has explored the role of respect in these interactions from one perspective, drawing primarily on Anishinaabe teachings. It has considered why respect is important, and it has examined some of the barriers to engaging with respect and how we might cultivate it more in our interactions. In his book *Embers*, the late Richard Wagamese wrote: "Teachings come from everywhere when you open yourself to them. That's the trick of it, really. Open yourself to everything, and everything opens itself to you."[72] Teachings about respect can come from many places. The work of living with mino-audjiwaewin is ongoing. Like most skills, it requires deep, continual practice.[73] There are times we each will falter, and times we will notice our strength. May we find encouragement and gentleness in community as we work to respectfully understand one another across our differences, and work towards our essential collective goals as part of the human family.

NOTES

1 Brené Brown, "The Courage to Not Know" (13 February 2020), online (blog): *Brené Brown* <https://brenebrown.com/blog/2020/02/13/the-courage-to-not-know/>.

2 Rafferty Baker, "A Who's Who of the Wet'suwet'en Pipeline Conflict," *CBC News* (26 February 2020) online: <https://www.cbc.ca/news/canada/british-columbia/wetsuweten-whos-who-guide-1.5471898>.

3 Simon Little, "Indigenous Youth Occupy B.C. Legislature Steps in Support of Wet'suwet'en Hereditary Chiefs," *Global News* (7 February 2020) online: <https://globalnews.ca/news/6523209/indigenous-youth-occupy-bc-legislature-wetsuweten/>.

4 John Borrows, *Freedom and Indigenous Constitutionalism* (Toronto: University of Toronto Press, 2016) at 50.

5 Alex Neve, "Open Letter Urges Canadian, B.C. and Alberta Governments to Heed UN Racism Committee's Call to Respect Indigenous Rights," online: *Amnesty International* <https://amnesty.ca/news/open-letter-urges-canadian-bc-and-alberta-governments-heed-un-racism-committees-call-respect>.

6 *Coastal GasLink Pipeline Ltd. v Huson*, 2019 BCSC 2264.

7 See for examples: Jessica Asch et al (Indigenous Law Research Unit & Shuswap Nation Tribal Council), *Secwépemc Lands and Resources Law Research Project* (Tk'emlúps: Shuswap Nation Tribal Council, 2016) [Asch et al]; Dean Billy, Lindsay Borrows, Jessica Clogg, & Helen Copeland, *Revitalizing Indigenous Law for Land,*

Air and Water: St'at'imc Legal Traditions Report (Lillooet: St'a'timc Chiefs Council, 2018), online: <https://www.wcel.org/sites/default/files/publications/2018 _statimc_relaw_legaltraditionsreport.pdf>; Frank Brown & Y Kathy Brown, *Staying the Course, Staying Alive, Coastal First Nations Fundamental Truths: Biodiversity, Stewardship and Sustainability* (Victoria, BC: Biodiversity British Columbia, December 2009), online: <http://www.llbc.leg.bc.ca/public/pubdocs /bcdocs2010/463007/bbc_staying_the_course_web.pdf>.

8 "Rude Behavior in Every Day Life and on the Campaign Trail," The Associated Press-NORC Centre for Public Affairs Research at the University of Chicago, online: <https://apnorc.org/projects/rude-behavior-in-everyday-life-and-on-the-campaign-trail/>. See also: Rousiley C.M. Maia & Thaiane A.S. Rezende, "Respect and Disrespect in Deliberation across the Networked Media Environment: Examining Multiple Paths of Political Talk" (2016) 21:2 Journal of Computer-Mediated Communication 121; Linda Lauren, "Respect and Social Media," *HuffPost* (6 December 2017), online: <https://www.huffpost.com/entry/respect-and-social-media_b_9315164>.

9 I use the term warrior here, knowing some of the many positive and powerful ways of showing up with this title. See, for example, the recent publication by Anishinaabe linguist Anton Treuer, *The Language Warrior's Manifesto: How to Keep Our Languages Alive, No Matter the Odds* (St. Paul: Minnesota Historical Society Press, 2020). See also the documentary *Warrior Fathers*, directed by Chris Hsiung, performance by Thomas Snow (CBC, 2019), online: <https://gem.cbc.ca/media /absolutely-canadian/s19e30>.

10 Online: <https://www.nawash.ca/>.

11 R. Horton, "Anishinaabemowin: The Ojibwe Language," *The Canadian Encyclopedia Online* (18 December 2017), online: <https://thecanadianencyclopedia.ca/en/article /anishinaabemowin-ojibwe-language>.

12 Basil Johnston, *Anishinaubae Thesaurus* (East Lansing: Michigan State University Press, 2007) at 110 [Johnston, *Anishinaubae Thesaurus*].

13 Seven Generations Education Institute, "Seven Grandfather Teachings," online: < https://www.7generations.org/seven-grandfather-teachings/>.

14 The Seven Grandfather Teachings of the Anishinaabe have been discussed for many years. I use the term Seven Grandparent teachings to recognize the various genders that make up our Elders and wise ones. For more information on these teachings see, for example, Edward Benton-Banai, *The Mishomis Book: The Voice of the Ojibway*, 2nd ed (Minneapolis: University of Minnesota Press, 2010).

15 Kekek Jason Stark, "Anishinaabe Inaakonigewin: Principles for the Intergenerational Preservation of Mino- Bimaadiziwin" (2021) 82:2 Mont L Rev 293. See also, The Ojibwe People's Dictionary Online (University of Minnesota), <https://ojibwe.lib.umn.edu/main-entry/mino-bimaadiziwin-ni?>.

16 Hilary Jacobs Hendel, "Ignoring Your Emotions Is Bad for Your Health. Here's What to Do about It," *Time Magazine* (27 February 2018), online: <https://time .com/5163576/ignoring-your-emotions-bad-for-your-health/>.

17 In the popular Disney Pixar movie *Inside Out* (2015), an eleven-year-old girl
    named Riley moves from her home in Minnesota to San Francisco. The move
    is difficult for Riley, and her five core emotions of Anger, Fear, Joy, Disgust, and
    Sadness display themselves in new ways that confuse both the young woman
    and her parents. Riley's parents keep asking where their happy girl is. Through
    character dialogue, the film explores the importance of each emotion to Riley,
    and though Joy keeps trying to silence Sadness, she (Sadness) has an important
    role to play too (for example, in helping Riley develop empathy, moving through a
    transition period into adolescence as well as a geographic transition). It is poignant
    and I highly recommend watching it. For information on the science of the film,
    see Dacher Keltner and Paul Ekman, "The Science of 'Inside Out,'" *The New York
    Times* (3 July 2015), online: <https://www.nytimes.com/2015/07/05/opinion
    /sunday/the-science-of-inside-out.html>.

18 To support the point that anger can serve a valuable purpose, see Glen Coulthard,
    Red Skin, White Masks (Minneapolis: University of Minnesota Press, 2014).

19 Eric Mathieu, "Denominal Verbs in Ojibwe" (2013) 79:1 International Journal
    of American Linguistics 97. See also Margaret Noodin, *Bawaajimo: A Dialect of
    Dreams in Anishinaabe Language and Literature* (East Lansing: Michigan State
    University Press, 2014), ch 1.

20 Lindsay Borrows, *Otter's Journey through Indigenous Language and Law*
    (Vancouver: UBC Press, 2019) at xv.

21 R. Horton, "Anishinaabemowin: The Ojibwe Language," *The
    Canadian Encyclopedia Online* (18 December 2017), online: <https://
    thecanadianencyclopedia.ca/en/article/anishinaabemowin-ojibwe-language>.

22 James Boyd White, *Justice as Translation: An Essay in Cultural and Legal Criticism*
    (Chicago: University of Chicago Press, 1990) at 272.

23 For examples of Basil Johnston's publications (there are many), see: Basil Johnston,
    Ojibway Heritage (New York: Columbia University Press, 1976); Basil Johnston,
    Moose Meat and Wild Rice (Toronto: McClelland & Stewart, 1978); Basil Johnston,
    Ojibwe Ceremonies (Toronto: McClelland & Stewart, 1994); Basil Johnston, *The
    Bear-Walker and Other Stories* (Toronto: Royal Ontario Museum, 1995).

24 Johnston, *Anishinaubae Thesaurus, supra* note 12 at 110.

25 *Ibid* at 168.

26 *Ibid* at 205.

27 Here Basil Johnston explicitly references the deities as deserving of respect. We also
    learn many teachings about treating plants, animals, water, rocks, etc. with deep
    respect in Anishinaabe thought. See, for example, Mary Siisip Geniusz, *Plants Have
    So Much to Give Us, All We Have to Do Is Ask: Anishinaabe Botanical Teachings*,
    edited by Wendy Makoons Geniusz (Minneapolis: University of Minnesota Press,
    2015).

28 Seven Generations Education Institute, "Seven Grandfather Teachings," online:
    < https://www.7generations.org/seven-grandfather-teachings/>.

29 John Borrows, *Law's Indigenous Ethics* (Toronto: University of Toronto Press, 2019) at 217–18.

30 Rupert Ross, *Dancing with a Ghost: Exploring Indian Reality* (Markham ON: Octopus Books, 1992).

31 Several years later I was an articling student doing a sentencing hearing for an Indigenous client at the courthouse in Victoria, BC. I told the judge that I believed my client needed to be reminded of their capacity for goodness as they acknowledged the mistake they made. My supervising lawyer said afterwards that he thought it was an "interesting" line! Research on various countries' criminal justice systems that rely less heavily on punitive measures (such as incarceration) show the benefits of more 'open' models where detainees are able to live more like regular citizens. See, for example, Doran Larson, "Why Scandinavian Prisons are Superior," *Atlantic* (24 September 2013), online: <https://www.theatlantic.com/international/archive/2013/09/why-scandinavian-prisons-are-superior/279949/>.

32 I do not want to suggest that the Canadian legal system is always devoid of respect. It is not. It can be courteous, civil, and orderly. My point is that there are times where it could do much better. I admire the people working in the criminal justice field that uphold the dignity of those who move through it.

33 There are many potential sources to support the idea that justice systems are flawed. For a recent article, see Ardith Walpetko We'dalx Walkem, "Expanding Our Vision: Cultural Equality and Indigenous Peoples' Human Rights" (2020), online: *British Columbia Human Rights Tribunal* <http://www.bchrt.bc.ca/shareddocs/indigenous/expanding-our-vision.pdf>.

34 Bessel van der Kolk, MD, *The Body Keeps the Score: Brain, Mind and Body in the Healing of Trauma* (New York: Penguin Books, 2015).

35 I discuss wariness about forgiveness later in this article. See Courtney Jung, "Reconciliation: Six Reasons to Worry" (2018) 14:2 Journal of Global Ethics 252, online: <https://www.tandfonline.com/doi/abs/10.1080/17449626.2018.1507000> [Jung].

36 Daniel Kahneman, *Thinking Fast and Slow* (New York: FSG Publishing, 2013). Kahneman addresses cognitive biases, including the negativity bias (as well as the confirmation bias). For one review of his book, see Peter Diamandis, "Why We Love Bad News: Understanding Negativity Bias" (July 2013), online: *Big Think* <https://bigthink.com/in-their-own-words/why-we-love-bad-news-understanding-negativity-bias>.

37 For other introductory summaries of research on negativity bias, see Catherine Moore, "What Is the Negativity Bias and How Can It Be Overcome?" (30 December 2019), online: *Positive Psychology* <https://positivepsychology.com/3-steps-negativity-bias/>; Jacob Burak, "Humans Are Wired for Negativity" (4 September 2014), online: *Aeon Digital Magazine* <https://aeon.co/essays/humans-are-wired-for-negativity-for-good-or-ill>.

38 Krista Tippett in conversation with Ross Gay, "Tending Joy and Practicing Delight," *On Being with Krisa Tippett Podcast* (26 March 2020), online: <https://onbeing .org/programs/ross-gay-tending-joy-and-practicing-delight/#transcript>.

39 Ross Gay, *The Book of Delights: Essays* (Chapel Hill, NC: Algonquin Books, 2019).

40 See also Steven Pinker, "The Media Exaggerates Negative News. This Distortion Has Consequences," *Guardian* (17 February 2018), online: <https://www.theguardian .com/commentisfree/2018/feb/17/steven-pinker-media-negative-news>.

41 Rick Hanson, "Hardwiring Happiness" (2013), online (video): *TEDxMarin* <https://www.rickhanson.net/ted-x-marin/>; Alison Ledgerwood, "Getting Stuck in the Negatives (and How to Get Unstuck)" (2013), online (video): *TEDxUCDavis* <https://www.youtube.com/watch?v=7XFLTDQ4JMk>.

42 Centre for Mindfulness Studies, "The Evidence," online: <https://www .mindfulnessstudies.com/mindfulness/evidence/>; Alvin Powell, "When Science Meets Mindfulness," *Harvard Gazette* (April 2018), online: <https://news.harvard .edu/gazette/story/2018/04/harvard-researchers-study-how-mindfulness-may -change-the-brain-in-depressed-patients/>.

43 For information on Cognitive Behavioral Therapy (CBT), see the following resource from Anxiety Canada, online: <https://www.anxietycanada.com/articles /cognitive-behaviour-therapy-cbt/>.

44 Office of the Correctional Investigator, "Indigenous People in Federal Custody Surpasses 30% Correctional Investigator Issues Statement and Challenge" (21 January 2020), online: <https://www.oci-bec.gc.ca/cnt/comm/press/press20200121 -eng.aspx>.

45 Ellen Boeder, "Emotional Safety Is Necessary for Emotional Connection" (4 August 2017), online: *Gottman Institute* <https://www.gottman.com/blog/emotional -safety-is-necessary-for-emotional-connection/>; Brené Brown, "Dehumanizing Always Starts with Language" (17 May 2018), online: *Brené Brown* <https:// brenebrown.com/blog/2018/05/17/dehumanizing-always-starts-with-language/>.

46 Brené Brown, *Daring Greatly: How the Courage to Be Vulnerable Transforms the Way We Live, Love, Parent and Lead* (Penguin Publishing Audio, 2018). See also Emma McAdam (registered marriage and family therapist), "Therapy in a Nutshell" (16 November 2017), online (video): <https://www.youtube.com /watch?v=hEfCxEdDtGU> [McAdam].

47 There is interesting research on how interconnected we and the plant and animal world around us are. For example, there are complex networks of fungi in the forests that communicate with each other and sustain the biome that is fundamental to life. See, Peter Wohlleben, *The Hidden Life of Trees: What They Feel, How They Communicate, Discoveries from a Secret World* (Vancouver: Greystone Books, 2016); Adrienne Maree Brown, *Emergent Strategy: Shaping Change, Changing Worlds* (California: AK Press, 2017) [Brown], ch 3: "Fractals: The Relationships Between Small and Large."

48 McAdam, *supra* note 46.

49 Brown, *supra* note 47.

50 Jung, *supra* note 35.

51 Adrienne Maree Brown, "What Is/Isn't Transformative Justice?" (9 July 2015), online (blog): *Adrienne Maree Brown* <http://adriennemareebrown.net/2015/07/09/what-isisnt-transformative-justice/>.

52 M.K. Gandhi, *The Collected Works of Mahatma Gandhi*, Vol. 13 (New Delhi: Publications Division, Ministry of Information & Broadcasting, Government of India, 1999), at 241, online: <https://www.gandhiashramsevagram.org/gandhi-literature/mahatma-gandhi-collected-works-volume-13.pdf>.

53 Indigenous Law Research Unit, online: <https://www.uvic.ca/law/about/indigenous/indigenouslawresearchunit/index.php>.

54 Val Napoleon & Hadley Friedland, "Gathering the Threads: Developing a Methodology for Researching and Rebuilding Indigenous Legal Traditions" (2015) 1:1 Lakehead Law Journal, online: <https://www.uvic.ca/law/assets/docs/ilru/Gathering%20the%20Threads%20Lakehead%20Law%20Journal%202015%20Friedland%20Napoleon%20.pdf>.

55 For an example of one such report, see Asch et al, *supra* note 7.

56 Hadley Friedland & Val Napoleon, "An Inside Job: Engaging with Indigenous Legal Traditions through Stories" (2016) 61:4 McGill LJ 725 at 753–4, online: <https://lawjournal.mcgill.ca/article/an-inside-job-engaging-with-indigenous-legal-traditions-through-stories/>.

57 Chimamanda Ngozi Adichie, "The Danger of a Single Story" (2009), online (video): *TEDGlobal* <https://www.ted.com/talks/chimamanda_ngozi_adichie_the_danger_of_a_single_story>.

58 Frank Gouldsmith Speck, "Myths and Folklore of the Timiskaming Algonquin and Timagami Ojibwa" in *Canada Department of Mines Geological Survey Memoir 71*, No. 9 Anthropological Series (Ottawa: Government Printing Bureau, 1915) at 53–4.

59 For an interesting book on the role of one non-Indigenous anthropologist in BC, see Wendy Wickwire, *At the Bridge: James Teit and an Anthropology of Belonging* (Vancouver: UBC Press, 2019).

60 Dictionary.com defines "cancel culture" as "the popular practice of withdrawing support for (canceling) public figures and companies after they have done or said something considered objectionable or offensive. Cancel culture is generally discussed as being performed on social media in the form of group shaming," online: <https://www.dictionary.com/e/pop-culture/cancel-culture/>.

61 For an understanding of how many ways there are to say "have gas" in Anishinaabemowin, see Anton Treuer & Keller Pap, eds, *Aaniin Ekidong: Ojibwe Vocabulary Project* (St. Paul: Minnesota Humanities Centre, 2009) at 76.

62 Of course, respect isn't the only principle we learn from the story, and to focus on it exclusively in a more in-depth discussion would blind us to the other important practices and principles this story conveys.

63 Colonialism has played a large role in shaping lateral violence in our communities. See Melissa Ridgen, "Lateral Violence a 'Colonial Hangover' We Need to Heal: Prof," *APTN News* (9 January 2020), online: <https://aptnnews.ca/2020/01/09/lateral-violence-a-colonial-hangover-we-need-to-heal-prof/>.

64 Val Napoleon, "Demanding More of Ourselves. Indigenous Civility and Incivility," forthcoming book chapter in Dimitrios Karmis & Jocelyn Maclure, eds, *Civic Freedom in an Age of Diversity: The Public Philosophy of James Tully* (Montreal: McGill-Queen's University Press, 2023).

65 *Ibid.*

66 John Borrows, *Canada's Indigenous Constitution* (Toronto: University of Toronto Press, 2010) at 35–46.

67 *Ibid* at 24–8.

68 *Ibid* at 46–51.

69 *Ibid* at 51–5.

70 *Ibid* at 28–35.

71 Borrows, *Law's Indigenous Ethics, supra* note 29 at 14–16.

72 Richard Wagamese, *Embers: One Ojibway's Meditations* (Toronto: Douglas & McIntyre, 2013) at 58. I also note that after his passing from this world, Richard Wagamese's unfinished manuscript on the Seven Grandparent teachings was published. One of the chapters focuses on Respect: see Richard Wagamese, *One Drum: Stories and Ceremonies for a Planet* (Toronto: Douglas & McIntyre, 2019).

73 Chase Jarvis, *Creative Calling: Establish a Daily Practice, Infuse Your Life with Meaning, and Succeed in Work and Life* (Toronto: HarperCollins, 2019).

6 "How Could You Sleep When Beds Are Burning?" Cultural Appropriation and the Place of Non-Indigenous Academics

FELIX HOEHN

Like the members of the band Midnight Oil, I am not Indigenous, and yet we have each applied our craft – popular music and not-so-popular legal writing – to speak against the injustices colonialism has perpetrated on Indigenous Peoples.

Differences in format aside, the underlying message in my academic writing on Canadian law as it pertains to Indigenous Peoples is consistent with Midnight Oil's hit song "Beds Are Burning." The song is a call to fight injustice, to right a wrong, and not to be complacent while the dominant society continues to oppress Indigenous Peoples. Rob Hirst has explained what motivated him to write this song:

> I had been to an art exhibition which featured the story of the fascists during the Second World War, Mussolini and the fightback from the partisans. The guy who put the exhibition on explained to me that there was an expression from Italy about the fightback from those partisans, "How could you sleep when beds are burning?" and I thought we could write a song about the same idea of an ancient Australian community who had so much thrown at it but was still joyfully dancing in the desert, singing their songs and pushing back against all the shocking things that had been visited upon them ever since Europeans had arrived in this country.[1]

My writing lacks the colour and poetry of Midnight Oil's songwriting, and instead attempts to persuade with legal argument and weighty citations. Since its purpose is to address injustice, it is "normative" legal writing – it speaks not just to what the law is, but how it ought to be, or at least how I think it ought to be applied and interpreted.

My writing highlights the importance of recognizing the sovereignty of Indigenous Peoples, and this also aligns with the message of "Beds Are Burning." Just as the song's lyrics refer to facts and fairness, sovereignty is a *fact* that has been denied by legal doctrine founded on the doctrine of discovery. It is racist and fundamentally *unfair* for courts to treat unilateral Crown assertions of sovereignty as a source of law capable of overriding the sovereignty of Indigenous nations. By giving Crown assertions this unwarranted advantage, courts allow the Crown to escape the need to seek the consent of Indigenous Peoples for sharing their sovereignty, jurisdiction, lands, and resources.

To build a positive relationship between Indigenous Peoples in Canada and non-Indigenous Canadians, we must convince courts that the doctrine of discovery is no longer a part of Canadian law, and therefore unilateral Crown assertions lack legal legitimacy. Once unilateral assertions are no longer effective, the Crown must embrace the principle of the equality of peoples as it seeks agreements with Indigenous Peoples. These negotiations should seek a form of treaty federalism, to borrow Sa'ke'j Henderson's label.[2] Since a hierarchical relationship isn't consistent with the principle of the equality of peoples, the relationship should strive to become a genuine partnership.[3]

It follows that I want to consider questions relating to cultural appropriation and the place of non-Indigenous academics through a lens that accepts the reality of Indigenous sovereignty and views Canada as a nation aspiring to become a partnership that includes Indigenous nations.

My analysis has benefited from the insight of Professor Bruce Ziff that sovereignty is a better lens than property for understanding cultural appropriation. He observed that concerns voiced about cultural appropriation "focus on forms of taking that tend to fall outside the realm of the current law of property, or more specifically, the laws governing intellectual property (patents, trade-marks and copyright)," offering as an example a traditional Aboriginal song.[4] He suggests this may be an area in which the law of property does not have the capacity to adequately mediate conflicting claims.[5] What spoke to me most about his comments is his observation that some have argued that what is involved in cultural appropriation is a "'*conflict of sovereignties*' especially when Aboriginal practices are involved," and this leads him to ask: "What doctrines should govern: customary Aboriginal law, generic intellectual property legislation, or something altogether new?"[6]

Viewing cultural appropriation through the lens of sovereignty doesn't offer easy answers, but it offers a perspective which may be helpful in at least pointing us to where answers may lie on this question and on issues related to the role of non-Indigenous scholars.

I will try to answer the following questions:

1 Should *non-Indigenous* persons become scholars of Aboriginal law?
2 Should I always identify myself as non-Indigenous to be clear that I speak with a non-Indigenous voice?
3 Are there limits to the teaching roles appropriate for non-Indigenous scholars of Aboriginal law?

4   As a non-Indigenous scholar of Aboriginal law, to what extent should I be expected to participate in ceremonies or practices that are part of Indigenous cultures?

1.   Should *non-Indigenous persons* become scholars of Aboriginal law?

By Aboriginal law I mean the law of Canada as it pertains to Indigenous Peoples, to distinguish it from "Indigenous Law," which is the law of Indigenous Peoples.[7] Implicit in this question is that we need *Indigenous* scholars of Aboriginal law. I don't think this assertion needs to be defended, and so I will say only that Indigenous scholars can offer one thing all non-Indigenous scholars lack, and that is a worldview shaped by being part of Indigenous culture and having experienced the reality of what being an Indigenous person in Canada means.

I began my study of Canadian Aboriginal law when I entered the LL.M. Program at the University of Saskatchewan. I considered the rights of Indigenous Peoples an important matter, and a rapidly changing area of law worthy of study. I had some concerns that pursuing this topic would cause me to study and write about the rights of peoples to whom I did not belong. When I raised this with the then Associate Dean of Graduate Studies, he suggested I seek out Professor Sa'ke'j (Youngblood) Henderson at the Native Law Centre (now Indigenous Law Centre), to ask his opinion of whether he thought it was appropriate for me to do so. He encouraged me, and I stopped worrying about it for some time. My passion for the subject and the need for change grew as I studied it, and I am grateful for the support I have received from both Indigenous and non-Indigenous academics. Nevertheless, I confess there have been times when I have wondered whether my scholarship would have been received differently if I were Indigenous. I consider one of those occasions in the next section.

There are now many more and many excellent Indigenous scholars of Aboriginal law. It could be argued that their voices speak with greater cogency on the subject since they can bring their own knowledge of the effect of Canadian law on themselves and their families, communities, and nations. It might be argued that they also speak with greater legitimacy – who am I, as an outsider, to say what rights Indigenous Peoples need or should be entitled to?

Looking at the question through the lens of a partnership between equal peoples reminds us that Aboriginal law is too often mistakenly viewed as being mainly about "the rights of Indigenous Peoples." Instead, the discussion is really about how to build a just legal relationship or nation-to-nation partnership between Indigenous Peoples and non-Indigenous peoples in Canada. Relationships between equal peoples require scholars from each of the partners. To build and maintain a healthy relationship each of the partners must work to understand the dynamics of the relationship, how to nurture it, and how to manage the tensions that arise.

A partnership is not a competition, and so it's not a case of needing scholars from each "team" in some kind of contest. A partnership is a joint venture that seeks justice and prosperity that will ultimately benefit all the partners of Confederation. It is healthy for scholars to disagree, to debate, and to help each other find better answers. Diversity among scholars – that is, scholars from a number of Indigenous nations as well as non-Indigenous scholars – will invigorate the debate and make it more likely that the best legal arguments and solutions will emerge and dominate.

2. Should I always identify myself as non-Indigenous to be clear that I speak with a non-Indigenous voice?

This question arose because of a comment made by an anonymous peer reviewer of an article I had submitted to a law journal on an Aboriginal law topic. The reviewer commented that I ought to have identified myself early in the paper as settler, or as an Indigenous or non-Indigenous person. This took me by surprise. Would the answer to this question have affected the reviewer's opinion of whether the article should be published, and if so, how, or why? Wouldn't this information potentially defeat part of the purpose of double-blind peer reviews, which are designed to remove personal identities and characteristics and any possible prejudices these might evoke – favourable or unfavourable – from the equation?

A more benign interpretation of the reviewer's comment was that the purpose of revealing my status as either a settler or Indigenous person was not for the reviewer's use but for the benefit of the reader of the article once published. But why does the reader need this information?[8] My gut reacted negatively to the suggestion that I had to identify myself as Indigenous or not for an article about Aboriginal law, and in particular on an Aboriginal law topic largely focused on interpretation of the Canadian constitution. If I were writing about Indigenous Law, then this would naturally raise questions about how I came to learn that Law – was it part of my cultural heritage, and if not, how did I learn it and why should I be accepted as a voice on that topic?

However, on thinking further about this I realized my gut reaction may not have been entirely consistent with the logic of arguments I have made elsewhere. I have argued that we need a paradigm shift from the "settler" perspective offered by Canadian Aboriginal law, which continues to be based on the doctrine of discovery, to a paradigm that recognizes the equality and sovereignty of Indigenous Peoples.[9] In that context I have argued that these two paradigms are incommensurable, and that Indigenous and non-Indigenous Canadians grow up in different worlds that naturally lead them to see the world through different paradigms.

If Indigenous Peoples and non-Indigenous peoples are to an appreciable extent grounded in different paradigms, then maybe it does follow that each should identify themselves – so that the reader knows what perception of reality the paper's analysis is grounded in.

While I can see the argument, I'm not convinced by it. Maybe I haven't constructed it well enough, and maybe the anonymous reviewer or someone else could do it better so that I can be persuaded that this kind of identification is necessary or advisable. However, a persuasive argument would need to overcome my fear that focusing on the identity of the author before evaluating the strength of the argument makes it seem too much as though scholarship were being conducted in teams – and we need to know who is playing for what team so we know whom to cheer for. In other words, an early focus on identity feels unduly adversarial, as though differing identities will mean our legal analysis will inevitably be different and therefore more likely to conflict.

If we are peoples in partnership, then our task is to work together. Our common purpose as scholars should be to seek knowledge and understanding of the world, and as scholars of law this entails a quest for truth and justice. Of course, we all bring our life experiences and biases to this, and sometimes it's useful to consider those biases in ourselves and in other scholars. However, our biases shouldn't be the starting point. We should seek to consider the content of the scholarship and its merits first. After that, there may be room to acknowledge that for each of us our background colours our view of the world, and in some cases it may be useful to explicitly consider how our biases have influenced our analysis.

Therefore, my tentative answer to this question is that identification as settler or Indigenous in scholarly writing should not be mandatory, and should only be expected in exceptional situations in which the background of the author is relevant to the topic. One example is Larry Chartrand's article in the Supreme Court Law Review entitled "The Story in Aboriginal Law and Aboriginal Law in the Story: A Métis Professor's Journey,"[10] or perhaps articles about Indigenous Law. In other cases we should consider the merits of the legal argument and analysis as objectively as possible at the outset, without our evaluation being influenced by the identity and status of the writer – biases can be considered later.

3. Are there limits to the teaching roles appropriate for non-Indigenous scholars of Aboriginal law?

I have twice taught Aboriginal law, an upper-year course that previously had been taught by both Indigenous and non-Indigenous faculty. I have to admit to some degree of discomfort, especially since there were a few students in each class whom I knew to be Indigenous. Was it appropriate for me, a non-Indigenous male, to be teaching them Canadian law still so replete with colonialist content such as the *Indian Act* and the doctrine of discovery? After all, for the Indigenous students in my class this was part of their lived reality – while for me it was more something I have learned from books and law reports.

So was it appropriate for me to teach Aboriginal law? I admit to some lingering doubts on the question, but my answer is a qualified "yes." That answer flows from my guiding principles of the treaty and partnership relationship. Each party to the treaties and each partner in the relationship has a duty to study the law of Canada as it pertains to that relationship, to analyse it, to criticize it, and to seek to improve it. Having researched and analysed that law, a scholar may be competent and indeed well-placed to teach that subject – and to teach the same body of law to Indigenous and non-Indigenous students.

I would hasten to add that because of the continuing underlying colonialist and racist principles of Aboriginal law and the trauma this has caused for individual persons of Indigenous heritage – including those in the classroom – it should be taught with sensitivity to that reality. I don't know if my approach adequately addressed this, but I tried to do so by offering opportunities for all students to share their experiences and perspectives in classroom discussions and optional presentations. All students were expected to contribute to the discussion, but they had a choice as to the extent their contributions would count toward their final grade, and they were free to bring personal perspectives into the discussion or just to focus on the academic content of the course. I also attempted to address my non-Indigenous identity by bringing Indigenous voices into the classroom in the form of readings, video clips, and a guest speaker. I also considered it appropriate to offer critical analysis – insofar as I represented the non-Indigenous side of the partnership, I viewed it as my responsibility to point out the flaws in Aboriginal law.

Having said that, there are certainly things an Indigenous instructor could have brought to these classes that I could not. Since I can't speak to the impact of racist and colonialist legal doctrines from personal experience, the best I can do is to look for other sources for that. Also, the role of Indigenous sources of law is of increasing importance, and while I know a little about how Canadian law can incorporate different legal systems, I'm not qualified to speak to the form or content of Indigenous Law. At the same time, not every Indigenous instructor with expertise in Aboriginal law could speak with authority on Indigenous Law either. Even if they could, their expertise may well be limited to the laws of their own Indigenous nation.

Until recently, and without having given the matter a lot of thought, I was of the view that only an Indigenous instructor should teach the kind of course recommended by the Truth and Reconciliation Commission (TRC) Call to Action 28,[11] which calls upon Canadian law schools:

> to require all law students to take a course in Aboriginal people and the law, which includes the history and legacy of residential schools, the *United Nations Declaration on the Rights of Indigenous Peoples*, Treaties and Aboriginal rights, Indigenous law, and Aboriginal–Crown relations. This will require skills-based training in intercultural competency, conflict resolution, human rights, and anti-racism.

In response to this Call to Action, at the University of Saskatchewan's College of Law we have established a compulsory fist year course known as Kwayeskastasowin, which is Cree for "setting things right." I was not closely involved with the design of this course, but I shared the assumption of other faculty at the College that this should be taught be an Indigenous member of faculty. I based my assumption at least in part on the expectation that the course would introduce students to Indigenous cultural and legal traditions, and so it would appropriate to have an Indigenous person teach it.

I have slowly come to question the assumption that Kwayeskastasowin must be taught by an Indigenous faculty member, especially since I have heard anecdotally of some "pushback" from students on having to take this course, and unfortunately there have been reports of some racist comments inside and outside the classroom. I have heard reports of some students resenting having to take the class because it's not what they came to law school for, or because they see it as "political."

Looking at this class through the lens of a partnership and a nation-to-nation relationship, shouldn't the responsibility for educating future lawyers about the history and importance of that relationship fall equally on both partners? If it's hard to motivate some students who tolerate the class only because they can't get a law degree without it, shouldn't this challenge be shared equitably between the treaty or partnering peoples?[12] Sharing this task underlines its importance, and sends the message that "setting things right" is important enough to be everyone's job. Sharing this task would also set a good practical example for students of how Indigenous and non-Indigenous scholars can work together toward a common objective.

Almost all of the topics recommended for inclusion by Call to Action 28 can readily be taught by non-Indigenous faculty. These include the history and legacy of residential schools, the *United Nations Declaration on the Rights of Indigenous Peoples,* Treaties and Aboriginal Rights, Aboriginal–Crown relations, and training related to intercultural competency and anti-racism. Only the topic of Indigenous Law presents a barrier for non-Indigenous instructors. Karen Drake has explained that Indigenous Law cannot be properly learned as a "list of rules or principles, removed from their ontological, epis-temological, ethical, and logical foundations."[13] An understanding of Indig-enous Law requires an understanding of Indigenous ways of knowing, and this, in turn, may only be fully accessible to someone who understands the Indigenous language in which those laws are framed.[14] Nevertheless, some have concluded that Indigenous Law is teachable, and so maybe with enough effort and study a non-Indigenous person could become qualified to teach Indigenous Law.[15] In theory, then, it might be possible for an appropriately qualified non-Indigenous instructor to teach all the topics the TRC recom-mends including in such a class. Nevertheless, teaching reconciliation with-out the prominent participation of one or more voices that are Indigenous would seem incomplete and insincere, and would lack the benefits of sharing the task referred to above.

4. As a non-Indigenous scholar of Aboriginal law, to what extent should I be expected to participate in ceremonies or practices that are part of Indigenous cultures?

This question flows from my situation, but the same question could be asked about the expectations of non-Indigenous scholars in many disci-plines. This is especially the case in view of the effort of faculties and uni-versities to "indigenize" the academy, which sometimes include initiatives to involve faculty in Indigenous ceremonies like Smudges and Sweat Lodge ceremonies.

I have participated in numerous Smudging ceremonies at the beginning of meetings or workshops that have included Indigenous people. To date I have not participated in a Sweat Lodge ceremony. I have only been invited once, and that invitation was not a personal invitation extended to me by an Indigenous person but was part of an "indigenizing" process. I struggled with the question of whether I should feel obliged to attend since I did not feel comfortable with the prospect of taking part in this kind of ceremony. I reluctantly decided to go, but then changed my mind after I learned more about the specifics of this particular request. I'm still struggling with the question of whether or under what circumstances I might accept a future invitation.

Some might object to participating in Indigenous sacred practices on grounds that it is not consistent with their own belief system. Although I do not consider myself a religious person, nor have I made any kind of spiritual practices a regular part of my life, this objection would have parallels to my own feelings. I long ago made a deliberate choice to move away from my own religious background because I was not comfortable with the demands it made of me to accept its precepts on "faith" and to take part in certain ceremonies. Having chosen to reject the sacred or religious ceremonies of my own culture and background, I wonder whether I should give in to pressure to take part in sacred aspects of another culture.

While Smudges and Sweats both have sacred components in Indigenous cultures, I was much less reluctant to participate in a Smudge and have done so many times without giving it a lot of thought. On reflection, I think this is because Smudging had a clearer purpose in the context of the activity it took place in, and it was minimally intrusive. The Smudges took place as preludes to meetings that included Indigenous persons who initiated the Smudge and asked for my participation. I understood that Smudging may have sacred significance for them, and they understood it was not part of my culture or belief system but asked me to participate. I considered my participation a show of respect for the beliefs and practices of those I was meeting with, and as a sort of protocol to set the stage for a positive interaction. This may be similar to going along with a friend or family member who says grace before a meal, or an Elder who says a prayer before a gathering. Whether my personal belief system suggests that prayer in these circumstances is needed or appropriate is beside the point. I'm meeting with people who consider this important, and all they ask of me is that I bow my head in silence for a few moments to show respect for their beliefs and to set a good tone for what is to follow. Finally, considered through the lens of conduct appropriate to the interaction between sovereign partners, in my view it is fitting that at gatherings of both partners the ceremonies and protocols adopted reflect the cultures of both partners as much as reasonably possible. Subject of course to allergies or other medical conditions that might preclude participation, it is appropriate and conducive to a positive relationship for a non-Indigenous person to participate in a Smudging ceremony when invited to do so.

I view Sweat Lodge ceremonies differently, though I admit my understanding of them and their purposes is limited,[16] and maybe if I learned more about them I would better appreciate why I should participate. Indeed, as I will explain, this was the first problem with the invitation I ultimately refused. It gave the purpose of participating in the Sweat Lodge ceremony as "to begin learning Indigenous legal traditions." Certainly, this is a laudable purpose, and as someone who researches Aboriginal law and teaches Indigenous students I could see it would be valuable for me to learn more about Indigenous legal traditions. I was prepared to offer a few hours of my Saturday morning for that purpose, even if I felt significant discomfort about actually participating in a Sweat Lodge ceremony.

However, once I received more information about what the Sweat Lodge ceremony would entail, I changed my mind and declined the invitation. First, I learned that the time commitment would be close to twelve hours and included teachings, building the lodge, picking medicines, the ceremony itself, and finally a feast. We were told it was all or nothing – leaving early would not be acceptable. Also, the intrusion into my life was greater than just the activity itself. I was instructed not to use alcohol or drugs for four days before the Sweat Lodge, and the instructions also barred those in their "moon cycle" from taking part in the ceremony. This meant I was also being asked to be a party to what seemed to me, at least, to be gender-based discrimination, and this added to my discomfort.

This added information caused my unease about attending to outweigh the pressure I felt to go as a faculty member asked to take part in a collegial initiative and the purported benefit of beginning to learn about Indigenous legal traditions. Even if I see the objectives to be broader and as including learning about Indigenous cultural traditions more generally and fostering a positive relationship with Indigenous Peoples, I thought these objectives could be furthered in a less intrusive manner. Moreover, asking me to participate in a sacred ceremony without at least first teaching me to understand and appreciate the nature of the ceremony I would be agreeing to participate in threatens to demean the sacred nature of the ceremony and those who hold it sacred. Even from the little I knew about Sweat Lodge ceremonies, I did not feel comfortable attending one like a tourist might stop at a roadside attraction – perhaps with good intentions of learning about the place, but with little care, concern, or understanding of what one is walking into.

A Cree scholar's description of a Cree Sweat Lodge ceremony confirms its profound importance in that Indigenous culture. Janice Alison Makokis described a Sweat Lodge ceremony as a sacred place where Cree people "learn and practice what self-determination and governance mean."[17] According to the Cree author, much of her understanding of Indigenous epistemology came from ceremony, and

> only when one truly immerses and embraces his/herself within indigenous ceremony do they find the true meaning of an indigenous way of thinking and experiencing the world through a true anti-colonial framework. It is through the experiential knowledge acquired by participating in various ceremonies that you truly appreciate the importance of a philosophy based on ceremonial teachings found within the spiritual realm of an indigenous existence.[18]

This suggests a flaw in the approach of attending a Sweat Lodge "to begin learning Indigenous legal traditions" – as my invitation proposed. Makokis's description of the Sweat Lodge ceremony and of its importance in Cree culture generally indicates that this may indeed be a way to learn about Cree Laws and ways of thinking – but it is the advanced course, not the beginner's course. I'm still a beginner, I need to learn more before I could consider moving to the advanced level, and I'm not yet ready to decide if or when I would want or need to go to that level.

Viewed through the lens of sovereignty and partnership, participating in a Sweat Lodge ceremony looks different than participating in a Smudging ceremony. While Smudging also has spiritual meaning for Indigenous Peoples, a non-Indigenous person lacking a full understanding of the ceremony can still participate as a sign of respect and to express a shared desire for setting a positive and constructive tone for a meeting or discussion.

A Sweat Lodge ceremony, on the other hand, is a much more elaborate and intrusive activity which has profound meaning for Indigenous Peoples. It is not possible to do it justice in a few minutes of respectful participation, and it is not ordinarily a prelude or protocol expected before an interaction between Indigenous and non-Indigenous persons. Unlike Smudging, which a newcomer to Indigenous culture can readily learn to take part in, a Sweat Lodge is a much more complex process with profound significance for Indigenous culture, governance, and self-determination. To me it feels as though an invitation to participate in such a ceremony extended by an Indigenous person to a non-Indigenous person is an invitation to an intimate encounter that may allow a glimpse of the world from an Indigenous perspective.

A partnership and a positive relationship can be satisfied by the approach symbolized in the two-row wampum of a separate but equal relationship, which allows each of the parties to steer their own vessels. While attending the ceremony doesn't violate the promise not to steer the Indigenous vessel, it is analogous to entering it to see what the world looks like from that vessel. This might be a good thing, but it should not be done lightly or without adequate preparation. It therefore worries me that invitations to Sweat Lodge ceremonies are sometimes extended so casually to non-Indigenous people. While this is no doubt done with the best of intentions, I would argue that there is much education and discussion that should precede a decision to attend this kind of ceremony.

I might accept an invitation to a Sweat Lodge ceremony in the future, notwithstanding the reservations that caused me to decline the last one. Those reservations would still exist, but it might be possible to overcome them in the right circumstances. For example, in view of the intimate and profound nature of a Sweat Lodge ceremony, it would make a difference if the invitation came directly from an Indigenous person with whom I already had a relationship rather than being an organized event with a vague "indigenization" agenda. I would also need to be at a place in my life when I was ready to be open to appreciating and learning about the Sweat Lodge's spiritual and cultural dimensions, so that I could do justice to the generosity of the invitation as well as benefit from it.

Conclusion

As a non-Indigenous person benefiting from "white privilege," I have blind spots, despite the best of intentions, and it means I can never really understand the lived realities of Indigenous Peoples in Canada. Moreover, since my legal writing is admittedly normative, it is obvious that my scholarship is not just a neutral and amoral pursuit of truth. It seeks to find a just foundation for a positive relationship between Indigenous Peoples in Canada and non-Indigenous Canadians. It follows that what I write is designed to affect the reality of peoples whose identity is different from mine. Nevertheless, I do not believe it would be accurate to say I am appropriating Indigenous culture or voice. Instead, part of my normative purpose comes from a recognition that all partners to Confederation must turn their minds and their pens to the question of what laws would be conducive to reconciliation. Taking part in that discussion does not represent a conflict of sovereignties that might characterize cultural appropriation. Instead, it is a recognition of sovereignty and a desire to find laws that will help to reconcile those sovereignties.

Even though there are times when it may be appropriate to consider how an author's academic work is influenced by their context and worldview, I nevertheless want my work to be assessed on its own merit apart from that identity in matters such as peer review. We should always consider academic merit first and identity second, although there may be some areas such as writing on Indigenous Law where the identity of the author is more relevant to the evaluation of the work, especially if there are questions of appropriation of voice or qualification to speak with authority on the subject.

Perhaps the greatest risk of cultural appropriation occurs when I teach Aboriginal law, even if I can claim the same legitimacy in teaching the subject as I do in writing about it. The voices and experiences of Indigenous Peoples are critical, and there is a risk that they will be absent or dominated by the settler perspective.

The prospect of a non-Indigenous scholar teaching Indigenous Law raises particularly acute and perhaps insurmountable worries of appropriation of the Indigenous voice. While perhaps possible in theory, in practice it is hard to imagine this as acceptable in all but extraordinarily rare circumstances. This should not be perceived as a barrier for non-Indigenous faculty participating in the delivery of law classes recommended by the TRC to further reconciliation. On the contrary, a good case can be made that it is wrong to put the delivery of this kind of course solely on the shoulders of Indigenous faculty members.

Navigating issues of cultural appropriation is bound to be tricky, and mistakes are to be expected – and for all their successes, Midnight Oil was not immune from having taken some wrong turns in this regard. Their music reached millions, and they were able to use their access to the stage at the close of the Sydney Olympics in 2000 to play "Beds Are Burning" before 115,000 people in the stadium and an estimated 3.5 billion on television.[19] They wore black outfits prominently displaying the word "sorry" in white. This was a protest against the Australian prime minister's refusal to apologize to Aboriginal Australians on behalf of the government.[20] It took another eight years, but in 2008 Prime Minister Kevin Rudd finally delivered an official apology to the "stolen generations" of Indigenous Australians.[21] This Olympic performance was widely praised, but it came only after the band had learned from earlier missteps in their approach to Indigenous Peoples, including criticisms of stereotypical portrayals and that an earlier song inaccurately portrayed Tasmanian Aborigines as extinct.[22]

I like the suggestion that what ultimately matters are not Midnight Oil's blunders, but their efforts to find a strategy to heal the tensions within Australia's society.[23] The controversies generated can themselves be useful for generating discussion and a renegotiation of the borders between cultures.[24]

Midnight Oil was willing to learn from their mistakes and to try new approaches. We can all learn from this openness to adapt, especially with vexing questions like when it would be appropriate for non-Indigenous peoples to be invited into sacred spaces such as Sweat Lodges. Insofar as reconciliation requires us to be able to "better understand the perspective of the other side,"[25] this can be pursued through a variety of means. Education and dialogue can do wonders for furthering mutual understanding, and protocols like Smudging can help to set a positive tone for conversations. A Sweat Lodge is a more intimate encounter and maybe it should wait until an adequate groundwork has been laid and a good relationship has been established by other means.

Above all, the message of "Beds Are Burning" is that there is urgent work to be done. Non-Indigenous academics have a particular reason to be sensitive to issues of cultural appropriation, and we should seek strategies for building understanding that are most effective. While we should not let worries of making mistakes keep us from pursuing reconciliation with Indigenous Peoples, we should be alert for opportunities to learn and to do better.

NOTES

1 See Duncan Haskell, Interviewer, "How I Wrote 'Beds Are Burning' by Midnight Oil's Rob Hirst" (5 May 2019), online: *Songwriting* <www.songwritingmagazine .co.uk/interviews/how-i-wrote-beds-are-burning-by-midnight-oils-rob-hirst>.

2 James [sákéj] Henderson, "Empowering Treaty Federalism" (1994) 58 Sask L Rev 241.

3 The Supreme Court of Canada has developed "a growing appreciation that Aboriginal and non-Aboriginal people are partners in Confederation": *Daniels v Canada (Indian Affairs and Northern Development)*, 2016 SCC 12, [2016] 1 SCR 99 at para 37.

4 Bruce Ziff, *Principles of Property Law*, 7th ed (Toronto: Thomson Reuters, 2018) at 65.

5 *Ibid* at 66.

6 *Ibid* at 65.

7 The word Aboriginal is used here because of its use and definition within s 35 of the *Constitution Act, 1982* (being Schedule B to the *Canada Act 1982* (UK), 1982, c 11). Section 35(1) recognizes and affirms the existing Aboriginal and Treaty Rights of the Aboriginal Peoples of Canada, and s 35(2) defines Aboriginal Peoples as including "the Indian, Inuit and Métis peoples of Canada."

8 Although perhaps not directly applicable to a law review article, it may also be that the reviewer's perspective was influenced by the importance that at least some Indigenous Nations place on a personal introduction that includes one's name, family, and where one is from, such that this could be considered a protocol required by Indigenous Law. I am indebted to John Borrows for bringing this possibility to my attention.

9 See e.g., Felix Hoehn, *Reconciling Sovereignties: Aboriginal Nations and Canada* (Saskatoon: University of Saskatchewan Native Law Centre, 2012).

10 Larry Chartrand, "The Story in Aboriginal Law and Aboriginal Law in the Story: A Métis Professor's Journey" (2010) 50 Sup Ct L Rev 89; also published in Sanda Rodgers & Sheila McIntyre, eds, *The Supreme Court of Canada and the Achievement of Social Justice: Commitment, Retrenchment or Retreat* (Markham: Lexis-Nexis Canada, 2010).

11 *The Final Report of the Truth and Reconciliation Commission of Canada: Canada's Residential Schools: Legacy*, vol 5 (Montreal: McGill-Queen's University Press, 2015) at 281, online: <www.trc.ca>.

12 On the risk of marginalization faced by teachers of a stand-alone course on Indigenous Law, see Karen Drake, "Finding a Path to Reconciliation: Mandatory Indigenous Law, Anishinaabe Pedagogy, and Academic Freedom" (2017) 95 Can Bar Rev 9 at 26 and sources therein cited.

13 *Ibid* at 27.

14 *Ibid* at 30.

15 See Chapter 7, Karen Drake and A. Christian Airhart, "Who Should Teach Indigenous Law?" For a demonstration that Indigenous Law is teachable and transferable, see Hadley Louise Friedland, "Reclaiming the Language of Law: The Contemporary Articulation and Application of Cree Legal Principles in Canada" (PhD diss., University of Alberta, Faculty of Law, 2016) [unpublished]. According to Friedland, through an adapted method of legal analysis, Cree legal principles are "teachable, transferable and replicable" (*ibid* at ii).

16 It is difficult to generalize about Sweat Lodges since they are a part of many distinct Indigenous cultures and so come in different types, and may also take on different forms and purposes within individual cultures. As a broad generalization, a Sweat Lodge may be described as a sacred place that offers "deeply spiritual and cultural experiences." René R. Gadacz, "Sweat Lodge" in *The Canadian Encyclopedia*, online: <https://www.thecanadianencyclopedia.ca/en/article/sweat-lodge>.

17 Janice Alison Makokis, "nehiyaw iskwew kiskinowâtasinahikewina – paminisowin namôya tipeyimisowin: Cree Women Learning Self Determination through Sacred

Teachings of the Creator" (master's thesis, University of Victoria, Department of
Human and Social Development, 2008) [unpublished] at 11.

18 *Ibid* at 25.

19 Rob Hughes, "How Midnight Oil Made an Art of Mixing Politics with Music,"
    Louder (22 June 2017), online. <https://www.loudersound.com/features/how
    -australias-midnight-oil-made-an-art-of-mixing-politics-with-music>.

20 *Ibid.*

21 Teo Kermeliotis, "The Aboriginal Apology," *openDemocracy* (24 February 2008)
    online: <https://www.opendemocracy.net/en/the_aboriginal_apology/>.

22 Laetitia Vellutini, "Finding a Voice on Indigenous Issues: Midnight Oil's
    Inappropriate Appropriations" (29 July 2008), online: *Australian Public Intellectual
    Network* <https://web.archive.org/web/20080729090622/http:/www.api-network
    .com/main/index.php?apply=scholars&webpage=default&flexedit=&flex
    _password=&menu_label=&menuID=homely&menubox=&scholar=76> [Vellutini].

23 *Ibid,* citing Rosemary Van Den Berg, "Nyoongar; Perceptions of Reconciliation"
    (2000) 1 Meanjin 155.

24 Vellutini, *supra* note 22.

25 *Ibid,* citing Aden Ridgeway, "An Impasse or a Relationship in the Making?" in
    Michelle Grattan, ed, *Reconciliation: Essays on Australian Reconciliation* (Bookman
    Press: Melbourne, 2000) 14.

7 Who Should Teach Indigenous Law?

KAREN DRAKE AND A. CHRISTIAN AIRHART

1. Introduction

Should non-Indigenous instructors teach Indigenous Law? In 2015, the Truth and Reconciliation Commission of Canada called on law schools to make a number of topics mandatory within law programs.[1] These topics include not only state law affecting Indigenous Peoples,[2] but also Indigenous Law, meaning Indigenous Peoples' own laws. In response, Canadian law schools have introduced additional courses or mandatory program components on Indigenous Law. Who should teach these courses? Should only Indigenous instructors teach Indigenous Law?[3]

This issue arose recently at Mount Saint Vincent University in Halifax, although the context was an undergraduate course on the history of residential schools as opposed to a course on Indigenous Law. According to media reports, the university's decision to assign a non-Indigenous faculty member to teach the course drew criticism on social media.[4] Critics were reported to have said "only Indigenous people have the lived experience to understand the complex and cumulative ways they've been discriminated against."[5] In contrast, the Society for Academic Freedom and Scholarship (hereafter, Society) was reported to have argued that "a professor's race or ethnicity should not be a consideration when assigning a course" and the matter "should be judged on academic grounds alone."[6] Ultimately, the university endorsed the assigned instructor, as she had the support of "Indigenous and non-Indigenous faculty and administration."[7]

How can we decide between these competing views? To begin, we can identify the theories underpinning them. Doing so allows us to evaluate the arguments' foundational assumptions which can otherwise operate unnoticed, driving conclusions while remaining unexamined. Some might resist the project of theorizing Indigenous issues.[8] Scholars have posited the following reasons for this hesitancy: theory has been used to oppress Indigenous Peoples;[9] prospective theorists might fear inadvertently employing non-Indigenous theory;[10] theory can be thought to privilege one form of knowledge (the intellectual knowledge prized within academia) to the exclusion of Indigenous ways of knowing;[11] and finally, theorizing might seem self-indulgent, especially given the immediate, practical problems facing Indigenous communities.[12] A detailed examination of the many responses to these concerns is beyond the scope of this chapter.[13] We wish to highlight only one theme which intersects with some of these concerns, namely, the notion that theory might be antithetical to Indigenous lifeways. Following Leanne Betasamosake Simpson, we can consider theory in its most basic form as an explanation of phenomena.[14] On this view, theory is congruent with Indigenous lifeways. In this chapter, we focus on the Anishinaabeg to avoid a pan-Indigenous approach. Within an Anishinaabe lifeway, theory is interdependent and interwoven with physical, spiritual, and emotional ways of knowing.[15] As a result, the conventions of Anishinaabe theory differ from those of non-Indigenous theory.[16] We develop this point further in section three below. These differences do not detract from the value of theory within an Anishinaabe lifeway.

Returning to the respective arguments of the critics and of the Society at Mount Saint Vincent University, let's identify the theories underpinning their views.

The Society's position is arguably grounded in modernist views, such as liberalism and the premise that norms or metrics for measuring academic merit can operate objectively. Under certain versions of liberalism, the principle of equality protects us from discrimination on the basis of race or ethnicity, and thus differentiating among individuals on this basis is an illiberal violation of equality. The position of the critics, in contrast, is consistent with the strand of critical theory grounded in postmodernism, which denies the objective knowability of normative frameworks, including metrics for assessing academic merit. On this view, the lived experience of those who occupy a marginalized position gives rise to an epistemic standpoint not available to others. Thus, we can understand the scenario at Mount Saint Vincent University as an instantiation of the impasse between liberalism and critical theory.

The perils of theorizing Indigenous issues using liberalism are well-documented. Some scholars have attempted to ground Indigenous issues – such as Indigenous Rights[17] and mandatory Indigenous courses[18] – within the discourse of liberalism. Others have critiqued such attempts as overlooking or falling short of protecting Indigenous self-determination.[19] Moreover, liberalism is just as likely to restrict and distort[20] or completely undermine[21] Indigenous claims. Some liberal theorists might argue these results reflect a shortcoming not with liberalism but with Indigenous claims. On this view, the core epistemic premises of liberalism are normatively superior and thus conclusions which are critical of Indigenous claims merely reflect the inherent weakness of those claims. But liberalism's premises are not only contested by, but incommensurable with, at least some forms of Indigenous constitutionalism, such as those which Aaron Mills refers to as rooted constitutionalism [22] This incommensurability explains the restricted and distorted results of applying liberal logic to Indigenous claims and also reveals the lack of any neutral ground from which to evaluate the correctness of liberalism.[23] For these reasons, the project of theorizing Indigenous issues from within liberalism is contentious.

In contrast, Indigenous scholars are more likely to theorize Indigenous issues using critical theory. Perhaps not surprisingly, the potential pitfalls of using critical theory in this way are less discussed than the pitfalls of liberalism.[24] That said, some scholars – including Gordon Christie and Aaron Mills – have highlighted the incongruity between Indigenous lifeways and the post-structural premises of some strands of critical theory.[25] This chapter builds on their work. In section two we trace the postmodern epistemological commitments informing the strand of critical theory which prioritizes standpoint epistemology. Section three then considers the ostensible overlap between these postmodern epistemological commitments and the epistemology of one Indigenous People, the Anishinaabeg. Drawing on the works of Lana Ray and Paul Nicholas Cormier, Leanne Betasamosake Simpson, and Aaron Mills, we argue that the apparent resemblances between postmodern epistemological commitments and Anishinaabe epistemology belie foundational differences. As a result, the challenges of using critical theory to theorize Anishinaabe issues can be as significant as the challenges of using liberalism.[26]

Fortunately, liberalism and critical theory are not the only available options. Indigenous writers such as Patricia Monture-Angus, James (Sákéj) Henderson, Gordon Christie, Leanne Betasamosake Simpson, Glen Coulthard, and Aaron Mills have called on us to theorize Indigenous issues using Indigenous theory.[27] In the fourth section, we take up this call. Drawing on the works of Aaron Mills, we consider how the question "Who should teach Anishinaabe Law?" could be resolved using Anishinaabe theory, specifically Anishinaabe constitutionalism, as filtered through our understanding at this time. Following Mills, we use the term "constitutionalism" to refer to a society's normative framework for constituting itself as a political community; this normative framework is rooted in a people's lifeworld, including their ontology, epistemology, and ethics.[28] In our view, the application of Anishinaabe constitutionalism results in a more nuanced analysis than a simple dichotomy between Anishinaabe people being qualified to teach Anishinaabe Law and non-Anishinaabe people being unqualified to do so. According to our understanding at this time of Anishinaabe constitutionalism, to be qualified to teach Anishinaabe Law, one should have knowledge of Anishinaabe Law in accordance with Anishinaabe epistemology and one should also comply with Anishinaabe Laws. These criteria are not necessarily tied to one's identity. In some circumstances, a non-Anishinaabe person could satisfy these criteria.

We claim neither the objective truth of Anishinaabe constitutionalism nor its superiority over other theories. Nor do we deny these claims. Our goal is only to illustrate how Anishinaabe constitutionalism could be applied to resolve the question of who should teach Anishinaabe Law. If a community or a law school determines it wants to work within Anishinaabe constitutionalism, this chapter offers guidance. Since the Truth and Reconciliation Commission released its final report, law schools, other faculties, and entire universities have committed to reconciliation and to "indigenization."[29] As many others have explained, merely displaying Indigenous art or making land acknowledgments does not constitute indigenization.[30] Those who decide to commit to indigenization can avoid a superficial approach by implementing substantive Indigenous norms, or, in other words, by complying with Indigenous constitutionalisms.

We acknowledge an Anishinaabe community is entitled, as a self-determining people, to choose not to work within Anishinaabe constitutionalism, or to work within a different variation or vision of Anishinaabe constitutionalism or Anishinaabe theory than that discussed here. As such, an Anishinaabe People may exercise its agency to decide, for example, that only Anishinaabe people can teach their Law. Indigenous Peoples may choose to ground their laws, protocols, decisions, and conclusions in non-Indigenous theories such as critical theory or even liberalism.[31] That being said, one of the goals of this chapter is to illustrate the value of caution when engaged in such a project.[32] Non-Indigenous theory can be rooted in norms and premises which on their surface seem to complement Anishinaabe constitutionalism but produce divergent implications.[33] Our goal in sections three and four is to reveal one such instance of divergence.

2. Critical Theory and Postmodernism

The notion of identity as a necessary pedagogical qualification has its roots in a strand of critical theory which is grounded in postmodernist philosophy. To understand the potential disparity between these approaches and Anishinaabe constitutionalism, this section provides a brief outline of the evolution of postmodernist thought and certain of its critical theory offshoots.

Postmodernism eludes any single authoritative definition; for the purposes of this chapter, we follow Lyotard in characterizing it as an "incredulity towards metanarratives."[34] A metanarrative is a comprehensive and totalizing cognitive framework that purports to organize and explain phenomena.[35] Examples include science, religions, and political theories such as Marxism or liberalism, each of which systematically attributes explanations or meanings to discrete natural or social phenomena. Since the explanation or meaning is determined by reference to the metanarrative itself, its validity depends on the validity of the metanarrative. Thus, any intellectual framework claiming something is "true" must inevitably defend that claim on the basis that the framework itself is legitimate. From this premise, Lyotard argues any such discourse of legitimation is self-referential and ultimately incapable of objective proof.[36] Knowledge, understood so, is not objective; rather, it is relative to the phenomenological standpoint of the subject.

The inevitability of epistemic relativism was reinforced by the works of Jacques Derrida. In his seminal work, *Of Grammatology*, Derrida argues the communication of meaning itself, dependent as it is on language, is dependent on the relative and contextual meaning of words.[37] Language is structured as a system of oppositions and words are given meaning by reference to their opposites:[38] for instance, "north" can only be understood by reference to "south," and when one queries a dictionary to define "south," one finds similar referential language.[39] One word leads to another, and meaning is infinitely deferred and indeterminate. The infinite referentiality of language and the inability of meaning to exist outside of language dictate that all meaning is necessarily relative.[40] Derridean deconstruction, which examines textual ambiguities in order to reveal absurdities and contradictions within, is an attractive tool for challenging the social status quo because it causes us to view human social institutions and identity as semiotic concepts that are socially constructed and therefore subject to change.[41] Divorcing the words of a text from any single meaning effectively opens the text up to a multitude of interpretations – none more authoritative than any other – and situates the locus of meaning-determination in the mind of the reader.[42] This indeterminacy and subjectivity of meaning does not imply equality; Derridean oppositions exist in a "violent hierarchy. One of the two terms governs the other (axiologically, logically, etc.), or has the upper hand. To deconstruct the opposition, first of all, is to overturn the hierarchy at a given moment."[43]

The epistemic relativism of Lyotard and Derrida denies that knowledge can be objectively ascertained, nor can it be neutrally conveyed. While these insights are arguably useful for undermining the legitimacy and value claims of the status quo, they do not provide a theoretical basis for privileging identity as an epistemic category. Indeed, they do not seem capable of supporting any sort of broad claim about value or meaning without falling prey to their own critiques. At most, they weaken the case for privileging empirically based pedagogical qualifications by negating efforts to characterize them as anything more than arbitrary.

Making an affirmative case for replacing empiricism requires a normative argument; for this, contemporary postmodern thinkers lean heavily on the work of Michel Foucault. Foucault integrates the poststructuralist relativism exemplified by Derrida and Lyotard into a theory of social power dynamics.[44] In his view, meaning is constructed by historically contingent discourses.[45] These are "ways of constituting knowledge, together with the social practices, forms of subjectivity and power relations which inhere in such knowledges and the relations between them."[46] Discourses are not merely ways of designating meaning; they dictate the form of the object of which they speak.[47] Thus, discourse is a form of power because it controls individuals' subjective perceptions and, through them, their thoughts and actions.

This definition and the idea of the discourse itself form a sort of self-reinforcing circularity, something Foucault acknowledges and terms "power-knowledge."[48] Power relations dictate the potential objects of knowledge but are only able to do so by employing techniques of knowledge and discourse.[49] Knowledge and power thus form a duality of sorts and cannot be meaningfully separated from one another. Since discourse is a manifestation of power and there are a multitude of discourses, potentially contradicting each other and competing with one another, Foucauldian discourse theory can be understood in terms of a struggle for power. However, this struggle does not take place on an equal playing field. Dominant or hegemonic discourses are entrenched and operate to silence marginalized discourses: "[I]n every society the production of discourse is at once controlled, selected, organised and redistributed by a certain number of procedures whose role is to ward off its powers and dangers, to gain mastery over its chance events, to evade its ponderous, formidable materiality."[50] Prevailing social structures and norms, in this conception, stifle alternative ways of knowing and being because they continually reinforce the "truth" of the particular epistemic reality created by dominant discourses. As a result, the dominant epistemology becomes imposed on society in the sense that it appears natural and impartial; it is quite literally common sense.[51]

Discourse theory is particularly relevant to this discussion because identity itself is a form of discourse.[52] According to Foucault, differences, such as differing identities, necessarily create power relationships, leading to privileging of some identities and marginalization of others. Because of the ubiquity of a dominant discourse, it follows that everyone would have access to the subjectivity or "subject position" that it offers. The same is not necessarily true of marginalized discourses because the fact of their marginality arguably makes them inaccessible to many people.[53] The idea of marginalized subject positions existing within the dominant discourse has been used by critical theorists to argue that persons in those positions have a unique and superior vantage point, or "epistemic privilege," from which to view and understand the world.[54]

The salience of identity as an oppressive discourse in Western history, and perhaps particularly in the United States, leads critical theorists to posit that commonalities shared by individuals in a group can lead to the formation of a "group-based, collective standpoint."[55] The lived experiences of members of marginalized groups are theorized to give them distinct insights into the workings and structure of society which are otherwise obscured.[56] It is this epistemic privilege, gained through the subjective experience of being marginalized, which forms one apparent basis for claims that Indigenous identity should be a precondition for teaching Indigenous Law. This basis is an appeal to empiricism of sorts insofar as it claims an Indigenous scholar will have special knowledge which is largely unavailable to a non-Indigenous scholar by virtue of their group identity, thereby making that person a more suitable educator. We cannot conclude with certainty that this reasoning motivated critics of Mount Saint Vincent University, given the minimal account of their explanation provided by the media. But this line of reasoning is consistent with their reported explanation and supports their conclusion.

3. Anishinaabe Epistemology

At first glance, the epistemic commitments of critical theory discussed above might seem to overlap with those of Anishinaabe constitutionalism. But in fact, the assumptions about truth and knowledge underlying each of the two theories differ in foundational ways which in turn can produce different conclusions about who should teach Anishinaabe Law. This section first discusses the theories' apparent similarity which manifests as an emphasis on lived experience. It then outlines the epistemological premises of Anishinaabe constitutionalism underlying this emphasis and contrasts those premises with critical theory's epistemic commitments. Section four explores Anishinaabe constitutionalism's response to the question of who should teach Anishinaabe Law.

Both critical theory and Anishinaabe constitutionalism emphasize lived experience. For example, according to the strand of critical theory discussed in section two above, the lived experience of those whose identities are marginalized gives them a unique epistemic standpoint which is not available to others. Similarly, we can draw out the emphasis on lived experience from an Anishinaabe story, "Nanaboozhoo and the Maple Trees," recounted by Lana Ray and Paul Nicholas Cormier.[57] The following is just a sketch of the story: Nanaboozhoo came upon a village where no one was fishing, working in the fields, or gathering berries. Instead, they were all lying on their backs on the ground under maple trees with their mouths wide open, letting thick syrup drip directly from the trees into their mouths.[58] At that time, what came from maple trees was not the thin, watery sap that comes from them now, but thick, sweet syrup.[59] Nanaboozhoo was concerned, so he poured many buckets of water into the trees until the syrup turned into thin, watery sap.[60] Now when people want syrup, "they will have to gather many buckets full of the sap in … birch bark baskets … They will have to gather wood and make fires to heat the stones to drop into the baskets. They will have to boil the water with the heated stones for a long time to make even a little maple syrup."[61] Ray and Cormier explain the maple syrup is akin to knowledge.[62] Learning methods which prioritize only the intellect – such as consuming information from a lecture, text, or online module – are akin to lying on the ground and letting syrup drip into one's mouth.[63] In contrast, the process of collecting the sap, firewood, and rocks, tending the fire, heating the rocks, and boiling the sap into syrup is akin to the aspect of Anishinaabe knowledge which requires personal engagement in the learning process.[64] This process is at least as important as a product or outcome which can take the form of information cognizable to the intellect.[65] The focus on personal engagement in the learning process here emphasizes one's lived experience.[66]

Despite the shared focus on lived experience, the strand of critical theory discussed here and Anishinaabe constitutionalism each reach different conclusions about who should teach Indigenous Law. This disparity is the result of different epistemological premises underlying the focus on lived experience. As discussed above, critical theory's emphasis on lived experience stems from its concern with the epistemic standpoint of marginalized identities, which in turn stems from poststructuralism's skepticism about the objective knowability of ontological and normative claims, or, in other words, an incredulity towards metanarratives. In contrast, the emphasis on lived experience within Anishinaabe constitutionalism does not stem from a similar scepticism. Anishinaabe constitutionalism affirms the knowability of its normative and ontological commitments.[67] Some refer to an Anishinaabe normative, ontological, and epistemological framework as an Anishinaabe worldview.[68] Similarly, Leanne Betasamosake Simpson uses the term "Nishnaabewin" to refer to "all of the associated practices, knowledge, and ethics that make us Nishnaabeg and construct the Nishnaabeg world."[69] We understand each of these terms – "Anishinaabe constitutionalism," "Anishinaabe worldview," and "Nishnaabewin" – to refer essentially to the same thing: an ontology and ethics which are knowable in accordance with Anishinaabe epistemology. In other words, Anishinaabe constitutionalism includes knowable content. Here we reach a divergence between Anishinaabe constitutionalism and poststructuralism.[70]

If the normative and ontological commitments of Anishinaabe constitutionalism are knowable, one may wonder how the emphasis on lived experience relates to Anishinaabe constitutionalism. The answer is that Anishinaabe epistemology encompasses more than just intellectual ways of knowing; it also includes physical, spiritual, and emotional ways of knowing.[71] We understand Ray and Cormier to be emphasizing these latter three forms of knowledge generation in their analysis of "Nanaboozhoo and the Maple Trees." Ray and Cormier's discussion reveals that physical, spiritual, and emotional ways of knowing involve more than the kind of lived experience affirmed by critical theory.[72] Similarly, we understand this to be Leanne Betasamosake Simpson's point when she describes Anishinaabe ways of knowing: "This is not just experiential knowledge or embodied knowledge. It is not just individual knowledge rooted in my own perspectives and experiences with the abusive power of colonialism."[73] Learning involves internalizing Anishinaabe norms in a way that allows each of us to actualize our unique gifts.[74] Simpson explains how each individual is responsible for generating meaning within their own lives by engaging their minds, bodies, spirits, and emotions in knowledge-generating practices, such as "visiting, ceremony, singing, dancing, storytelling, hunting, fishing, gathering, observing, reflecting, experimenting, visioning, dreaming, ricing, and sugaring, for example."[75] When someone carries a teaching to the point where they easily embody it, then they are responsible for sharing the teaching, primarily by modelling it.[76] This is what it means to "wear your teachings," as Elder Edna Manitowabi puts it.[77] The key here for our purpose is that within Anishinaabe constitutionalism, there are teachings, or substantive norms, to be internalized.[78] What is lived within Anishinaabe constitutionalism is not a discourse or identity of marginalization, but practices that allow us to both generate and embody substantive norms which are knowable in accordance with Anishinaabe ways of knowing.

As Ray and Cormier explain, all four ways of knowing – physical, spiritual, intellectual, and emotional – contribute to Anishinaabe knowledge generation.[79] Intellectually derived knowledge is not valueless.[80] The goal is to maintain balance between the four ways of knowing.[81] Intellectual knowledge is not privileged over other ways of knowing.[82] These four ways of knowing are interconnected and interdependent.[83] This explains the inseparability between theory and practice, mentioned above in section one. This interconnection means Anishinaabe theory engages more than just the intellect.[84] Simpson's story of working with Elders of Long Lake #58 provides a vivid illustration. Each time she asked the Elders a theoretical question – about governance or treaties – they talked about trapping or took her fishing.[85] Simpson explains: "I loved all of it, but I didn't think they were answering my questions. I could see only practice. I couldn't see their theory until decades later. I couldn't see intelligence until I learned how to see it by engaging in Nishnaabeg practices for the next two decades."[86] This interdependence between theory and practice means Anishinaabe theory "isn't just for academics; it's for everyone."[87]

4. Who Should Teach Anishinaabe Law According to Anishinaabe Constitutionalism?

As mentioned above in section three, Anishinaabe constitutionalism affirms substantive norms. Until now, we have referred to these norms loosely as "teachings" or "laws." To answer the question, "Who should teach Anishinaabe law?" we need to examine these norms with more precision. To do so, we draw from Aaron Mills's tree model of legality.[88] A society's lifeworld – including its epistemology and ontology – is represented by the roots of a tree.[89] Focusing on ontology, creation is imbued with an inherent normative order known by various names, such as the "great law" or the "original instructions."[90] The original instructions tell us we have a responsibility to identify, develop, and use our unique gifts.[91] Next, the trunk corresponds to a society's constitutional order.[92] At this level, the logic of mutual aid provides further guidance on how to actualize the original instructions within our lives.[93] We each have a responsibility to give our gifts to meet the needs of others in accordance with the responsibilities of our kinship relationships, including our extended kinship relationships.[94] Moving up, the branches represent legal processes, including a society's processes for generating, interpreting, and modifying its laws.[95] Here, the normative force of Anishinaabe Law comes from persuasive compliance – or in other words, from internalizing the responsibilities from the level of the trunk – as opposed to external coercive authority such as that exercised by an executive branch of government.[96] Finally, the leaves of the tree represent a society's laws, or in other words, instances of exercises of one's responsibilities.[97] These exercises of responsibility lack the prescriptive determinacy of rights insofar as they do not exist in the form of universalizable rules applied equally to each person.[98] Our gifts and needs differ within different relationships and change over time, and thus our responsibilities are contextual and ever-changing.[99] This prescriptive indeterminacy is reflected in the Anishinaabemowin words most often used for "Law" – inaakonigewin or dibaakonigewin – which refer not to law in the sense of rules but to a careful exercise of judgment.[100]

With this brief sketch in mind, we can clarify that what can feasibly be taught within a mandatory law school course are mostly the norms at the levels of the roots and trunk. We use the term "law" to make the content of an Anishinaabe "Law" course cognizable to a non-Indigenous perspective and to distinguish it from a course on cultural competency.[101] But if law is understood as what happens at the level of the leaves, then students can at most only begin the process of learning Anishinaabe Law in a mandatory course. Instructors of such courses can and do engage in the modelling described by Simpson,[102] but these courses typically last for only a few months, or two semesters at the most. Simpson discusses how the process of internalization at the level of the branches, which then gives rise to the ability to exercise inaakonigewin at the level of the leaves, happens over a prolonged period of time, such as decades.[103] Perhaps more significantly, the process of internalization at the level of the branches occurs in accordance with persuasive compliance. In other words, it is entirely voluntary. In our understanding, to impose this work of internalization on others – for example, by requiring students in a mandatory course to take steps towards internalizing Anishinaabe constitutional norms – would be antithetical to the function of persuasive compliance and to associated Anishinaabe norms such as non-interference and individual agency.[104] Of course, teachers can describe the processes at the levels of the branches and leaves to students, but given the holistic nature of Anishinaabe epistemology discussed above, such descriptions do not constitute teaching Anishinaabe Law. This is reflected in the names of law school courses, which typically avoid the term "Law" and instead use names such as "Indigenous Legal Traditions," "Indigenous Legal Orders," "Anishinaabe Constitutionalism," or "Kwayeskastasowin Setting Things Right," for example.[105]

We are now in a position to answer the question, "Who should teach Anishinaabe law?" or more accurately, "Who should teach Anishinaabe constitutionalism?" Given that Anishinaabe constitutionalism affirms substantive norms at the levels of the roots and branches, one should have knowledge of these norms in order to teach them. This knowledge should be generated in accordance with Anishinaabe epistemology. Thus, merely researching and reading about Anishinaabe constitutionalism in accordance with non-Indigenous academic conventions is not sufficient to generate the relevant knowledge. One must engage not only intellectual but also physical, spiritual, and emotional ways of knowing in a process of voluntarily internalizing the norms (at the level of the branches) and through using one's judgment to make decisions and carry out actions in accordance with those norms (at the level of the leaves) over an extended period of time.[106] Moreover, Ray and Cormier as well as Simpson emphasize the relational nature of this knowledge.[107] We exercise judgment to make decisions in accordance with our various mutual aid responsibilities that flow from different relationships. Thus, knowledge is generated through a network of interrelated relationships with community members who are also endeavouring to uphold their mutual aid responsibilities in accordance with Anishinaabe constitutionalism.[108] Of course, one can strive to uphold Anishinaabe norms within non-mutual aid communities, but the attendant challenges will sometimes make doing so impossible.[109]

A final requirement for teaching Anishinaabe constitutionalism flows from the Anishinaabe epistemology discussed above. To generate knowledge, one should engage in not only intellectual but also physical, spiritual, and emotional ways of knowing. These latter three ways of knowing entail upholding Anishinaabe constitutionalism. Thus, one who teaches Anishinaabe Law should identify the relationships engaged by their teaching, and then identify and uphold their mutual aid responsibilities within those relationships. A key relationship in this context is one's relationship with Anishinaabe communities. A course on Anishinaabe constitutionalism generates a benefit for the law school in the form of tuition paid by the students taking the course, and a benefit for the instructor in the form of their salary, among other career benefits. What are the needs of Anishinaabe communities? What are the gifts of the instructor and of the law school which could meet those needs?

Applying these criteria, we find the result is not a simple dichotomy between Anishinaabe People being qualified to teach Anishinaabe constitutionalism and non-Anishinaabe people being unqualified to do so. Merely being Anishinaabe does not guarantee one has the relevant knowledge. In other words, having a lived experience of marginalization as an Anishinaabe person, while potentially relevant to teaching certain topics, is not sufficient to qualify one to teach Anishinaabe constitutionalism. Not surprisingly, some Indigenous people have not had the opportunity to engage in holistic ways of knowing within their communities because of Canadian laws,[110] such as laws compelling attendance at residential schools,[111] the purpose of which was to eradicate Indigenous lifeways,[112] as well as laws separating Indigenous people from their communities, such as the *Indian Act*'s marrying out rule.[113] Indigenous people should not be penalized if their limited physical, spiritual, and emotional knowledge of Indigenous constitutionalism is due to the use of state force against them and their families. Instead, they should be supported by state bodies, including law schools, even if they are only at the beginning of their process of engaging in physical, spiritual, and emotional ways of knowing. For example, Indigenous instructors can supplement their own knowledge by arranging for Anishinaabe knowledge keepers to visit with their students within Anishinaabe communities or in the classroom, and law schools can support these initiatives by providing the funds and other support needed for honorariums, food, transportation, and other logistics.[114]

Not being Anishinaabe[115] does not disqualify one from developing the relevant knowledge.[116] Non-Anishinaabe people and non-Indigenous people can undertake the process of learning Anishinaabe constitutional norms through practices that engage all four ways of knowing. Granted, some Indigenous knowledge is available only to certain people in certain circumstances.[117] This type of restriction, though, is not applicable to at least some of the norms at the levels of the roots and trunk that inform inaakonigewin or dibaakonigewin, which are enacted by each and every member of a mutual aid community.[118] Moreover, if treaties are to be understood from the perspective of Indigenous Peoples, then non-Indigenous parties to the treaties have a responsibility to learn at least as much of the norms at the levels of the roots and trunk as necessary to identify and uphold their responsibilities under the relevant treaty.[119] Thus, Anishinaabe identity is not a precondition for participation in at least some aspects of Anishinaabe lifeways.

That said, the reason for supporting Indigenous instructors while they are still at the beginning of the process of engaging in physical, spiritual, and emotional ways of knowing does not apply to non-Indigenous people. Moreover, it can be more difficult for non-Indigenous people who do not have pre-existing connections to an Anishinaabe community to develop the required community relationships and thus to uphold mutual aid responsibilities over a sustained period of time.[120] Thus, it may be much less common for non-Indigenous people to have the required knowledge and thus to be qualified to teach

Anishinaabe Law. It is not, however, impossible. Many non-Indigenous faculty members at Osgoode Hall Law School have established ongoing, long-term, mutual aid relationships with Indigenous communities, relationships which foster an environment conducive to engaging in not only intellectual but also physical, spiritual, and emotional ways of knowing. In the interests of space, we mention only two examples, but acknowledge there are many others. In 2014, Dr. Andrée Boisselle, along with Dr. John Borrows, his daughter Lindsay Borrows, and other members of their family, initiated an Anishinaabe Law Camp at Neyaashiinigmiing as a collaboration between the Chippewas of Nawash First Nation and Osgoode Hall Law School.[121] The Camp provides an introduction to Anishinaabe legal concepts for students and faculty members over the course of three days.[122] As part of this education, students perform work to assist community members, ranging from physical labour to assisting with strategic initiatives. Similarly, in Dr. Estair Van Wagner's Natural Resources Law course, students complete assignments on topics identified by Indigenous communities, their lawyers, or external organizations working in partnership with Indigenous communities. At the end of the course, the completed assignments are provided to the community. This is a small sample of some means used by non-Indigenous and Indigenous faculty members, staff, and students to uphold mutual aid relationships with Indigenous communities.

5. Conclusion

The question of who should teach Indigenous Law has wide application. It affects not only those who teach the relatively few courses focused solely or primarily on Indigenous Law, but also all law instructors who want to incorporate Indigenous content into their courses. Although the text of the Truth and Reconciliation Commission's Call to Action 28 suggests it calls for a single mandatory course, an approach that integrates Indigenous content throughout a law school's curriculum is arguably consistent with the spirit of Call to Action 28. Isolating Indigenous Law within one or more stand-alone courses can result in the marginalization of that material.[123] A better approach combines stand-alone Indigenous Law courses with the integration of Indigenous Law throughout a law program.[124] The majority of instructors within Canadian law schools are not Indigenous. Grounding our analysis within Anishinaabe constitutionalism means these non-Indigenous instructors are not precluded from incorporating Anishinaabe legal content into their courses.

Our discussion of Anishinaabe epistemology can offer guidance for these instructors. In his empirical study of faculty members' attitudes to Call to Action 28 and to the indigenization or decolonization of law school curricula, Adrien Habermacher reveals some responses grounded in non-Anishinaabe assumptions.[125] Habermacher reports that several interviewees called for more resources and "expressed frustration in response to ineffective or insufficient support for those professors who wanted to revise their materials and practices in order to give a greater place to Indigenous legal traditions."[126] For example, one faculty member "sought help from a staff member at UAlberta's Center for Teaching and Learning, who specialized in helping educators bring Indigenous perspectives into their teaching."[127] However, this faculty member viewed the suggestions offered by the staff member as not "relevant to the subject areas of the course" and thus not as helpful as expected.[128]

According to our understanding of Anishinaabe constitutionalism, law schools in Anishinaabe territory have a responsibility to provide the supports and resources needed to allow instructors to develop their capacities for engaging with and eventually teaching Anishinaabe constitutionalism. But the holistic nature of Anishinaabe epistemology means instructors who want to teach Anishinaabe constitutionalism must complete not only the required intellectual work but also the emotional, physical, and spiritual work. Learning Anishinaabe constitutionalism is not supposed to be simple. One is not supposed to be able to lie on one's back with one's mouth hanging open, letting syrup flow in. Institutions have a responsibility to show instructors where the maple trees are, but institutions are not responsible for boiling down the sap and delivering individual bottles of syrup to instructors. For those who are ensconced within an epistemology that privileges intellectual knowledge, it might be difficult or even initially impossible to recognize the significance of emotional, physical, and spiritual ways of knowing. If one has only ever worked with syrup, one initially might be unable to see the relevance when presented with trees or watery sap alone. Likewise, those who have only worked with doctrinal law might mistakenly assume that prescriptively indeterminate norms within a fundamentally different worldview are not "relevant to the subject areas of the course." But those who want to teach Indigenous constitutionalism have a responsibility to collect sap from the trees and make their own syrup.[129] Both Indigenous and non-Indigenous instructors can make their own syrup by instantiating the norms of the roots and trunk within their decisions and actions informing their courses and their teaching.

NOTES

We are very grateful to Tanzim Rashid for his excellent research assistance. We also thank the editors of this collection and the participants of the workshop that gave rise to it for their valuable feedback and insights. Any errors are our responsibility.

1 *Truth and Reconciliation Commission of Canada: Calls to Action* (Winnipeg: Truth and Reconciliation Commission of Canada, 2015) at 3 [*Calls to Action*]:

28. We call upon law schools in Canada to require all law students to take a course in Aboriginal people and the law, which includes the history and legacy of residential schools, the *United Nations Declaration on the Rights of Indigenous Peoples*, Treaties and Aboriginal rights, Indigenous law, and Aboriginal–Crown relations. This will require skills-based training in intercultural competency, conflict resolution, human rights, and anti-racism.

2   *Calls to Action* (referring to "Treaties and Aboriginal rights" and "Aboriginal–Crown relations").

3   For a related discussion of whether Indigenous Law should be taught primarily within Indigenous communities, and whether Indigenous Law should be taught in law schools at all, see John Borrows, *Law's Indigenous Ethics* (Toronto: University of Toronto Press, 2019) at 185–8 [Borrows, *Ethics*].

4   The Canadian Press, "Mount Saint Vincent University under Fire over Residential Schools Course Taught by White Professor," *The Star* (11 May 2018), online: <www.thestar.com/halifax/2018/05/11/mount-saint-vincent-university-under-fire -over-residential-schools-course-taught-by-white-professor.html>.

5   *Ibid.*

6   "Halifax University gives White Prof Go-Ahead to Teach Residential Schools Course," *CBC* (15 May 2018) online: <www.cbc.ca/news/canada/nova -scotia/mount-st-vincent-non-indigenous-professor-residential-schools -course-1.4664761>.

7   The Canadian Press, "Non-Indigenous Professor Gets Go-Ahead to Teach Residential Schools Course," *The Star* (15 May 2018) online: <www.thestar.com /news/canada/2018/05/15/non-indigenous-professor-gets-go-ahead-to-teach -residential-schools-course.html>.

8   See Linda Tuhiwai Smith, *Decolonizing Methodologies: Research and Indigenous Peoples*, 2nd ed (London: Zed Books, 2012) at 39 [Tuhiwai Smith]; Gordon Christie, "Indigenous Legal Theory: Some Initial Considerations" in Benjamin J. Richardson, Shin Imai & Kent McNeil, eds, *Indigenous Peoples and the Law: Comparative and Critical Perspectives* (Portland: Hart Publishing, 2009) at 211 [Christie, "Indigenous Legal Theory"].

9   See Tuhiwai Smith, *ibid* at 39; Christie, "Indigenous Legal Theory," *ibid* at 211.

10   Christie, "Indigenous Legal Theory," *ibid* at 211–12.

11   *Ibid* at 211, note 35.

12   *Ibid* at 213.

13   For a discussion of the reasons theory is important for Indigenous Peoples, see Tuhiwai Smith, *supra* note 8 at 40.

14   Leanne Betasamosake Simpson, "Land as Pedagogy: Nishnaabeg Intelligence and Rebellious Transformation" (2014) 3:3 Decolonization: Indigeneity, Education & Society 1 at 7 [Simpson, "Land as Pedagogy"].

15   *Ibid* at 7.

16 *Ibid.*

17 See e.g., Will Kymlicka, *Multicultural Citizenship: A Liberal Theory of Minority Rights* (Oxford: Oxford University Press, 1995).

18 Nicholas Tanchuk, Marc Kruse & Kevin McDonough, "Indigenous Course Requirements: A Liberal-Democratic Justification" (2018) 25:2 Philosophical Inquiry in Education 134.

19 See Patrick Macklem, "Normative Dimensions of an Aboriginal Right of Self-Government" (1995–6) 21 Queen's LJ 173 at 214–15; Dale Turner, *This Is Not a Peace Pipe: Towards a Critical Indigenous Philosophy* (Toronto: University of Toronto Press, 2006) at 70.

20 See Gordon Christie, *Canadian Law and Indigenous Self-Determination: A Naturalist Analysis* (Toronto: University of Toronto Press, 2019) at 339–41 [Christie, *A Naturalist Analysis*]; Andrew Christian Airhart, "Lifeworlds Apart: Reconciling Rawlsian Liberalism with Anishinaabe Constitutionalism" (2019) [unpublished] at 15–17.

21 Jeremy Waldron, "Superseding Historic Injustice" (1992) 103:1 Ethics 4; Tom Flanagan, *First Nations? Second Thoughts*, 2nd ed (Montreal: McGill-Queen's University Press, 2008); Canada, *Statement of the Government of Canada on Indian Policy*, 1969 (Ottawa: Queen's Printer, 1969), online: <www.aadnc-aandc.gc.ca/eng /1100100010189/1100100010191>.

22 Aaron Mills, "The Lifeworlds of Law: On Revitalizing Indigenous Legal Orders Today" (2016) 61:4 McGill LJ 847 at 855, n 14 [Mills, "Lifeworlds"]; Aaron James (Waabishki Ma'iingan) Mills, *Miinigowiziwin: All That Has Been Given for Living Well Together: One Vision of Anishinaabe Constitutionalism* (PhD diss., University of Victoria, Faculty of Law, 2019) [unpublished] at 15, 98ff, [Mills, *Miinigowiziwin*].

23 Mills, *Miinigowiziwin, ibid* at 26.

24 But see Eve Tuck & K. Wayne Yang, "Decolonization Is Not a Metaphor" (2012) 1:1 Decolonization: Indigeneity, Education & Society 1 at 16 (criticizing projects which "hybridize … decolonial thought with Western critical traditions" and thus make 'decolonization' into a metaphor).

25 Christie, *A Naturalist Analysis, supra* note 20 at 399; Mills, *Miinigowiziwin, supra* note 22 at 215ff; Aaron Mills, "Rooted Constitutionalism: Growing Political Community" in Michael Asch, John Borrows & James Tully, eds, *Resurgence and Reconciliation: Indigenous-Settler Relations and Earth Teachings* (Toronto: University of Toronto Press, 2018) 133 at 147–52 [Mills, "Rooted Constitutionalism"]; Gordon Christie, "Law, Theory and Aboriginal Peoples" (2003) 2 Indigenous LJ 67 at 107–112 [Christie, "Law, Theory"].

26 Christie, "Law, Theory," *ibid* at 101, 112.

27 Mills, "Rooted Constitutionalism," *supra* note 25 at 152–3; Leanne Simpson with Edna Manitowabi, "Theorizing Resurgence from within Nishnaabeg Thought" in Jill Doerfler, Niigaanwewidam James Sinclair & Heidi Kiiwetinepinesiik Stark,

eds, *Centering Anishinaabeg Studies: Understanding the World through Stories*
(East Lansing, Michigan: Michigan State University Press, 2013) 279 at 279;
Christie, "Indigenous Legal Theory," *supra* note 8 at 197; James (Sákéj) Youngblood
Henderson, "Post-Colonial Indigenous Legal Consciousness" (2002) 1 Indigenous
LJ 1; James Youngblood Henderson, *First Nations Jurisprudence and Aboriginal
Rights: Defining the Just Society* (Saskatoon: Native Law Centre of Canada,
2006); Patricia Monture-Angus, *Journeying Forward: Dreaming First Nations'
Independence* (Black Point, NS: Fernwood Publishing, 1999) at 55–6.

28 Mills, "Lifeworlds," *supra* note 22 at 862; Mills, *Miinigowiziwin, supra* note 22 at 41–3.

29 Adam Gaudry & Danielle Lorenz, "Indigenization as Inclusion, Reconciliation, and
Decolonization: Navigating the Different Visions for Indigenizing the Canadian
Academy" (2018) 14:3 AlterNative 218 at 218. For a testament to the "sea change"
brought about by the Truth and Reconciliation Commission's final report, see
Nicole O'Byrne, "Teaching Aboriginal Law in an Age of Reconciliation" (2019) 9:1
Antistasis 56 at 61. For a comparison of "indigenizing" and "decolonizing" efforts
within law schools, see Jeffery G. Hewitt, "Decolonizing and Indigenizing: Some
Considerations for Law Schools" (2016) 33 Windsor YB Access Just 65 at 69–71.

30 See Leanne Betasamosake Simpson, *As We Have Always Done: Indigenous Freedom
Through Radical Resistance* (Minneapolis: University of Minnesota Press, 2017) at
15 (comparing a research project in which Elders merely offer a prayer and smudge
at the beginning to a project that centers the knowledge of Elders) [Simpson, *As
We Have Always Done*].

31 For a defence of an anti-fundamentalist approach that eschews restricting
Indigenous Peoples to any one theory, see John Borrows, *Freedom and Indigenous
Constitutionalism* (Toronto: University of Toronto Press, 2016) at 11; Borrows,
Ethics, supra note 3. See also Simpson, *As We Have Always Done, ibid* at 31 (writing
"Indigenous peoples … can choose to use the conventions of the academy to
critique the system of settler colonialism and advance Indigenous liberation, and I
believe this is valuable work").

32 Christie, "Indigenous Legal Theory," *supra* note 8 at 196, 217.

33 Christie, "Indigenous Legal Theory," *ibid* at 213–14. However, Christie adds the
qualification that it is possible to adopt non-Indigenous theory such as critical
theory in a circumscribed way which does not commit the theorist to a non-
Indigenous worldview: *ibid* at 213–14.

34 Jean-François Lyotard, "The Postmodern Condition: A Report on Knowledge,"
translated by G. Bennington & B. Massumi, in W. Godzich & J. Schulte-Sasse, eds,
Theory and History of Literature (Minneapolis: University of Minnesota Press,
1984) vol 10 at xxiv.

35 *Ibid* at xxiii–xxiv.

36 *Ibid*.

37 Jacques Derrida, *Of Grammatology*, translated by Gayatri C. Spivak (Baltimore:
The Johns Hopkins University Press, 1997) at 216–19.

38 *Ibid* at 154–7. Sa'ke'j Henderson's discussion of Algonquian languages, which
    includes Anishinaabemowin, reveals that these languages do not reflect the
    oppositional structure described by Derrida, given that they "are centered on the
    process of being or the verbs": James [sákéj] Youngblood Henderson, "Míkmaw
    Tenure in Atlantic Canada" (1995) 18 Dalhousie LJ 196 at 220–1. We are indebted
    to John Borrows for this insight.

39 *Ibid.*

40 Arthur Bradley, *Derrida's Of Grammatology* (Edinburgh: Edinburgh University
    Press, 2008) at 71.

41 Christopher Butler, *Postmodernism* (Oxford: Oxford University Press, 2002) at
    20–1.

42 Roland Barthes, "The Death of the Author" in *Image, Music, Text*, translated by
    Stephen Heath (New York: Hill & Wang, 1977) at 142–8.

43 Jacques Derrida, *Positions*, translated by Alan Bass (Chicago: University of Chicago
    Press, 1981) at 41.

44 Chris Weedon, *Feminist Practice & Poststructuralist Theory* (Oxford: Blackwell
    Publishers, 1987) at 107 [Weedon].

45 Michel Foucault, *The History of Sexuality: An Introduction*, vol 1, translated by
    Robert Hurley (New York: Pantheon Books, 1978) [Foucault, *History of Sexuality*].

46 Weedon, *supra* note 44 at 108.

47 Michel Foucault, *The Archaeology of Knowledge*, translated by AM Sheridan Smith
    (London: Routledge, 2002) at 54.

48 Foucault, *History of Sexuality*, *supra* note 45 at 98–9.

49 *Ibid* at 98.

50 Michel Foucault, "The Order of Discourse" in Robert Young, ed, *Untying the Text:
    A Post-Structuralist Reader* (Boston: Routledge & Kegan Paul, 1981) at 52.

51 Nicola Gavey, "Feminist Poststructuralism and Discourse Analysis" (1989) 13:4
    Psychology of Women Quarterly 459 at 464.

52 *Ibid.*

53 *Ibid.*

54 See e.g., Patricia H. Collins, *Black Feminist Thought: Knowledge, Consciousness,
    and the Politics of Empowerment*, 2nd ed (New York: Routledge, 2000) [Collins];
    Brenda J. Allen, "Feminist Standpoint Theory: A Black Woman's (Re)view of
    Organizational Socialization" (1996) 47:4 Communication Studies 257 [Allen].

55 Collins, *ibid* at 24.

56 Allen, *supra* note 54 at 259.

57 Lana Ray & Paul Nicholas Cormier, "Killing the Weendigo with Maple Syrup:
    Anishinaabe Pedagogy and Post-Secondary Research" (2012) 35:1 Can J Native
    Education 163 at 165, citing Michael J. Caduto & Joseph Bruchac, *Keepers of
    the Earth: Native American Stories and Environmental Activities for Children*
    (Colorado: Fulcrum Publishing, 1989) at 145. Ray and Cormier describe their
    methodology as "an Anishinaabe process of knowledge creation": *ibid* at 164. For

an account of a methodology which applies the case brief method – commonly used within a common law legal education – to Indigenous stories, see Hadley Friedland & Val Napoleon, "Gathering the Threads: Developing a Methodology for Researching and Rebuilding Indigenous Legal Traditions" (2015–6) 1:1 Lakehead LJ 16. For an example of an application of this latter methodology, see Hadley Friedland, *The* Wetiko *Legal Principles: Cree and Anishinabek Responses to Violence and Victimization* (Toronto: University of Toronto Press, 2018).

58 Ray & Cormier, *supra* note 57 at 165.

59 Ray & Cormier, *ibid*.

60 Ray & Cormier, *ibid*.

61 Ray & Cormier, *ibid*.

62 Ray & Cormier, *ibid*.

63 Ray & Cormier, *ibid* at 165, 166–7. See also Karen Drake, "Finding a Path to Reconciliation: Mandatory Indigenous Law, Anishinaabe Pedagogy, and Academic Freedom" (2017) 95 Canadian Bar Review 1 at 24–5.

64 Ray & Cormier, *supra* note 57 at 165, 169.

65 Ray & Cormier, *ibid* at 170.

66 See Simpson, "Land as Pedagogy," *supra* note 14 at 7, 11, 16, 23 (explaining the significance of lived experience within Nishnaabewin).

67 Mills, *Miinigowiziwin, supra* note 22 at ch 6. See also Christie, "Law, Theory," *supra* note 25 at 107 (making this point regarding the lifeways of Aboriginal Peoples generally). We are using the term "ontological" in the sense of conceptualizing that which exists. As an English term associated most closely with western philosophy, we acknowledge that its use here could have a distorting effect, as many aspects of ontology in the sense of a branch of metaphysics are inapplicable to our discussion. The value of using the term "ontological" here is similar to the value of using the term "law" within discussions of Indigenous teachings, even though "law" is potentially distorting insofar as much Indigenous teachings operate very differently from the positivistic and prescriptive ways Canadian law operates: see text accompanying notes 95–101.

68 See Ray & Cormier, *supra* note 57 at 168, 172.

69 Simpson, *As We Have Always Done, supra* note 30 at 23.

70 See Mills, "Rooted Constitutionalism," *supra* note 25 at 148–52; Christie, "Law, Theory," *supra* note 25 at 110, 112.

71 Ray & Cormier, *supra* note 57 at 168, 169; Simpson, *As We Have Always Done, supra* note 30 at 28.

72 See also Mills, "Rooted Constitutionalism," *supra* note 25 at 150 ("being Indigenous means more than privilege and oppression").

73 Simpson, *As We Have Always Done, supra* note 30 at 30.

74 Ray and Cormier, *supra* note 57 at 170; Simpson, *As We Have Always Done, ibid* at 4. See also John Borrows, "Creating an Indigenous Legal Community" (2005) 50 McGill LJ 153 at 158–9 (telling a Cree story about where to hide gifts

so that humans will not misuse them when they are found; the last proposal was to hide the gifts within humans so that when they do the work required to find the gifts, they will not misuse them); Hannah Askew, "Learning from Bear-Walker: Indigenous Legal Orders and Intercultural Legal Education in Canadian Law Schools" (2016) 33 Windsor YB Access Just 29 at 35, 41 (recounting stories about working with Anishinaabe knowledge-keepers (Jean Borrows and Neepitapinaysiqua) at Neyaashiinigmiing which illustrate the significance of internalizing Anishinaabe norms as opposed to relying on the coercive force of an external authority to enforce norms).

75 Simpson, *As We Have Always Done, ibid* at 29; Simpson, "Land as Pedagogy," *supra* note 14 at 11.

76 Simpson, "Land as Pedagogy," *ibid* at 11.

77 Simpson, "Land as Pedagogy," *ibid*; Simpson, *As We Have Always Done, supra* note 30 at 29.

78 Simpson with Manitowabi, *supra* note 27 at 288.

79 Ray & Cormier, *supra* note 57 at 168.

80 Ray & Cormier, *ibid* at 167. See also John Borrows, *Canada's Indigenous Constitution* (Toronto: University of Toronto Press, 2010) at 242 (explaining that the Earth's agency can be respected and knowledge about the Earth's receptiveness to decisions can be generated through not only ceremonies and observation, but also through scientific evidence) [Borrows, *Indigenous Constitution*].

81 Ray & Cormier, *supra* note 57 at 168.

82 Christie, "Law, Theory," *supra* note 25 at 107–8.

83 Simpson, *As We Have Always Done, supra* note 30 at 20.

84 Simpson, "Land as Pedagogy," *supra* note 14 at 7.

85 Simpson, *As We Have Always Done, supra* note 30 at 18.

86 Simpson, *As We Have Always Done, ibid* at 18–19.

87 Simpson, "Land as Pedagogy," *supra* note 14 at 7.

88 Mills, *Miinigowiziwin, supra* note 22 at 39.

89 Mills, *Miinigowiziwin, ibid* at 41–3; Mills, "Lifeworlds," *supra* note 22 at 862.

90 Mills, *Miinigowiziwin, ibid* at 69–70; Aimée Craft, "Navigating Our Ongoing Sacred Legal Relationship with Nibi (Water)" in *UNDRIP Implementation: More Reflections on the Braiding of International, Domestic and Indigenous Laws* (Centre for International Governance Innovation, 2018) 53 at 59.

91 Mills, *Miinigowiziwin, ibid* at 69–72, 74.

92 Mills, *Miinigowiziwin, ibid* at 41–3.

93 Mills, *Miinigowiziwin, ibid* at 96–8.

94 Mills, *Miinigowiziwin, ibid* 88, 114, 117, 119.

95 Mills, *Miinigowiziwin, ibid* 45.

96 Mills, *Miinigowiziwin, ibid* at 161, 163–4.

97 Mills, *Miinigowiziwin, ibid* 46.

98 Mills, *Miinigowiziwin, ibid* at 139.

99 Mills, *Miinigowiziwin*, *ibid* at 139.

100 Mills, *Miinigowiziwin*, *ibid* at 143–4.

101 See Simpson, *As We Have Always Done*, *supra* note 30 at 24 (writing that Nishnaabeg intelligence "is not a series of teachings or laws or protocols; it is a series of practices that are adaptable and to some degree fluid"). For a critical examination of cultural competence courses as a response to Call to Action 28, see Pooja Parmar, "Reconciliation and Ethical Lawyering: Some Thoughts on Cultural Competence" (2019) 97 Can Bar Rev 526.

102 See text accompanying notes 76–7.

103 See text accompanying note 86; Simpson, *As We Have Always Done*, *supra* note 30 at 19, 29.

104 For a story reflecting the significance of non-interference and individual agency, see Basil Johnston, "Pitchi – Robin" in *Ojibway Heritage* (Toronto: McClelland & Stewart, 1976) at 128–31.

105 University of Saskatchewan, online: <https://programs.usask.ca/law/juris-doctor /jd.php>.

106 Simpson, *As We Have Always Done*, *supra* note 30 at 29.

107 Ray & Cormier, *supra* note 57 at 166; Simpson, "Land as Pedagogy," *supra* note 14 at 10–11.

108 See Simpson, "Land as Pedagogy," *ibid* at 11; Borrows, *Ethics*, *supra* note 3 at 184, 186–7; Simpson with Manitowabi, *supra* note 27 at 289.

109 For an example of the damage that results when one person attempts to uphold mutual aid responsibilities in a relationship with another person who does not treat the relationship as one of mutual aid, see Johann Georg Kohl, *Kitchi-Gami: Wanderings Round Lake Superior* (London: Chapman & Hall, 1860) at 61–4.

110 See Borrows, *Ethics*, *supra* note 3 at 180.

111 *Indian Act*, RSC, 1985, c I-5, ss 118, 119, repealed, 2014, c 38, s 17.

112 Truth and Reconciliation Commission of Canada, *What We Have Learned: Principles of Truth and Reconciliation* (Truth and Reconciliation Commission of Canada, 2015) at 5.

113 Bob Joseph, *21 Things You May Not Know about the Indian Act* (Port Coquitlam, BC: Indigenous Relations Press, 2018) at 19–23.

114 For example, one of the authors, Drake, acknowledges that her knowledge of Anishinaabe constitutionalism currently draws more from intellectual ways of knowing and less from spiritual, emotional, or physical ways of knowing. She is a Bill S-3 member of Wabigoon Lake Ojibway Nation. Her great-grandmother lost her status due to the *Indian Act*'s marrying-out rule and thus was separated from her community. Growing up without a connection to her community, Drake did not have the opportunity to spend those decades internalizing the norms of Anishinaabe constitutionalism. To supplement her knowledge, when teaching Anishinaabe constitutionalism, she provides opportunities for her students to learn from those who have more experience enacting inaakonigewin.

For example, she brought her students from the Bora Laskin Faculty of Law at Lakehead University to visit with members of the Fort William First Nation at the sugar bush within their territory: see Drake, *supra* note 63 at 32; Borrows, *Ethics*, *supra* note 3 at 164. Most recently, while teaching at Osgoode Hall Law School, she invited Aaron Mills and Lori Mishibinijima to serve as uncle and aunty respectively for her students. These roles entailed an ongoing relationship with the class during the course.

115 This statement raises questions about the contours of Anishinaabe identity. While a full examination of this issue is beyond the scope of this chapter, Damien Lee's work on customary Anishinaabeg adoption resonates with a view of Anishinaabe citizenship informed by Anishinaabe constitutionalism, as opposed to a conception based on blood quantum or notions of race: Damien Lee, "Adoption Is (Not) a Dirty Word: Towards an Adoption-Centric Theory of Anishinaabeg Citizenship" (2015) 10:1 First Peoples Child and Family Review 86.

116 See Borrows, *Ethics*, *supra* note 3 at 179; Hewitt, *supra* note 29 at 72.

117 See Borrows, *Indigenous Constitution*, *supra* note 80 at 149 (explaining that "for many First Nations of the West Coast, only people who have earned the right to receive hereditary names are permitted to speak about and use certain knowledge"). For additional reasons why Indigenous Peoples might restrict access to their Laws, see Borrows, *ibid* at 148.

118 Mills, *Miinigowiziwin*, *supra* note 22 at 96–7.

119 We are indebted to Lori Mishibinijima for this insight and have reproduced it here with her permission. For additional reasons why non-Indigenous peoples should learn Indigenous Laws, see Borrows, *Indigenous Constitution*, *supra* note 80 at 142–3.

120 *Cf* Hewitt, *supra* note 29 at 72.

121 Osgoode Hall Law School, "The Anishinaabe Law Camp," online: <www .osgoode.yorku.ca/programs/juris-doctor/experiential-education/anishinaabe -law-camp/> [The Anishinaabe Law Camp]. For a discussion of the benefits of land-based learning, as well as a description of the Anishinaabe Law Camp with the Chippewas of Nawash at Neyaashiinigmiing, see Borrows, *Ethics*, *supra* note 3 at ch 5, especially at 166–8; John Borrows, "Outsider Education: Indigenous Law and Land-Based Learning" (2016) 33 Windsor YB Access Just 1. More recently, Osgoode Hall Law School has also held an annual Anishinaabe Law Camp at Mnjikaning in collaboration with the Chippewas of Rama First Nation; this camp is led by members of the Chippewas of Rama First Nation and facilitated by Professor Jeffery Hewitt.

122 "The Anishinaabe Law Camp," *ibid*. The camp has been run every September since 2014, although it did not take place in 2020 due to the COVID-19 pandemic.

123 Drake, *supra* note 63 at 26.

124 Drake, *ibid* at 26–8. See Adrien Habermacher, "Understanding the Ongoing Dialogues on Indigenous Issues in Canadian Legal Education through the Lens

of Institutional Cultures (Case Studies at UQAM, UAlberta, and UMoncton)" (2021) 57:1 Osgoode Hall Law Journal, at 73–4 (identifying a growing emphasis on "the indigenization or decolonization of the traditional law courses").

125　Habermacher, *ibid.*

126　Habermacher, *ibid* at 77.

127　Habermacher, *ibid* at 78.

128　Habermacher, *ibid.*

129　See Simpson with Manitowabi, *supra* note 27 at 287, 289.

8 Reflections on Cultural Appropriation

MICHAEL ASCH

Introduction

In October 2019, Kent McNeil and John Borrows held a workshop entitled "Indigenous Voice, Cultural Appropriation, and the Place of Non-Indigenous Academics." Its theme was "to address issues of voice and cultural appropriation that many of us struggle with, with a sense of hope, even as we explore the challenges." Although not a participant at the original workshop, I was subsequently invited to make a contribution to the collection of essays that developed out of it.

Initially, I took this call as a challenge for me to reflect on "cultural appropriation and the place of non-Indigenous academics" only in a narrow sense; that is, to invite me to reflect on experiences related to my research and how I find my voice amid the challenges. And this paper will discuss that. However, I now see that the topic itself emerges from a broader, even more profound issue: how our status as settlers generates the challenges to voice that we, as academics, face in our research. And connected to that question is the link between the contractual relationship that provides the community consent now essential to undertaking ethical research and the yet-undeveloped relationship imagined through Confederation-era treaty agreements. That, then, is the topic of this contribution.

So let me begin with the term "cultural appropriation." Among many possible normative definitions, I found this one most helpful. It states that cultural appropriation "refers to a particular power dynamic in which members of a dominant culture take elements from a culture of people who have been systematically oppressed by that dominant group."[1] So "cultural appropriation" narrowly defined in the context of this project refers to "taking" from an Indigenous culture by non-Indigenous academics.

One might conclude this means by definition that any use of any aspect of Indigenous cultures by anyone who is not Indigenous constitutes appropriation and is therefore wrong. In other words, it might refer to a need to completely silence outsider voices that originate in the "dominating" (not dominant) culture on any matter related to Indigenous culture (in the largest sense), regardless of what those individuals are saying. While the term is often used in that way (as are labels like "privilege" and "strategic essentialism"), that is not the interpretation I am applying here. Instead, my intent is to explore the conditions under which the term "cultural appropriation" does not apply to the actions of non-Indigenous, settler outsiders. So, at its heart the topic is calling upon academics such as myself to explain how we come to the view that what we communicate on Indigenous issues does not constitute the kind of "taking" that constitutes "cultural appropriation." Or to put it another way, when do we have the standing to intervene (I would presume in an authoritative academic voice) on topics pertaining to Indigenous issues and what are its parameters?

It seems to me, straight off, that the academy has developed a pretty airtight way to put an end to such a reflection before it begins – at least with regard to research. It is organized around the notion that what is not cultural appropriation (and therefore does not constitute taking) flows from a completed formal process through which we gain prior consent from an appropriate authority to conduct our research – and thus lay a claim to the legitimate right to speak to our findings. The method is codified in the 2018 Tri-Council Policy Statement: Ethical Conduct for Research Involving Humans[2] that resulted from an agreement between the public research funding community and Indigenous authorities. In fine, this agreement is contained in a "contract" in which the terms of engagement are strictly stipulated. Thus, it presumes that, so long as one remains faithful to these terms, a settler academic has the authority to speak on topics related to the "Indigenous." It goes so far as to indicate that an outsider academic may even publish results that conflict with community understandings, so long as the community's objections are made clear in the researcher's communications.[3]

It is certainly true that, when adhering to this policy, we indemnify ourselves from the charge that we are "taking" without permission. In this sense, the policy has become the "hoop to jump through" that permits researchers to "get on with" their principal objective, to research and publish in an Indigenous setting, without being called out or boycotted when we speak of our findings. When I served on an early iteration of a national committee constituted by the Tri-Council to come up with a proposal on what constituted ethical research with Indigenous (and other) communities, I came to understand that, for most researchers, this policy puts an end to the matter, full stop.[4]

I have a different view. Formal agreements are a first "step" in the process of relationship building through which I may come to believe that I have a legitimate place in a conversation around Indigenous issues. It is process that, in my imagination, is akin to the relationship building that Indigenous and some of the Crown parties envisioned would be developed by treaties at the time of Confederation. Although I don't know another way to proceed with the degree of comfort that Western conceptualizations of permission now require, I wish I could, for what we now have in place pushes to the margins what in my experience is essential to the process of finding one's voice: the growth that inheres within the very uncertainties in determining when (if ever) one has the responsibility to speak about what one has been taught.

This chapter focuses on four formative experiences from my childhood and early adult years through which I have developed my understanding of how (among other matters) I, as a non-Indigenous scholar, ought to conduct my engagement with Indigenous issues. It is intended to be experiential and personal, not prescriptive. It will include a brief discussion of how the kind of relationship I have come to understand flows from the exercise of treaty relations, which in my view offers a productive way to reframe matters pertaining to "cultural appropriation" discussed here. Then, in closing I will say a few words regarding the recent use of allegations of "cultural appropriation" to seek to silence non-Indigenous academics and how that has affected me in my academic life.

Experience 1: "Solidarity Forever"

I was born in New York City in 1943 and grew up in a community that was targeted in the so-called Red Scare. Its central tactics were the public shaming (through forced testimony at government hearings) and public silencing (by naming on a blacklist) of those considered by the accusers to be Communists or Communist sympathizers and thus as "dangers" to the state. In other words, while the analogy is not perfect, the members of my community were accused of cultural appropriation, or at least the cultural misrepresentation of American values and institutions, to whom the injunctions of public shaming and public silencing associated with "othering" were to be applied.

Consequently, from early childhood I witnessed at first hand the silencing of voices for holding views that were not acceptable to powerful others. Assertion of the right, in face of this silencing, to speak out what we understood to be the truth played a central role in my personality formation. This experience planted in my mind that one could either allow oneself to be silenced or speak out and take the consequences. For me, this meant, at least in my self-image, that I would be someone who would not let any authority limit my right to express my point of view.

This conviction was further deepened by the fact that my father, Moses Asch, who directed Folkways Records, positioned himself to be the vehicle for the voices silenced by McCarthy to find public expression. These explicitly included, among others, voices such as those of African American blues singers, Indigenous Peoples, and political progressives – that is, musical expressions that those in power and in the larger public sought to silence. His goal was to provide means to enrich the understanding of humanity of those in the larger community who felt constrained by the limitations of what was offered through more commercial (and censored) outlets. And, as has been said by many communities, my father also intended to provide information essential to the survival of communities under attack as they move(d) through turbulent times.

But I did not just learn from my father. My mother fearfully took in their shared experience of being progressives as well as being Jewish in a then hostile, gentile world. For her, while speaking out was always on the table, survival meant to step very cautiously; a sensibility I inherited. But there was of course more than that. On the fearful side, there was, for example, the unforgettable experience of being followed by FBI agents when I was three (obviously I was not the target); and, more generally witnessing the consequences of the Blacklist, such as seeing parents (well, mostly fathers) of school mates who sat at home with no work and no income just because standing on principles put them on lists that made employment impossible. On the defiance (or at least perseverance) side, there were the teachers in my school, Little Red School House, who got together to teach there when they could not get jobs in the public school system. In short, as I am sure is true of many others in my community, the fight or flight response (or as I will call them the defiance or fear responses) bookend my immediate gut reaction to any challenge, perceived or actual, to my authority to express what is on my mind.

But I need to emphasize that there was an elision in this thinking. It is well illustrated in what was to me and many others our most important symbol of survival through defiance: the Pete Seeger Christmas Carnegie Hall concerts. Here, thousands of community members joined together as one to sing along with Pete to songs of hope and resistance that ranged from "Wimoweh" and "Solidarity Forever" to "Die Gedanken Sind Frei" ("Thoughts Are Free"). The elision was this: we had no consciousness that in singing a song like "Wimoweh" we might be taking without permission. It was not so much that we believed we had that right because Die Gedanken Sind Frei, but because, as in the chorus of "Solidarity Forever," "the union makes us strong": we saw the act of singing "Wimoweh" as building solidarity with other oppressed communities to work together for the liberation of us all. It was a view reinforced through concerts and talks from members of such communities, and of course by bringing their music to the public through phonograph records. Given this understanding, it is my belief that our reaction to a charge of "cultural appropriation" would have been to feel a sense of betrayal from allies rather than shock at a realization that we might be trafficking in something that belonged to others without their permission.

Experience 2: "We Shall Overcome"

The first time I recall being conscious of the possible salience of what we now call "cultural appropriation" was in the mid-1960s. It came via the American Civil Rights Movement, and again Pete Seeger is central to my narrative. Seeger's involvement in the cause was multifaceted. Beginning in the late 1950s, he focused on promoting equality for African Americans through his singing and playing as well as by organizing countless concerts and appearing at many demonstrations and fundraisers. Perhaps, Seeger's singular contribution to the Movement was his introduction of "We Shall Overcome" to it. This song originated in a gospel hymn entitled "I'll Overcome Some Day" written at the turn of the twentieth century. With the change of the pronoun "I" to "We" and new lyrics, it entered into the musical repertoire of the labour movement in the 1940s. However, it did not become the anthem for the Civil Rights Movement until Seeger (along with another non-Black civil rights activist, Guy Carawan) introduced it in 1959.[5] Through acts such as these Seeger became an important contributor to the cause, admired virtually universally by its members. And, consistent with the values within which I was raised, I (along with many others) considered Seeger to be a role model for how to act in solidarity with allies. The notion that anything he did in the Movement might constitute cultural appropriation never would have crossed my mind.

Then, in 1965 things suddenly changed. Elements in the Movement's leadership (among them Stokely Carmichael) began to question the role of non-Blacks in general. In effect, they called for the retreat if not the silencing of outsider voices regardless of the work they were doing to support the cause. This demand hit Seeger soon after he had joined the 1965 march from Selma to Montgomery to support voting rights at the invitation of Martin Luther King Jr. As I understand, at that point Seeger was singled out for criticism by the leadership of a central organization, the Student Non-Violent Coordinating Committee (SNCC). In addition to the charge that he was too prominent, some questioned his motivation in that, from their point of view, his involvement also "benefitted" his career. Ultimately, however, the leadership did not ask Seeger to step aside so much as to step back.[6]

Seeger did not resist these criticisms. While maintaining his commitment to the cause, he did agree to step back, and he also resolved any concerns those elements of the leadership had with his professional involvement. At least publicly, the rationale for his actions, as explained to me, was that, given his prominence, contesting these matters publicly would distract attention from the Movement's goal. Seeger *also* shifted his focus to his long-standing concern with environmental renewal. While the Hudson River has national importance, for Seeger it was local as well in that he had lived on the banks of the Hudson virtually his entire adult life. I recall him saying at that time that he was motivated by a deep belief that the earth belonged to us all, and that it definitely needed healing if the human race were to survive.

Still, I remember being outraged at the time by the way Seeger and other non-Black allies were treated by this segment of the Movement.[7] And although I believed Pete acted honourably, I was disappointed that, rather than stand on principle, he seemed to acquiesce. My view has changed over the years. I now see that, regardless of one's sensibilities, as a general rule it is only right to take guidance from community leaders, even when it requires standing back; and so now I see (as I believe he did at the time) that Seeger's decision was less an act of acquiescence than one of respect. Or to put it another way, ultimately the Seeger experience allowed me to include in my value system the possibility that, whether or not I feel it is a betrayal, there are times when it is quite appropriate even for an ally to seek to limit self-expression.

Experience 3: "The Indians Will Be with Us Forever"

I took my first anthropology course in 1963 (my third year at the University of Chicago) from an anthropology professor named Sol Tax. As Pete Seeger is my role model for acting politically, so Tax is my professional mentor. He gave me the gift of understanding that it is possible to be an academic anthropologist who can marry politics and scholarship with integrity. Tax worked closely with Native Americans around the United States.[8] For example, he co-organized the famous American Indian Chicago Conference in 1961.[9] It resulted in a Declaration of Indian Purpose that asserted in the strongest terms that "Indian People" would not willingly assimilate[10] – a proposition that was quite controversial at a time when this was thought to be inevitable. He also developed a method for anthropological research with Indigenous communities. Called "Action Anthropology," it insisted not only that local people be involved in research in all its aspects (as is the case with community-based research), but that the research be done at the community's initiative, with researchers acting under the direction of the leadership and using their skills to work through issues identified by its members.[11] It is work that demands a long-term commitment as well as accepting up front that a community has the authority to determine the length and nature of the anthropologist's engagement with it.

I recall Dr. Tax bringing to my consciousness early in that first course the idea, counter to the assimilationist presupposition prevalent at the time, that, as he put it, "The Indians will be with us forever." Along with this perspective, Tax suggested that it was the job of anthropologists to support them, thereby explaining the rationale for Action Anthropology. The idea galvanized me. I know that was the moment I thought to myself that I had to commit to this cause and work to promote their right to survive and to thrive as Peoples.

In his courses, Tax also introduced me to the unique way in which Indigenous Peoples conceptualized their political relationship with the United States. I had been taught my whole life that the USA's greatest problem was to overcome the political and historical fact of slavery by working to ensure that African Americans have political equality. It was a vision of an America that, having overcome segregation, would become integrated politically in the sense that each citizen would have equality of civic standing, regardless of the colour of their skin or other attributes: democracy meant, one person, one vote. But, as Tax described, Indigenous Peoples were proposing a different approach, based on a nation-to-nation relationship that was neither segregationist nor integrationist in perspective. It had never crossed my mind that there would be any group other than white racists who would not want the political standing we advocated for in solidarity with African Americans, much less that there could be an alternative approach to political relations that moved in such a direction. It was a brand new idea: one I welcomed and committed myself to – for I saw it as a way out of the oppositional politics in which ethnonational relations are enacted.

Consequently, later in my senior year, I asked Tax, who had urged me to go on to graduate school, what I might do in a practical way to further the cause. He invited me to join a project led by Robert K. Thomas (a member of the Cherokee Nation and a student of Tax) with the Cherokee community in north-eastern Oklahoma.[12] So, in the fall of 1965, I went there and was welcomed by Thomas to work along with Hiner Doublehead, Al Wahrhafig, and himself on what was called the Carnegie Project.[13] This project, which ostensibly focused on promoting English language education among Cherokee youth, equally intended to assist Cherokee in maintaining their language and culture. My assignment was to have been to promote the music of Cherokee Blacks, particularly by organizing a music festival featuring their music. But I did not stay long enough even to begin. Later in the month I was reclassified 1A by the Selective Service and in order to avoid being drafted I landed up at Columbia University, where I became a doctoral student in January 1966.

Notwithstanding its brevity, my stay in Oklahoma proved formative in that it confirmed at first hand two of Tax's basic teachings regarding relations between anthropologists and communities. The first concerns on whose behalf one is working. In discussing the history of the project (which began in 1963) when I first arrived, Thomas explained that he had originally consulted with W.W. Keeler, the Principal Chief of the Cherokee Nation (and also president of Phillips Petroleum) as well as other officials of the Tribal Council but found that they were strongly opposed to the project (in part because they supported a future directed toward assimilation). However, that did not deter him. The team was there at the invitation of the part of the local community he was serving and the project was aimed at assisting it to further aspects of their culture (such as by language retention) they saw as crucial for their survival. Therefore, the project would continue unless the community withdrew its support and cooperation. From this I took away that a community's goals may be at odds with those of its official leadership, and that on such occasions it is sometimes appropriate to rely on community support for the work, even when the larger political structure disagrees.

Second, even in the brief time I was there, I spent much time travelling with team members as they worked their way up and down rural roads to visit and engage with community members. I was struck by the warmth of the interactions and by the willingness of all to work together. This offered me a glimpse as to how I might live in an Indigenous community. But it also reminded me that, as Tax had taught, working within the tradition of Action Anthropology is more than working on projects. It entails building long-term relationships (this project lasted over twenty years).[14] And, to reference the theme of this chapter explicitly, this process can enable a researcher/practitioner to better understand what does and does not constitute "taking without permission," as well as create a foundation upon which misunderstandings can be resolved through mutual trust.

Experience 4: "Because It Is Important for You to Know"

The last experience that informs my reflection on "cultural appropriation" comes from the year my wife Margaret and I lived in Wrigley (or Pedzéh Kı́) in the Mackenzie Region of the Northwest Territories between August 1969 and 1970. It begins with my decision to undertake fieldwork in Fort Norman (now Tulita), based on an interview I had with June Helm, the leading Athapaskanist, as to the best sites from a practical point of view.

At that time, this region was remote and access to it for a long-term stay was more like that encountered in travel to some regions in Africa and Asia than in North America.[15] As is the case today, doing research also required prior official authorization. At that time, this was controlled by officials in the government of the Northwest Territories and was generally exercised without input from an Indigenous community. Consequently, I wrote the local official in charge of the Fort Norman region (called the Area Administrator). Given the state of mail service, it took many months to receive a reply. His response was cautiously supportive of my request and of the availability of housing, but he gave no indication as to whether he had informed the Indigenous community of our pending arrival.

Armed with that letter, Margaret and I headed North to Tulita. However, upon our arrival in Edmonton, the Area Administrator informed me that his promised support (particularly accommodation) would not be forthcoming. After a frantic search for another venue, the Acting Area Administrator of the Fort Simpson region offered to authorize the project and to provide rental accommodation in the small community of Wrigley (or Pedzéh Kį), located about 200 km south of Tulita. So in early August we hitched on a government charter flight from Fort Simpson and arrived in town. Once there, we were shown to our accommodation (a small house) by the power plant operator, who was as close to a government representative as there was in this unincorporated community of roughly 150 Dene and, now including ourselves, seven Euro-Canadians (as we called ourselves then).

I recall seeking out Chief Edward Hardisty soon after our arrival to explain my project and, if possible, gain consent from himself and Council for my research. He was taken aback. My request was novel in his experience. He also expressed misgiving at making such a determination on behalf of the community, either by himself or through a decision of their Chief and Council. This meant that I would never be in a position to obtain formal consent from representatives of the Dene community.

However, simultaneously a different consent process became manifest. The fact is that our arrival in this very remote community attracted much notice. Indeed, on the very first day children (many of whom spoke English), came to our house to visit, play, and scope us out. Within those first days, community members, including Elders (or old timers, as they were called in English at that time) visited and politely (in English as translated by the children) asked us to explain our presence. Still others invited us to accompany them on their travels, for example, to fishnets along the Mackenzie River and, in Margaret's case, to snare lines. All of this was very friendly; but it was all sussing us out. So, permission for the research was not granted by formal agreement, but emerged over time and largely through quotidian acts. Consequently, I never gained a level of confidence that I had permission to do this research that flows from the "certainty" that derives (at least from a Western point of view) from an agreement stipulated in a formal contract.

Still, there were moments, such as when I was instructed to bring my tape recorder to the community hall so that I could tape a drum dance, where the sense that I had been given permission became almost as clear as if I had a written agreement upon which to rely. The first such moment was of particular note. It came indirectly through the Roman Catholic priest from Fort Simpson who visited Wrigley roughly every second Sunday. On meeting me early on in our stay, he declared harshly that he really disliked anthropologists as all they did was take from people and never give back. Then on his very next visit he took a very different tone with us. It seems he was disarmed after he had heard from community members that they liked and welcomed us and supported my work. In short, it took time, and there were many tests, but ultimately we gained permission in the sense that community members were supportive of my project and comfortable with our living together in the same place.

Our experience in Wrigley also helped Margaret and me to better understand that, beyond gaining permission, it is crucial to gain an understanding of one's responsibilities to what we are taught and those who teach us. While we learned this largely through daily interactions with community members, two examples that made the point very clear come to mind.

The first involves an exchange with a wise hunter and medicine person, Wilson Pellissey. One day in the midst of our stay, Wilson was called to help cure another community member. He knew very well that I was interested in recording all music. Consequently, he sent a youngster to my house to invite me to record the ceremony, including the songs he sang to call his medicine animal. I was very excited, as such opportunities occurred rarely. But soon the youngster returned to say that Wilson had withdrawn his invitation. He was worried that if I played the tape when he was not present, the medicine animal would come and I wouldn't know what to do.

Were I to conceptualize Wilson's decision through the lens of "cultural appropriation," I would likely read his act as the withdrawal of his permission to record, full stop. But I think such an interpretation completely misreads his intent. His intent was not to deny something to me but rather to protect me from the consequences of an act that, had he given his permission, might ultimately endanger me. That is, his action flowed from his sense of responsibility to the knowledge and to me. In other words, it was an act of caring.

The second example takes the idea of caring in another direction. It comes through my third mentor, Mrs. Jessie Hardisty. While there is no space here to discuss the scope of her teachings, speaking in generalities, Jessie gave us an understanding of what it means to be a responsible, compassionate, ethical human being. She was my main teacher in Wrigley, in part because, for reasons I will not explain here, she was fluent in English as well as her own language, notwithstanding that she was then in her eighties.

Jessie had a deep understanding of Dene kinship structure and a knowledge of how people were related through kinship that extended across generations and over hundreds of kilometres. She soon discovered that I was deeply interested in that aspect of kinship theory known at that time as "alliance theory," which focused in particular on how kinship relations can create bonds that link groups with one another. Soon, the structure of Dene kinship terms and relations in Wrigley and surrounding communities, in both their theoretical and practical dimensions, became a central topic of conversation.

On bringing up the topic once again during one of the nearly daily visits Margaret and I made to her house, I came to the realization that, while she would look at me when I was asking a question about kinship, Jessie would invariably turn to Margaret to answer it. I guessed that the reason for her action might be that kinship knowledge at this level was women's knowledge and so is not something that should be told to a man (which she never said directly).

Wondering if this was correct, I asked Jessie what she would do if her son asked her the same questions. She replied that she would tell him it was just gossip and ask him to go away and leave her alone. I responded, "what if he persisted?" She said, "I would tell him (using Dene terms) only who is his mother's brother and who is his father's brother, and tell him that is all he needs to know" (this is a significant distinction in this kinship terminology, for it determines – partly – how an individual is linked to groups). So, I asked, "why are you telling me?" She responded: "Because it is important for you to know."

That answer penetrated me. Why was it so important for *me* to know? I began at that moment to wonder what she intended, and I have been thinking about this ever since. First, I have concluded that, in contrast to the situation with Wilson, Jessie trusted that what I had learned about kinship through my Western lens was adequate for me to handle her teachings on this topic responsibly. Second, I am convinced that she had offered me these teachings for a reason beyond merely conveying information, but, at the same time, did not explain to me what that was; it was my job to figure that out.

Over the years, I have wrestled with what her intent was. At this point, I have come to believe that her larger purpose was to task me with using what I had learned to help convey to the larger world, as exemplified in Dene kinship relations, how harmony and disharmony within the human community and beyond can be regulated elegantly and with dignity through a process based on relationality (and hence, as it developed, my intense focus on treaty relations). Following from this principle, in receiving this understanding I became obliged to share it forward. And, as I have come to believe, that, speaking more broadly, was the teaching that community members sought to convey to us. Far from worrying about our taking without asking, they were concerned that, to the degree they agreed we could do so responsibly, we would pass on what we were taught, thereby offering to the larger world a glimpse into a way of living they valued *profoundly* and wished to share. In short, our involvement in daily life provided a grounded exercise through which we could better understand and value a social life connected through a treaty relationship, and commit ourselves to sharing it more broadly. At the same time, I am certain that, had it become apparent that I had a secret research agenda, the community's welcome would have been quickly withdrawn.

Were I to conceptualize Jessie's decision, like Wilson's, through the lens of "cultural appropriation," I would likely read her act solely as permission to document, full stop. But again, such an interpretation completely misreads intent. As I see it, her intent was to invite me to pass what I had learned on to others in a respectful way. Thus, as with Wilson, her decision flowed from her sense of responsibility to the knowledge and to me. It too was an act of caring.

Finally, as with Action Anthropology, we learned that working in a community establishes relationships that in some cases endure through a lifetime.

Therefore, the length of engagement cannot be limited to a specific temporality even when such terms are stipulated in a written agreement.

Conclusions

In my introduction, I stated that the primary goal of this chapter would be to explore some of the conditions under which the term "cultural appropriation," does not apply to the actions of non-Indigenous, settler outsiders. After mentioning that "gaining permission" is the condition normally offered by members of the research community, I then discussed the development of my thinking on the subject, at least with regard to my own practices. This concluded with a detailed discussion of what Margaret and I learned from members of the Wrigley community where we lived for one year when we were in our mid-twenties.

I would say that the conditions I understand to be central for acting in a non-appropriative way come down to adhering to two factors. First, I cannot treat teachings as commodities in the sense that Marx discusses the term in "The Fetishism of Commodities."[16] Teachings are not objects but are processes that are enmeshed in the fabric of a lifeway. Any attempt to pull them out as though they are isolated may well constitute "cultural appropriation," even when permission has been given. Second, while some ideas, such as political relations based on relationality, resonate deeply beyond any one community, it is not possible for me to ever assume that I have fully "captured" the meaning of what I have been taught, much less that I have communicated it accurately to people who live within a Western tradition of thought. However, this does not mean that I do not try, especially when their appeal is compelling. In fact, that is, in my understanding, exactly what the people in Wrigley, particularly Jessie Hardisty and Wilson Pellissey, encouraged me to do.

These factors now guide my practice. I write what I have come to understand, not so much in the expectation that I got it "right" (although I am happy when knowledgeable people nod in agreement), but rather so that we can continue a conversation to get to a better mutual understanding – a process that I consider, again, an instantiation of the treaty relationship. But, I know that there are topics around which, as with Wilson's medicine song, I have been given too little knowledge to even begin a conversation and so I am silent. As well, there are times when my confidence may be only sufficient to offer a simple reflection that might begin a conversation. But always, I make it clear that whatever I am offering is an "understanding" that I have come to, not a final answer, and that it is one I am trying to render in Western thought. When I communicate in this way, I have a degree of confidence that I am not engaging in "cultural appropriation" and have every expectation that a fair-minded person would agree.

In closing, I will turn briefly to how I have felt when allegations of cultural appropriation were used in what I perceive to be in an effort to silence me even though I had adhered to the principles I have discussed. I will say, in fairness, that in a career that spans nearly a half century this tactic has been overtly directed at me only once in an academic setting. This took place when I was talking to a class of mostly Indigenous graduate students about treaty relations soon after the publication of *On Being Here to Stay*. After a pro forma introduction by the Indigenous professor who had invited me, I began to discuss what had led me to write the book and what I hoped it would achieve. Almost before I could begin two Indigenous students in the class stopped me and then accused me of talking on the topic without the authority to do so. They demanded that I detail for them to whom I was "accountable" for what I had written. I fully expected that the professor, himself Indigenous, would have stepped in – after all he had invited me. When he didn't, I was stunned. Emotionally I reverted back to my earliest days and felt "betrayed." I kept silent on the matter but continued my presentation.

What struck me was the anger that was being directed at me. It seemed to be shared by many others in the class and by the professor. At the time, the anger seemed misplaced, but on reflection, I can understand. And now I am limiting myself to asking why it has emerged only recently. The fact of the matter is that, for a very long time, seeking the exclusion of outsider voices was not prominent in Indigenous-settler discourse; in fact, our voices were encouraged. Having witnessed (and experienced) this exclusionary move in civil rights discourse in the 1960s, as well as the development of academic agendas based on strategic essentialism,[17] I was grateful for its absence here.

I have asked myself what, from a sociological point of view, accounts for the difference in timing? I have come up with this answer. In both cases, the rise of this form of discourse reflects a change in political circumstances. Each movement began in solidarity between communities, and ended when that form of solidarity proved insufficient to achieve justice. For the Civil Rights Movement, I associate that move with the growing realization by the mid-1960s that solidarity based on moral arguments was not sufficiently powerful on its own to overcome racism. As Julius Lester wrote in 1966:[18]

Now it is over. The days of singing freedom songs and the days of combating bullets and billy clubs with Love. We Shall Overcome (and we have overcome our blindness) sounds old, out-dated and can enter the pantheon of the greats along with … union songs. As one SNCC veteran put it after the Mississippi March, "Man, the people are too busy getting ready to fight to bother with singing anymore."

Still, I need to add that, while it reflected and still reflects the view of many in the African American community, that view was nor is by no means universal;[19] and, as what is taking place in the USA as I write attests, there remains hope that an alliance among Black and non-Black will together create the conditions to achieve justice.

In Canada, a moment similar to the one in the '60s did not come until decades later. I attribute this largely to the understanding, central in important strains in Indigenous thought, that the political solution lies not in separation but rather in the establishment of a nation-to-nation relationship based on treaty. But there also is a difference in the time it took to reach such a moment. In contrast to the States, the period from my arrival in Canada in 1969 to the passage of the 1982 *Constitution Act* and the Constitutional Conferences that followed was one of growing optimism among Indigenous Peoples and their allies that Indigenous Rights (Aboriginal and Treaty Rights in the language of that time) would be resolved justly, through a nation-to-nation relationship. When this approach proved unsuccessful, it was followed by a decade or more when it was expected that the courts would move us toward that goal. As with the Civil Rights Movement, the exclusionary move became prominent only when it became clear to many (probably in the mid-2000s) that even this process would not succeed. However, as in the United States, there remain many who see this as a moment to keep the alliance together and press on. It seems to me that this book is one small step in that direction.

In sum, I believe there is very little one can do objectively to reverse what is a deeply held and evidence-based understanding among many Indigenous Peoples of the realpolitik within which we are now immersed. Like Seeger, I believe that it is futile and perhaps even irresponsible to contest cultural appropriation labelling, regardless of how that makes me feel. To do so constitutes a distraction that misdirects away from our shared goal of achieving a just relationship. That is, I see now as a moment for me to encourage the renewal of conversations with even the most sceptical Indigenous voices by redoubling my effort to upend a political system that, having been built on the most fundamental appropriation of all – the taking of Indigenous lands without their permission – continues to silence their voices on the most crucial conversation for us all: how we will all live together on lands that we, the recent settlers, now call home.

NOTES

I would like to thank Margaret Asch, Emma Feltes, and Carl Urion for their comments and suggestions. I appreciate them greatly.

1 Maisha Z. Johnson, "What's Wrong with Cultural Appropriation" (14 June 2015), online: *Everyday Feminism* <https://everydayfeminism.com/2015/06/cultural -appropriation-wrong/>. For a detailed discussion see "Cultural Appropriation," online: *Wikipedia* <https://en.wikipedia.org/wiki/Cultural_appropriation> and

"Cultural Appropriation of Indigenous Peoples in Canada," online: <https://www
.thecanadianencyclopedia.ca/en/article/cultural-appropriation-of-indigenous
-peoples-in-canada>.

2 Tri-Council Policy Statement Ethical Conduct for Research Involving Humans
(2018) online: <https://ethics.gc.ca/eng/policy-politique_tcps2-eptc2_2018.html>.

3 Tri-Council Statement cited ft 2 in chapter 9.17 "If disagreement about
interpretation arises between researchers and the community and it cannot be
resolved, researchers should either (a) provide the community with an opportunity
to make its views known, or (b) accurately report any disagreement about the
interpretation of the data in their reports or publications. This should not be
construed as giving the community the right to block the publication of findings.
Rather, it gives the community the opportunity to contextualize the findings."

4 I also was a member of research initiative entitled "Intellectual Property Issues in
Cultural Heritage" or "IPINCH." Led by George Nicholas, the seven-year project
explored issues such as what constitutes cultural appropriation. Certainly the ethos
and the practice of members stretched well past the mere concern about passing
through hoops. The group produced many relevant documents, one of which is
entitled "Think before You Appropriate: A Guide for Creators and Designers": it is
relevant to the theme of this paper, can be accessed at this website: <https://www
.sfu.ca/ipinch/resources/teaching-resources/think-before-you-appropriate/>.

5 As Carl Urion pointed out in an email to me dated 29 September 2020, "the gospel
song was written by a widely-admired and influential 19th century African American
pastor, whose songs, like this one, were Black church standards that had currency in
the African American community generally, not just in church. It's my understanding
that the new version was introduced by Lucille Simmons, an African American tobacco
factory worker and labour organizer, in 1945." For a discussion of the song's history and
provenance see, online: <https://en.wikipedia.org/wiki/We_Shall_Overcome>.

6 For a discussion of this moment, see online: <https://libcom.org/blog/lessons
-leftism-pete-seeger-black-power-movement-09052017>.

7 My anger at what I saw as a betrayal was only heightened by the fact that frequently
they justified their actions by allegations that were substantively anti-Semitic
(including some singling out Pete Seeger's Jewish manager).

8 In fact, in contrast to his wholesale condemnation of the field of anthropology,
Vine Deloria Jr. supported the work of Sol Tax and even offered a eulogy at
his funeral. Joshua Smith, "Standing with Sol: The Spirit and Intent of Action
Anthropology" (2015) 57 Anthropologica 445 [Smith].

9 Nancy Oestreich Lurie, "Sol Tax and Tribal Sovereignty" (1999) 58:1 Human
Organization 108. Also see: <https://en.wikipedia.org/wiki/Sol_Tax>.

10 Statement reads in part: "We, the Indian People, must be governed by principles in
a democratic manner with a right to choose our way of life." Declaration of Indian
Purpose (p. 4) online: <https://files.eric.ed.gov/fulltext/ED030518.pdf>.

11 Smith, *supra* note 8.

12 For a detailed discussion of this Project, please see Daniel M. Cobb, "Devils in
    Disguise: The Carnegie Project, the Cherokee Nation, and the 1960s" (2007) 31:3
    American Indian Quarterly 465.

13 Clyde Warrior, discussed in Sa'ke'j Henderson's chapter in this book, was also a
    part of the Project.

14 Smith, *supra* note 8, 454, ft 1.

15 For example, moving there successfully required a level of logistical planning that
    included pre-determining that accommodation was available and that one had
    adequate provisions for the year. This meant having purchased a year's supply of
    food and other necessities that were trucked up from Edmonton, our jumping-off
    point, and then packed on a Mackenzie River barge.

16 See Karl Marx, *Capital*, vol 1, p 48, online: <https://www.marxists.org/archive
    /marx/works/download/pdf/Capital-Volume-I.pdf>.

17 Strategic essentialism can be defined in different ways. Here I am following the
    term as it is defined in the Wiley Online Library and particularly the description
    that "strategic essentialism advocates provisionally accepting essentialist
    foundations for identity categories as a strategy for collective representation in
    order to pursue chosen political ends." It is a stance that has frequently been
    deployed to silence outsider voices. Online: <https://onlinelibrary.wiley.com/doi
    /abs/10.1002/9781118786352.wbieg1170>.

18 Julius Lester, "The Angry Children of Malcolm X," Excerpted from Sing Out!
    Magazine (co-published by my father), online: <http://nationalhumanitiescenter
    .org/pds/maai3/overcome/text5/angrychildren.pdf>.

19 See Angela Davis, for example. For a recent discussion of her continuing efforts to
    support solidarity among groups, see online: <https://www.nytimes.com
    /interactive/2020/10/19/t-magazine/angela-davis.html>.

9 Turning Away from the State: Cultural Appropriation in the Shadow of the Courts

JOHN BORROWS

1. Introduction: Appropriation and Ambiguity

Cultural appropriation is the use of a people's traditional dress, music, cuisine, knowledge, and other aspects of their culture, without their approval, by members of a different culture.[1] There have been prominent examples of people criticized for appropriating Indigenous culture in recent years.[2] People take what belongs to others and this must stop. We must find effective ways of critiquing artists, musicians, journalists, fashion houses, authors, academics, politicians, and others who exploit Indigenous Peoples in these ways. Without judging specific cases, this chapter highlights a particular challenge when addressing cultural appropriation: achieving proportionality when court-derived markers of Indigenous identity are narrow and troublingly pervasive.

Proportionality is an important value.[3] It might be described as balance, holism, relationality, or two-eyed seeing in some Indigenous contexts.[4] Good judgment includes attentiveness to the scale, scope, sphere, or dimensions of the question to which decisions are addressed. Where warranted, we must not shy away from incisive critique, chastisement, and reproof. Abusing Indigenous Peoples' cultures and ways of life should not be vindicated, justified, or excused. This is true even if cultural appropriation is done innocently, in good faith, or for a broader public purpose. Harmful acts do not occur in a vacuum; there is a broader pattern underlying these harms. Indigenous culture is continuously manipulated or misappropriated, thus replicating the dominance of non-Indigenous peoples over Indigenous Peoples in Canada and beyond.[5]

At the same time, critiques of how people relate to culture must be proportionate. Conclusions must "fit" within the context in which they are applied. We must not turn condemnation of reprehensible acts into scorn, contempt, disdain, or hate. People on all sides of this issue have a right to be different, contrary, experimental, atypical, disagreeable, wrong, and even repellent in how they present themselves. We must find ways of disagreeing without undermining another person's life, well-being, or security. In criticizing others, we must be careful that we do not overreach. There is nothing wrong with disagreeing strongly and vociferously. In fact, we should welcome such practices. This is often necessary, given the gravity of harms experienced by Indigenous Peoples and the failures to understand or act on them.

However, in heated exchange, we might sweep too much into our critiques. Humans make mistakes. In addition to considering other people's humanity, we should be careful that disagreements do not turn into censorship. This could harm us all. Degraded conversational environments could prevent others from saying things we might benefit from hearing, even if what they say is upsetting, unkind, or disagreeable.

There is also place for responding to other people's harmful acts or expressions with love, truth, bravery, humility, wisdom, honesty, and respect, the gikoomisinan gimishomisinan kikinoomagewinan or seven grandmother/grandfather teachings of the Anishinaabe.[6] There is power in loving someone with whom we strongly disagree. Some of our treaty relationships create obligations to respect people who have strikingly different world views and goals.[7] Humility, bravery, and wisdom can give us power to deal with ourselves and other people in a new light, even if their actions are offensive.[8] Indigenous Peoples have standards, principles, criteria, measures, norms, and benchmarks to process disputes. This is to say, as Indigenous Peoples we have Law. We should consider how Indigenous Peoples' Law and lifeways might guide our engagement with others. Indigenous Law is an underutilized resource in our debates and activities related to cultural appropriation, even among Indigenous commentators. It must be revitalized to bring into focus Indigenous Peoples' humanity as reasoning and reasonable people who make judgments and take action to create fairness in their relationships.

In addition to acting with humanity, with proportionality, without censorship, and in accordance with Indigenous Law, we must also take care to ensure that we do not choose ways of critiquing cultural appropriation which can be turned against us as Indigenous Peoples. In particular, we must be careful about adopting ideas from Canadian law which characterize Indigenous Peoples in past-tense terms. Some of these approaches could silence us and undermine self-determination. We must never forget that power is arrayed against Indigenous Peoples in ways that are often beyond our control. What benefits us today might harm us tomorrow. Thus, this chapter expresses a caution related to Canadian law's categorization of Indigenous Peoples when dealing with Indigenous Peoples and cultures. Canadian law has narrowly construed Indigeneity in ways that ultimately benefit non-Indigenous law and governance.

When criticizing cultural appropriation we must be careful not to replicate the very frameworks and arguments used to oppress Indigenous Peoples. We must not reproduce the same analytical structures that have caused dispossession in the first place. As noted, the state's legal framework has deployed rigid legal categories to define and control Indigenous Peoples.[9] This must end: Indigenous Peoples must be self-determining and not get caught in state-defined webs. That is, we must turn away from state structures and frameworks that blind us to how they reproduce cultural appropriation.

This chapter argues that claims of cultural appropriation hide as much as they reveal. Cultural appropriation is a malleable term that should raise significant suspicions about its usage when it is detached from context. Cultural appropriation "call-outs" occur within different frameworks. We should not automatically assume the rightness or righteousness of this term's use in our hands or in the hands of others if they connect to broader state dispossession. Call-outs related to cultural appropriation which draw on Canadian law regarding Indigeneity can serve power struggles that transcend the words or phrases used. We can only make sense of these actions in context; we should not assume critiques of cultural appropriation are universally good.

My worry is that allegations of cultural appropriation that draw on court-inspired and state-derived identity markers can undermine our ability to participate or contribute to a desired end with others. Appropriation's polarity can be easily reversed; claims of cultural appropriation can be used for or against us. While we must reject unjust uses of tradition, expression, or heritage, we must not choose arguments and frameworks which weaken or violate Indigenous Peoples' Law.

As noted, allegations of cultural appropriation can humiliate, subsume, or silence those with whom we disagree, and break Indigenous Law in the process. In these circumstances, imprudent or undue critique can be a blunt and oppressive tool. It can lead to polarization and define in-groups and out-groups in ways that create moral enemies of those targeted by this label. In some situations, cries of cultural appropriation may even be an instrument of authoritarianism if coupled with xenophobic appeals to purify the culture and people associated with a particular point of view.

This is to say that the Indigenous legal context of our engagements should guide our responses. We must be careful not to universalize critique in essentializing fundamentalist or overly abstract ways. We must not dilute the force of our critiques by failing to match the means chosen for our communication with their ultimate ends. We must be the change we hope to see. There is power in being the change we hope to realize. Thus, one of this chapter's claims is that *how* we say something can be as important as *what* we say. Form and substance matter in human communication, and we must attend to both in our disagreements. Acting congruently by matching means with ends may be the most substantial critique we can offer when it comes to questions of cultural appropriation.

Cognitive science suggests that persuasion rests on making favourable mental connections and breaking unfavourable ones. In our efforts to draw attention to incompatibilities and dissonance related to cultural appropriation we need to attend to the science of connectivity, as the literature about persuasion suggests. Making as well as breaking connections is necessary to help ourselves and others overcome their pre-existing biases. Persuasion ultimately rests on tone, concessions, building of common ground, attentiveness to tradition, deployment of balancing schemes, sharing, likeability, attitude towards one's adversaries, reciprocity, etc.[10]

We have much to learn when addressing questions of cultural appropriation. Unless we want to change others through coercion, compulsion, or duress, which I would strongly reject, we must be aware of how we structure and present our arguments in this field.

This chapter describes some of the problems associated with cultural appropriation in Canada's constitutional regime. After considering how Canadian courts are implicated in cultural appropriation, we will see how those who want to protect Indigenous culture can fall into the same conceptual traps.

2. Indigenous Rights, Culture and Constitutional Hypocrisy

My first argument is that Canadian courts selectively appropriate culture to marginalize Indigenous Peoples in their relationships with others. This has implications for how some Indigenous Peoples disputing cultural appropriation get caught in frameworks which potentially undermine their own self-determination.

Cultural appropriation by courts and governments should be constitutionally inappropriate. Yet the Canadian state appropriates what it does not own, for its own use, without permission.[11] Canadian governments have taken Indigenous lands and imposed non-Indigenous rule without legal justification.[12] Crown assertions of sovereignty do not acknowledge Indigenous authority on Indigenous Lands despite pre-existing and ongoing relationships with their historic territories.[13]

While the Supreme Court of Canada upholds Crown appropriations of Indigenous land and governance, it precludes Indigenous Peoples from claiming constitutional protection for practices, customs, or traditions that "arose solely as a response to European influences."[14] Cultural practices that were not "integral to distinctive cultures prior to European arrival in North America" are incapable of receiving constitutional protection. Appropriation is therefore a one-way street in Canada. The Crown can "take something from a culture and use it as [its] own" (i.e., governance and land),[15] while Indigenous Peoples are precluded from using their culture to control their own lands and governance.

This produces hypocrisy, discrimination, inequality, prejudice, and injustice in Canada's constitutional regime.

For example, if an Indigenous group choses to fund its governance through a casino, this activity is constitutionally unacceptable because Indigenous Peoples did not regulate gambling prior to European contact.[16] This was the result in the *Pamajewon* case. On the other hand, if an Indigenous People fished for commercial purposes, this *may* form the basis for a constitutional right in the present day, *if* the Indigenous People in question fished for commercial purposes before encountering Europeans.[17] This is what happened in the *Gladstone* case. The difference between these two scenarios is that some Indigenous groups fished commercially before European arrival, while casinos did not exist in North America before Europeans arrived here.

As noted, there is a double standard allowing the Crown to appropriate Indigenous resources while prohibiting Indigenous Peoples from adopting so-called European organizational forms. The court's selective use of culture is arbitrary, one-sided, unbalanced, disproportionate, and unjust.

The court's framework shows how so-called cultural appropriation is constitutionally impermissible for Indigenous Peoples in Canada while it is permissible for the Crown. The Supreme Court of Canada denied Anishinaabe constitutional protection for the adoption and adaption of cultural forms (small-scale gambling) to practices that did not exist before European contact (governance of high-stakes gaming). Since casinos were not "integral to the distinctive culture" of Anishinaabe Peoples when Samuel D. Champlain visited them in 1615, they could not be appropriated as constitutional rights in the 1990s.

There is something deeply discriminatory about the court's willingness to assume Crown title in North America when Europeans did not own or govern Indigenous Land before contact, nor secure proper permissions for such action. The Crown did not run casinos before European arrival in North America, particularly on Indigenous Peoples' lands; however, the court assumes parliament and not Indigenous Peoples can regulate high-stakes gaming on Indigenous Land.

The Supreme Court's focus on the cultural purity of "distinctive aboriginal societies ... prior to the arrival of Europeans," as in the *Van der Peet* case, undermines Indigenous constitutional protection.[18] It undermines contemporary Indigenous Peoples' political voices. It also gives non-Indigenous governments a pass. They do not have to satisfy tests of cultural authenticity. They do not have to confront the troubling question of how their own jurisdictional authority relies on racialized abstract notions of self-proclaimed superiority when it comes to land holding and governance.[19] It is troubling for courts to act as if there is an authentic or integral aspect to Indigenous governance, rooted in once-upon-a-time practices. This empowers non-Indigenous governments, who freely create complex legal regimes without having to justify how this relates to abstract and superior notions of European or Canadian culture.

The Supreme Court of Canada's policing of the bounds of Indigeneity, and expansion of the Crown's adaptability, strips Indigenous Peoples of their social, political, economic, and legal power. It erases nuance, closes minds, censors adaptability, reinforces segregation, supports disengagement, and thwarts growth. The court's position is wrong on its very face because it is always an integral part of any culture to adopt or adapt new ideas and practices from other groups. Indigenous Peoples should be able to adapt and be flexible in how they constitute themselves and their affairs.[20] The court's diminishment of Indigenous fluidity occurs at the same time as it upholds the appropriation of Indigenous Land and governance over these same lands. This is cultural appropriation writ large.

In making these observations, let me say that there seems to be something of what might be described as a "cancel culture" in the Supreme Court's judgments dealing with Indigenous Rights. A cancel culture is based on the idea is that "if you do something that others deem problematic, you automatically lose all your currency. Your voice is silenced. You're done."[21] While the court's language is measured, polite, polished, and urbane, Indigenous Peoples suffer some of the same effects as those who are called out in contemporary political debates for daring to adopt or adapt the culture of some other group. To cancel is "to destroy the force, effectiveness or validity of something."[22] In these cases, Indigenous Peoples' claims were called out for being culturally inauthentic. While the court did not use the term appropriation, it was unwilling to recognize constitutional rights for practices, customs, and traditions that were "non-Indigenous" when Europeans arrived on their shores.

3. Drawing Analogies: Speaking about Cultural Appropriation in the Shadow of the Courts

My second and related argument is that Indigenous call outs related to cultural appropriation can alarmingly draw on some of the very same logic used by the Supreme Court of Canada to dispossess Indigenous Peoples. Language and frameworks critical of cultural appropriation, used by some Indigenous Peoples, can mirror Canadian processes that uphold Indigenous Peoples' marginalization. This is problematic and demonstrates that we should turn away from the state when it comes to questions of cultural appropriation.

In drawing attention to criticisms of Indigenous cultural appropriation I want to reiterate that there is no doubt that Indigenous identity has been wrongfully appropriated in Canada throughout the generations[23] and in the present day.[24] There is no disputing this fact. It is a huge problem and must stop. Stealing Indigenous identity is abhorrent. In the following section I am merely trying to draw attention to the logic used to challenge cultural appropriation and show how it corresponds to frameworks used by courts to dispossess us as Indigenous Peoples. My implication is that we can end up further entrenching our own marginalization in the process. Two examples related to Indigenous citizenship demonstrate this problem. In reviewing these examples, I want to be clear: I am not taking any position with regard to the substance of who is "in" or "out" when it comes to any particular community. My sole goal is to draw attention to the state-centric frameworks used to draw these distinctions.

There have been many controversies about Indigenous identity in eastern Canada, particularly when considering Métis identity.[25] The Métis National Council (MNC) recently suspended the Métis Nation of Ontario (MNO) from membership on the Council for, among other things, "concerns about the way the Ontario Métis government defines people as Métis."[26] The vice president of the MNC said that accepting people the MNO defined as Métis communities is "something we must clearly be fearful of as a people."[27] MNO citizenship decisions were labelled identity theft and a risk to Métis birthrights. An MNC Press release stated: "By not following the Métis National Definition, Ontario is, wrongfully, purporting to grant Métis Nation Citizenship to people living in eastern Ontario who are not part of the Métis Nation. Their communities in which they live are shamefully and wrongly claimed to be part of the historic Métis Nation. These communities are not, have never been, and can never be a part of our Métis Nation's history and Homeland."[28] The MNC called this "swamping of the Métis Nation by non-Métis people" an invasion, usurpation and "cultural appropriation."[29] These strong words explicitly draw upon the language of cultural appropriation while trying to support Métis claims to self-determination. I support Métis self-determination. I worry about problematic self-indigenization that appropriates Indigenous citizenship and identity. Individuals and groups can make claims to Indigeneity that are self-serving and damaging to the broader self-determination of the group. At the same time, I am drawing attention to the fact that some of the language used by adversaries in this debate replicates ideas about cultural purity found in the Supreme Court of Canada.

The MNC says, "'Métis' means a person who self-identifies as Métis, is distinct from other Aboriginal peoples, is of historic Métis Nation Ancestry and who is accepted by the Métis Nation."[30] The MNC says this definition of "Métis" was confirmed by the leading Métis rights case, R v Powley, which set out the components of membership as self-definition, ancestral connection, and acceptance by a contemporary "Métis" community.[31] When you examine the Powley case in greater depth, you can see that it relies on assumptions of what was "integral to the distinctive culture" of communities after contact and before effective European control (during which time the court said the Métis People came into existence).[32]

As we have seen, the "integral to a distinctive culture test" is the Canadian Supreme Court's own invention, which freezes Indigenous identity at a particular point in time. As discussed in the last section of this chapter, the court's determination of who and what is culturally appropriate allows Canada to assume governance and steal (appropriate) lands and resources without having to justify its claims. The MNC is using the *Van der Peet/Pamajewon* framework as reproduced in *Powley* to decide who is Métis. I recognize there are seductive incentives to using Canadian law because it is recognized by the broader nation state and thus easier to enforce. Moreover, I am not claiming that the MNC and MNO do not have to draw lines in determining citizenship. They must make these tough decisions. There are legitimate questions regarding cultural appropriation and citizenship within Métis or other Indigenous groups. These are serious issues and have to be addressed by each group.

Furthermore, I am not saying that Indigenous Peoples cannot adopt or adapt useful principles from Canadian courts in advancing self-determination. We are creative people who know how to turn arguments on their head. We have long experiences working with tricksters, and we are aware of how to subvert or overturn challenging situations. Thus, I have often argued that Indigenous Peoples can transform aspects of Canadian law to suit their own purposes.[33] We can use our power to flexibly work to achieve ends that are not intended by those who seek to constrain our freedom. At the same time I have highlighted the dangers involved in taking this course.[34]

Canada has a deeply colonial constitution. It seeks to maintain the fiction that all governing power derives from the Crown.[35] In this light, sometimes, Indigenous use of Canadian law simply deepens colonialism. In my view, the "integral to the distinctive culture test" in the *Van der Peet/Pamajewon/Powley* cases creates Canada's most pernicious limitation on Indigenous Rights. These cases freeze Indigenous identity by reference to the Crown's own expansive flexible powers. They show that the Crown's political breadth and advancement is based upon and contrasted with Indigenous Peoples' diminishment. We must reject the "integral to the distinctive culture" test and turn away from the state on this point. It holds Indigenous polities in past-tense terms and reinforces Canada's overarching claims to define who we are as Indigenous Peoples.[36] This is cultural appropriation. The test is a severe limitation on Indigenous voices.

Therefore, what I am questioning are the grounds on which debate about citizenship and cultural appropriation occurs. I worry when Indigenous communities adopt a colonial lens that gives the state the power to determine Indigeneity based on troubling racialized assumptions. I acknowledge that some groups might be using the *Van der Peet* "integral to a distinctive culture" test without meaning to adopt the decisions' underlying reasoning. Yet this would be a mistake. Ends may be mismatched with means when Métis and other

Indigenous groups challenge other people's claims by using the Supreme Court of Canada's flawed cultural frameworks.[37] It is disturbingly ironic to criticize people for engaging in cultural appropriation while using constitutional logics that marginalize Indigenous Peoples in the broader scheme of things – like limiting their rights by reference to Canadian state power (contact, assertion of Crown sovereignty, or a date of so-called "Crown effective control over Indigenous Peoples"). Surely, there are better grounds than colonialism for working through issues of cultural appropriation.

Similar issues of claims of cultural appropriation appear when addressing citizenship issues among the Qalipu Mi'kmaq of Newfoundland. In 2011 the Qalipu secured recognition as a landless band through an order-in-council pursuant to the Agreement for the Recognition of the Qalipu Mi'kmaq Band. Despite this federal recognition, the Qalipu were rejected by the Mi'kmaq Grand Council, the traditional government of the Mi'kmaq People, and by the Assembly of Nova Scotia Chiefs. They have the right to make this decision, and I want to be clear that I strongly support Mik'maq self-determination. At the same time, as I am arguing, I worry about how self-determination is advanced. Indigenous self-determination is at its strongest when it advances decolonization. Unfortunately, like the Métis example, the *Powley* case looms large in determining who is officially Mi'kmaq and recognized as Indigenous in this dispute.[38]

A points system that draws upon the *Powley* decision's criteria is used to determine who is qualified for membership in the Qalipu Band. Among the measures used to acquire membership points is a "copy of a Newfoundland newspaper article pre-dating the 23 June 2008 signature of the Agreement reporting the participation of the applicant as a member of the Mi'kmaq Group of Indians of Newfoundland in ceremonial, traditional or cultural activities of the Mi'kmaq of Newfoundland."[39] The points system exists because a number roughly equal to one-fifth of Newfoundland's population, or over one hundred thousand people, applied to be members of the Qalipu Band under the 2011 Agreement. If all these applicants were accepted, this would have made the Qalipu by far the largest band in Canada.

The large numbers of applications led the Qalipu and the federal government to reconsider questions related to who was entitled to be founding members of this community. As the parties wrestled with Qalipu citizenship, as noted, they used the Supreme Court of Canada's "integral to a distinctive culture" framework as found in the *Powley* case. Remember, this case freezes rights related to Métis political culture in the time before it came under the effective control of European laws and customs.[40] *Powley* used the *Van der Peet* case as a template and made European law and customs the measure for determining Métis identity constitutional protections.[41] This implies that Métis practices, customs, and traditions that occur after "the imposition of European law and customs" cannot generate constitutional rights from this time forward. Aboriginal rights do not find their source "in a magic moment of European contact, but in the traditional laws and customs of the aboriginal people in question."[42] The Supreme Court of Canada appropriates Métis culture for colonial purposes in the *Powley* decision by allowing the continual transformation of European political and legal culture while simultaneously creating a cut-off date beyond which Métis cultural self-determination cannot grow. There is a troubling irony in using the state's criteria to assert control over membership when these same standards ultimately freeze Indigenous Law and culture in a European dominated framework.

For example, in the case of *Abbott v Canada (AG)* the Federal Court noted that Qalipu membership included "criteria of self-identification as a member of an historic community, acceptance of the individual by that community and aboriginal ancestry established by the Supreme Court of Canada decision in *Powley*."[43] As part of the original Qalipu enrollment process, "applicants were submitting standard form affidavits, with blank spaces to insert names, describing hunting, fishing, and picking berries as maintaining a Mi'kmaq way of life."[44] An Enrollment Appeal Master eventually "determined that standard form affidavits stating simply that an applicant hunts, fishes and picks berries, which are not exclusively Mi'kmaq pursuits, are not determinative of involvement in and acceptance by the Mi'kmaq community."[45] This seems like a reasonable conclusion. As a result, as noted, this led to the negotiation of a supplemental Agreement in 2013, to better determine Qalipu membership criteria. A directive pursuant to the 2013 Agreement was eventually produced to ensure that "[t]he connection that an applicant must show with a Newfoundland community of the Mi'kmaq Group has to be significant in quality and quantity; it must be true, profound and not of recent vintage."[46] In addition, the directive noted: "An applicant must demonstrate strong ties with the Mi'kmaq Group of Indians of Newfoundland that pre-date or were contemporaneous with the signing of the Agreement and continued up to the date of the Recognition Order."[47] The new criteria had residency considerations attached to them. As noted, over 100,000 applications were reassessed in light of the 2013 supplemental Agreement and associated directive. This resulted in 78,632 of those applicants being ineligible for membership in the Qalipu Band.[48]

When Mr. Abbott applied for a review of his rejected reassessment, the Federal Court upheld decisions that turned down his application to be in the category of a "founding member" of the Qalipu Band. The court affirmed the Appeal Master's decision, who wrote that Mr. Abbott's "affidavits are completely silent on the subject of how he [Mr. Abbott] maintains a Mi'kmaq way of life; silent on membership in an organization promoting Mi'kmaq interests; knowledge of Mi'kmaq customs, traditions and beliefs. There is no mention of participation in cultural or religious ceremonies or pursuit of traditional activities. [The applicant] hunts, fishes, and berry picks, but these are pursuits engaged in by thousands of Newfoundland citizens and are not exclusively Mi'kmaq."[49] As a result, the Federal Court found that "Mr. Abbott has failed to establish that the Parties' decision to issue the Directive was tainted by any desire to reduce the number of successful non-resident applicants or to impose unreasonable requirements on them."[50]

Aside from the colonial legal arguments, it may be that the Qalipu Enrollment Committee, Appeal Master, and Federal Court came to the proper conclusion concerning Mr. Abbott's citizenship. I take no issue with the result. In fact, the use of standard form "fill in the blank" applications raises serious concerns about the ease by which someone could appropriate Qalipu cultural identity. However, the issue I am highlighting is how claims of cultural appropriation are addressed using criteria the Canadian state has used to take Indigenous Land and suppress Indigenous governance.

We must not lose sight of the fact that the category of non-Indigenous is the default criteria for who rightfully occupies land and claims governance of this country. Unlike the narrow framing of who is considered Indigenous, the category "non-Indigenous" can grow and does not have to justify its numbers or connection to history to be considered legitimate. This allows the Federal Court to uphold the decision to deny Mr. Abbott citizenship because "[t]he Parties intended when negotiating the AIP [Agreement-in-Principle] to give effect to the group membership criteria set out in the decision of the Supreme Court of Canada in *R v Powley*."[51]

It is important to understand that factually, on the ground, what counted against Mr. Abbott securing recognition as a founding Qalipu member was his move to Ottawa to obtain an engineering degree. The question of non-residency was the most significant strike against Mr. Abbott in his quest to be recognized as Qalipu. Apparently, living in Newfoundland is more Mi'kmaq than securing post-secondary education in territories beyond those traditionally occupied by a community.[52] Despite Qalipu being a landless Indian Band, Mr. Abbott would likely have received more membership points had he lived in Qalipu homelands.

Neither the Qalipu registrars nor the federal government insisted that securing an engineering degree or moving outside Mi'kmaq territory was not integral to distinctive Qalipu culture prior to the arrival of Europeans. Nevertheless, the effect of the Qalipu membership criteria measures Indigeneity by these standards. It assumes someone is more deserving of receiving a higher Indian status if they live in their traditional territory. This result holds, even though the Supreme Court of Canada has decided, in a case called *Corbiere v Canada*,[53] that denying Indigenous people political rights because of residency could be discriminatory.

For example, in the *Corbiere* case, the court wrote:

> Off-reserve band members have important interests in band governance. ... They are co-owners of the band's assets. The reserve, whether they live on or off it, is their and their children's land. The band council represents them as band members to the community at large, in negotiations with the government, and within Aboriginal organizations. Although there are some matters of purely local interest, which do not as directly affect the interests of off-reserve band members, the complete denial to off-reserve members of the right to vote and participate in band governance treats them as less worthy and entitled, not on the merits of their situation, but simply because they live off-reserve. [This assumption] reaches the cultural identity of off-reserve Aboriginals in a stereotypical way. It presumes that Aboriginals living off-reserve are not interested in maintaining meaningful participation in the band or in preserving their cultural identity, and are therefore less deserving members of the band.[54]

From reading the *Corbiere* case one might conclude that deciding who has a higher or lower level of Qalipu status based on residency is discriminatory. Despite this problem, the *Abbott* case concluded that denying Mr. Abbott Founding Member status "was not haphazard" because "[t]he Parties considered the importance placed by the Supreme Court of Canada in *Powley* on the past and ongoing participation in a shared culture and in the customs and traditions of a community."[55]

4. Conclusion

Appropriating Canadian frameworks for patrolling cultural boundaries reinforces the state's appropriation of Indigenous culture. The Canadian state has long attempted to define what an Indigenous community is and define the membership of these communities by reference to blood, ancestry, culture, or other sociologically flat kinds of references. It has done this to marginalize, diminish, assimilate, and extinguish Indigenous communities. Unfortunately, Indigenous Peoples can internalize colonial messages about what it means to be an Indigenous community and be a citizen of such a community. These frameworks exclude or discipline others through a logic which underlies colonialism.

The narrowing of Indigeneity based on attenuated and antiquated markers of belonging is unfortunately a part of contemporary politics. Though generated by Canadian courts, they can be found in some Indigenous reserves, Métis communities, and Indigenous urban landscapes. These artificial markers get passed along and reinforced through populist means using social media-driven algorithms to patrol community belonging using state-derived logics and frameworks.

This chapter has argued that we should be suspicious of how ideas of cultural appropriation are used in public debate in Canada. Since calling attention to cultural appropriation is not always an unalloyed good, we must exercise greater care in how we think about and use this concept. Indigenous Peoples' own laws, which attend to their past, present and future political, cultural, social, and economic aspirations, should be revitalized as part of this work. Those who use the state's frameworks when addressing the unjust appropriation of cultural goods might themselves be generating injustice, bigotry, and discrimination in the process. This is ironic, given that calling attention to cultural appropriation aims at overturning these very harms. This is why this chapter suggests we turn away from the state when discussing issues of cultural appropriation and urges care about how we talk about culture when considering questions of appropriation in Canada and beyond.

NOTES

1 Jennifer Brant, "Cultural Appropriation of Indigenous Peoples in Canada" (7 June 2021), online: *Canadian Encyclopedia* <https://www.thecanadianencyclopedia.ca /en/article/cultural-appropriation-of-indigenous-peoples-in-canada>.

2 For examples, see Maurice Switzer, "Opinion: Indigenous Cultural Police and Joseph Boyden," *Anishinabek News* (5 September 2018), online: <http:// anishinabeknews.ca/2018/09/05/opinion-indigenous-cultural-police-and-joseph -boyden/>; Alexander Narzayan, "White Painter Loses Art Show over Cultural Appropriation Debate," *Newsweek* (5 May 2017), online: <https://www.newsweek .com/cultural-appropriation-outcry-succeeds-cancelling-gallery-show-white -painter-594924>; Adina Bresage, "Inuit Artists Boycott Indigenous Music Awards over Cultural Appropriation," *Star* (27 April 2019), online: <https://www.thestar .com/entertainment/music/2019/04/02/inuit-artists-boycott-indigenous-music -awards-over-cultural-appropriation.html>.

3 Aharon Barak, *Proportionality: Constitutional Rights and Their Limitations* (Cambridge: Cambridge University Press, 2012); Carl Schmitt, *The Crisis of Parliamentary Democracy* (Cambridge, MA: MIT Press, 1988) at 40.

4 For a general discussion of Indigenous research methods discussing these ideas see Margaret Kovach, "Doing Indigenous Methodologies" in Norman K. Denzin & Yvonna S. Lincoln, eds, *The SAGE Handbook of Qualitative Research* 5th ed (London: SAGE, 2018) at 214; Deborah McGregor, "From 'Decolonized' to Reconciliation Research in Canada: Drawing from Indigenous Research Paradigms" (2018) 17:3 ACME 810; Joanne Archibald, *Indigenous Storywork: Educating the Heart, Mind, Body, and Spirit* (Vancouver: UBC Press, 2008) at 11, 140; Cheryl Barlett, "Two-Eyed Seeing and Other Lessons Learned within a Co-learning Journey of Bringing Together Indigenous and Mainstream Knowledges and Ways of Knowing" (2012) 2 Journal of Environmental Studies and Science 331.

5 An excellent discussion of cultural appropriation in the US context is Angela
   R. Riley & Kristen A. Carpenter, "Owning *Red*: A Theory of Indian (Cultural)
   Appropriation" (2016) 94:5 Texas L Rev 859.

6 John Borrows, *Law's Indigenous Ethics* (Toronto: University of Toronto Press,
   2019).

7 See generally Robert Williams Jr., *Linking Arms Together: American Indian Treaty
   Visions of Law and Peace, 1600–1800* (New York: Oxford University Press, 1997).

8 Lindsay Borrows, "Dabaadendiziwin: Practices of Humility in a Multi-Juridical
   Legal Landscape" (2016) 33 Windsor YB Access Just 149.

9 John Borrows, *Freedom and Indigenous Constitutionalism* (Toronto: University of
   Toronto Press, 2016) at 19–49.

10 Linda L. Berger & Kathryn M. Stanchi, *Legal Persuasion: A Rhetorical Approach to
   the Science* (New York: Routledge, 2017).

11 Cambridge Dictionary, "Appropriate," online: <https://dictionary.cambridge.org
   /dictionary/english/appropriate> [Cambridge].

12 John Borrows, "The Durability of Terra Nullius: Tsilhqot'in Nation v British
   Columbia" (2015) 48 UBC Law Review 701.

13 John Borrows, "Sovereignty's Alchemy: An Analysis of *Delgamuukw v British
   Columbia*" (1999) 37 Osgoode Hall Law Journal 537.

14 *R v Van der Peet*, [1996] 2 SCR 507 at para 73 [*Van der Peet*].

15 Cambridge, *supra* note 11.

16 *R v Pamajewon*, 1996 CanLII 161 (SCC), [1996] 2 SCR 821. As the Supreme Court
   of Canada approvingly recorded, at para 29, there "is no evidence to support a
   conclusion that gambling generally or high stakes gambling of the sort in issue
   here, were part of the First Nations' historic cultures and traditions, or an aspect of
   their use of their land."

17 *R v Gladstone*, 1996 CanLII 160 (SCC), [1996] 2 SCR 723.

18 *Van der Peet*, *supra* note 14 at para 60.

19 See Robert J. Miller, Jacinta Ruru, Larissa Behrendt & Tracey Lindberg, *Discovering
   Indigenous Lands: The Doctrine of Discovery in the English Colonies* (Oxford:
   Oxford University Press, 2010); Lindsay G. Robertson, *Conquest by Law: How the
   Discovery of America Dispossessed Indigenous Peoples of Their Lands* (New York:
   Oxford University Press, 2007).

20 Raymond Orr & Yancey Orr, "Compositional Stasis and Flexibility in American
   Indian Tribes" (2021) 68:2 Ethnohistory 191.

21 Sarah Hagi, "Cancel Culture Is Not Real – At Least Not in the Way People Think,"
   Time Magazine (21 November 2019), online: <https://time.com/5735403/cancel
   -culture-is-not-real/>.

22 Merriam-Webster Dictionary, "Cancel," online: <https://www.merriam-webster
   .com/dictionary/cancel>.

23 See generally James Young & Conrad Brunk, eds, *The Ethics of Cultural
   Appropriation* (West Sussex, UK: Blackwell Publishing, 2012).

24 Daryl Leroux, *Distorted Descent: White Claims to Indigenous Identity* (Winnipeg: University of Manitoba Press, 2019).

25 See Michel Bouchard, Sebastien Malette & Guillaume Marcotte, *Bois-Brûlés: The Untold Story of the Métis of Western Québec* (Vancouver: UBC Press, 2020); Chris Anderson, *"Métis": Race, Recognition, and the Struggle for Indigenous Peoplehood* (Vancouver: UBC Press, 2015); Adam Gaudry & Darryl Leroux, "White Settler Revisionism and Making Métis Everywhere: The Evocation of Métissage in Quebec and Nova Scotia" (2018) 3:1 Critical Ethnic Studies 116.

26 Canadian Press, "Métis Leaders Raise Concerns about National Council, Call for Reform," *CBC* (26 January 2020), online: <https://www.cbc.ca/news/canada /manitoba/metis-national-council-concerns-reform-1.5441080>.

27 *Ibid.*

28 Métis National Council Press Release, "Métis Nation Citizenship – The Real Issue," *Newswire* (20 January 2020), online: <https://www.newswire.ca/news-releases/metis -nation-citizenship-the-real-issue-827254370.html>.

29 *Ibid.*

30 Métis National Council, "Métis Nation Citizenship," online: *Métis Nation* <https:// www2.metisnation.ca/about/citizenship/>.

31 *Ibid.* See *R v Powley*, [2003] 2 S.C.R. 207 [*Powley*].

32 *Powley, ibid* at paras 37, 38, 43, 44.

33 Canada's written and unwritten constitution can be transformed to advance broader Indigenous aspirations: John Borrows, *Recovering Canada: The Resurgence of Canadian Law* (Toronto: University of Toronto Press, 2002); John Borrows, *Canada's Indigenous Constitution* (Toronto: University of Toronto Press, 2010); John Borrows, *Freedom and Indigenous Constitutionalism* (Toronto: University of Toronto Press, 2016).

34 John Borrows, "The Trickster: Integral to a Distinctive Legal Culture" (1997) 8:2 Constitutional Forum 27 at 32.

35 John Borrows, "Canada's Colonial Constitution" in John Borrows & Michael Coyle, eds, *The Right Relationship: Reimagining the Implementation of Historical Treaties* (Toronto: University of Toronto Press, 2017) at 17.

36 John Borrows, *Indigenous Law and Governance: Challenging Pre-contact and Post-contact Distinctions in Canadian Constitutional Law* (Montréal: Les Éditions Thémis, 2017).

37 Kerry Sloan effectively critiques the *Powley* case's bias against Métis people in "Always Coming Home: Metis Legal Understandings and Community and Territory" (2016) 33:1 Windsor YB Access Just 125.

38 Supplemental Agreement Between the Federation of Newfoundland Indians, a body corporate under the laws of Newfoundland and Labrador, with its head office at 3 Church Street, Corner Brook, Newfoundland and Labrador, A2H 2Z4, and Her Majesty the Queen in Right of Canada, as represented by the Minister of Indian Affairs and Northern Development, online: <http://qalipu.ca/qalipu/wp-content /uploads/2016/11/Supplemental_Agreement.pdf>.

39 *Ibid.*
40 *Powley, supra* note 31 at para 37.
41 *Ibid* at paras 18, 37.
42 *Van der Peet, supra* note 14 at para 247 (McLachlin J, dissenting).
43 *Abbott v Canada (Attorney General)*, 2019 FC 1302 (CanLII) [*Abbott*].
44 *Ibid* at para 41.
45 *Ibid* at para 44.
46 *Ibid* at para 51.
47 *Ibid.*
48 *Ibid* at para 77.
49 *Ibid* at para 130.
50 *Ibid* 145.
51 *Ibid* at para 150.
52 *Ibid* at para 157–62.
53 *Corbiere v Canada (Minister of Indian and Northern Affairs)*, [1999] 2 SCR 203.
54 *Ibid* at para 18.
55 *Abbott, supra* note 43 at para 172.

10 Writing on Indigenous Rights from a Non-Indigenous Perspective

ROBERT HAMILTON

On the northern edge of Miramichi Bay, the wind blows onto the shore not so much in gusts as in a consistent push, as if a giant standing in the Bay were in the midst of a long, steady exhale onto the shore. If you look to the east, the sea and sky mix together like the fresh and salt water in the Miramichi River's estuary some thirty kilometres to the south-west. Look a little southward, to the right, and you'll see Portage Island, a protected refuge for migrating shore birds. The eastern edge of the island is eroding, the small place that has been set aside for these birds, who once thrived all along these shores, slowly wasting away. They are powerless to protect the small home they have left in the face of encroachments that are beyond their control. A little farther to the right, past Fox Island and Bay du Vin Island, almost directly to the south, is the mouth of the Bay du Vin River. It's too small to see from the northern shore. If you were there, though, and if a waning tide hadn't left the waters too shallow, you could jump off the Highway 117 bridge into the warm, salty estuary. From Bay du Vin, the lights from the houses and streetlights on the north shore are visible at night. On the north side sits the Esgenoôpetitj, or Burnt Church, First Nation. A Mi'kmaq First Nation of just under two thousand people on New Brunswick's north-eastern coast, it is known to most Canadians, and even most New Brunswickers, only because of the lobster fishing conflict there that followed the Supreme Court's recognition of Mi'kmaw treaty fishing rights in 1999. Fewer still know that Esgenoôpetitj is in the Mi'kmaw district of Siknikt, one of seven districts in the traditional territory of the Mi'kmaq, a territory which spans present-day Nova Scotia and Prince Edward Island, eastern New Brunswick, and the Gaspé Peninsula.

Bay du Vin is part cottage country, part fishing community. My understanding of the many complex relationships and ideas that make the conceptual and physical crossing of the Miramichi Bay so much more challenging than it might appear at first glance was sharpened one night at a cottage on Bay du Vin when I asked the cottage's owner, my friend's mother, if the lights across the

Bay were from Burnt Church. I had a sense of the location of the community, having visited it a couple of years before. She was incredulous that I, a middle-class white kid from the capital city of Fredericton – a staid government and university town – had been to Burnt Church: "What were *you* doing *there*?" I think back to this now when I get a similar question, one that admittedly might seem unrelated at first glance: "Do you have Indigenous ancestry?" This question normally comes in a law school or at an academic conference, someone wondering why I would be involved in Indigenous Rights work. In both questions is an underlying sense that a line between groups has been transgressed in a way that, if not unacceptable, is at least curious: what would a white kid being doing on an Indian reserve? Why would a white scholar do Indigenous Rights work? I use the term "white" intentionally here, not to solidify distinctions based on race, but because it is central to the logic that lies below the questions. The presumption is that there must be some justification: there is an *us* and *them*, to be sure, and to be among or work with *them* is something that requires explanation.

It is how consideration of these issues relates to my work as a legal academic that I want to explore here. The workshop this chapter emerged from was first framed as being about cultural appropriation and Indigenous voice. It morphed through the two days of conversation to include reflections on why we engage in this work at all. Our personal stories were understood as centrally relevant to how we choose to engage in this area; how we choose to use our voices, where we draw on the voices of others and in what ways, and what animates this engagement were all understood as being informed by our experiences. And so, I come back to the question: "What were *you* doing *there*?"

New Brunswick in the 1990s

Though the explanation for any given event or circumstance is always replete with contingencies that complicate any neat narrative one might establish after the fact, there are a couple of events that caused me to be *there* (and, as a result, made my being *here* – as a professor of Aboriginal law at the University of Calgary Faculty of Law – must more likely). New Brunswick in the 1990s saw frequent and substantial Mi'kmaq and Wolastoqey (Maliseet) activism. I was thirteen when Thomas Peter Paul, a Mi'kmaw man from the Pabineau First Nation, was acquitted on charges of unlawfully taking timber from Crown lands. In upholding the acquittal at the New Brunswick Court of Queen's Bench, Justice Turnbull held that the Indigenous signatories to the 1725/26 treaties, the Mi'kmaq and Wolastoqey, had a treaty-protected right to land in the province. Of Crown land, Justice Turnbull wrote: "there are several ways one could describe the status of rights in Crown land. A legally correct way would be to consider Crown lands as reserved for Indians."[1] And, perhaps most

Sign posted by a Wolastoqey logging company

evocatively, "[t]he trees on Crown land are Indian trees."[2] These are remarkable statements, confirming important aspects of the Indigenous understandings of the nature of the Peace and Friendship treaty relationship. The decision provided an opportunity for much needed economic activity, and many Mi'kmaw and Wolastoqey entrepreneurs and woodsmen were quick to act. Cutting sites popped up on "Crown" land in several locations.

This was an unwelcome development for the government and the influential forestry industry. While the case was on appeal in the New Brunswick Court of Appeal, the government sought to prevent logging; the loggers, excited that long-standing legal restrictions had been lifted and anxious to take advantage of the economic opportunities this created, were not willing to pause while awaiting the results of the appeal. My father had close friends among the Wolastoqey loggers, and he spent time documenting the ensuing conflict on video. This was my introduction to "Aboriginal Rights": I "met" the organizers, activists, and loggers through the camera. It became more tangible when we joined a crowd of hundreds gathered outside the Entertainment Centre and Bingo Hall at the St. Mary's First Nation for a rally. We joined a convoy that drove through Fredericton and then about an hour to a parcel of Crown land where loggers began to fell trees. The six singers on the big drum created an indelible soundtrack, by turns uplifting and haunting, as their songs were interspersed with the sounds of chainsaws and cheering crowds as trees came down. There was a sense of collective action and optimism. People were proud. And then Justice Turnbull's decision got overturned at the Court of Appeal.

Next came the lobster fishing dispute. Again, a hard-won court victory, this time at the Supreme Court of Canada. In the *Marshall* decision, the court recognized that Indigenous signatories to the 1760–1 Treaty have a right to a limited commercial fishery.[3] As in the period following the *Thomas Peter Paul* decision, fishers seized the opportunity. A community-run lobster fishery quickly developed in Esgenoôpetitj, a fishery violently opposed by non-Indigenous fishermen around Miramichi Bay and by the Department of Fisheries and Oceans (DFO). One scene, in particular, drew national attention as a DFO boat swamped and sunk a small Mi'kmaw skiff, its occupants leaping into the Miramichi Bay just at the moment of the collision. More so than in the Crown lands dispute, here we saw a militarized response like that which has unfortunately been seen in so many instances across the country. Once again, my father was there, filming. He would come home every couple of weeks, and I would watch the footage. On a couple of occasions, he took my brother and me with him. This is how *I* came to be *there*.

Finding Voice(s)

These experiences observing government responses to Indigenous attempts to lift themselves and their communities up through exercising rights and collective action made me aware of some of the injustices that pervade our legal and political structures. Earlier, at George Street Junior High School, I was introduced to the existence of racism and prejudice; they pervaded the informal politics of the student body and disabused any reasonable observer of the notion – easily acquired if raised in a nearly all-white suburb of a small Canadian city – that racism was a thing that happened in other places, at other times. With the Crown lands and lobster fishing disputes, I made the connection between what I saw at school – the fights, the taunts, the casual racism – and the way society was structured. I learned later of the history of mistreatment of Indigenous Peoples and the overwhelming statistics that speak to the effects of historical and ongoing marginalization, but it was those early impressions – of disenfranchisement, exclusion, exploitation, and prejudice – that stuck with me. I realize that, as an explanation for my engagement with Indigenous Rights issues, this framing may have an air of the *White Man's Burden* to it. It is not meant to evoke that, nor is it meant to overlook what a privileged position I was in to learn about racism from the outside rather than having a working knowledge of its effects for my entire life as a victim of it. The issue, for me, is one of implication; it is about a realization of being implicated in something unjust. This implication carries obligations to speak and act against injustice and oppression. There is a cost to remaining silent, a cost that has caused me to try to find a voice.

But, how to do that? How to speak in a meaningful way? How to avoid doing more harm than good? How can I answer these questions when I have not suffered any of the disadvantages of oppression and have, in fact, benefited considerably from it? My namesake arrived in the Miramichi – unceded Mi'kmaw territory – in about 1829, and on September 12 of that year purchased one half of "Lot 2" in Upper Halcomb on the Little Southwest Miramichi River, no more than an hour's drive on today's roads from Burnt Church. My family tree includes New England planters who migrated to Nova Scotia in the 1760s to receive free farm land vacated through the expulsion of the Acadians, Loyalists who were granted free land throughout the lower Wolastoq (Saint John) River valley, a family who received land – which they were never able to pay for – under a farm settlement program for veterans of the First World War, and Irish and Acadians who settled on New Brunswick's north shores, not far from the Pabineau First Nation that Thomas Peter Paul called home. Structural inequalities ever since have made it easier for me to get jobs and university degrees and made it less likely that missteps would define my future. The intergenerational benefits of being "propertied" are well known. I own property now in unceded Wolastoqey territory, land once freely granted to a Loyalist settler in violation of the treaty promise that no lands would be settled without the prior consent of the Wolastoqey.

In thinking through these questions of how and where to engage in light of my position, I'm reminded of a speech that Stokely Carmichael (as he was then known) gave at UC Berkeley in 1966. Carmichael argued:

In order to understand white supremacy we must dismiss the fallacious notion that white people can give anybody his freedom. A man is born free. You may enslave a man after he is born free, and that is in fact what this country does. It enslaves blacks after they're born. *The only thing white people can do is stop denying black people their freedom.*

I maintain that every civil rights bill in this country was passed for white people, not for black people. For example, I am black. I know that. I also know that while I am black I am a human being. Therefore I have the right to go into any public place. White people don't know that. Every time I tried to go into a public place they stopped me. So some boys had to write a bill to tell that white man, "He's a human being; don't stop him." That bill was for the white man, not for me. I knew I could vote all the time and that it wasn't a privilege but my right. Every time I tried I was shot, killed or jailed, beaten or economically deprived. So somebody had to write a bill to tell white people, "When a black man comes to vote, don't bother him." That bill was for white people. I know I can live anyplace I want to live. It is white people across this country who are incapable of allowing me to live where I want. You need a civil rights bill, not me. The failure of the civil rights bill isn't because of Black Power or because of the Student Nonviolent Coordinating

Committee or because of the rebellions that are occurring in the major cities. *That failure is due to the white's incapacity to deal with their own problems inside their own communities.*[4] [emphasis mine]

This is a brilliant and subversive shift in perspective that challenges the foundations of the hegemonic liberal rights discourse and undermines the (too often hypocritical) moral claims of the dominant society. Carmichael understood that allowing dominant white society to construe civil rights as being *given* to African Americans only served to cement existing power structures and unjust social relations by maintaining the dominant society in its role as the ultimate arbiter, not only of the rights framework, but of the structure of political, economic, and human relations more broadly. As Carmichael saw, when a dominant group purports to recognize the rights of a marginalized group, and in so doing construes itself as "allowing" that marginalized group to engage in certain activities pursuant to those rights, the dominant group reserves for itself the political and legal power to shape and control the recognition and exercise of rights. This risks allowing the dominant society to absolve itself of wrongdoing while constraining the possibilities for structural change.

In the context of Indigenous Peoples in Canada, adopting this perspective means that rights, such as those recognized in s.35 of the *Constitution Act, 1982* are not *granted to* Indigenous Peoples: they are limitations placed on non-Indigenous peoples. When Donald Marshall Jr. fished and sold 463 pounds of eels for $787.10 in Pomquet Harbour, Nova Scotia, on 24 August 1993, *he knew* he had a treaty-protected right to fish and sell those eels. It was the DFO who needed to be told to leave him alone. Section 35, in important respects, *is for them.* The conflict at Esgenoôpetitj, and the many others like it, can be viewed through this lens. In that instance, the Supreme Court of Canada confirmed a treaty-protected right to fish for limited commercial purposes: the DFO continued to enforce, with considerable violence, their interpretation of the law based on their own understanding of how much s.35 limited their behaviour. Section 35 clearly placed a limit on the DFO; it said: "when those people are fishing, leave them alone." The DFO insisted, "we can still tell them when and how much to fish." Whose behaviour do Aboriginal Rights seek to regulate? When s.35 says that Aboriginal and Treaty Rights are "affirmed," it affirms what Indigenous Peoples have been asserting all along. It is not asking them to change their behaviour; rather, it is constraining state actors. This is not meant to undermine the work that Indigenous Peoples put into having s.35 written into the Constitution, nor is it meant to suggest that s.35 cannot be a site for the production of generative intersocietal laws and norms. Rather, it is meant to highlight an orientation, a way of seeing what state law is and is not doing.

What does this mean for a non-Indigenous legal academic? It raises two immediate issues: objectives and audience. What ought the objectives of a legal academic working in Indigenous Rights be? Non-Indigenous academics should be aware that their goal – if they want to work toward decolonization, economic justice, and emancipation – is first the modification of *non-Indigenous* behaviour. It is not about identifying pathologies or shortcomings of the marginalized. My commentary, therefore, is directed toward the dominant society: they are the primary audience, and it is their (our) behaviour that most concerns me. The specific objective is to clear the ground, so the varied exercises of Indigenous resistance, revitalization, and resurgence can take hold, free from undue constraint, transforming their communities and nations while transforming our shared political and legal frameworks in the process. Only when we get to this latter transformation – which some might label reconciliation – can the process become more dialogical.[5]

What does that look like in practice? We can start by saying what it does not involve: it is not about prioritizing normative or evaluative judgments about Indigenous modes of resistance, revitalization, and resurgence. The best ways to structure Indigenous communities internally and in relation to the state, the appropriate theoretical models to guide political action, the role of direct action, and, increasingly, the meaning of terms such as "reconciliation," "resurgence," and "Indigenous Law" are all subject to intense debate, contestation, and negotiation. Some Indigenous Peoples will seek a renewed emphasis on tradition, some more participation in a market economy; some will use direct action, some will pursue litigation; some will be trappers, some artists, some accountants. Some Indigenous Nations strive for greater separation from Canada, some for greater integration. Some seek complicated mixtures of many of these things as they navigate the demands of contemporary society and complicated questions of identity and belonging, all under the weight of entrenched bureaucratic colonial control. It is not, as I see it, the role of the non-Indigenous academic (or journalist, politician, business leader, or citizen) to attempt to impose their own views on these issues. Self-determination means precisely that: the freedom to determine a course of action according to one's own values. What this will lead to in specific cases is variable and unpredictable: the concern is to recognize agency, not police how it is exercised.

This is not – as some might suggest – to adopt a lazy relativism. It is not to say that anything that an Indigenous person or group does is acceptable merely because they are Indigenous. Such a position would be patronizing. Indigenous people are people, for better and for worse, and the decisions they take can be challenged. My suggestion, however, is that non-Indigenous thinkers not prioritize this by focusing our energy on these issues. It may well be that, acting according to their own freedom and values, Indigenous communities adopt practices that are profoundly illiberal or inhumane and are deserving of condemnation. Bracketing for a moment the fact that many of these pathologies are induced by colonialism – take, for example, the abuse of custom elections codes to establish "chiefs for life" in some places or contests over membership in some communities – these situations will, in my assessment, be exceedingly rare. In almost all cases the differences will be between approaches that all fall within a reasonable range of outcomes, even if we may disagree with the approach on the basis of our own values, perspectives, and understandings. In these instances, we might take Carmichael's advice that the dominant society must first "deal with their own problems inside their own communities." Put another way, there are traits of Canadian society that make meaningful forms of reconciliation and resurgence difficult to achieve. Ongoing colonialism makes it difficult for Indigenous Peoples and people to thrive. That ought to be the first and primary concern.

But what does this look like? And, importantly for the context of this collection, how and where can Indigenous voices be drawn on in this project? Further, how can such an admonition be understood in the context of deeply entangled relationships – between both groups and individuals – and the need to create shared means of healthy co-existence? Carmichael's position takes us only so far unless we are prepared to accept an "us" and "them" perspective, when in practice Indigenous Peoples and non-Indigenous peoples overlap in complicated relationships of interdependence, oppression, cultural sharing (and appropriation), and reciprocity. Yet, it remains the case that state law and many processes it permits and facilitates have engrained colonial practices that must be overcome and that the responsibility for this lies with non-Indigenous Canadians in important respects. In the context of legal scholarship, this means identifying those aspects of the law which perpetuate unjust relations and exploitation. Where is the law stopping people from exercising their human rights, in the case of Indigenous Peoples their rights of internal self-determination? Where is the law undermining freedom and dignity for Indigenous individuals and collectives? The contributors and editors of this collection have done an incredible amount of work interrogating and critiquing Canadian law with these types of questions in mind.

Of course, people will have a wide range of opinions about how this is best achieved, opinions based on their own values, learning, and experiences. Different conceptions of liberalism, constitutionalism, economic development, capitalism, rights, social justice, the meaning and possibilities of law, and the role of the state – to name only a few of the many hinges upon which there will be substantial disagreement – will all inform distinct views on how Indigenous self-determination and freedom can best be achieved. Indeed, the meaning of self-determination will itself be subject to ongoing debate and negotiation and will change over time. These differences will shape what legal mechanisms one believes will best help Indigenous Peoples reach their goals and what aspects of state law must be modified to that end.

Yet, we must be careful here: it can be a very fine line between advocating for the change we would like to see and advocating space for Indigenous Peoples to make their own decisions. To take one example, a person may think that Indigenous communities would be best served by capitalizing on the desire of governments and corporations to build pipelines through their territories. Such developments might bring jobs and royalties that could help the nation provide services to its citizens and improve their standard of living. The distinction I want to emphasize is between holding that belief (and advocating for it if one feels the need) and arguing that Canadian law ought to allow such pipelines to be built even over the objections of the concerned Indigenous parties. This latter view seems always to be grounded, at least implicitly, in a belief that it would benefit the Indigenous Peoples in question (regardless of whether they believe that to be the case), that their rights can be legitimately set off against the needs of the "broader society," or both. There is a perceptible and crucial difference between arguments outlining perceived benefits of a resource development project for Indigenous Peoples and others, and arguments in favour of a legal regime that would allow those perceived benefits to be imposed against the wishes of Indigenous Peoples. The former, along with articles that seek to explain the current state of state law in respect of such developments as clearly as possible, seem to me to be well within the domain of legal academics. The latter risk denying freedom rather than promoting it. Politics – which is what these types of disputes are about – ought to be grounded in persuasion; the impulse to move to compulsion should be resisted. Those who promote the view that Indigenous Peoples *ought not* to have the freedom to make political determinations about what occurs in their territories risk using the law as a tool of compulsion to support their own political positions.

To return to the questions of objective and audience, then, as a non-Indigenous legal academic working in this field, I focus on how the Canadian legal system can, to the greatest extent possible, stop denying Indigenous freedom. The audience in this is the one Canadian law is being written *for*, in the sense of Carmichael's orientation. Indigenous Peoples should never be put in the positions of supplicants, asking the dominant society for recognition.[6] Rather, the focus of non-Indigenous thinkers, writers, and activists ought to be how to best get Canadian law out of the way, to clear the Canadian legal order of its most pronounced colonial functions, so that it inhibits Indigenous self-determination to the least extent possible.

Of course, this does not mean that it is a one-way dialogue. Listening is crucial. Dialogue is essential. To understand how we must modify behaviour, we must clearly understand how that behaviour is impacting people. While it is crucial to understand the impacts of colonialism from Indigenous perspectives, we have to be attentive to what we ask of Indigenous Peoples in two important senses. First, they shouldn't carry the weight of telling us, as Carmichael would have it, how to deal with our own problems inside our communities; if we continue to support laws and policies that perpetuate the dispossession of lands and resources, that is a pathology of the non-Indigenous community. If we continue to accept what ought to be shocking statistics regarding Indigenous representation in prisons and child welfare systems, comparatively low educational outcomes, high rates of suicide, and poor health outcomes relative to the rest of society, it is a pathology of the non-Indigenous community. This is not to say that Indigenous communities have no role to play in remedying and responding to these harms. It is only to say that non-Indigenous communities must focus on their own contribution. We cannot place on Indigenous Peoples alone the weight for explaining how and why colonialism is harmful and how it can be overcome.

Second, non-Indigenous peoples must listen carefully and not react defensively and in a way that insists Indigenous resistance to encroachments on their freedom and dignity be expressed in only a limited range of palatable ways. As Robert Jago has written in response to an outcry among many established Canadian media figures alleging that he had "crossed a line" in his response to a Conrad Black missive, Indigenous Peoples should never be put in a position of having to justify their existence or humanity.[7] Jago's argument runs this way: too often, people from a dominant social group will try to circumscribe the ways in which the oppressed respond to their oppression. They will demand that responses be "civil," be couched in legal language, and accept certain givens about the relationship. But, Jago says:

> [Consider] what it feels like to have people in the press say that it is my job as a First Nations person and sometime writer, to reply civilly to something so powerfully uncivil. The impact you have on me – and I think many other First Nations people – every time you tell us to debate the worth of our race, is to make us feel subhuman. The value of First Nations people as humans should never be open to debate. To say that I have a duty to reply to these claims of Black's requires you to make a premise out of his conclusion – that our humanity is debatable. I will not debate the humanity of First Nations people with anyone. I will not defend it, I will not disprove those people that say we don't belong in this world, I will not ever again. It is not an open question, and no matter how florid the text that surrounds the proposition, it is never civil. These are people who ... have taken it upon themselves to talk down to minorities, tell us how to behave, and direct us to what you consider to be more effective forms of protest. But effective for whom is an open question.[8]

For the purposes of a legal academic or lawyer, the point is crucial: when we ask an Indigenous person to "defend" a given legal position, what is it that we are putting up for debate? When we ask them to engage with the legal system, what are we asking of them? Take, for example, the fact that Indigenous Peoples must go into court to prove their rights. Recall the nature of the *Van der Peet* test,[9] which only protects as rights those activities that the court deems so central to an Indigenous

Peoples' existence that the group would *be other than they are* without being able to engage in them; they would cease to exist as a distinct and identifiable people if they could no longer practice the activity in question. Aboriginal Rights, that is, are framed as protecting activities that are *constitutive of* Indigenous culture and identity. What position are Indigenous Peoples put in when we deny the existence of these rights, demand that they take onerous and costly steps to prove them, and then seek to justify the "infringement" of those that are proven? When we hold that such rights are only afforded the diminished procedural protections of "consultation" so long as they remain merely "asserted"? When we argue in favour of legal positions that challenge the existence of Indigenous Peoples *as peoples*, what exactly is it that we are putting up for debate? We should clearly identify what is being debated and how past patterns of oppression shape our understandings of what is at issue. When taking up legal or academic arguments that feel "neutral," "abstract," or "academic," we should think carefully about what responding to those arguments asks of others.

Again, what strikes me as foundational to understanding this is the ability to listen and to accept that, whatever expertise one might have, Indigenous Peoples have the most direct knowledge about the impacts of law on Indigenous Peoples. As Mi'kmaw poet Rita Joe writes, "we are the ones who know about ourselves."[10] A recognition of this requires two things. First, it demands a level of humility on behalf of non-Indigenous people about what we know and don't know. It bears repeating that this is not to say that we ought to accept as true without question anything an Indigenous person tells us: the diversity of opinions among Indigenous Peoples would quickly show the absurdity of any such position. Rather, it is to say that we should listen carefully and resist the impulse to "correct" or challenge a perspective shared with us until we have taken the time to carefully consider, not only the perspective, but the reasons why it may seem troubling or wrong to us or make us uncomfortable. We have to listen deeply and be prepared to allow new perspectives to cause us to see familiar things in different ways.

The second thing that this recognition requires is that we allow the process of critiquing and challenging Canadian law – of seeing where and how it undermines freedom and dignity and ought to be reformed – to be guided by Indigenous voices. Accepting that we ought to be guided by Indigenous voices and perspectives on legal issues that pertain directly to them, we need to consider how to do this in an appropriate way. There is a caution to note here at the outset, which is that we have to be careful not to emphasize only those Indigenous voices that agree with our own prior beliefs. This is easier said than done: the diversity within Indigenous communities means that one will always be prioritizing, amplifying some voices at the expense of others. We will find most persuasive those arguments and perspectives that align with our own. What strikes me as central is that, while we may well amplify Indigenous voices that accord with our own outlook, we must be careful not to cast the others aside or pretend they don't exist. This is particularly true if our disagreement is based on essentialized conceptions of Indigenous identity – because they don't fit within a mold of what we consider authentic Indigeneity. There are, for example, a diverse range of Indigenous voices and perspectives concerning the several pipelines being built in the country. While we may well find some voices more apposite than others in arguing for Indigenous self-determination, we should be careful not to sideline those voices whose conclusions we disagree with: it is important, for example, to acknowledge the deep and complicated divisions in Wet'suwet'en society about the Coastal GasLink pipeline and, while we may find one "side" of the debate more persuasive than the other, we must be careful not to amplify that side because it supports our own views about the pipeline rather than because it is an expression of self-determination.[11] Indigenous self-determination should be defended as good in and of itself and as a precondition to healthy Indigenous-settler relations, not as instrumental to the goals of an environmentalist group or mining company.

We have to ensure that we engage not with Indigenous voice, but with a plurality of Indigenous voices, recognizing the historical and cultural distinctiveness between Indigenous Peoples and the complex diversity of Indigenous people. Some – admittedly not all – concerns with cultural appropriation can be addressed this way: there is no risk of appropriating a monolithic Indigenous voice, as no such voice exists. Distinct Indigenous Peoples have stories, songs, artwork, and so on that may well be inappropriate for use by outsiders or in certain contexts. This can only be ascertained through engagement and dialogue with those specific people.

I want to end, then, where I began: "What were *you* doing *there*?" "Do you have Indigenous ancestry?" In these questions I read an imperative to remain separate and apart. Engaging in this work in a meaningful way means finding ways to live and work together, to accept both deep entanglements and mutual autonomy. It means working against an expectation that *you* not be *there* and, instead, finding respectful ways to develop processes of reconciliation with Indigenous Peoples. This requires focusing on state law and its colonial traits so that space can be made for Indigenous revitalization without interference, but it also requires working to undermine the premises in the two questions – that it is curious for *me* to be *there*. When that no longer requires an explanation, we will have made significant progress.

NOTES

1 *R v Paul (T.P.)*, 1997 CanLII 17799 (NB QB) at para 70.
2 *Ibid.*
3 *R v Marshall*, [1999] 3 SCR 456.

4 Stokley Carmichael, "Black Power" (1966), online: *Black Past* <https://www
.blackpast.org/african-american-history/speeches-african-american-history/1966
-stokely-carmichael-black-power/>.

5 I have used a few terms here – resurgence, revitalization, and reconciliation – that
have contested meanings in the literature and in practice. For an overview of the
varied meanings and the importance of recognizing these concepts as existing on
a contested terrain, see John Borrows and James Tully's introduction in Michael
Asch, John Borrows, & James Tully, eds, *Resurgence and Reconciliation: Indigenous-
Settler Relations and Earth Teachings* (Toronto: University of Toronto Press, 2018).

6 I think this holds regardless of where we sit on critiques of the "politics of
recognition" (see e.g., Glen Coulthard, *Red Skin, White Masks: Rejecting the
Colonial Politics of Recognition* (Minneapolis: University of Minnesota Press, 2014);
Leanne Betasamosake Simpson, *As We Have Always Done: Indigenous Freedom
through Radical Resistance* (Minneapolis: University of Minnesota Press, 2017)
at 175–89 [Simpson]), or what model or framework of resurgence (e.g., fervently
separatist or conciliatory in orientation) we adopt.

7 Robert Jago, "In Defence of Ad Hominem" CANADALAND (28 September 2017),
online: <https://www.canadalandshow.com/in-defence-of-ad-hominem/>.

8 *Ibid.* Leanne Betasamosake Simpson forcefully makes a similar point in the
context of a discussion about the impact of shame and how colonialism causes
Indigenous Peoples to carry and feel shame. She writes, "the primary message in
[negative] stereotypes is *you are wrong*, not even *you've done something wrong* but
you are wrong ... The impact of being immersed for several generations now in
continual, daily messages to varying degree of *you are wrong* is that individually
and collectively we carry large amounts of shame inside of us." Simpson, *supra* note
6 at 186.

9 *R v Van der Peet*, [1996] 2 SCR 507, at paras 55–9.

10 Rita Joe, *Song of Rita Joe: Autobiography of a Mi'kmaq Poet* (Charlottetown:
Ragweed Press, 1999) at 96.

11 The divisions in Wet'suwet'en society over the development of the Coastal
Gaslink pipeline were made highly visible when some Wet'suwet'en protested the
development of the pipeline through direct action and were forcibly removed
from the pipeline's path by the Royal Canadian Mounted Police. Of course, all
Indigenous communities, like all political communities, have a range of opinions
and perspectives about controversial issues. In this case the divisions were
highlighted in large part because the issue brought to the fore divisions between
traditional governance and governance bodies established under the *Indian Act*.
Further, these divisions and differences of opinion were emphasized by those
outside the community, frequently seeking to delegitimize the direct action by
pointing to divided opinion in the community or to justify the opposition by
arguing that those opposed to the project represented the traditional authority
structures in the Nation and were therefore more legitimate than the colonially

imposed *Indian Act* governance bodies, most of which supported the project. In each case, the divisions that are present in many Nations were brought into sharp relief in the context of a highly charged political environment. For commentary and legal analysis see: Kate Gunn & Bruce McIvor, *Reconciliation on Trial: Wet'suwet'en, Aboriginal Title, and the Rule of Law* (Vancouver: First Peoples Law, 2020), online: <https://www.firstpeopleslaw.com/public-education/publications>.

11 Guided by Voices? Perspective and Pluralism in the Constitutional Order

JOSHUA BEN DAVID NICHOLS

The cause of Indigenous self-determination is one species of the larger project of human freedom, and so it is a project that can be helpfully taken up from an endless variety of perspectives.[1] The struggle for freedom on Turtle Island has always been one of a strange multiplicity of alliances and kinship relations that do not neatly break down into the seemingly discreet categories of Aboriginal and non-Aboriginal.[2] If we fail to take this into account and opt for the simplistic Aboriginal/non-Aboriginal (which operates much like member/alien or friend/enemy) distinction, then we are quickly drawn back into the darker tradition of Western political thought with its slogan of freedom for some and fear of the many (Hobbes, Mill, Kant, etc.). This world view skips over the factual plurality and diversity of everyday human relations and presents a government that can speak with a single voice and unilaterally determine its responsibility to those outside (and often within) its limits. If we do not want to accept this as the foundation for Aboriginal constitutionalism, then we need to engage in the far more difficult work of relating who is speaking to what they are saying.

Part of that challenge in Canada is to carefully consider how the courts are defining who "Aboriginal peoples" are in terms of the *Constitution Act, 1982*. I think this requires a more critical assessment, precisely because the idea that the courts, or for that matter the Crown, are able to legally define who is or is not Aboriginal directly contradicts the most basic implications of the right of self-determination; namely, the right to determine membership internally. While many have attempted to evade this legal definition by resorting to the Aboriginal/Indigenous distinction, I believe that this concedes too much ground, as it seems to imply that the term "Aboriginal Peoples" can be externally defined whereas "Indigenous Peoples" cannot. In other words, this concession implies that "Aboriginal Peoples" are a "cultural minority" with a species of Charter-like rights. I maintain that this is only *one possible interpretation* of the *Constitution Act, 1982*, and it is one that is inconsistent with both the history of Canada and the fundamental assumptions of its constitutional order. The simple fact is that the right of self-determination applies to "Aboriginal peoples" in s. 35(2) of the *Constitution Act, 1982,* and this right only makes sense if it allows groups to determine their own membership. In this chapter I will start by exploring what the phrase "Aboriginal perspective" means in Canadian constitutional law and what these ways of understanding it imply. I then conclude with some more general reflections on how pluralism interacts with our common understandings of perspective and identity.

Interrogating the "Aboriginal Perspective"

What does the phrase "Aboriginal perspective" mean? This question will doubt-lessly strike some as being so obvious that we can either respond by saying that it refers to "the perspective of Aboriginal Peoples" or simply assume that our interlocutor is using some rhetorical gambit and ignore it altogether. But the self-evident fact that Aboriginal Peoples have Aboriginal perspectives does little to settle the issue and there is no sure way of determining which questions are sincere and which are merely linguistic props. Questions involving perspec-tive are, at the best of times, shot through with common uncertainties. Whether we are talking about the reliability of eyewitness testimony (which forces us to make use of the equally unreliable measure of credibility) or the distinction between the literal and intended meaning of our words, there is simply no way to settle the matter once and for all. These uncertainties are so familiar to us that they almost go without saying.

We spend so much of our time pointing, describing, and explaining what we saw, how we saw it, or what we really meant that the question of perspective seems somehow confrontational. It is as if we are seated in a cramped and fea-tureless room, responding to the questions of someone who is little more than a dark silhouette behind the blinding glare of a desk lamp that has been repur-posed as a spotlight: "What did you *really* see?" "What did you *really* mean?" "Are you *sure*?" And so on. The all too familiar confines of the interrogation room – which we know from every police procedural drama – forces us to sort what we *think* we saw from what was *really* there. But this is by no means the crucible of truth; it is simply Plato's cave with the furniture moved about. When the light is behind us, we are cast as spectators who mistake shadows for the world, blissfully ignorant, but when we are turned around to face the light it seems like what we really saw or meant has no standing, like we are somehow as insubstantial as the shadows we cast. But this is an effect that is produced by the staged nature of the problem. Thought experiments and theatrical stages both rely on a set of baked-in presuppositions.

In the case of the interrogation room, we are led to believe that *the* fact-of-the-matter is somehow secure, already there, all we need to do is to state it clearly and then we are free to leave. Those behind the light are not subject to error in the same way we are; they *know* things and all they need is for us to admit them. The hidden presuppositions of this particular stage trick are exposed as soon as we ask why the request for legal representation is equated with guilt – the innocent have nothing to hide, or at least so we are told. But legal representation is not merely a technical means for evading confession. The fact is that in the real world, perspective cannot be separated from fact – the very idea that it could be forces us to try to find the God's-eye-view that would settle the matter. Law enforcement is a difficult job precisely because police officers are also reliant on their limited and all-too-human point of view. This is further complicated by the rather obvious fact (obvious at least for those of us in the legal profession) that laws do not interpret themselves. There simply is no fact that is simply given to us: everything is subject to interpretation, but this does not mean that there are no such things as chairs, laws, or for that matter, *perspectives*. It just means that we cannot provide a definition that applies in all cases, so we need to go back to the rough ground of *actual contexts* and *real cases*. In other words, the meaning of the phrase "Aboriginal perspective" is not subject to a singular definition, it is *case sensitive* and as such it is open to a plurality of possibilities.

The "Aboriginal Perspective" in the Courts

We can begin to get a sense of the stakes involved when the phrase "Aboriginal perspective" is put into play by looking at how it is used in judicial decisions. For example, in *Van der Peet* Chief Justice Lamer (citing Professor Mark Walters) held that

> the only fair and just reconciliation is [...] one which takes account of the aboriginal perspective while at the same time taking into account the perspective of the common law. True reconciliation will, equally, place weight on each.[3]

In this instance the phrase "Aboriginal perspective" is given its content by being put into an equal relationship with the "perspective of the common law." This makes sense on an intuitive level as it carries with it the implication that the concept of reconciliation, much like that of justice, requires the *balancing of perspectives*. But the actual meaning of this process of balancing hinges on the judicial practices that are put in play to determine the legal content of a right. As the (former) chief justice explains:

> The definition of an aboriginal right must, if it is truly to reconcile the prior occupation of Canadian territory by aboriginal peoples with the assertion of Crown sovereignty over that territory, take into account the aboriginal perspective, yet do so in terms which are cognizable to the non-aboriginal legal system.[4]

This sentence is far more densely packed than our first example, and so we will need to take our time breaking it down. First, we see that the overall purpose of an "aboriginal right" is to reconcile the "prior occupation of Canadian territory by aboriginal people" with "the assertion of Crown sovereignty over that territory." The asymmetry of this comparison is obvious and unexplained within the confines of this case; as with many decisions in this area, the most decisive propositions are simply stated and backed by unanalysed citations. But limiting ourselves to the cited text, we can see that Aboriginal Peoples derive rights from "occupation" and the Crown does so with the "assertion of sovereignty" over the territory. Naturally this leads us to ask how and why "occupation" is different from the "assertion of Crown sovereignty." In other words, why are we not reconciling sovereignties?[5] The answer to this question is, at least in part, found in the *Sparrow* court's assertion that "there was from the outset never any doubt that sovereignty and legislative power, and indeed the underlying title, to such lands vested in the Crown."[6] The authorities that they cite for this (puzzling) proposition are instructive: *Johnson v M'Intosh*,[7] the *Royal Proclamation of 1763* and three specific pages from *Calder v Attorney-General of British Columbia*.[8] Forgoing a detailed analysis, these simply boil down to the Crown's unilateral determination that Aboriginal Peoples did not have sovereignty over their lands because they were uncivilized. This racist proposition is not placed into the legal space of reasons; rather, it is set as an unquestionable assumption that the court (mistakenly) takes as a condition precedent to its own jurisdiction. The "Aboriginal perspective" does not apply to this proposition – it is simply taken as a background assumption.

Moreover, in the above citation from *Van der Peet* the relationship between the "aboriginal perspective" and that of the common law is not equal; rather, the terms of the latter are being set as the conditions for the recognition of the former. This is, after all, how a cognizability requirement works. If we say that we are taking account of the German language in terms of what is cognizable in English, we are necessarily excluding those German words and phrases that do not have cognizable equivalents in English.[9]

Given these complications, how exactly are judges to understand the *Van der Peet* imperative that "Courts must identify precisely the nature of the claim being made in determining whether an aboriginal claimant has demonstrated the existence of an aboriginal right"?[10] Due to the one-way-street approach taken to the requirement of cognizability, much of the actual content of the "Aboriginal perspective" will be stripped away in the process of *precisely* characterizing the claim. The "precision" that the court has in mind here is more than a little reminiscent of Procrustes and his infamous one-size-fits-all bed. The results of this process are about as "fair and just" as the phrase "integral to a distinctive culture" is clear and unambiguous[11] (e.g., consider the recharacterization of the claim in *R v Pamajewon* and more recently in the second trial level decision in *Ahousaht*).[12] The simple fact is that in the Canadian courts the phrase "Aboriginal perspective" has been understood as a term of art within the law of evidence, which is thus subject to the limitations imposed by judicial discretion. This leaves us with the asymmetry of the "Aboriginal perspective" being merely a *perspective*, whereas the common law perspective is law.

The "Aboriginal perspective" must take the stand in a court that is designed to treat the perspective of its adversary as law. The lack of fairness and justice here is glaring, and it can tempt us to dismiss the courts, the common law, and the entire constitutional order as inherently colonial. If we adopt this stance then it seems that we have two categorically distinct groups: Aboriginal and non-Aboriginal. This may well seem to be a natural distinction to make. After all, there are numerous historical, cultural, and linguistic distinctions that attach to these terms, but this multitude of differences does not provide us with a *strict definition*. In order to set a bright-line distinction between these two groups, we would need some kind of essence or distinct property that could be used to precisely determine who was or was not in a given group. This is a dangerous fiction. It is the mirror image of the notion of a unified and singular Canadian voice, which expresses the national interest that fixes the boundaries of Aboriginal Rights. The fact is that whether we are using the term Canadian or Aboriginal, these are *perspectives*, and this plurality goes all the way down; there is no singular Aboriginal voice just as there is no singular Cree or Haida voice. It could seem that this emphasis on the plurality of perspectives makes all group distinctions melt into thin air, leaving us with a world in which anyone can say anything. In other words, there are no boundaries to determine responsible and irresponsible speech. But this is simply not the case: rather, it means that the process of making that determination cannot be centred on the question of who is speaking (and that the identity of the speaker cannot be settled with a single noun). We also must place significant weight on what is being said and in which context.

The fact is that linguistic differences go all the way down to the individual level, as no two individuals can be said to speak the *same* language; they speak languages that are similar enough for them to interpret one another with relative ease, but they do still need to interpret one another. The fiction of singular national languages is part of the package of fictions that maintain the nation-state. The factual plurality and diversity of linguistic differences is important when it comes to the question of determining the limits of legitimate speech because it means that this determination is case sensitive. In other words, there is no final arbiter that can step outside and fix the limits of what is or is not an "Aboriginal perspective." There are only judgments on what is or is not acceptable and those who make and/or reaffirm these judgments are responsible for them.

Pluralism, Identity, and Perspectives

I do not mean to make the obvious cases of non-Aboriginal academics speaking about Aboriginal Peoples or appropriating their knowledge disappear. This pernicious species of pseudo-scientific description relies on the bankrupt notion that it is possible to objectively interpret the behaviour of others without asking them what they are actually up to. That is, it relies on the notion that truth is lived in one language but not in the other. I am trying to tease out what is implicit in the very notion that we are speaking to one another across linguistics differences. In other words, what is implicit in the very possibility of meaningful communication between different linguistic communities. The only way that we are able to understand the speech of others is to attribute reasonableness to their words. If we do not recognize their sense-making capacity, then we deprive ourselves of a check on our own worldview. Another way of putting this is that meaning is only possible when it is shared. Without *mutual* intelligibility, we are left with the absurdity of a self-asserted claim to authority. For example, the sentence "I am king" cannot be taken as grounds for authority without responsibility because it is only possible as an expression in the background where this speech act makes *sense* (as Clifford Geertz reminds us, you cannot mutiny in a bank). Self-proclaimed authority is as unintelligible as a private language or the possibility that we are all just brains in vats. The everyday practice of interpretation shows us that authority can only ever make sense within a relationship of responsibility because it requires *mutual recognition*. Without that, we have the absurd and bloody fiction of Hobbes's state of nature, which can only do its work within the vacuum of our imagination. In reality, such a condition is impossible as the basic facts of language and kinship cut against its central claims.

The preceding discussion can help us come to terms with the meaning of the phrase "Aboriginal perspective" in Canadian law. The fact that the term cannot be strictly defined makes the practice of maintaining a categorical distinction between the "Aboriginal perspective" and the common law perspective implausible. The open-textured nature of the "Aboriginal perspective" serves to highlight the absurdity of the foundational claims of the Crown's assertion of sovereignty. By participating in this process Aboriginal plaintiffs cannot be understood as simply accepting the Crown's assertions as a proposition that they agree with or consent to. For example, it would be a mistake to assume that employees who are following their employer's regulations are endorsing those regulations – this assumption would simply blind us to the effects of a work-to-rule strike. Likewise, we must not assume that those Aboriginal Peoples who bring forward cases within the Canadian legal system are thereby endorsing its assertion of jurisdiction – it is also possible that they are following the courts' rules so as to highlight the limits of the courts' jurisdiction and thereby draw attention to the arbitrary basis of Crown sovereignty. In other words, framing the space available for a given perspective can undoubtedly play a very large role in shaping its interpretation, but it *cannot strictly define it*. If the phrase "Aboriginal perspective" has been transformed into a legal term of art, this cannot be understood as somehow blocking the *actual* perspective of Aboriginal individuals or groups from having legal effect. This blocking (or substitution of) the actual perspective for a constructed one would be akin to the courts strictly interpreting all individuals before the court with its own definition of the "reasonable person." The most cursory survey of the struggle for civil rights – whether it be Magna Carta, the Constitution of the United States, or the Charter – should make this point abundantly clear. This does not mean that the existing legal system is "fair and just" (whatever that could possibly mean) – rather, it means that the practice of legal interpretation is necessarily open-textured and perspectival. Law can be given rigid limits, but these limits are "given" or "set" by practices of interpretation and thus the meaning of law necessarily remains open to contestation. As Aristotle understood, the sheer diversity of situations and perspectives require law (*nomos*) to be supplemented by equity (*epieikeia*), which allows the general rules of law to be interpreted in a manner that fits the circumstances of the case.

In closing, I do not see any final way of defining the term "Aboriginal perspective." That is, if we take the realities of pluralism into account, I see no clear and obvious way of simply settling the issue once and for all. The question of what the "Aboriginal perspective" means is something that requires a case-by-case approach and about which, in many cases, reasonable people can disagree. For example, consider how the Canadian courts have struggled with the idea of individual members asserting collective rights in *Behn v Moulton*[13] or the distinctions between band councils and traditional leadership in *Coastal Gas-Link Pipeline Ltd v Huson*.[14] Accordingly, I think it is unhelpful to attempt to determine who is speaking from an "Aboriginal perspective." Instead, we need to carefully consider the distinctions between speaking *for, as, to, with, about,* and *at*. If I *speak as* a particular sort of person, then in order to have credibility I need to have some mixture of qualities and/or experiences that pass the recognition criteria of others within that group. If I *speak for* another, then my ambit of speech is circumscribed by and through that relationship (e.g., as a representative of some sort). If I am *speaking to* another person, this again comes with a host of different rules that apply in different contexts (e.g., a conversation, a vow, an interrogation, etc.). If I am *speaking with* another, then I must begin with the presumption that my interlocutor is rational and their beliefs are largely true, and then as we talk, we will both adjust our working theories of interpretation so that we can understand one another and share our worldviews. If I am *speaking about* another, then I am giving my own interpretation of their words/actions. Finally, if I am *speaking at* another, then I am most often issuing commands, pronouncing sentences, designating categories of subjects or one of the other sovereign performances of state or other authority, which often qualify the requirement of mutual recognition by supplying a background theory that frames the targets of the speech as subjects.

Each of these ways of speaking can go wrong in a wide variety of ways, but the work of making the determination of what is responsible and irresponsible must be conducted on a case-by-case basis, and those who make those determinations must do so in their own voice and not lay claim to some free-floating definition of the "Aboriginal perspective" to jump over the demands of real dialogue. If self-determination is going to have meaning, then it must enable Peoples to make determinations within their communities and via their legal and political norms. Whatever the "Aboriginal perspective" means, it is clear that it cannot be both strictly defined and self-determining. If it is the former, then it is little more than a theatrical ploy of colonial ventriloquism. If it is the latter, then acting as if we can start from who speaks from an authentic "Aboriginal perspective" is simply reenacting that same colonial ploy. The real work of self-determination cannot start from neatly defined labels to fix the identity of the speakers in advance; rather, it requires that we make room for the deep pluralism and strange multiplicities that give living meaning to perspectives and speech within and between the constitutional traditions of peoples.

NOTES

1 In this chapter I use "Aboriginal peoples" to refer to the three groups that the
   Constitution Act, 1982 identifies in s. 35(2) as the "Indian, Inuit, and Métis Peoples
   of Canada." I acknowledge that the term "Indigenous Peoples" is often used to
   refer to groups who define their membership internally with their own legal
   and political traditions, have historical connections with specific lands, and are
   adversely affected by state or state-authorized actions on their lands. I argue that
   the distinction between these terms is unhelpful and that real self-determination
   necessarily requires us to refuse this distinction. Accordingly, I use the term
   "Aboriginal peoples" as a phrase that refers to peoples with the right of self-
   determination which cannot be curtailed by legalistic attempts to externally define
   it. In this way Aboriginal and Indigenous can be understood as synonyms that have
   distinct histories of contestation over their use.
2 The literature that could be referred to here is vast, but for a small sample of some
   of the best of it see: James Tully, *Strange Multiplicity: Constitutionalism in an Age
   of Diversity* (Cambridge: Cambridge University Press, 1995); Michael Asch, *On
   Being Here to Stay: Treaties and Aboriginal Rights in Canada* (Toronto: University

of Toronto Press, 2014); and Peter Russell, *Canada's Odyssey: A Country Based on Incomplete Conquests* (Toronto: University of Toronto Press, 2017).

3 *R v Van der Peet*, [1996] 2 SCR 507 at para 50 [*Van der Peet*].

4 *Ibid* at para 49.

5 I am borrowing Felix Hoehn's helpful phrasing here. See *Reconciling Sovereignties: Aboriginal Nations and Canada* (Saskatoon: Native Law Centre, University of Saskatchewan, 2012).

6 *R v Sparrow*, [1990] 1 SCR 1075.

7 8 Wheat. 543 (1823).

8 [1973] SCR 313.

9 The trouble with the notion of translating Aboriginal Rights into the common law came to the forefront in *R v Marshall; R v Bernard*, [2005] 2 SCR 220, and the strongly critical reception of the court's reasoning: Cf. Brian Slattery, "The Metamorphosis of Aboriginal Title" (2006) 85 Can Bar Rev 255 at 279–81.

10 *Van der Peet, supra* note 3 at para 50 (underlining removed).

11 In *R v Sappier; R v Gray*, 2006 SCC 54 the Court came very close to conceding this point as it struggled to make sense of the reference to "core identity" in *Mitchell v M.N.R.*, 2001 SCC 33. I'd like to thank Professor Kent McNeil for bringing this important point to my attention.

12 *R v Pamajewon*, [1996] 2 SCR 821; *Ahousaht Indian Band and Nation v Canada (Attorney General)*, 2018 BCSC 633.

13 In *Behn v Moulton Contracting Ltd.*, 2013 SCC 26, the Court was dealing with issues concerning standing and abuse of process arising from the appellants (who, with the exception of one, were members of the Fort Nelson First Nation) blocking access to the respondents (a logging company) to harvest timber. The court noted that while Aboriginal Rights are group rights, there may be cases where they have an individual aspect that has legal effect, but in this case, they found the use of the blockade constituted a self-help remedy and found against the appellants.

14 In *Coastal GasLink Pipeline Ltd. v Huson*, 2019 BCSC 2264, the plaintiff (Coastal Gaslink Pipeline Ltd., formerly TransCanada Pipelines Ltd.) obtained provincial permits for the construction of a pipeline that crosses the territory of the Wet'suwet'en People. The Wet'suwet'en have a government that combines heredity and *Indian Act* Band Council systems. The defendants are representatives within the traditional side of the Wet'suwet'en government, and they argue that their consent is necessary under Wet'suwet'en Law and have blocked access to the plaintiff. In applying the test for injunctions, Justice Church needed to determine three factors (the *prima facie* strength of the plaintiff's case, irreparable harm, and the balance of convenience), and in those determinations the nature of the defendants' rights is pivotal. Church J. found that the defendants' claim to standing within the Wet'suwet'en government was so contested that it was unclear what

their position was and that their claim to the defense of Indigenous Law failed because Indigenous Law does not have legal effect until it is incorporated into Canadian law via legislation, treaty, or judicial decision. For a comparative analysis of the problems in these cases, see Joshua Nichols & Sarah Morales, "Finding Reconciliation in Dark Territory: *Coastal Gaslink*, *Coldwater* and the Possible Futures of DRIPA" (2021) 53:4 UBC L Rev 1185.

12 NONU WEL,WEL TI,Á NE TX̱,EȻEŁ:
Our Canoe Is Really Tippy

KQWA'ST'NOT AND HANNAH ASKEW

The following piece is co-authored between kQwa'st'not Charlene George (t-Sou-ke Peoples) and Hannah Askew (settler of English and Scottish ancestry). The authors have been working together for the past two years to help facilitate cross-cultural organizational transformation for Sierra Club BC, an environmental charity located on Lekwungen territory. As kQwa'st'not observed at the outset of our work, NONU WEL,WEL TI,Á NE TX̱,EȻEŁ (our canoe is really tippy) as we try to journey together, so we must strive to better balance our relationship with each other and with Western and Indigenous knowledge systems and ways of knowing. This is a process that can be both difficult and uncomfortable, and requires hard work, an open mind, humility, and willingness to change.

Our hope is that in sharing some of our personal stories and experiences, others undertaking similar work in diverse institutional settings may find useful insights. Our piece alternates between our two voices and shares our different experiences of the transformational work. An intentional choice to use Indigenous English[1] has been made by kQwa'st'not. *As you read our piece, we gently suggest that you reflect on four questions: Who is in your community? Who is your neighbour? What will things look like in one hundred years? What is working well?* We begin our reflections now by sharing with you a story that has been central in guiding our work.

kQwa'st'not: This story and its teachings comes from my grandparents and was shared with me in my teen years. Clookshla is Raven ... his wife is daughter of Dog Salmon ... his sister is Crow who has many children. Clookshla lived in the great time of the beginning when Changer still walked the tum'ilth [sacred earth] ... he experienced many, many lessons that are shared to help us human relatives learn.

CLOOKSHLA AND THE SHADOW PEOPLE

Clookshla would go out in the canoe for a four-day trip. There was a village he passed one time. Nobody was around but there was smoking from a house but no people showing. Clookshla was out for a couple days. On his way home he passed that village again. It was still smoking.

"I wonder why .... there isn't any people living there." A few days after he made the trip again ... bringing his wife. This time he was going to stop there and look at it. He reached the village where the smoke was ... no people walking around. He got to the shore and pulled his canoe up a little bit. He walked up to the house. The door was closed. He got in and looked around. Nobody... but fish was hanging in some baskets ... dried fish in baskets. He said to himself, "Nobody owns this dried fish ... I'll take it all with me." He went down to the beach and said to his wife: "Come up with me ... there's lots of dried fish ... empty houses ... we'll take it all."

"All right ... we've got enough. You get in the bow. I'm going to shove this canoe out and jump in and start paddling. We must go home as quickly as we can because we have a Big load." Wife felt somebody touch her ... made her sit down ... tied her legs down. "Start paddling. We've got to get home quick!" But wife couldn't, she was tied up. Somebody reached over ... pulled her against Clookshla. Feeling her near he said: "What are you doing? Why don't you get busy and paddle!?"

"I can't ... my legs are tied." Clookshla looked at his wife and saw the ropes tied on her feet. He stopped paddling. Instead of going ahead his canoe was going backwards. It was pulled right back to the beach. Somebody started unloading the canoe but Clookshla couldn't see them. He saw the baskets of dried fish float in the air and go back in the house ... no one was packing it. The people took the dried fish back where Clookshla got it from and when it was all taken out ... the canoe was shoved out – empty.

Learning to Be a Human Relative

Hannah: kQwa'st'not shared the story of "Clookshla and the Shadow People" when we were just beginning to grapple with our colonial history as an environmental organization, specifically our history of advocating for the creation of designated "wilderness parks." This advocacy happened in the absence of recognition of Indigenous Law, governance, and occupation. In many cases, parks were created without the consent of the Indigenous Nations affected and Indigenous Peoples were forcibly removed from their lands. This harmed not only people but also the land, cutting off ecosystems from beneficial Indigenous management practices that had shaped them over millennia.

Sierra Club BC is a fifty-three-year-old Canadian conservation organization, sharing an even longer history with its United States counterpart, which was formed by the Scottish-American naturalist John Muir in California in 1892. The original purpose of the club was to facilitate mountain hiking for its members; however, it quickly expanded to advocacy for parks creation to shield certain spaces from intensive logging, mining, and sheep and cattle grazing. Sierra Club BC was brought into being by American draft dodgers in Vancouver in 1969, and the members first action was to organize against logging in an area of Squamish, Musqueam, and Tsleil-Waututh territory, ultimately contributing to the creation of Cypress Bowl Park. From its inception, the roots of Sierra Club have been tangled up with the violence of colonization and the erasure of Indigenous Law and governance, but we are collectively trying to shift into a more respectful way of being.[2]

kQwa'st'not: I see the organization in the process of "Coming of Age" – a transformational time. I shared the story of "Clookshla and the Shadow People" to encourage reflection for the Sierra Club family. If we are to truly transform ourselves as human ... be human relatives ... how do we do this? To be "singular-based humans" is the goal of Western society ... this is evidenced by what is valued. Like the teaching in the story, where are singular-based humans now? We can get stuck ... why?

Like Clookshla, do we perpetuate the belief that if IT doesn't appear to belong to a being (human or other-WISE) ... can IT be claimed/named/categorized/diminished so it is comfortable for a designed society/mindset called colonialism? Can we simply gather up a new basket full of IT ... from an uncomfortable place of transformational change (required to bring us humans) to be in balance with our interconnected relatives? Perhaps we need to weave a new basket (way of thinking/sense of value and respect) and be as persistent in re-designing society from the past possession-based worldview.

Hannah: With kQwa'st'not's permission, Sierra Club BC shared the story of "Clookshla and the Shadow People" in a 2019 reflection and statement of accountability called *Balancing the Canoe: Acknowledging Our History and Changing Course for Our Future*.[3] In this document, we acknowledge the harm caused by our organization, and by the Western environmental movement more broadly, in describing areas of land on Turtle Island as "wild," "untouched," and "empty": this was untrue and misleading because the land was already being governed and stewarded by the Indigenous Nations who had looked after their territories for millennia in accordance with their own legal orders. In *Balancing the Canoe*, we commit as a Sierra Club BC family to acknowledging and taking responsibility for past and ongoing harms, and to changing course for the future by learning as an organization to recognize, respect, and uphold Indigenous legal orders in the lands where we live and work together.

Seeing through Watchers' Eyes

Genuinely following through on this commitment is difficult and complex under our current organizational practices, and many of the questions kQwa'st'not raises in relation to the story involve deep challenges to assumptions that are built into the DNA of our organization. For example, her question regarding how we can transform ourselves from humans to human relatives highlights a struggle that surfaces regularly in our work. How can we do this while operating in a Western context and worldview that prioritizes individual human needs and wants and simultaneously de-prioritizes collective and community needs, including those of our non-human relatives? While change is often slow, difficult, and uncomfortable, we are deeply committed to it. We recognize that our current ways of thinking and operating as a Western environmental organization have not resulted in the change we need, the greatest evidence being that during our fifty-three years in operation, the ecological crisis has substantially worsened rather than improved and is now reaching a critical point both in terms of rapidly accelerating climate change and species extinction.

An example of where we are striving to better transform into our role of human relatives is in our relationships to other-than-human beings. As a traditionally Western-science-based organization that communicates in English, we rely on thinking and language that can create a sense of separation between humans and other beings. In her powerful short essay, "The Grammar of Animacy," the Potawatomi botanist Robin Wall Kimmerer observes that "English

doesn't give us many tools for incorporating respect for animacy. In English, you are either a human or a thing. Our grammar boxes us in by the choice of reducing a non-human being to an *it*, or it must be gendered, inappropriately, as a *he* or a *she*."[4] Later in the same essay, she elaborates:

> The animacy of the world is something we already know, but the language of animacy teeters on extinction – not just for Native peoples, but for everyone. Our toddlers speak of plants and animals as if they were people, extending to them self and intention and compassion – until we teach them not to … When we tell them that the tree is not a *who*, but an *it*, we make that maple an object; we put a barrier between us, absolving ourselves of moral responsibility and opening the door to exploitation. Saying it makes a living land into "natural resources." If a maple is an *it*, we can take up the chain saw. If a maple is a *her*, we think twice.[5]

As we transform as an organization, we need new stories and frames to help guide us into more intimate and respectful relationships with our non-human relatives. One powerful tool for helping us and others to do this is through kQwa'st'not's interactive, collaborative art piece grounded in Coast Salish Law and knowledge, *Seeing through Watchers' Eyes – Beyond the Worlds*.

In confronting the climate and extinction crisis, the first question we must ask ourselves is "Where do we begin?" The thirty-two-foot collaborative mural and its accompanying, publicly available online tool, *Seeing through Watchers' Eyes – Beyond the Worlds*, designed[6] by kQwa'st'not, help to answer this question by inviting learners into a new way of seeing and relating to the natural world.

Through a nine month collaborative process,[7] the mural was painted at Spencer Middle School on the territory of the Lekwungen-speaking Peoples (Songhees and Esquimalt Nations). *Seeing through Watchers' Eyes* shares a complex and deep story seen through the eyes of Coast Salish SNA'WY'ALTH (practice and teaching) with the Wild Man and the Wild Woman. It invites voices and views about nature and our place in it that have been notably absent in the environmental movement. The mural and accompanying online learning tool are there to help learners engage with different perspectives, using place-based learning from Indigenous Peoples from Esquimalt and Songhees (Lekwungen); Tslartlip, Pauquachin, Tseycum, Tsawout, and (W̱SÁNEĆ); Malahat (MÁLEXEⱢ); and Beecher Bay (SCIA'NEW).

The mural tells the story of the land on which it lives, including the story of the diverse beings that inhabit the land such as various birds, plants, trees, fish, animals, insects, and supernatural beings. The curriculum that comes with the mural was created using Coast Salish protocols and includes options for three different learning styles: linear, Indigenous, and intuitive. English, Senćoten, Hul'q'umi'num, Klallam, tSouke, Lekwungen, and Nuu-chah-nulth languages are used to tell the story, designed to bridge cultures by creating common ground through sharing images, stories, audio clips, and videos, leading to common understanding. *Seeing through Watchers' Eyes* is being used by Sierra Club BC's environmental education program in various school districts and communities across southern Vancouver Island.

kQwa'st'not: The learning tool *Seeing through Watchers' Eyes* helps us think through the questions I posed at the beginning of this piece – *Who is your community? Who is your neighbour? What will things be like in one hundred years?* and *What is working?* Coast Salish protocol and actions hold sacred the family connections to all the beings transformed at the time of initial great change in the time of XÁ,EL,S (changer/creator/transformer). Many parts of these teachings were shared with the Sierra Club "family" through the creation/unveiling/celebration and subsequent deeper dive into *Seeing through Watchers' Eyes*. This work was created through the initial process of "bringing human folks along" on the intuitive journey of giving voices to the neighbours of non-human relatives just outside our modern box houses ... These relatives are choked with our human societal needs for consuming much ... this is the warning that ḰENI is telling us about. The "storm" (or one storm) has reached us ... we are "grounded" or in a "pause" right now. How do we move "forward"? Perhaps, family/community/governance/societal structures may be reimagined with an intercultural view of Wild Woman and Wild Man who borrow us their "glasses" or lens to see what is in front of our eyes but may not be seen. Bringing our tippy canoe into balance or at least shifting into the waves and paddling together makes a lighter journey for us by collaboratively working with all our unique gifts.

In this time of change, there is a hunger from people for heart education/ learning/nourishment, which is also spiritual connection. The present Western system of thinking mostly acknowledges only the mind education and values. *Seeing through Watchers' Eyes* uses English; however, the English language primarily focuses on describing concepts in front of the eyes. I needed to relate this to what lives behind the eyes,[8] so a mixture of languages has been used to enhance/enrich the learning experience of "re-reminding" people by connecting them to inner knowing. Indigenous languages used in *Seeing through Watchers' Eyes* include include Senćoŧen, Hul'q'umi'num, Klallam, tSouke, Lekwungen, and Nuu-chah-nulth. Additionally, the inclusion of "Indigenous English" throughout was purposeful in bridging English/scholarly prose to a new lens or colour of lens within the safety of emic place. The choice of these languages reflects my cultural personal connections and responsibilities and also strives to authentically centre the learning to this sacred land (tum'ilth) where the mural lives.

Hannah: The opportunity for Sierra Club BC to participate in the creation *Seeing through Watchers' Eyes* was profound as it represented a chance for us to engage with Indigenous Law in a concrete and applied way and to have our own thinking enriched by its insights and logic. While it was an important first step for us to admit in *Balancing the Canoe* our organization's historical and ongoing failures to recognize the operation of Indigenous legal orders on the territories on which we live and work, we needed an invitation to begin to engage with and learn from them. By generously extending this invitation to us, along with the communities she collaborated with, kQwa'st'not helped us to begin to see the land, our relations, and our obligations in a way that was new to us as an organization. This process helped us begin to imagine new ways to do our work. It has also opened up new possibilities for us in terms of imagining ways that we might constitute ourselves as a society and order our relations with all of our relatives. *Seeing through Watchers' Eyes* is set in the past, present, and future simultaneously, and in a powerful way reveals that relations have been constituted differently in the past and may be differently constituted again at some time in the future. It showcases interactions and reciprocity between humans and other relatives. It opens up our imaginations and understanding to a different realm of possibility for ecological governance and our place within it. My ability to engage with *Seeing through Watchers' Eyes* as a non-Coast Salish settler person was greatly enhanced by my prior experiences of learning Anishinaabe Law from the community of Neyaashiinigmiing.[9]

Cookie Time

Hannah: An important teaching moment that kQwa'st'not created early in our work together has become jokingly referred to by the staff as "cookie time" or "the cookie test." One week, while I happened to be away, kQwa'st'not dropped by the Sierra Club offices on a Friday afternoon with an enormous batch of cookie dough. She gathered together the staff who were in the office that afternoon and asked everyone who was able to take some home over the weekend to bake and bring it back in order to have them ready to share with all the children at the middle school who had helped with the painting of the mural *Seeing through Watchers' Eyes*. kQwa'st'not explained that because she only had one small oven in her home, it would be difficult for her to bake the many hundreds of cookies by herself. At the time, kQwa'st'not was new to the organization and few of the staff had had an opportunity to develop a relationship with her. The staff were quite surprised by her request. While a few agreed, most said that for different reasons they were unable to help. kQwa'st'not left most of the cookie dough in the fridge with an invitation for anyone who was able to help. She said that she would be back on Monday to pick up the baked cookies. On Monday, she returned and picked up the baked cookies from those who had been able to help, as well as the unbaked dough still sitting in the fridge. She then baked the remainder of the cookies herself, to share with the children at the school in celebration at the unveiling of the mural.

When I returned to the office the following week, a number of perturbed staff came to speak to me about the baking request, pointing out to me that baking cookies was not a part of their job description and explaining that they felt somewhat guilty not to have helped. They were also surprised and uncomfortable to have been asked, since it was out of the ordinary. Since I had not spoken with kQwa'st'not about the cookies, I was not sure what had happened but promised to speak with her and find out more. When we talked, kQwa'st'not explained to me that she had wanted to share a teaching with the staff which would simultaneously invite them into Coast Salish protocol of providing food for guests (the children) at a gathering, as well as help them to re-imagine their relationships with her and other staff members in a more intimate and familial way. This teaching would materialize as people pitched in and helped one another in ways that were not in their specific job descriptions and work hours. They would learn as they engaged in a more holistic way outside of their formal roles. The invitation was completely optional. If they chose to participate, it offered an opportunity to staff to experience their roles and relationships to one another and herself in a different way. kQwa'st'not did not directly explain this to the staff – they came to this understanding over time by learning other stories and teachings that kQwa'st'not shared. Many of the staff eventually began to affectionately refer to the incident as "the cookie test." In addition to this teaching, kQwa'st'not also modelled a more familial way of relating. At times she invited the staff and board into her home. She showed us parts of her nation's territory. She shared food with us and brought her relatives (including her young grandchildren) into the office at different times.

Sierra Club "Family"

In addition to working directly with the board and staff on organizational transformation, we also engage with the thirteen thousand members of Sierra Club BC. In this section, we describe our experience of the 2018 fall annual general meeting for the Sierra Club membership, which was hosted in Lekwungen territory and at which kQwa'st'not delivered the keynote speech. This event was significant because it was where we first formally announced to the membership the new direction we were embarking on and the transformational work we would be doing together.

kQwa'st'not: A portion of my conversation and invitation to the folks that gathered that evening included two stories and an example of creating/embracing family that may not come from your "belly button." First to set the intention, my daughter's friend/sister Amina joined me in place of my daughter that evening. Her roots are the other side of the sacred land TENEW and across TŁÁŁSE ~ sacred saltwater … I called on her to help me as a "daughter" to share and support … This became very important later as an example when we introduced the value of Sierra Club being a "family" … embracing the importance of having family to stand beside you as you do your "work" … facing the community with a solid structure of family made up from many uniquely gifted individuals that collaboratively embrace their joint "work" …

My first story was the introduction of who is your neighbour. My own neighbours include Mr. Bear … in this case my sharing was of a late night visit … After many frustrating moments as a single mom working late night with an overwhelming number of tasks, Mr. Bear decided to visit following my unconscious invitation … The Raccoon family previously visited often to enjoy the many leftovers my young family had generously donated to my outside "can." With broom in hand I crossed my door's threshold using my big mom voice saying "Out of there" … and paused … this is Mr. Bear not Raccoon family … protocol is very different … or is it? I decided to continue "This will make you sick young Bear!" I said … Mr. Bear backed up and left, after hearing my caring "I will leave you some good food but don't ever crunch my 'can' again … hyjka." To this day we have mutual respect and understanding of each of our protocols … even now with my "good smelling" compost bin my protocol is respected by Mr. Bear family (& Raccoon family too) … My question: how do you interact with your neighbours/who are your neighbours/who is in your community?

My second story was the re-reminder that each human understands everything from their own "lens" … This story shows two lenses … A man from the military wishing to do his best, be collaborative and inclusive, asked many times for one of my relatives to come take part in a celebration – to bless the water is what he thought should happen to be respectful. This invitation was not answered by ANYONE in my family … This was frustrating for the man …

doing his best. Instead of being offended by seemingly ignored invitations he asked a question "Should I be asking another person to come do this work? We've worked so hard to invite?" As you might have guessed I reframed the question. Consider that TŁÁŁSE is so sacred that we as humans need to introduce ourselves to and ask permission when we wish to journey ... that this sacred water is the same as we were first nurtured in our mothers' bellies ... The thought would then be, "How could we thank the sacred water from both east and west in our celebration of the military?" This was the question that could be responded to ... and was responded to with further learning by my family of how sacred this TŁÁŁSE is. Without the shift in lenses, how could we hope to bridge gaps ... Many, many of my relatives shift to make translations for those in dominant worldview ... Now the invitation is to have those with this dominant lens make the effort to see differently or recognize that there is another lens to see with.

Hannah: kQwa'st'not's sharing of these stories and the ways of relating they portray caused interest, appreciation, curiosity, and some discomfort among our membership. Sierra Club BC is an organization that historically and currently identifies as science-based. Keynote speakers at our annual general meetings have typically been trained biologists, marine scientists, naturalists, and well-known environmental activists and leaders. While many attendees expressed gratitude for the teachings that were shared, some expressed concern about the implications of this way of knowing for the organization's science-based approach.

Additionally, immediately following kQwa'st'not's talk, a couple of awkward jokes were made loudly by one or two audience members about the idea of water, or even a mouse, being considered as a relative. In the moment, I was unsure of how to respond to these comments. An Indigenous friend who was in the audience shared with me later that night that it hurt her to hear important teachings shared by an Indigenous woman joked about in this inappropriate way. She wondered if I and other non-Indigenous staff could communicate this directly to our membership in future spaces to ensure that Indigenous colleagues, teachers, and guests felt welcome and respected. I am grateful for my friend's feedback – it's helped me to better understand how I can show up[10] in a good way at subsequent events. In discussing with kQwa'st'not the lack of understanding and prejudice that Indigenous knowledge sometimes encounters within the Western environmental movement, she counselled perseverance, strength, patience, boundaries, and kindness.

kQwa'st'not: Transformation doesn't happen in a linear way, but in a spiral. We have followed many spirals of a transformational cycle or loops in our work at Sierra Club BC. The stimulating event has come in a few ways ... the first way was conversations with sister Hannah, second was "cookie time," third was the introduction to SC family/community at the annual general meeting, and many more also. We have used transformational learning theory as our guide. Briefly, the five stages of transformational learning/change are as follows: activating event, inner reflection, deep conversation, thinking/brainstorming a potential plan, trying it out … And then repeat. I have added this Indigenous thinking from my uncle … "there's no wrong way to do sometin rit" … Loosely translated as there are no "mistakes" but only opportunities to learn/go/adjust thinking/try again and/or be unique thinking. Added to this is the thinking of SNIU (sna'wy'ulth – good teachings passed on from generations before) … that each respected person adds to the whole basket … that the basket ends up being so full it overflows when we re-remember (hear echoes of deep truths from within) that we are so "wealthy" that no modern dollar systems can relate.

Growing into Balance

Hannah: At the beginning of 2020 we were able to adopt and launch Sierra Club BC's new strategic plan.[11] It commits us to engage with, respect, and uphold Indigenous legal orders on the territories on which we live and work. The new strategic plan also commits us to both learn from and live in greater respect and reciprocity with our non-human relatives. As Illustrated by kQwa'st'not, many of the non-human relatives depicted in *Seeing through Watchers' Eyes* are also found in the strategic plan with accompanying teachings. For example, on the cover is both a photo and artwork of Heron~SNEKE with a caption that explains that this being can teach us about lifelong balance and graceful commitment to transformational movements.

In formally launching our new strategic plan, following kQwa'st'not's guidance, we attempted to follow Coast Salish protocol to the best of our ability and knowledge. In advance of the physical launch, we travelled in person to extend invitations in a number of communities and provided advance copies of our strategic plan. We asked a Bighouse speaker to announce our work to invited guests at the formal launch, which was hosted at the Songhees Wellness Centre, and we prepared both refreshments and a giveaway for those who were able to accept our invitation to attend. Both staff and board members did the best they could to show up as hosts according to Coast Salish protocol. Witnesses were asked to watch carefully, remember, and reflect back what they saw of the work being done. It was a special night for Sierra Club BC as it helped us to experience that relating to one another and our neighbours in a different way, guided by Coast Salish protocol, produced deeper bonds and new possibilities for collaboration.

kQwa'st'not: The launch of the strategic plan allowed us to publicly announce our work, give space/place for disagreement or corrections, and express thankfulness to all who helped. Cousin Rick was our speaker and he spoke from the heart. Some of the neighbours who attended, such as one Tsimshian woman, said that it was the first time she could imagine being part of an environmental organization because she saw a cultural connection and more openness in our approach. Moving forward, we are accountable to the guests who attended.

Final Thoughts

Hannah: The process of truly engaging with the teachings of the "Clookshla and the Shadow People" remains ongoing. The transformative work we have undertaken as an organization at Sierra Club BC to recognize and learn from Indigenous Law, knowledge, and ways of being in relationship has only just begun. Yet it has already had a profound impact on us. We are grateful for the knowledge shared with us and the invitations extended to us to engage in this work in a respectful way. We are open to being changed by the new relationships into which we are entering, in ways that we cannot right now fully predict or imagine. We trust that each small step we take will help lead us to a more balanced, grounded, and respectful place from which to do our work.

kQwa'st'not: I think of the change that is happening as being the rock that rolls into the pond (qwaa – sacred water). The waves associated with this would be the tide that gently rolls in to cover the relatives that need refreshing … not the turbulent storm that rushes and re-makes the beach and beings that make their homes in the tidal zones. We all hope to move gently together in a new way.

NOTES

1 Charlene George, *Rebuilding Our THEE LELUM ~ Collaboratively Moving Forward ~ YÁ ŁTE SE ŚELŚ TEN̲ (we're going for a walk) ~ Developing Stewardship Framework Together: ÍY SCÍÁĆEL ~ transforming ourselves to greet and embrace this new day; Steps to Lifelong Learning by asking: where do we start?* (Victoria: Royal Roads University, 2019), online: <https://viurrspace.ca /handle/10613/20856?fbclid=IwAR1_almEz4eU12lrsy9kH-NVsTkabD7fb0IBeS9s NxtueOb7V5RN9IBYtYk>.

2 Sierra Club BC, *Growing into Balance – Sierra Club BC's Strategic Plan: 2020–2023.* Artwork by kQwa'st'not (Victoria BC, 2020), online: <https://sierraclub.bc.ca /balance/> [Sierra Club BC]. See also Sierra Club BC, *Sierra Club BC Annual Report 2019*, online: <https://sierraclub.bc.ca/uploads/2019-Annual-Report _Sierra-Club-BC.pdf>.

3 Sierra Club BC, *Balancing the Canoe: Acknowledging Our History and Changing Course for the Future.* Artwork by kQwa'st'not (Victoria BC, 2019), online: <https:// sierraclub.bc.ca/balancing-the-canoe/>.

4 Robin Wall Kimmerer, *Braiding Sweetgrass: Indigenous Wisdom, Scientific Knowledge and the Teachings of Plants* (Minneapolis: Milkweed Editions, 2013), 56.

5 *Ibid* at 57.

6 kQwaʾstʾnot (2019), online: <sierraclub.bc.ca/watcherseyes>.

7 Described *ibid.*

8 The descriptive term, "behind the eyes" (Caroline Myss, personal communication, 13 February 2018), aided me in describing the impactful oral traditions in Coast Salish ways of knowing.

9 Hannah Askew, "Learning from Bear-Walker: Indigenous Legal Orders and Intercultural Legal Education in Canadian Law Schools" (2016) 33:1 Windsor YB Access Just 29, online: <https://wyaj.uwindsor.ca/index.php/wyaj/article/view/4808>.

10 Be an ally.

11 Sierra Club BC, *supra* note 2.

13 Sharp as a Knife: Judge Begbie and Reconciliation

HAMAR FOSTER

1.

If we are going to move towards reconciliation, we should not choose a tactic based on discomfort.

Lee Maracle, Stó:lō poet and author

I began writing this in the autumn of 2019, a few weeks before the October workshop. It was difficult to know how to start, so, as you can see, I resorted to the Trickster. In the common law tradition, to appropriate property is to take it without permission and without compensation.[1] Theft, essentially. The tricky part is deciding what counts as property, and therefore whether permission is required, especially where different legal traditions are involved.[2] I think the sun is property in neither the common law nor the Indigenous legal tradition, so Raven may be off the hook. Or maybe not. See appendix 1, below.[3]

I have been interested in the legal history of Native-Newcomer relations, especially in British Columbia, for a long time. But lately I have been feeling that I am observing it through bifocals. Through one set of lenses, it is clear that on so many fronts Canada is moving too slowly to effect reconciliation – a reality re-emphasized by the protests and blockades against the Coastal Gaslink pipeline in February and March of 2020. This is certainly how many younger Canadians see our country, and everything from the scandal of drinking water on reserves to the failure to implement Supreme Court decisions on Aboriginal title unless horsewhipped by events, make it easy to see why. Perhaps the worst example of all is that since the Bryce Report a century ago it has been clear that morbidity and mortality rates in residential schools were what Bryce called them, a national crime. And in May of 2021 the Tk'emlúps te Secwépemc announced that they had located what may be over two hundred unmarked graves on the grounds of the Kamloops Indian Residential School. That so many non-Indigenous Canadians were shocked and astonished by this is also shocking, given the Bryce Report and the Truth and Reconciliation Commission's 2015 report.

Yet, when I look through the other set of lenses, it is equally clear that a sea change has occurred since I was an undergraduate in the 1960s. Compare, for example, the consultations with First Nations carried out by government when the original Trans Mountain pipeline was approved in the 1950s (there were none) with what happens when mega-projects, such as the expansion of this same pipeline, are proposed today (whatever one may think about the efficacy of such consultations). Or compare the building of the W.A.C. Bennett Dam in the 1960s to the shelving of the Northern Gateway pipeline more than half a century later. And consider that when Tom Berger walked into court to try the *Calder* case more than fifty years ago, most people, whether

Indigenous or non-Indigenous, lawyers or laypersons, could not imagine the version of Aboriginal title and rights that characterizes Canadian law and politics today.[4]

If proof be needed, I offer what a judge wrote in a unanimous decision in 1971, a full century after BC joined Canada. From the moment colonial laws authorized Crown land grants, he said, "the Indians of ... British Columbia became in law trespassers on and liable to actions of ejectment from lands in the Colony other than those set aside as [Indian] reserves."[5] That these laws made no mention of what was then called Indian title, let alone extinguishing such title, did not matter.[6] It was an astonishing thing to say, but at the time it caused barely a ripple of dissent among the non-Indigenous Canadian public.[7] Of course, the fact that change has taken place does not mean that all is well: see above.

Why the current law of Aboriginal title was unimaginable fifty years ago depends largely upon whether one was Indigenous or non-Indigenous. For most of the latter, it was because the law of Aboriginal title – like residential schools – was not even remotely on their radar, although it was there to be found in the case law, where for decades it had slept among the spiders and the mice, in archives and old books. For most of the former, it was because years of official denial had made what began as a reasonable hope for a just resolution of the land question recede into the future and appear increasingly unlikely. As long ago as 1929, provincial and federal policies seemed to have extinguished almost all such hope. In that year the Kitwancool Land Committee, some of whom had been jailed for resisting reserve surveys two years before, were especially discouraged. Noting that their laws were not so different from English laws regarding ancestral lands, they lamented that the "Good Queen Victoria" was no longer alive.[8]

2.

It was on that day, Monday, 8 October 1900, that Swanton met the finest poet he would ever meet, in any language or tradition.

Robert Bringhurst, *A Story as Sharp as a Knife*,
referring to Skaay of the Qquuna Qiighawaay

My original subject for this collection of essays was Volume 1 of Robert Bringhurst's trilogy on Haida oral literature, *A Story as Sharp as a Knife: The Classical Haida Mythtellers and their World*.[9] I chose it because the trilogy and the critical reaction to it raised all three of the themes of the workshop, and especially the role of the non-Indigenous scholar in conversations about Indigenous art, languages, history, and law. What did Bringhurst do? He translated thousands of lines of Haida stories told by the "Mythtellers" of Xhaaydla Gwaayaay, or "the

Islands on the Boundary between Worlds," to linguist John Reed Swanton at the beginning of the twentieth century. Then he wrote about what it meant to him.[10]

Swanton's focus was on Ghandl of the Qayahl Llaanas, baptized in English as Walter McGregor, and Skaay of the Qquuna Qiighawaay, called by the missionaries John Sky. When Bringhurst published these works and his reflections on them, a heated controversy ensued. I recall reading about it at the time, but I did not appreciate what he had done until a couple of years ago, when I read the second edition of *A Story as Sharp as a Knife*. Twice. I think this book is remarkable (in a good way). As anthropologist Hugh Brody wrote in the *National Post*, "Just about every verse is touched with magic ... The voices of the Haida glow in this book." But not everyone agrees. As a Haida history student at UVic put it, Bringhurst "is the supposed 'great' Canadian author that everyone seems to be drooling about [and he] has taken it upon himself to translate and rewrite our history, without consultation with us, and is proceeding in making a fortune with his three glossy books."[11]

This assessment is harsh, but it captures one of the two main objections to what Bringhurst did: that he should not have translated and written about Haida myths without Haida permission. The other is that he took liberties with the translation and wrongly characterized the stories told by Ghandl and Skaay as works of oral literature that draw heavily on communal myths, rather than as communal myths or stories *simpliciter*. In other words, myths are not poems, say the critics, nor are tellers of myths poets.[12]

Haida artist Bill Reid was Bringhurst's friend and teacher. He and Reid worked together for over a decade and published a book, *The Raven Steals the Light*, in 1984. Bringhurst also edited a collection of Reid's writings after the latter's death in 1998.[13] Citing Reid in support, he says this in a "Political Afterword" to the second edition of Vol. 1:

> It is ... true that *literature* is not the word that most Haida people use nowadays to speak of their verbal inheritance ... The fact that I was reading and celebrating this inheritance *as literature* was exciting to Bill Reid, but to many other Haida (and to some anthropologists and linguists) it has seemed misguided at best. The fact that I have called the stories *poems*, identified and singled out their speakers, researched their biographies, and celebrated them as *poets* has seemed to some especially perverse and intrusive. For some, this sense of intrusion, and the anger that came with it, may never wear off. Within the Haida community, that reaction is not hard to understand. People whose culture and identity have been relentlessly squeezed over more than a century, and then, with equal mindlessness, romanticized and commercialized for the tourist trade, are entitled to be angry and suspicious for as long as they can bear to feel that way. But the view that no outsider should speak of the Haida mythtellers without Haida permission is not the view that I was taught by my Haida teacher and not a view to which I subscribe.[14]

In *Surviving as Indians*, Menno Boldt provided a justification for such a position. He argued that non-Indigenous scholars can write about Indigenous issues because the "principle of a common humanity requires scholars to transcend the boundaries of their identity to find common human ground."[15] Edward Said, in *Culture and Imperialism*, takes it up a notch. "I have no patience," he wrote, "with the position that 'we' should only or mainly be concerned with what is 'ours,' any more than I can condone reactions to such a view that require Arabs to read Arab books, use Arab methods, and the like. As C.L.R. James used to say, Beethoven belongs as much to West Indians as he does to Germans, since his music is now part of the human heritage."[16]

To understand Bringhurst's perspective, one needs to know the back story of what Swanton did, and how this enabled Bringhurst to translate and write about the stories Ghandl, Skaay, and others told to him 121 years ago. But I wrote most of the above before the workshop. Afterwards, cloistered at home because of the COVID-19 pandemic and instructed by Kent and John to submit essays that are "more personal and experiential than academic," I realized that I had to change gears. Intriguing as the Bringhurst book is, I am not especially qualified to address it, nor does it speak to my own experience.

So I moved on to a different story, also with sharp edges: the decision of the Benchers of the Law Society of BC in April of 2017 to disassociate the Society from Sir Matthew Baillie Begbie, BC's first legally trained judge, and to remove his statue from the foyer of its headquarters.[17] The Benchers' action was prompted by his having presided in 1864 at the trials of six Tsilhqot'in warriors that resulted in the conviction and execution of five of them, executions that the Royal Commission on Aboriginal Peoples compared to the hanging of Louis Riel.[18] This is more within my bailiwick than whether Ghandl and Skaay were the Haida Sophocles and Shakespeare. But, for me, it is also more fraught.

As a lawyer and historian who has written about Begbie, often critically, and who testified for the Tsilhqot'in in *Tsilhqot'in Nation v British Columbia*, speaking up for him has felt more than a little awkward.[19] Defending a colonial judge the public now sees as having been shamed by the Law Society is, let's face it, not a good look. It invites the sort of reaction that Mohawk Taiaiake Alfred had to Alan Cairns's *Citizens Plus: Aboriginal Peoples and the Canadian State*. I regard Cairns's book as an early attempt to grapple with the challenges of what we now refer to as truth and reconciliation. Alfred does not. His review was entitled "Of White Heroes and Old Men Talking." In it he describes Cairns as a "grumpy geezer" and says that people like him should "stop talking and get out of our way." Cairns was unsure whether "our" meant Indigenous scholars or Indigenous people generally but, either way, he said, "I interpreted this as a negative review."[20] That sounds about right.

3.

The narratives of journalism (significantly called "stories"), like those of mythology and folklore, derive their power from their firm, undeviating sympathies and antipathies. Cinderella must remain good and the stepsisters bad. "Second stepsister not so bad after all" is not a good story.

Janet Malcolm, *The Silent Woman*

A few weeks after the Law Society's decision to remove Begbie's statue because of "his negative relationship with Indigenous people in British Columbia," the judiciary approved the installation of a bust of Chief Justice McEachern in the Law Courts.[21] I am sure the irony of this is not lost on many readers. But for those on whom the irony *is* lost: in 1991 Chief Justice McEachern ruled that any rights the Gitxsan and Wet'suwet'en may have had before 1846 were implicitly extinguished by colonial ordinances, and that oral histories on their own are not good evidence of title. There were therefore no constitutionally protected Aboriginal rights or title whatsoever in BC. If any decision created a "negative relationship" between a judge and Indigenous people, it was this one.[22]

But I need to be very clear. Commemoration and history are different things: the former deals with national or cultural mythology and symbolism; the latter, when done properly, seeks to understand the past on its own terms. So it was appropriate for the Law Society to decide that a colonial judge is no longer the right symbol for BC's legal profession in the twenty-first century. Especially one whose role was as important as Begbie's in instituting British law. True, there is evidence that some Indigenous people appreciated the arrival of British law and order, and not only to keep American miners in line. For example, in interviews with three Nlaka'pamux Elders in 1893 conducted by James Teit, who spoke their language fluently, one elder, Tsillagheskit, said that feuding and violence were so bad by 1858 that he thought "it was good for the Indians that the Whites came into the country and law, peace and order was brought in." He told Teit that it gave the communities "a chance to ... live easier & better."[23] Speeches made annually on Queen Victoria's birthday at New Westminster in the 1860s are similar. In addition to asking the new governor to protect their land, one chief in 1864 was reported as saying, "Please to protect us against any bad Indians, or any bad white men ... [and] Please to give good things to make us become like the good white men as exchange for our land occupied by white men."[24] Nonetheless, Begbie – not as an individual but as BC's first legally trained judge – represents or symbolizes a colonial regime of governance that, over time, largely – but by no means completely – replaced Indigenous law with British law. A regime that, after a century of shouting, finally, and slowly, has begun to quiet down and listen.

I am also not interested in renewing criticism of Chief Justice McEachern's decision at trial in the *Delgamuukw* case.[25] My subject, instead, is how the Benchers' decision was made and, in particular, the reasons contained in the advisory committee report that they relied upon. Their decision was motivated, quite properly, by the need for truth and reconciliation and by the need to listen. But in my view the report and the way the decision was announced are in tension with these objectives, and addressing this unavoidably raises the issue of the role of the non-Indigenous scholar. We therefore need to remind ourselves that the report of the Truth and Reconciliation Commission stresses that "shaming and pointing out wrongdoing were not the purpose of the Commission's mandate."[26] Indeed, none of the report's ninety-four Calls to Action require the removal of statues, which Chief Commissioner Murray Sinclair has described as "counterproductive to … reconciliation."[27] Moreover, Calls to Action 79–83, which deal with commemoration, stress inclusion and the integration of Indigenous perspectives rather than the exclusion of others. Had the Benchers simply expressed respect for Begbie as BC's first chief justice, but explained that a colonial judge, especially one obliged to preside over the 1864 trials, was no longer an appropriate symbol for the foyer of the Law Society building, this might have remained an essay about Bringhurst.

Because they did not do this, I tried to write about Begbie and the Law Society long before the workshop but gave up when the draft began to rival *War and Peace* in length. Kent and John's invitation to be experiential and personal seemed to be permission to try again. So what I offer here is the *Coles Notes* version, conceding that I have cheated somewhat – okay, more than somewhat – by resorting to copious endnotes. I realize that I may be no more successful at getting it right this time around than I was in my last abandoned attempt. But that is for others to judge.

4.

In thinking about American Indian history, it has become essential to follow the policy of cautious street crossers: Remember to look both ways.

Patricia Limerick, *The Legacy of Conquest:*
The Unbroken Past of the American West (NY 1987)

The main reason given in the report the Benchers acted on for removing Begbie's statue is that he "found [the Tsilhqot'in warriors] guilty" of murder and "ordered their execution." But he did not do this.

The trials at Quesnelmouth in 1864 were jury trials. It was the jury who found the warriors guilty, not Begbie, and in 1864 death was the mandatory sentence for murder. If the jury convicted, the presiding judge had no discretion respecting punishment. So although Begbie did pronounce the mandatory sentence, as he was required to do, he neither found the warriors guilty nor did he decide to order their execution.

The report also states, incorrectly, that he sentenced six men to death at Quesnelmouth in 1864. It was in fact five: Klatsassin (or Klatsassan), Piell, Telloot, Tahpit, and Chessus (currently spelled Lhats'as?in, Biyil, Tilaghed, Taqed, and Chayses). Begbie also discharged two others for want of evidence, and a third was acquitted after a juror took to heart Begbie's instruction that the evidence against him was insufficient. A sixth man, Chief Ahan, was tried along with another named Lutas at New Westminster in 1865 and hanged, but Begbie did not preside. Lutas was pardoned because of his youth and because, in Governor Seymour's view, "a sufficient number of lives had been taken to atone" for the attacks in 1864.[28] It was the colonial governor, not Begbie, who had the discretion to commute the death sentences and who set the date of execution if clemency were denied.

No mention was made of any of these facts when the decision to remove the statue was announced in 2017. Such omissions may seem minor, and perhaps they are, on their own. But many of the press accounts that I read at the time were equally bereft of detail. They made little or no mention of the nature of the attacks that began what came to be called the Chilcotin War, or the reasons for the attacks, including the unforgiveable threat by someone to bring back the smallpox. According to the warrior leader, Lhats'as?in, twenty-one Tsilhqot'in were involved. They killed nineteen colonists and possibly Kylmtedza, the Tsilhqot'in wife of one of the colonists. Only one Tsilhqot'in warrior, Chacatinea, was killed. (He had been among those who had ambushed a party of traders subsequent to the main attack on the Homathko River.) Begbie noted that it was a threat to bring back the smallpox that had triggered the attacks, adding that there was a similar threat "said to have been made to them previous to the [epidemic of 1862–3], when half their numbers (on a moderate computation) perished."[29] This statistic, like the unmarked graves in Kamloops, is yet another all too invisible aspect of our mutual history.

I know some might object that "war" is the wrong term for what happened, given that so few Tsilhqot'in were directly involved. But this objection substitutes what war has meant in non-tribal cultures for what it meant to the Tsilhqot'in: surprise attacks by a small group of warriors on another nation qualified as war, even though a chief such as Lhats'as?in did not have the authority to commit other Tsilhqot'in chiefs and their people to join in.

Briefly, what happened was this. Denied food, angry at the intrusion on their lands, and frightened by the threat to bring back the dreaded smallpox, the war party, which included men who had worked on the projected road, mingled with the workers at supper the evening beforehand.[30] Then, just before dawn, they prayed, blackened their faces and attacked the sleeping encampments. Once they had killed everyone they could, they mutilated the bodies: heads were cut off, limbs amputated, and in the case of one especially despised individual, not only was his heart cut out and partially eaten, but by some accounts his penis was amputated and inserted in his mouth. These attacks were followed a few weeks later by two more.[31] In the world of the Tsilhqot'in, such disturbing details are the identifying signs, not of crime, but of intertribal, i.e., international, war. They are indispensable context for assessing both the perspective of the attackers and, equally, the perspective and reaction of the colonial authorities.[32]

Gold Commissioner William Cox, who headed one of the two expeditions sent to capture the war party, appeared, or at least pretended, to regard the conflict as this sort of war. He testified that before the warriors came to his camp, he had sent them a message stating that, if the guilty did not surrender, he would "follow them up and kill the men, women and children."[33] That was how tribal warfare had been conducted in the past, but to Begbie such a course of action would have been unthinkable. He believed one had to strive for due process, even as he realized that all the complex and ancient rules of English criminal procedure could not, and perhaps should not, be observed.[34] The only documented lynching in BC I am aware of in Begbie's day was carried out by an American mob who crossed the border in 1884, broke a fifteen-year-old Stó:lō boy out of police custody, and hanged him.[35] This was a vigilante alternative to an imperfect trial that was resorted to all too often in the US and, after the fact, may even have tempted Governor Seymour. When he informed the Colonial Office in September of 1864 that he might find himself compelled to "invite every white man to shoot each Indian he may meet," he added that, if he did, he would only be following the example set by the Governor of Colorado. The secretary of state for the colonies professed not to know what Seymour meant – a clear rebuke – and instructed him to adhere to "the line of conduct hitherto pursued."[36] The proclamation announcing Colorado Governor John Evans's policy was published in the *British Colonist* on 17 September 1864. The headline, "The Way Our Neighbours Settle Indian Difficulties," may well have been intended to refer to more than just the policy in Colorado.

For example, in 1862, two years before the trials at Quesnelmouth, a military court had sentenced 303 Dakota Sioux to death for their participation in the Dakota War in Minnesota. The military wanted all of them speedily hanged, but President Abraham Lincoln, although preoccupied with the American Civil War, would approve the execution of only thirty-eight. The remainder were jailed and on more than one occasion were attacked by mobs while in military custody. One of the criteria Lincoln used for commuting the Dakota death sentences was whether the accused had killed during a surprise attack or "massacre" (as the Tsilhqot'in did), or during a battle with the army. Only the former were executed, and it was the largest mass execution in US history. All the Dakota reservations were abolished, and the Dakota were expelled from the state of Minnesota.[37] And a year later, in 1863, volunteer soldiers from Fort Douglas in Salt Lake City surrounded four bands of Shoshone at Bear River in Idaho and killed between 250 and 500 people.[38]

Some of the press accounts of the Law Society's decision in 2017 that I referred to above not only attributed the convictions and death sentences to Begbie, but described them as "wrongful," implying that he had personally done something reprehensible, that is, something over and above a legal error that might result in a new trial today. Neil Postman has called this sort of thing "decontextualized information."[39] In providing some missing context, I do not mean to imply that facts about the criminal justice system in 1864 get to the heart of the matter. They most emphatically do not. But they do need to be addressed.

There was no right of appeal from a criminal jury conviction in 1864, nor would Anglo-Canadian law provide such a right until 1892.[40] But because there were no trials (as contemplated by the common law) in the Tsilhqot'in legal regime, it follows that there were no appeals in it, either. (When more supreme court judges were appointed at confederation with Canada in 1871, convictions could then be reviewed in the Full Court by writ of error. But this procedure was confined to errors on the face of the record, and "record" was narrowly defined: for example, it did not include the wrongful admission of evidence or a jury misdirection.) Such procedural issues – what Jeremy Bentham called the arcane technicalities of "Judge & Co." – would of course not have mattered to the Tsilhqot'in. Nonetheless, and setting aside the key issue of jurisdiction (to which I will return in Part 5), what sort of error might have qualified as theoretically appealable today? I think there is at least one possible ground and two other aspects of the case that are vulnerable to criticism, even if these two cannot be characterized as *legal* errors.

The Chilcotin War began with surprise attacks on the road builders' ferry, their base camp, and their advance camp, and it ended with surprise arrests. The latter provide a potential ground of appeal because the evidence adduced at trial included some inculpatory statements by the warriors. These statements could have been excluded because the men had come into the colonial posse's camp believing they were attending peace talks, not surrendering. Although there is some debate as to what the source of this misunderstanding was, the fact that the warriors did misunderstand is clear and was controversial even at the time. Begbie, for example, reported that "[b]oth Mr. Cox and Klatsassin ... expressly state ... that the latter was completely in the dark as to the consequences of his entering Mr. Cox's camp on the 15th August." He added that Klatsassin (Lhats'as?in) at no time alleged "any breach of faith" by Cox.[41] Nonetheless, a report in the *British Colonist* at the time concluded that "the account given by our informant of the means by which Mr. Cox obtained possession of the eight Indian prisoners ... does not look very well."[42]

In the mid-nineteenth century there was no Charter of Rights, and the law respecting confessions was in flux. Generally, a statement was involuntary and therefore inadmissible only if it were induced, either by hope of advantage (a promise) or fear of prejudice (a threat) held out by a person in authority. But the real complaint in 1864 was not the statements; it was that someone led the warriors to believe they were coming to peace talks when the intention was not to negotiate but to arrest them. The inducement, therefore, was with respect to surrendering, not speaking.[43] Moreover, the statements appear to have played a minor role in the trials. For example, the British Colonist for 25 August 1864 reported that Lhats'as?in had said on arriving that "I have brought seven murderers, and I am one myself," but Begbie did not allow this to go to the jury.[44] Obviously a mistranslation, it would be admissible only against Lhats'as?in in any event. It is true that today the statements, even if voluntary, could be excluded if they were induced by a "trick" that would "shock the community" and bring the administration of justice into disrepute. But this is a very high bar.[45] And there was substantial other evidence on the counts where the jury did convict. At the trial of Tahpit (Taqed), for example, Nancy, a Tsilhqot'in woman who was William Manning's wife, testified that she saw Tahpit kill him. And after the trials, the condemned prisoners conceded their roles in the attacks.

The first of the two other grounds for criticism is Begbie's inclusion of Telloot (Tilaghed) with the others because he had been convicted of attempted murder only. Begbie did have an odd sort of discretion on this one count: he could have simply recorded the jury's verdict rather than pronounce it in open court, which would have reduced the penalty to life imprisonment. He had done this at least once before, in 1859, when a jury had convicted an Indigenous man of attempted murder.[46] He also knew that in England a judge would probably have done this.

Begbie may not have known that in 1861 the number of capital offences had been reduced by statute in the UK to four, excluding attempted murder and thereby making execution for it legally impossible; strictly speaking, this did not matter. English statute law was received only as it existed at the reception date of 17 November 1858, so in 1864 attempted murder was still a capital offence in BC. Still, Begbie could have simply recorded the sentence. It therefore seems that because British Columbia in the 1860s was not England, he felt he could not distinguish Telloot from the others in terms of responsibility. So he did not, leaving him in the same position as his companions, that is, at the mercy of the governor.

By the time another case of attempted murder came before the governor and his council, Begbie must have become aware of the 1861 statute because he advised that in England the death penalty was no longer imposed "unless life had actually been taken." Although the prisoner, Mootsack, is described as a boy, and there was evidence of mental disturbance, the majority of the council remained in favour of the death penalty notwithstanding this. Governor Musgrave disagreed: he was critical of what he saw as the council's double standard regarding Indigenous offenders and commuted the sentence. He added that he "understood the Chief Justice to agree with him in the propriety of this course."[47]

Begbie's decision not to recommend clemency is another point of contention, but it also does not qualify as a legal error, however much one might wish he had done otherwise. His report to the governor respecting the convictions reveals hesitation, stating as it does that it "seems horrible to hang five men at once – especially under the circumstances of the capitulation. Yet the blood of twenty-one [sic] whites calls for retribution." He concludes his report by telling the governor, "I do not envy you your task of coming to a decision" about whether to carry out the executions.[48] In my view, none of these decisions crossed the line between judicial error and judicial abuse of authority; more importantly, none speaks to the real reason that, over the years, the executions became an open wound for the Tsilhqot'in: that men who saw themselves as warriors defending their country had been treated as criminals worthy only of the gallows. As Judge Anthony Sarich put it when he inquired into criminal justice issues in the region in 1992, even then there was "still barely concealed anger and resentment about the trickery" that led to the hangings in 1864.[49]

I do not think that the Benchers' failure to make it clear that it was the jury who found the warriors guilty, or that the death penalty was mandatory, was deliberate. "The largest difficulty in legal history," a legal historian has written, "is precisely that we look at past evidence in the light of later assumptions, including our own assumptions about the nature and working of law itself."[50] It can therefore be easy to forget the facts discussed above about criminal procedure in 1864. And to forget that, if the prosecution proved that the accused caused the death of the deceased, the burden of proof shifted to the defence to disprove murderous intent.[51] And that accused persons could not take the stand to try to disprove this intent because they could not testify under oath until 1893 – all accused persons, Indigenous or not. Given these possible memory lapses, the Benchers, relying on the committee report, may have assumed that because judges can try murder cases without a jury today, they could in 1864 as well; they may have also thought that Begbie had discretion as to sentence (although even now the penalty for murder is mandatory, so this is harder to credit).[52] Or perhaps both the Benchers and the committee members were so focused on the need to listen to what the Tsilhqot'in were saying and to appreciate the symbolism involved, they simply did not direct their minds to these other factual issues. This seems more likely.

Nonetheless, their imprecision has led to misunderstanding and confusion. After the decision to remove the statue was announced I spoke to a number of people, and almost everyone, lawyers included, whose only source of information about the events of 1864 was the media, believed that the decision to convict and sentence the men to hang was Begbie's, and his alone. Which is not true. Some also did not know what the hanged men were alleged to have done. A poster that appeared in April of 2017 next to the official plaque about Begbie near the old courthouse in Victoria's Bastion Square is an extreme example of this because, without elaborating, it describes the executions as the result of a "land dispute." As such, it can give the impression that the men were executed simply for opposing the road through their territory. It therefore illustrates both the importance of context and the need to distinguish between facts and perspectives. I have reproduced and commented on this poster in appendix 2.[53]

The allegation that Begbie convicted the warriors of murder and decided to have them executed is not simply a matter of perspective: it is factually incorrect. The jury convicted and the governor ordered the execution. The report also concludes that Begbie "epitomizes the cruelty of colonization" and gives more reasons for condemning him. Some of these involve misinformation, but most are better characterized as misleading or incomplete rather than incorrect because they involve a mixture of facts and opinion: for example, the assertion that Begbie's relationship with BC's Indigenous people generally is "negative." The report produces no evidence to support such a sweeping generalization. The Law Society's decision to remove his statue has nonetheless prompted others – notably the City of New Westminster – to follow suit. Of course, if one knows nothing about Begbie other than what was contained in the Law Society's announcement, the issue probably seems straightforward.

I have been researching and writing about BC's legal history for over forty years, and I have come across only one example of an Indigenous person saying anything negative about Begbie. It was in 1879, after Charlie McLean and three others killed a constable. Charlie told a stock-raiser from whom they had taken guns and ammunition that they would kill anyone who came after them. Charlie added this: "Do you think that grey-headed son-of-a-bitch Judge Begbie will ever get the drop on me? They will never take me alive." He then lowered his rifle and said "a shot out of that would send [Begbie] straight to the right hand of Jesus Christ." Not long afterwards, Charlie, his brothers Alan and Archie, and Alex Hare surrendered to a posse of over seventy-five men, mainly ranchers and members of the Nicola First Nation, including a prominent chief, Chill-e-heetsa (Chilihitza).[54]

My research has been primarily, although by no means exclusively, documentary; so it is quite possible that accounts based on oral histories, particularly in the Chilcotin, contain harsh views of Begbie. *Nemiah: The Unconquered Country* is one such account. Published in 1992 and written by Terry Glavin and the Xeni Gwet'in of the Nemiah Valley, the primary plaintiffs in the Tsilhqot'in land claim, *Nemiah* deals with the Chilcotin War of 1864 and is based extensively on

Tsilhqot'in oral history. But Begbie is not mentioned in it, let alone criticized. Nor does Glavin recall him being brought up during the interviews he conducted. It therefore seems that, until quite recently, even the Tsilhqot'in did not single Begbie out for censure.[55]

Begbie also goes largely unmentioned in the *Report of the Cariboo-Chilcotin Justice Inquiry* (1993), even though "in every village" the commissioner visited the people had "long memories" and maintained that the hanged men were warriors "defending their land and people." The only exception is Judge Sarich's statement that "even Begbie was concerned about the fairness of the trial," which is a reference to Begbie's hesitation about the circumstances of the warriors' capitulation, i.e., the disturbing fact that they came into the authorities' camp believing they were attending peace talks.[56] The advisory committee report does not refer to *Nemiah*. It does cite the *Sarich Report*, but only for its recommendation that the warriors be pardoned. It does not note the lack of focus on Begbie. And according to the priest who ministered to the condemned men in 1864, when Tahpit, the oldest, mounted the scaffold in Dakelh territory, he asked the Dakelh in the crowd, who were traditional enemies of the Tsilhqot'in, to tell "the Chilcoatens to cease anger against the whites."[57]

The advisory committee report goes on to state that, for "mainstream society, Judge Begbie represents the introduction of law and order to the province of British Columbia," which, to the extent that the mainstream is aware of him, may well be true. But it adds that this "perception is based on the assumption that there was no law and order in the region prior to the arrival of Europeans, which completely ignores the existence of Indigenous peoples and Indigenous laws." This may be how "mainstream society" perceives pre-contact British Columbia. It is not how Begbie did.

In 1858 imperial officials knew little or nothing about the Indigenous peoples of BC and their laws, and they admitted as much in colonial despatches. That is one of the reasons why the British government provided so little guidance on the subject and gave Governor James Douglas, the "man on the spot," such extraordinary executive and even legislative authority. Moreover, the Colonial Office did not send a trained legal professional to the new colony to counter any perceived threat to law and order posed by Indigenous people. Begbie was sent because of the sudden influx of at least thirty thousand non-Indigenous – mainly American – gold seekers. His legendary role (partly factual, partly apocryphal) in carrying out this responsibility is why "mainstream society" may perceive him as they do. In other words, and contrary to the implication in the report, the Colonial Office was concerned about the threat of violence and American annexation posed by lawless non-Indigenous miners, *not* "lawless" Indigenous people.[58]

They were not lawless, and Begbie knew this. From the fur trade era until at least the 1880s, the documentary record is replete with references to "Indian law" and "tribal law" by people such as fur traders, colonial officials, and even some journalists who actually knew something about the various nations. Judges knew this as well. Had there been no gold rush in 1858 and no perceived threat to law and order posed by non-Indigenous miners, it is unlikely that Begbie would have been sent when he was. A legally trained judge was not despatched to Vancouver Island until 1865, sixteen years after that colony had been established.

To support the contention that, for "many Indigenous people, Judge Begbie epitomizes the cruelty of colonization," the report goes further, asserting that he "completely disregard[ed] Indigenous laws." No evidence other than the 1864 trials is produced in support of the first charge.[59] As for the second, it is true that Begbie was a British judge in a colony of the British Empire, and that British law was the law he was sworn to apply. It is also true that he saw that law as superior, and looked forward to its eventually replacing "the [Indians'] own old methods of investigation and punishments and licenced retributions and compensations."[60] But it is not true that he completely disregarded Indigenous law. I think Begbie would have agreed with what a prominent local lawyer said in 1873 about how the criminal law should be applied to Indigenous persons. "As the Indians in their tribal condition have established almost universally a system of recompense for almost all offences," he wrote, "why should not that system be carried out and only those offences brought before the Supreme Court which couldn't be dealt with in this manner?"[61] I say Begbie would have agreed because he said something similar and because, although he told jurors that they had to follow British law, he allowed evidence of what Indigenous law was to go before the jury and regarded it as relevant to whether clemency was appropriate.

Begbie recommended clemency, or remained neutral, in almost half of the capital cases he presided over in the colonial period. Fifty-two men were charged with murder between 1859 and 1872. Of these five were acquitted, nine were convicted of manslaughter only, and thirty-eight were convicted of murder. In eleven of the latter (nine Indigenous and two Chinese) Begbie recommended clemency and the governor and council agreed. He opposed clemency for twenty of the twenty-seven who were hanged, and either remained neutral or his recommendation for clemency was rejected in the remainder.[62] In other words, he recommended clemency or remained neutral in eighteen of the thirty-eight murder convictions. (In the decade after confederation the supreme court bench expanded from one judge to five, so Begbie's role in murder cases declined significantly.) People may disagree on whether this record is sufficiently harsh to justify the descriptor, "hanging judge." But he was not known as such during his lifetime. The phrase was the invention, after Begbie's death in 1894, of journalists and tourism promoters who wanted BC's colonial history, which looked tame compared to the "Wild West" south of the border, to be more exciting.

Begbie also intervened in the prosecution process on occasion to have charges against Indigenous persons reduced so as to avoid mandatory penalties and make more flexible sentences possible.[63] For example, in 1872 a Tsimshian man named Qutlnoh killed a medicine man he believed had bewitched his sisters, causing their deaths. Because this was his right under tribal law, Begbie and Justice Crease did not support imposing the mandatory death penalty. Their reason was best expressed by an old fur trader in his own submission to the governor general. Qutlnoh's act was not unreasonable, given the laws and beliefs of his people, said William Fraser Tolmie. It also seemed "in the abstract unjust that the rigor of modern British law should be brought to bear" on him. Especially, he added, "when it is remembered how many generations of the most civilized nations of Europe it took to get over this same superstitious belief in witchcraft which of old led to deeds that ... are now ... considered as altogether wrong."[64] Qutlnoh's sentence was therefore commuted to life imprisonment, and a year later Anglican missionary William Duncan and Begbie arranged for a petition that successfully urged that his sentence be further reduced to residence at Metlakatla under Duncan's supervision.

I can find nothing in the report to suggest the authors considered any of this. Neither, it would seem, did the Benchers. Perhaps they did not have time. Perhaps it would have made little or no difference, in any event. Nonetheless, I respectfully suggest that these cases hardly indicate a complete disregard for Indigenous laws. Of course, this does not change the fact that Begbie was a colonial judge applying colonial law. But I think it is necessary context for assessing just what sort of judge he was and whether the report's characterization of him in this respect is a fair one.

Begbie also urged justices of the peace to refrain from interfering with "chiefs exercising their customary jurisdiction" over minor offences unless the chief had imposed a penalty that was excessively severe. This directive *is* acknowledged by the authors of the report in a footnote. But it is dismissed as one of the examples Begbie's "supporters" cite to illustrate his "purported" compassion toward Indigenous people.[65] I don't think Begbie was being compassionate, purportedly or otherwise. He was simply being practical and acting on his belief in due process, the rule of law, and formal equality before the law. In three of the other examples of purported compassion the authors list he was also stating his opinion, respectively, that the government had acted badly with respect to the Songhees Indian reserve in Victoria; that the "Indian population" in general was intelligent and industrious; and that the law banning the Potlatch was poorly drafted.[66]

I think this last example is important. In the case of *R v Hamasak* an Indian agent, R.H. Pidcock, arrested Hamasak and charged him with violating the Potlatch ban. Pidcock then used his status as a justice of the peace to take a guilty plea and impose the maximum jail term permitted by law. Begbie set aside the guilty plea, a highly unusual thing to do at the time, and discharged Hamasak. He also criticized the anti-Potlatch law as vague and unfair and condemned Pidcock for an "abuse of justice." This decision rendered the law unenforceable until it was amended after Begbie's death.

In *The Fourth World: An Indian Reality*, co authors George Manuel and Michael Pooluns discuss this case. Manuel was a former elected Chief of the Neskonlith Indian Band and a member of the Shuswap (Secwépemc) Nation. He was one of the founders of the World Council of Indigenous Peoples and until 1981 was president. He also served three terms as president of the Native Indian Brotherhood (now the Assembly of First Nations) and was president of the BC Union of Indian Chiefs from 1979 to 1981. Published in 1974 with a forward by prominent Native American author Vine Deloria Jr., *The Fourth World* was a call to action, and it honours individuals who have advanced the cause of justice for Indigenous people. Most of the honourees are Indigenous, such as Johnny Chilihitza and Basil David of the Interior Tribes of British Columbia, Peter Kelly and Andrew Paull of the Allied Indian Tribes of British Columbia, and many others. A few, however, are not. One of these is Matthew Baillie Begbie, whom the book describes as a "proper justice."

The Fourth World addresses the *Hamasak* case in some detail. After referring to the incentives that the Indian agents offered for co-operation in potlatch prosecutions, the authors conclude: "We honour our grandfathers, who refused to persecute their brothers for money. We honour our grandfather [Hamasak], who endured Pidcock of whom we will speak no more. We honour Judge Begbie as a fitting grandfather for our European neighbours."[67]

The reason the report dismisses this sort of evidence (his "purported compassion toward Indigenous people") would appear to be Begbie's description of Lhats'as?in as "the finest savage I have met with yet." According to the authors, his "use of the term ' savage' is a clear indication that he was influenced by racist ideologies of his era." They also accuse him – again with no evidence – of being a "social Darwinist." I think this makes the word "savage" carry much more weight than it can bear. A century after these trials, for example, anthropologist Claude Levi Strauss entitled his book on the structural similarity of the thought processes of "primitive" and modern human beings *The Savage Mind*. And as David Milward has noted, two of the criticisms of Chief Justice McEachern's

> handling of the evidence [in the *Delgamuukw* case is] that he had a tendency to snip isolated quotes from source materials and then take those quotes at face value. Seen through the lens of academic history, both are cardinal sins. From the historians' perspective, a quote is an integral part of a broader whole: it cannot be properly understood without situating it, and understanding its place, within a much broader whole.[68]

I agree. In my opinion, by focusing as they have on one de-contextualized word, the authors of the report have resorted to a "scissors and paste" approach to the past. Jeremy Webber makes the point this way: "We [lawyers] are so used to employing the past instrumentally ... to support whatever argument we want to make today – that we can do very bad history, ignoring context, treating words as though their use in 1905 were the same as their use today, and failing to distinguish how the decisions of the past were often made in profoundly different institutional contexts."[69] In this case a contextual approach would note that the equivalent of "savage" in the Chinook Jargon is, as any Jargon dictionary will confirm, "siwash" (from the French, *sauvage*). The Jargon was an international language spoken by both Indigenous and non-Indigenous people in the nineteenth and early twentieth centuries, and "siwash" meant "Indian." As historian Jean Barman has said, "when Chinook was commonly spoken along the Pacific Northwest, the Chinook word 'Siwash' was not a derogatory term" – although it did become one.[70]

Still, I believe Begbie *was* influenced by the racial ideologies of his era, including the distinction between savagery and civilization. He also believed that "races" who consumed alcohol were superior to those that did not; or at least that "the use of alcohol is compatible with great improvement all along the line, and that water-drinking does not preserve a nation from every sort of degradation." He shared this eccentric opinion, which was clearly influenced by contemporary ideas about the superiority of Christianity and Anglo-Saxon civilization, with a royal commission on liquor towards the end of his life. Begbie himself drank wine and beer but rarely spirits. He opposed prohibition both on principle and because he thought it would cause more harm than it prevented.[71]

The reason I believe Begbie was influenced by racial thinking is that virtually everyone, Indigenous and non-Indigenous, was. And is. But to varying degrees. Celia Haig-Brown and David A. Nock have argued that "biological racism in eighteenth and nineteenth century attitudes ... was hegemonic ... until sometime around the Second World War. It was really only the fairly slow retreat of biological racism after 1945 ... that has made [it] seem so remote and politically incorrect to modern day, educated Canadians. However, 'scratch one of our ancestors' and we are apt to find a biological racist."[72] But only "apt to find." Being influenced by the racial ideas of one's day and being a biological racist are not the same thing. And apart from noting his use of the term "savage," the report provides no evidence that Begbie was the latter. Nor does it address the question of just what Begbie's views really were.

I cannot say with certainty what they were either, but the evidence suggests that he was influenced by the stadial theory of cultural development. Stadial theory was a product of the eighteenth century Scottish Enlightenment that enjoyed a resurgence when Begbie was in university in the 1830s. Biological racism is timeless, but the version associated with "social Darwinism" came along later. Both are Eurocentric, but they are different. Biological or "scientific" racism regards the hierarchy of races as fixed: once inferior, forever inferior. Stadial theory held that societies move gradually and naturally through stages from hunting (savagery) to herding (barbarism) to agriculture, and then, finally, to commerce.[73]

Another factor is that Begbie was an Anglican, and his racial ideas appear to have been similar to those often expressed by Anglican missionaries who, although both imperialist and Anglophile, rejected the biological racism and social Darwinism that in the latter half of the nineteenth century were eclipsing other ideas. According to Brett Christophers they believed that people "were distinguished from one another by religious belief, not by genus or skin colour." Christophers acknowledges that the Anglican discourse, while not one of race, was certainly one of empire, but he argues that the concept of human unity that underlies the rationalization of missionary work in general and conversion in particular "contradicted the thrust of contemporary racial theory."[74] Haig-Brown and Nock make a similar point: "Missionary teachers, now often reviled, generally held that Aboriginal cultures were less advanced than those of the white settlers (as did the biological racists) but stressed the capacity of Aboriginal students (as the biological racists did not) to ascend the ladder of civilization and held out the prospect of equality of the races."[75] In short, they were convinced of their religious and cultural superiority, not their immutable racial superiority.

This approach is of course also, and rightly, unacceptable today, but it is neither biological racism nor social Darwinism. When one looks at what Begbie actually had to say when he *did* generalize about people who were not European – notably the Chinese and the Indigenous peoples of BC – one will find class bias and idiosyncrasies about such things as water and alcohol, certainly, but nothing like the virulent racism that infected so many. For example, English traveler John Bensley Thornhill complained in 1913 – twenty years after Begbie's death – that British Columbia "has no use for the namby-pamby way in which the Dominion Government handles the Indian question, and I think that I am right in saying that everyone would be pleased if they segregated the sexes and let them die out altogether."[76] That Begbie would ever say – or even think – something like this is unimaginable.

His defence of the Chinese is especially striking because his public pronouncements attracted criticism. And it seems he may also have given support privately. A possible example involves one Charles Frederick Moore. Towards the end of his life Begbie employed Moore as his secretary; yet with only one exception, I cannot find Moore in the standard published accounts of BC's social and legal history, not even in David Williams's comprehensive biography of Begbie. The exception is a brief mention in an article published in 1947, in which the author, historian Sydney Pettit, notes that Begbie was known as a "secret giver, often helping the unfortunate with gifts of money." One such recipient was a C.F. Moore, whom Pettit describes as "an obscure person, it seems, who had suffered a great deal from misfortune."[77] Pettit apparently did not know Moore had been Begbie's secretary; that he had had a career as a writer, photographer, and colonial administrator in Hong Kong; or that when he relocated to BC he qualified as a notary public and passed his preliminary examination for the Canadian civil service. I do not point this out to be critical because Moore really does have a low historiographical profile.[78] I do so only because there is a possible explanation for what Pettit saw as Moore's unexplained obscurity and alleged misfortune: his wife was Chinese and they had seven interracial children. In his will Begbie left Moore interest on $4,000 and the use of one of his houses, rent free, for life. He and his family appear to have lived there most of his remaining years, possibly right up to Moore's death in 1916.[79]

Begbie's public stances on discrimination are better known. For example, in refusing to allow the City of Victoria to use a bylaw to deny pawn brokers' licences to Chinese applicants, he condemned the "racial jealousy" behind the move.[80] Citing international legal norms, he concluded that the law was an infringement "of personal liberty and the equality of all men before the law."[81] Writing about this case eighty years later, a Manitoba judge asked readers to "[p]lease remember that these words, which have a modern ring, were spoken in a British Columbia Court in 1888."[82] Three years earlier Begbie had told a royal commission of inquiry that "Industry, economy, sobriety and law-abidingness are exactly the four prominent qualities of Chinamen as asserted both by their advocates and their adversaries. Lazy, drunken, extravagant, and turbulent: that is, by the voices of their friends and foes, exactly what a Chinaman is not. That is, on the whole, I think, the real cause of their unpopularity."[83] For expressing these views, the Victoria *Daily Times* for 22 May 1885 reported that the chief justice was denounced "in scathing terms" at a public meeting, and a day later noted that there was a resolution "fastening the blame for future bloodshed on the heads of our judicial rulers." On his last circuit in 1889, when he was seventy-one, Begbie renewed old acquaintances in the Cariboo, describing the Chinese who had been there since the gold rush thirty years earlier as "better British Columbians than nine-tenths of the later arrivals."[84]

In 1859, the same year that he and Magistrate Peter O'Reilly convicted a white miner of assault solely on the testimony of Indigenous witnesses, Begbie wrote that "the Indian population ... have far more natural intelligence, honesty, and good manners, than the lowest class – say the agricultural and mining population – of any European country I have ever visited, England included."[85] Class conscious and perhaps even a tad pompous, yes, but a racist who epitomizes the cruelty of colonization, of whom lawyers should be especially ashamed? Compared to whom? Nor does Begbie seem to have changed his views: in 1885 he referred to Indigenous people as "a race of laborious independent workers" who were "self-supported and self-supporting."[86]

To invoke the spectre of social Darwinism to condemn Begbie's behaviour in the 1860s is, in my opinion, more of a rhetorical device than an argument. It is rather like calling everyone on the left a communist or everyone on the right a fascist – especially as the report makes no attempt to link the doctrine to anything Begbie ever said or did. Perhaps part of the problem is the term itself: one scholar has even suggested that "[o]verall, the label of 'Social Darwinism' is unhelpful and misleading."[87] I doubt this is always the case, but I think it is here because the authors of the report provide no evidence in support of their characterization of Begbie apart from his statement that Lhats'as?in was "the finest savage I have met with yet." They also seem to conflate stadial theory with biological racism. After citing a passage from Kent McNeil's article, "Social Darwinism and Judicial Conceptions of Indian Title in Canada in the 1880s," they quote a passage from a book published in 1871 that describes the stadial theory, not biological racism.[88] But as the title of Kent's article indicates, he was discussing Indian title in Ontario in the 1880s, by which time the biological racism to be espoused by the likes of John Bensley Thornhill was in ascendance.[89]

The judges Kent focusses on – notably Chancellor Boyd, the trial judge in the St. Catherine's Milling case – had never walked, paddled, or rode on horseback through bush to hold court, or hunted and fished to provision the court party, or sat around a campfire with Indigenous people, or tried to learn Indigenous languages, or advocated for reserve lands, as Begbie had.[90] They were cossetted urban men, mainly from Toronto, with, at most, a summer camp on Georgian Bay.[91] As BC Supreme Court Justice H.P.P. Crease remarked about the thousands of miles that assize judges had to cover on foot, horseback and canoe in BC: "I have travelled right through Canada from End to End – have lived for over three years in Canada West, and journeyed along Lake Huron and Lake Superior before steamboats were; and met nothing harder there."[92]

Another critic of the advisory committee summed up what was problematic about the report by saying that it reads more like an appellate factum than an attempt at an objective assessment of Begbie. It is perhaps best described as forensic history.[93] And as Judge Sarich himself remarked, quoting Claude Levi-Strauss, "The denial of complexity is the greatest tyranny."[94]

5.

It is possible to recognize people's contributions at the same time as recognizing their flaws.
Annette Gordon-Reed, author of *Thomas Jefferson
and Sally Hemmings: An American Controversy* (1997)

I abandoned my original bloated attempt to come to terms with the committee report because I was unable to resolve the tension between my disappointment with its flawed portrait of Begbie and my support for what motivated the Benchers' decision. One question led to another, and I ended up wandering down a number of rabbit holes. I have nonetheless taken a second stab at it because I believed I had some modest expertise to offer, and I wanted to contribute to truth and reconciliation, which the Truth and Reconciliation Commission has defined as "an ongoing process of establishing and maintaining respectful relationships."[95]

In discussing different perspectives and assessing the power of symbols in a respectful way, we have to listen to those who feel injured by the symbols, which the authors of the report clearly did. But we also have to ascertain the relevant facts, elusive as they can sometimes be. We have to get as many of these as right as we can before we move on to the more difficult task of trying to understand and compare perspectives – which, admittedly, influence our understanding of all but the plainest facts. We also have to be careful that we do not slide into the error of saying yes, we each have our perspective, but mine is the truth. Yours is simply a perspective. I think this is close to what the authors of the report have done. This is what I am trying *not* to do. And I recognize that I may not have entirely succeeded.

If so, I can report another failure. For years a statue of Begbie stood to the right of the main staircase in the foyer of the law school at the University of Victoria, and a Coast Salish spindle whorl and blanket were on the left. This tableau was the product of a joint student/faculty initiative, with significant Indigenous input, in 1997, when a cleansing ceremony that was heavily attended was held to install the blanket and spindle whorl, with WSÁNEĆ Elders presiding. The spindle whorl and statue represented, respectively, the Indigenous and the common law traditions in BC. In 2009 the Begbie statue was vandalized and stolen. It was never recovered and, twelve years later, when truth and reconciliation are even higher on our mutual agenda, an acceptable replacement has yet to be found: the space that was designed to represent the common law tradition remains vacant. I regret that this failure is one in which I, as a member of the Art & Public Space Committee from 2009 to 2012, was very much a part.

In reacting to a one-dimensional prosecution, one runs the risk of replying in kind, of becoming an equally one-dimensional defender. I get that. And as a non-Indigenous retired academic, I have found it especially challenging to be critical of the committee's report. I know some of the people who were members of the committee, both Indigenous and non-Indigenous, and I respect them. For my part, I have not only written about Indigenous rights and title, but I have taught and spoken about these issues for more than forty years to anyone who would listen; and not only at law schools, law and history conferences, and events put on by such organizations as Project North and the Aboriginal

Rights Coalition. I have talked as well to elementary and high school classes, Church groups, chartered accountants, service clubs and the like. Over the years I have also written numerous op-ed pieces on this subject. So criticizing a decision made in the name of truth and reconciliation is difficult.

To revert for a moment to Bringhurst's book, the title of which is a play on an old Haida proverb. It is said to be based on a story about a man who told his son the world was as sharp as a knife, adding that if he were not careful, he could fall off. The son was sceptical, and when he kicked the earth to show how stable it was, a splinter entered his foot, and he died.[96] In like fashion, my criticism of the committee report makes me wonder if – metaphorically speaking – I should be wearing steel-toed boots. I also wonder if any of the Benchers and the members of the advisory committee that produced the report may have felt the same way and were concerned about the reaction if they did not denounce Begbie sufficiently strongly.

I can understand how removing a colonial symbol associated with the Chilcotin War furthers the cause of reconciliation, but distorting the reputation of someone who is perhaps the most prominent elder (or, to use George Manuel's term, grandfather) of BC's legal profession does not. When I was asked in 2008 to be the dinner speaker at the annual Education Conference for Provincial Court Judges at Government House, I was given a choice between two topics, one of which – Begbie – was clearly favoured. Although Lieutenant Governor Steven Point did not attend the dinner itself, he began the evening with a speech welcoming his former judicial colleagues. My notes indicate that one of the things I said was that Begbie "was not the passionate defender of native rights that Sir William Martin, the first chief justice of New Zealand was; nor could he entirely escape the ethnocentric ethos of his times. But his record is much better that that of his contemporaries in Australia, the US, and the rest of Canada. And when his career is subjected to close examination, he stands out as both insightful and sympathetic when compared to most British Columbians of his day." That was and is my perspective. There are clearly others. But let's share our perspectives, and tell our stories, and find common ground if we can.

Begbie could certainly be short-tempered when dealing with lawyers whose submissions he perceived as wrong-headed; I have provided details of some of his less than judicial outbursts in the articles I referred to earlier in this essay.[97] But he was also capable of humility. At a function in 1876 the latter character trait enabled him to address the former. When the City Council of New Westminster read a formal address congratulating him on his knighthood, he used the occasion to apologize, publicly, for his injudicious behaviour in two civil cases tried there more than a decade earlier. Referring to them, Begbie said that "he had done things he and the citizens of New Westminster were sorry for, and [asked] forgiveness for his human proneness to err."[98] It also seems unlikely that he would have wanted a statue to be erected of him. His instructions regarding his funeral were that "no other monument than a wooden cross be erected on my grave, that there be no flowers and no inscription but my name, dates of birth and death and 'Lord be Merciful to Me a Sinner.'"[99]

So I agree that Begbie is no longer an appropriate symbol for the profession in an era of truth and reconciliation. But the statue is not the issue. The issue is: was he the man portrayed in the report? In addition to the present essay I therefore wrote a much shorter piece on just one of the cases that got Begbie in trouble. It appeared in *The Advocate*, the bi-monthly publication of the Vancouver Bar Association, in May of 2020.[100] My hope was that, without lecturing readers about the shortcomings of the advisory committee's report as I have done here, I could use just one case to demonstrate that Begbie's relationship with Indigenous people is much more complex – and much less dark – than the authors of the report seem to believe. I would go farther: I think that, on the evidence, Begbie was more unpopular with significant and vocal elements of the settler community and the press of his day than he ever was with Indigenous people.

Author Charlotte Gray's advice speaks to this issue but rather more bluntly: "If we want the future to respect our moment in history, perhaps we should expand our knowledge of the past before we launch into spasms of outrage."[101] Or, if that is too harsh, how about what Yale historian Joanne Freeman has said: "Balance is everything when unraveling the meaning of a life."[102] So while assessments of Begbie's place in history and the profession need to face up to the negative, they must also include the positive. An example of the latter is what Queen's University President George Grant reported after he had met Begbie onboard a steamship on the Fraser River. His name, said Grant, was "held in profound respect by the miners, Siwashes, and all others among whom he had dealt out justice."[103] Not so unlike George Manuel's assessment.

At one point in my journey round Begbie I was contacted by Bruce Fraser, who, along with some others, was concerned about what they saw as a decision made with good intentions but "without independent historical enquiry or consultation with the members" of the Law Society. This group included former Chief Justice Lance Finch, Tom Berger, former BC Court of Appeal Justice Martin Taylor, former BC Provincial Court Judge Cunliffe Barnett, and a number of others.[104] We urged the Benchers, not to restore the statue, but to support what we saw as true reconciliation by facilitating an open discussion of who Begbie was and how we should see him, warts and all, in the twenty-first century. This proposal was accompanied by a paper written by former Chief Justice Finch, setting out in more detail why this should be done. The proposal contained this statement:

Our retired Chief Justice notes in his paper that statues are seen as a sign of respect, [and] their removal is seen as a sign that respect is no longer due. As each generation discovers, no historical figure is without flaws, and this is no doubt true of

Chief Justice Begbie. But it would be a mistake for the profession to allow [his] life and work to be dismissed in the way this has been allowed to happen.[105]

It may be that the Benchers did not mean that respect is no longer due, but that is clearly how their decision was seen.

After sending this proposal to the Law Society, Bruce and David Hay met with its president and executive director, who expressed no interest in it. Among other things, they said that the main opposition was coming from members of the Bar with a one-to-ten-years call, members who – the implication seemed to be – look on us as over the hill. This response meant that our only recourse was to the membership. So we attended the virtual Annual General Meeting of the Law Society in October of 2020. At that meeting, and with the considerable assistance of Bruce and Martin Taylor, Tom Berger moved and I seconded a resolution (a) criticizing both the wording of the Benchers' 2017 announcement and the report this announcement was based on, and (b) proposing a new committee to find an inclusive symbol for the profession to replace Begbie. (But not to come up with some sort of "official" Law Society position on Begbie. History should be left to historians, not another committee of lawyers.) The resolution passed with 1,774 votes in favour and 637 against.

Still, I have to admit that there *are* times when I feel, if not exactly over the hill, rather like Taiaiake Alfred's grumpy geezer, obsessed with defending the reputation of a long-dead judge, one most British Columbians neither care about nor, probably, have even heard of until recently. And writing as I am in the aftermath of the "Black Lives Matter" protests and the announcement concerning the Kamloops Indian Residential School, I concede that this issue no longer feels as important to me as it did four years ago. Or even four months ago. But I have persevered for two reasons. The first is that, as a lawyer, it seems remiss not to. The *Canons of Legal Ethics* for lawyers in BC state that "Judges, not being free to defend themselves, are entitled to receive the support of the legal profession against unjust criticism and complaint." Deceased judges are uniquely unable to defend themselves, and Begbie, I believe, has been criticized unjustly. The second reason is that once we start misrepresenting facts because we believe our cause justifies it, we begin to lose ourselves. And we risk, down the road, having people conclude that they have been misled, which jeopardizes rather than facilitates reconciliation.

In my opinion, understanding the killings in 1864 and the subsequent trials is not helped by portraying Begbie as an unfair, social Darwinist judge who completely disregarded Indigenous law and who epitomizes the cruelty of colonization. That is not the sort of judge he was. Nor does understanding the continuing significance of these trials turn on the technical rules and practices of colonial criminal law (and by discussing these issues earlier in this essay I know I risk being misunderstood on this point). Begbie could have excluded the impugned statements, exempted Telloot (Tilaghed) from the death penalty, and recommended clemency. But this does not get to the heart of the matter. The Rev. R.C. Lundin Brown, who ministered to the condemned men for several weeks before their execution, noted that some colonists thought that because the killers were "savages threatened with extinction and eager to strike the first blow, savages who were under the impression that they were making war with the whites," they should not be executed. Although Lundin Brown grew to respect the men, and Lhats'as?in in particular, he disagreed. He tutored them in scripture and prepared them for baptism, but because of the brutality of the surprise attacks they carried out, he believed that they "amply deserved their doom."[106]

It was tragic that so many died as a result of the Chilcotin War, no matter how one apportions the blame: nineteen colonists and one warrior were killed and six warriors were executed. The attacks and the trials could likely have been avoided if the colonial authorities had respected the territory of the Tsilhqot'in, made a treaty, and secured formal permission to construct the road from Bute Inlet to the Cariboo gold fields – a road that, for both financial and engineering reasons, may not have been completed in any event. Because this was not done, men who saw themselves as making a defensive war against unwelcome and uncharitable visitors were confronted by an insecure colonial regime that could classify their actions only as murder. A regime whose only sanction was the degrading penalty of death by hanging, thus denying the warriors' status as defenders of their country.

This, I think, is the key to understanding the real issue. It was not that legal rules internal to British law may have been misapplied. Nor that there was no overlap between Tsilhqot'in and colonial law: if a homicide fit the definition of murder in either system, the penalty was often death.[107] It was rather that both the Tsilhqot'in and the colonial authorities regarded themselves as sovereign in the Chilcotin, and therefore not subject to the others' laws and definitions. So what was war to the Tsilhqot'in was crime to the colonial government. The former perspective can be glimpsed in Lundin Brown's account of what "some" colonists thought, and it is front and centre in what Chief Ervin Charleyboy said at trial in *Tsilhqot'in Nation v BC* in 2005. In one of the only two testimonial references to Begbie that I can find in 334 days of trial, he echoed the words of the warrior leader, Lhats'as?in. What the men executed in 1864 had done was not murder, he said, but war. So the Supreme Court of British Columbia did not have jurisdiction to try them.[108]

However, coming to grips with conflicting claims to sovereignty and the distinction between war and murder is more than a little challenging. The federal and provincial governments have both exonerated the men executed in 1864 and 1865, and this obliges us to address the question: if Begbie's court did not have jurisdiction in the 1860s, just when *did* Canadian courts acquire jurisdiction over the Tsilhqot'in or, for that matter, any other First Nation?[109] It seems we find it is easier to condemn our predecessors for the decisions they made than assess, as objectively as we can, the decisions we make today. Yet we are confronted with what are essentially the same issues.

The Benchers, for example, have not criticized Justice Marguerite Church, who issued an injunction in December of 2019 against supporters of the Wet'suwet'en House Chiefs claiming legal authority over the territory that the Coastal GasLink pipeline is crossing.[110] Nor am I suggesting for a moment that they should. But consider: stopping a road authorized by a colonial government through Tsilhqot'in territory was the issue in 1864, and stopping a pipeline authorized by a provincial government through Wet'suwet'en territory was the issue in 2019. Whose territory this was, and whose law applied, was the issue in 1864, as it was in 2019, and still is. Moreover, the Tsilhqot'in were divided in 1864, just as the Wet'suwet'en are now. Some supported, and some did not support, the warriors who engaged in the attacks long ago in the Chilcotin.[111] Some support, and some do not support, the blockades near the Morice River Bridge today. We have the advantage of more than 150 years of hindsight and have not squared this circle, yet we send Begbie to Coventry for not doing so?

6.

[Sacred bundles] are our memories, our stories, our learning on this journey. They are everything we hold as special, as holy, as timeless. Each part is vital because it helps make us who we are. Opening up and sharing them is a ceremony in its purest sense. That's true for all of us. Indian or not.

Richard Wagamese, *One Native Life*

Bruce Fraser has noted that in 2014 the Dakelh agreed to hold a ceremony formally forgiving the Tsilhqot'in for the Chinlac massacre in 1745, and that the Tsilhqot'in in turn agreed to forgive the Dakelh for the retaliation that followed.[112] In 1904 Father A.G. Morice, an Oblate missionary who had attained some proficiency in the Tsilhqot'in language and whose sources were the elders among whom he worked in the 1880s, described what had happened at Chinlac. The Tsilhqot'in had conducted an attack on the village to avenge the death of one of their own. The attackers had killed everyone they could find – men, women, and children – and were said to have left a message: "[H]anging on transverse poles resting on stout forked sticks planted in the ground, were the bodies of the children, ripped open and spitted through the out-turned ribs in exactly the same way as salmon drying in the sun. Two such poles were loaded from end to end with that gruesome burden." When the Dakelh retaliated three years later, they were said to have erected three poles of dead children.[113] Similar raids and counter raids took place in 1826 and 1827 between the Tsilhqot'in and the Dakelh, in which "[s]calping and mutilation were practised on both sides."[114] The agreement that was signed in 2014 also pledged the two Nations to work together. In other words, forgive the past, and work on the present and a better future.

Frank Calder was asked in 2003 how he felt about the Supreme Court of Canada's "three to three" ruling on extinguishment of Indian title in the *Calder* case thirty years earlier. Frank replied that it was "a major victory." He explained:

> You see, we didn't establish the Indian reservations. Those guys that we faced in court, they did it … To confine people inside that boundary, you have to be on top of them. You're both in the gutter. Right? If somebody's holding down that First Nation inside that reservation, somebody's got to be on his back and that guy on his back is controlling the law books. So the three-to-three decision meant that he had to get off my back and we'd turn around and face each other and talk. That was the birth of the negotiations, which in my book is the major number one victory of the *Calder* case.[115]

Turn around and face each other, and talk. This wise advice applies to much more than treaty negotiations between Indigenous peoples and non-Indigenous governments. It is what took place at the workshop in Saskatoon that generated these essays, a workshop in which Indigenous and non-Indigenous scholars and writers "faced each other and talked." We certainly did not agree on everything, but I think we did agree that there is more than one "Indigenous voice" and more than one non-Indigenous voice, too.[116]

I find that Frank's words lead me back to what I thought my topic would be in September of 2019: Robert Bringhurst. Bringhurst says that Bill Reid thought everyone born in North America or who moves here "should be taught to understand the achievements of indigenous North American societies … and should learn the gruesome history of indigenous and colonial interrelations. We should all, he said, accept and absorb those traditions – and be accepted by them in turn – as part of the price of living where we live. We should do it because, if we did, we could, in his words, 'become *North Americans* at last instead of displaced Europeans.'"[117]

The need for this sort of historical understanding of the darker aspects of our history is critical. To take but one more example: 150 years after it happened, Stephen Hume wrote an excellent account in the *Vancouver Sun* of the devastating smallpox epidemic in 1862–3 that likely killed at least 60 per cent of the Indigenous people in BC.[118] The mortality rate was probably greater than during the Black Death in Europe in the fourteenth century, and its effect on BC's Indigenous peoples was catastrophic. That history is still very much with us. When I sent the link to this article to my law school colleagues, one who had gone to school and university in BC asked an excellent question: "How did I grow up in this province without being told about this?" How, indeed?

Referring to his own situation, Bringhurst adds this to Bill Reid's perspective:

Treating native American mythtellers as individual artists, thinkers and poets doesn't just threaten entrenched opinions and upset a few comfortable chairs. It upsets the détente between colonizers and colonized, now that the war between them is theoretically over. It implies that the wall between them is built out of misinformation and would, if we let it, simply fall down. This threatens identities, not just positions. But perhaps what it offers is richer and truer – more truthful about the past, more honest with the future – than what it undermines.[119]

I don't know if Bringhurst is right about the Haida mythtellers, I really don't. But being as truthful as we can about the past – our mutual past – and honest about what we can achieve together seem crucial to me if reconciliation is to have a lasting foundation. As former Cree Chief Blain Favel said about Ottawa's plan to exonerate Chief Poundmaker for his role in the 1885 rebellion: "It should not be viewed as an act of 'good guy, bad guy,' with the bad guy apologizing," he said, but as "an act of literal reconciliation and nation building because we are saying this is our common history."[120] I know not everyone will agree. But I think it is the best way forward. And – Taiaiake Alfred to the contrary notwithstanding – this can be achieved only if both Indigenous and non-Indigenous scholars engage in the sort of respectful listening and discussion that took place at the workshop.

The last note I have of those discussions is that at the end Sa'ke'j (James Youngblood Henderson) thanked non-Indigenous people who work hard on these issues "because we can't give them back that time." In words I carry in my heart he concluded, "We are grateful, even if it sometimes looks as if we are not." I am just as grateful for all that the Indigenous people in my life have taught me, including those who helped me put together and teach my first Aboriginal law course over thirty years ago. Even if some of what I have said in this essay makes it look as if I am not.

Appendix 1

Raven Stealing the Sun by Nusi

Appendix 2

The "Hanging Judge" Poster

Commentary: The "Hanging Judge" Poster

Begbie thought that land was one of the two key causes of the conflict. (The other more immediate or triggering cause was the threat to bring back the smallpox.) He noted that one of the victims had located his homestead on Tah-pit's family's land and wrote "land quarrel" after the verdict: Begbie's Bench Book, BCPA, GR 2025, Vol. 4 (*Regina v Tah-pit*). The media of the day, on the whole, agreed. *The Daily Chronicle* stated that the main goal of the Tsilhqot'in was "to put a stop to a road through the Chilcoaten territory, for which no compensation had been offered" (20 [?] May 1864), and the *British Colonist* denied that "plunder was the actuating motive," stating that it was the same cause as in other British colonies: "the real or supposed encroachment of the white man upon their property" (30 May 1864).

The poster makes no mention of the colonists killed, creating the impression that the men were executed for property offences. Understandably, given that the Law Society made the same error, the poster also confuses who does the convicting in a jury trial, and what determines the punishment in a capital case. As many others have done, the unknown creator of the poster further implies that Begbie was known as the "Hanging Judge" during his lifetime. He was not.

Finally, the courthouse in Bastion Square is not where this happened. It was built only a few years before Begbie died, a quarter century after the trials at Quesnelmouth in 1864. A small point, I know, but the poster risks giving the impression that Begbie insisted on having persons charged with offences brought to him in the capital, whereas he travelled thousands of miles on foot, horseback, and by canoe to bring his court to every settled part of BC.

On the other hand, in asserting that there was no land cession treaty with the Tsilhqot'in, the poster is quite accurate; nor were the Tsilhqot'in consulted about the construction of the road. It is also true that the accused who came before Begbie in capital cases during the colonial period (1858–71) were – like the colony's population as a whole – primarily Indigenous.

The juxtaposition of this poster with the plaque erected by the government commemorating Begbie's contribution to law and order in nineteenth century British Columbia is striking and should stimulate the sort of public discussion members of the Law Society – not just the Benchers and the advisory committee – have yet to have. It can act as a springboard, both for sorting out (as best we can) what the facts were, and for understanding these two contrasting perspectives on our colonial history. A springboard, in other words, for both truth and reconciliation.

NOTES

I would like to thank Katherine Cook, Jeremy Webber, Bruce Fraser, QC, Kevin Gillese, Martin Taylor, QC, Keith Thor Carlson, and Ross Tweedale for their comments and criticisms. Of course, any errors that remain are mine. An earlier version of this essay was presented to a virtual meeting of the members of the University of Toronto Legal History Workshop on 30 September 2020. I would like to dedicate this final version to the late Tom Berger, OC, QC, whose career was a monument to the cause of Indigenous rights.

1 Expropriation, on the other hand, is the compulsory taking of property *with* compensation.

2 I tried to compare the Indigenous and non-Indigenous legal traditions in "One Good Thing: Law and Elevator Etiquette in the Indian Territories" in Rutherdale, Abel & Lackenbauer, eds, *Roots of Entanglement: Essays in the History of Native-Newcomer Relations* (Toronto: University of Toronto Press, 2018) 289 [originally published in *The Advocates' Quarterly* in 2010].

3 The painting in the appendix is *Raven Stealing the Sun*, by my son-in-law, Heiltsuk artist Nusi (Ian Reid – no relation to Bill Reid). Ian also found the "Nice Sun, Be a Shame If Someone Stole It" image on the Internet, but we now cannot locate the source. Notwithstanding his help with these images, the opinions expressed in this essay are mine, and mine alone.

4 An example of someone looking intently through this other lens is Chris Sankey, formerly an elected counselor of the Lax Kw'alaams Band, who wrote: "Instances and incidents of real racism – discrimination enshrined in law, policies of overt oppression, and true hatred, rather than microaggressions and misunderstandings – are much lower in Canada today than in almost any other country. Compared with 40 years ago, the space created and shared with Indigenous peoples is enormous. We are gaining real authority to exercise self-determination." Chris Sankey, "The Road to Reconciliation Has Been Marred by Eco-Colonialism," *Globe & Mail* (12 February 2022), online: <https://www.theglobeandmail.com/opinion/article-the-road-to-reconciliation-has-been-marred-by-eco-colonialism/>.

5 *Calder et al v AGBC* (1971), 13 DLR (3d) 64 at 94 (BCCA), *per* Tysoe, JA.

6 Nor did it matter to a trial judge fully twenty years later: on this sort of extinguishment by implication, see the text accompanying note 22, below.

7 Two years later, when the *Calder* case reached the Supreme Court, Hall, J., described Tysoe, J.A.'s assertion as "a proposition which reason itself repudiates": (1973), 34 DLR (3d) 145 at 217 (SCC).

8 The Kitwancool Land Committee to the Provincial Government (2 December 1929), Library and Archives Canada (GR 10, Vol. 11047, File 33–1). As for why there was hope in the early years, see chapter 8 of Keith Thor Carlson, *The Power of Place, The Problem of Time: Aboriginal Identity and Historical Consciousness in the Cauldron of Colonialism* (Toronto: University of Toronto Press, 2010) and his essay, "'The Last Potlatch' and James Douglas's Vision of an Alternative Setter Colonialism," in Peter Cook, et al, eds, *To Share Not Surrender: Indigenous and Settler Visions of Treaty Making in the Colonies of Vancouver Island and British Columbia* (Vancouver: UBC Press, 2021) at 288–328.

9 2nd ed. Vancouver: Douglas & McIntyre, 2013. Originally published in 1999. The trilogy is entitled *Masterworks of the Classical Haida Mythtellers* (volumes 2 and 3 contain the collected works of the two main Haida poets that Bringhurst translated).

10 Labeled the Queen Charlotte Islands by the British, the archipelago now has its third name: Haida Gwaii. Bringhurst addresses his use of the term, "myth," at 419–20 of Vol. 1.

11 Undated and unpaginated clipping from *The Martlet*, the UVic student newspaper. Others prone to drool include Margaret Atwood, who called Vol. 1 a "book of wonders," and – obviously but less publicly and much less famously – me. This is the Wikipedia account of the controversy, online: <https://en.wikipedia.org /wiki/Robert_Bringhurst>. For journalist Terry Glavin's assessment, see online: <https://bcstudies.com/book_film_review/masterworks-of-the-classical-haida -mythtellers/>.

12 Bringhurst cites Edward Sapir's assertion that the *locus* of culture "is not in a theoretical community of human beings known as society ... [but] in the interactions of specific individuals and ... in the world of meanings which each one of these individuals may unconsciously abstract" (quoted in *A Story as Sharp as a Knife, supra* note 9 at 65–6).

13 *Solitary Raven: The Essential Writings of Bill Reid*, 2nd ed (Vancouver: Douglas & McIntyre, 2009).

14 *A Story as Sharp as a Knife, supra* note 9 at 423 [emphasis in original].

15 Alan C. Cairns, "Aboriginal Research in Troubled Times," in *Roots of Entanglement, supra* note 2 at 417, quoting from Boldt's *Surviving as Indians* (1993).

16 Edward Said, *Culture and Imperialism* (New York: Vintage Books, 1994) at xxv.

17 The Benchers also decided to stop giving miniature Begbie statues to recipients of the Law Society Award and to change the code word ("Begbie") used to trigger safety procedures in the building.

18 *Bridging the Cultural Divide: A Report on Aboriginal People and Criminal Justice in Canada* (Ottawa: 1996) at 7*ff*.

19 *Tsilhqot'in Nation v BC*, [2014] 2 SCR 257. The trial decision is at 2007 BCSC 1700. Some of my articles in which Begbie appears include "The Kamloops Outlaws and Commissions of Assize in Nineteenth Century British Columbia" in D. Flaherty, ed, *Essays in the History of Canadian Law*, Vol. 2 (Toronto: Carswell, 1983), 308–64; "The Struggle for the Supreme Court: Law and Politics in British Columbia 1871–1885" in Louis A. Knafla, ed, *Law and Justice in a New Land: Essays in Western Canadian Legal History* (Toronto: Carswell 1986), 167–213; and "'The Queen's Law Is Better than Yours': International Homicide in Early British Columbia" in Phillips, Loo, & Lewthwaite, eds, *Essays in the History of Canadian Law*, Vol. 5, *Crime and Criminal Justice* (Toronto: Osgoode Society, 1994) at 41–111 ["The Queen's Law"].

20 All of the quotations in this paragraph are from "Aboriginal Research in Troubled Times," *supra* note 15 at 403.

21 The quoted phrase is from the ten-page, unsigned memorandum of the Advisory Committee on Truth and Reconciliation to the Benchers. Posted in 2017 on the LSBC website, it has since been removed.

22 See Ian Mulgrew, "BC's Top Judges to Honour Author of 'Nasty, Brutish, Short'
    Decision," *Vancouver Sun* (5 June 2017), online: <https://vancouversun.com
    /opinion/columnists/ian-mulgrew-busted-begbie-decision-grand-chief-cast-pall
    -over-top-judges-mceachern-move/>. The trial decision is *Delgamuukw v B.C.*
    (1991), 79 DLR (4ᵗʰ) 185 (B.C.S.C., subsequently reversed on appeal, and a new
    trial ordered). For criticism of the decision at trial see – to take only one of many
    examples – Don Monet and Skanu'u, *Colonialism on Trial: Indigenous Land Rights
    and the Gitksan and Wet'suwet'en Sovereignty Case* (Gabriola Island: New Society
    Publishers, 1992).

23 See Wendy Wickwire, *At the Bridge: James Teit and an Anthropology of Belonging*
    (Vancouver: UBC Press, 2019) at 101–7 and 167.

24 From the *British Columbian*, 28 May 1864, quoting "Great Chief English."
    The speech was made in a Salishan language and then translated into the
    Chinook Jargon before being rendered into English, so this source is not
    as reliable as Teit. For more detail concerning the annual Queen Victoria's
    birthday speeches see *The Power of Place, The Problem of Time, supra* note 8
    at 222ff.)

25 My own critique, "It Goes Without Saying: The Doctrine of Extinguishment by
    Implication in *Delgamuukw*," is in Frank Cassidy, ed, *Aboriginal Title in British
    Columbia: Delgamuukw v The Queen* (Lantzville, BC: Oolichan Books, 1992) 133
    [originally published in 1991 in *The Advocate*].

26 *Honouring the Truth, Reconciling for the Future: Summary of the Final Report of the
    Truth and Reconciliation Commission of Canada* (Ottawa: Truth and Reconciliation
    Commission of Canada, 2015) at vi.

27 Online: <https://www.huffingtonpost.ca/2017/08/29/sen-murray-sinclair-shonour
    -indigenous-heroes-instead-of-debating-john-a-macdonald_a_23189684/> (no
    longer accessible).

28 Minutes of the Executive Council of the Colony of British Columbia for 12 July
    1865 in James E. Hendrickson, ed, *Journals of the Colonial Legislatures of the
    Colonies of Vancouver Island and British Columbia 1851–1871*, 5 vols. (Victoria:
    Provincial Archives of British Columbia, 1980), Vol. 4 at 35.

29 From a crossed-out passage in Begbie to Governor Seymour, 30 Sept. 1864, BCPA,
    Colonial Correspondence [Begbie], F14F.

30 As one survivor of the main attack testified at the trials, "They gave no sign of
    being bad or hostile towards us." *Begbie's Notes of the Trial of Four of the Accused*,
    28 Sept. 1864, Bench Book, BCPA, GR 2025, Vol. 4.

31 Sources: Terry Glavin and the People of the Nemiah Valley, *Nemiah: The
    Unconquered Country* (Vancouver: New Star Books, 1992) at 108–12; Edward
    Sleigh Hewlett, "The Chilcotin Uprising of 1864" (1973) 19 BC Studies 50 at 54–60;
    Mel Rothenburger, *The Chilcotin War: The True Story of a Defiant Chief's Fight to
    Save His Land from White Civilization* (Langley: Mr. Paperback, 1978) at 52, 55, 69,
    72, and 76; John Sutton Lutz, *Makúk: A New History of Aboriginal-White Relations*

(Vancouver: UBC Press, 2008) at 134; and Sage Birchwater, *Chilcotin Chronicles* (Halfmoon Bay: Caitlin Press, 2017) at 43–58.

32 On the latter perspective, see Tina Loo, "The Road from Bute Inlet: Crime and Colonial Identity in British Columbia" in *Crime and Criminal Justice, supra* note 19.

33 Begbie's trial notes, *supra* note 30. There are other accounts of what Cox said, but this was his testimony at trial.

34 For some examples of this, see my "The Queen's Law," *supra* note 19 at 71–80.

35 Keith Thor Carlson, "The Lynching of Louis Sam" (1996) 109 BC Studies 63.

36 Seymour to Cardwell, 9 Sept. 1864, BCPA, GR 1846, 60/19 and Cardwell to Seymour, 1 Dec. 1864, C.O. 398/2 at 271). Seymour's motivation may have been financial: vigilante justice was cheap. Based on what the Vancouver Island treaties had cost, the amount spent by the colonial treasury on the Chilcotin War would have been "sufficient to extinguish the Indian title to all the land" in BC (George Edgar Shankel, "The Development of Indian Policy in British Columbia," PhD diss., History Dept., University of Washington, 1945 at 74).

37 See, *inter alia*, Dee Brown, *Bury My Heart at Wounded Knee: An Indian History of the American West* (New York: Holt & Co., 1991) chap. 3 (esp. 59–61), and the powerful poem, "38" by Layli Long Soldier at 38; The On Being Project, online: <https://onbeing.org>.

38 Online: <https://www.sltrib.com/news/2018/05/09/its-almost-like-youre-walking -into-the-earth-shoshone-tribe-utah-architects-design-an-interpretive-center-for -the-site-of-the-bear-river-massacre/>.

39 Neil Postman, *Amusing Ourselves to Death: Public Discourse in the Age of Show Business* (New York: Penguin, 1985) at 8.

40 There was no separate court of appeal in BC until 1909. SBC 1907, c.10 provided for a court of appeal but was not proclaimed in force until 1909.

41 Begbie to Seymour, 30 Sept. 1864, *supra* note 29.

42 The Victoria *Colonist*, 7 September 1864.

43 Eight years later Begbie stated explicitly that the warriors had been "induced to surrender." See his memorandum in *British Columbia: Report of the Hon. H.L. Langevin, C.B., Minister of Public Works* (1872) at 27.

44 Michael L. Ross, "Colonialism's Insults: The Clash of English and Chilcotin Law in 1864 British Columbia," (n.d., unpublished) at 66, note 137. The warriors admitted "killing" the colonists (a question of fact), but not "murdering" them (a question of law). Killing in wartime is not generally murder in either legal regime.

45 See, *e.g.*, *R v Oickle*, [2000] 2 SCR 3,

46 David Williams, *"The Man for a New Country": Sir Matthew Baillie Begbie* (Sidney: Grays, 1977) at 118.

47 Minutes of the Executive Council of the Colony of British Columbia for 1 Dec. 1869, in James E. Hendrickson, ed., *Journals of the Colonial Legislatures, supra* note 28 at 136–7.

48 Begbie to Seymour, *supra* note 28. Begbie may have confused the number of
    warriors (21) with the number of dead colonists (19). He repeats the error in the
    memorandum referred to *supra* note 43.

49 The *Report of the Cariboo-Chilcotin Justice Inquiry* (1993) at 8.

50 S.F.C. Milsom, *A Natural History of the Common Law* (New York: Columbia
    University Press, 2003) at xvi.

51 The reverse onus rule did not change until 1935. Murder trials were also extremely
    short by today's standards. The trials in 1864 seem to have taken two days, but even
    by the 1880s a typical murder case in Ontario took only one to three days: M.L.
    Friedland, "A Century of Criminal Justice" (1982) 16 LSUC Gazette 336 at 339.

52 The death penalty was mandatory for murder in Canada until nearly a century
    after 1864, when parliament distinguished between capital and non-capital murder
    for the first time in 1961 (Bill C-92). It was abolished in 1976, and the penalty for
    murder became mandatory life imprisonment.

53 I am grateful to Keith Thor Carlson for bringing this poster to my attention.

54 The quoted words are from the deposition of Thomas Trapp, 13 Dec. 1879, BCA,
    Add MSS 54, Folder 6/34. For details, see "The Kamloops Outlaws," *supra* note 19.
    Charlie McLean and his two brothers were all sons of Donald McLean, who was
    the only casualty of the two expeditions sent to capture the Tsilhqot'in in 1864.
    Their mother was Indigenous. Mel Rothenburger (*supra* note 31) is a descendant.

55 *Nemiah: The Unconquered Country, supra* note 31, and a telephone conversation
    with Glavin in November of 2018.

56 The *Report of the Cariboo-Chilcotin Justice Inquiry, supra* note 49 at 8 and 30.
    After the trial Begbie asked Lhats'as?in whether he would eventually have had to
    surrender and reported that his answer was yes. Begbie concluded from this that
    "if they were not fairly hunted down on the 15th August they were on the verge
    of being so." I wrote in 1994 ("The Queen's Law," *supra* note 19 at 74) that this
    rationalization seems unconvincing, and I remain of that view. It reveals that he
    was clearly troubled by what had happened.

57 Hewlett, *supra* note 31 at 71. Again, there are the usual translation issues.

58 The title of an article by Barry Gough makes the point: "Keeping British
    Columbia British: The Law-and-Order Question on a Gold Mining Frontier"
    (1975) 38:3 Huntingdon Library Quarterly 269. More recently, see Daniel
    Marshall, *Claiming the Land: British Columbia and the Making of a New El
    Dorado* (Vancouver: Ronsdale Press, 2018), which focuses on 1858. By 1859 the
    claim that American miners were lawless was proving to be an exaggeration:
    "[I]t appeared that there was on all sides a submission to authority ... which,
    looking to the mixed nature of the population, and the very large predominance
    of the Californian element, I confess I had not expected to meet" (Begbie to
    Governor Douglas, 25 April 1859, quoted in Hamar Foster, "Law Enforcement
    in Nineteenth Century British Columbia: A Brief and Comparative Overview"
    (1984) 63 BC Studies 3 at 9.

59 In my opinion, the capital cases involving Indigenous defendants that became grievances tended to be those directly related to colonial land policy, and from 1864 the architect of this policy was Joseph Trutch: see "The Queen's Law," *supra* note 19.

60 From a memorandum by Begbie dated 11 September 1876 and cited in Loo, "The Road from Bute Inlet," *supra* note 32 at 128.

61 The signature is illegible, but it appears to be that of Montague Tyrwhyt Drake: see "The Queen's Law," *supra* note 19 at 83–4.

62 Williams, *supra* note 46 at 141.

63 For examples of reduced charges, see Jonathan Swainger, "A Distant Edge of Authority: Capital Punishment and the Prerogative of Mercy in British Columbia, 1872–1880" in Hamar Foster & John McLaren, eds, *Essays in the History of Canadian Law,* Vol. 6 (Toronto: The Osgoode Society, 1995) 204 at 210–12, where he discusses the cases of four Tsimshian men who had killed colonists as revenge for the smallpox epidemic. Swainger also states that in BC's first decade as a province neither of the two white men convicted of a capital crime had their sentences commuted, whereas eight of the ten Indigenous men did.

64 *Ibid* at 212–13. These cases are also discussed in Williams, *supra* note 46 at 103, 109–11, and 139, where Qutlnoh is spelled Qtl-noh. The authors of the report may not have known about Dr. Swainger's work, but they clearly had access to Williams's.

65 In a footnote the report cites Williams, *supra* note 46 at 102–5, for this and four other examples of his dealings with Indigenous people that are given little weight by the authors.

66 For the Songhees case see *Caskane and Others v Findlay and McLellan*, BCA, Begbie Bench Books, Vol. 13, 17 Nov. 1885 at 127 (also reported in the *Daily Colonist* on 20 Nov. 1885). This decision is interesting as courts have no authority to issue an injunction against the Crown, which was using agents to force development on the Songhees reserve. As Begbie put it, "I do not see how an agent can be restrained if no injunction would lie against the principal." But the agents were private contractors so he did it anyway, apparently gambling that the government would back off. It did.

67 New York: The Free Press, 1974 at 74. (In 2018 the University of Minnesota Press re-issued this book with a new afterword and introduction.) Pidcock said that Begbie's decision had rendered the potlatch law "a dead letter." Douglas Cole & Ira Chaikin, *An Iron Hand upon the People: The Law against the Potlatch on the Northwest Coast* (Vancouver: Douglas & McIntyre, 1990) at 35–6.

68 David Milward, "Review of Mary-Ellen Kelm & Keith D. Smith, *Talking Back to the Indian Act: Critical Readings in Settler Colonial Histories*" (2020) 206 BC Studies at 133–4, and citing Robin Fisher, "Judging History: Reflections on the Reasons for Judgment in *Delgamuukw v BC*" (1992) 95 BC Studies 43. See also the text accompanying *supra* note 50.

69 Jeremy Webber, "The Past and Foreign Countries" (2006) 10 Australian Journal
    of Legal History at 1–2. Bruce E. Johansen in *Forgotten Founders: How the
    American Indian Helped Shape Democracy* (Cambridge, MA: Harvard, 1982)
    provides a specific example: "[Benjamin] Franklin's writings on American
    Indians were remarkably free of ethnocentrism, although he often used words
    such as 'savages,' *which carry more prejudicial connotations in the twentieth
    century than in his time*" [emphasis added], online: <https://ratical.org/
    many_worlds/6Nations/FFchp5.html>. (I am grateful to Martin Taylor, QC, for
    directing me to this reference.)

70 *Vancouver Courier* (4 Oct. 2017). See also Charles Lillard with Terry Glavin, *A
    Voice Great within Us: The Story of Chinook* (Vancouver: New Star Books, 1998)
    and George Lang, *Making Wawa: The Genesis of Chinook Jargon* (Vancouver: UBC
    Press, 2009). Lillard concludes that "the derogatory and regrettable connotations of
    'siwash' are relatively new."

71 *Royal Commission on the Liquor Traffic*, Sessional Papers (No. 21), Vol. 3 (1894) at 503.

72 Celia Haig-Brown & David A. Nock, ed, *With Good Intentions: Euro-Canadian and
    Aboriginal Relations in Colonial Canada* (Vancouver: UBC Press, 2006) at 9.

73 See Paul McHugh, *Aboriginal Societies and the Common Law: A History of
    Sovereignty, Status, and Self-Determination* (Oxford: Oxford University Press,
    2005) at 121–2, and Mark Hickford, "'Decidedly the Most Interesting Savages on
    the Globe': An Approach to the Intellectual History of Maori Property Rights,
    1837–53" (2006) 27:1 History of Political Thought 122 at 124–5.

74 Brett Christophers, *Positioning the Missionary: John Booth Good and the Confluence
    of Cultures in Nineteenth-Century British Columbia* (Vancouver: UBC Press, 1998)
    at 22–5.

75 Haig-Brown & Nock, *supra* note 72 at 8–9.

76 John Bensley Thornhill, *British Columbia in the Making* (London: Constable & Co.,
    1913) at 145–6.

77 Sydney G. Pettit, "Dear Sir Matthew" (1947) 11 British Columbia Historical
    Quarterly 1 at 9.

78 Compare the "almost complete absence" of the mixed-race sons of fur trade
    marriages from the social record: Sylvia van Kirk, "Tracing the Fortunes of Five
    Founding Families of Victoria" (1997/8) 115 & 116 BC Studies 148 at 178.

79 The information on Moore is from the biographical sketch in the Charles Frederick
    Moore fonds in the BC Archives, and I am grateful to Darin Thompson, one of
    Moore's descendants, for alerting me to it. Interest on $4,000 at that time would be
    the equivalent of interest on about $125,000 today.

80 *R v Corporation of Victoria*, (1888), 1 BCR Part II 331 at 333. See also *Regina v Mee
    Wah* (1886), 3 BCR 403 at 412, in which Begbie set aside a conviction for operating
    a laundry without a licence. The prosecution had argued that, on its face, the law
    was racially neutral but of course everyone knew that virtually all the laundries at
    that time were run by Chinese.

81 *Ibid.*

82 Roy St. George Stubbs, "Sir Matthew Baillie Begbie" (1968–9) 3:25 Manitoba Historical Society Transactions, online: <http://www.mhs.mb.ca/docs/transactions /3/begbie_mb.shtml>.

83 Royal Commission on Chinese Immigration, 1885, at 71, online: <https://pier21.ca /research/immigration-history/royal-commission-on-chinese-immigration-1885>.

84 Williams, *supra* note 46, at 263, quoting from a letter from Begbie to his fellow supreme court judge, Henry Crease.

85 Quoted in Williams, *ibid*, at 100. This remark is a conclusion that follows other statements by Begbie about how hard-working, trustworthy and astute the "Indians" he dealt with on his first circuit in 1859 were. And it appears that he compared them to the "lowest class" of workers in England because most of the work they did for the court party was hard, physical "drudgery." Williams also notes (at 98) that a delegation of miners complained, unsuccessfully, to Governor Douglas about Begbie's decision to convict based solely on Indigenous testimony.

86 *Ibid* at 102.

87 Geoffrey M. Hodgson, "Social Darwinism in Anglophone Academic Journals: A Contribution to the History of the Term" (2004) 17 Journal of Historical Sociology 428. Hodgson writes that the term's "earliest appearance ... seems to be in an 1879 article in *Popular Science* by Oscar Schmidt."

88 (1999) 38:1 Journal of the West 68.

89 *Supra* note 76. For my take on Begbie and the issue of Indian title, see "Another Good Thing: *Ross River Dena Council v Canada* in the Yukon Court of Appeal, or: Indigenous Title, 'Presentism' in Law and History, and a Judge Begbie Puzzle Revisited" (2017) 50 UBC Law Review 293–319. (Note that there is an error at p. 311 of this article, where the text states that Begbie recommended clemency in 18 of 38 capital cases, rather than recommended clemency or remained neutral in these cases. I do not know how this error occurred in the editing process, but I accept full responsibility.)

90 For example, in 1879 Begbie supported T'exelcemc Chief William and Oblate Father Grandidier in having the government purchase land for the T'exelcemc: Birchwater, *Chilcotin Chronicles*, *supra* note 31 at 59–61.

91 On Boyd see chapter 4 of Donald B. Smith, *Seen but Not Seen: Influential Canadians and the First Nations from the 1840s to Today* (Toronto: University of Toronto Press, 2021), entitled, "Chancellor John A. Boyd and Fellow Georgian Bay Cottager Kathleen Coburn." The contrast with Begbie could not be greater. His court clerk recorded that on the very first circuit in 1859 Begbie set out for Fort Hope with the sheriff "and 5 Indians in one large canoe," and the rest of his party in another. They camped out most nights, and one evening "2 chiefs" and three others arrived on horseback wanting to have a "grand wawa" (Chinook for "talk") with Begbie; on another, Begbie went off – as he often did – to catch fish

for their supper: entries for 14 March, 8 April, and 15 April 1859 in "The Journal of Arthur Thomas Bushby" (1958) 21 *British Columbia Historical Quarterly* 83–198.

92   Crease to Edward Blake, draft dated 27 March 1877, BCPA, Add MSS 54, folder 12/66.

93   On forensic history see John Phillip Reid, *Patterns of Vengeance: Crosscultural Homicide in the North American Fur Trade* (Ninth Judicial Circuit Historical Society, 1999) at 16.

94   Judge Sarich said this in the introduction to his talk on the Cariboo-Chilcotin Justice Inquiry (*supra* note 49) at the Victoria branch of Project North, 20 January 1994, as reported in (1994) 5:1 Project North BC Newsletter 1.

95   *Supra* note 26 at 16.

96   *A Story as Sharp as a Knife, supra* note 9 at 373.

97   Listed *supra* note 19.

98   Williams, *supra* note 46 at 195, citing the *Mainland Guardian*, 20 May 1876. The City of New Westminster followed the Law Society's example and removed Begbie's statue in 2019.

99   *Ibid* at 274.

100 "A Man Like Greer" (2020) 78:3 Advocate 347.

101 Charlotte Gray, "We Need to Widen Our Views: Understanding Canadian History Requires Both Context and a Sense of Proportion," *Canada's History* (Feb.–March 2019) at 27.

102 Quoted in Cara Rogers, "Reinterpreting Jefferson," a Review of Robert MS McDonald, ed, *Thomas Jefferson's Lives: Biographers and the Battle for History*, online: <https://lawliberty.org/book-review/reinterpreting-jefferson/>.

103 George M. Grant, *Ocean to Ocean: Sandford Fleming's Expedition through Canada in 1872,* Enlarged and Revised Edition (Toronto: Belford Brothers 1877; facsimile edition, Rutland, Vermont: Charles E. Tuttle Co., 1967) at 319. (I am indebted to Donald Smith for this reference.)

104 *A Proposal to the Benchers for the Resolution of the Begbie Statue Controversy* (15 January 2020), cl. 3. Sadly, Lance Finch died on 30 August 2020, a week before the A.G.M. referred to in the next paragraph, and Tom Berger died on 28 April 2021, seven months after this A.G.M.

105 *Ibid* at cl. 9. See also Hamar Foster, Jeremy Webber & Heather Raven, "Comment: The Day the Lieutenant-Governor and the Chief Justice Danced onto the Stage," *Times Colonist* (25 Sept. 2020).

106 R.C. Lundin Brown, *Klatsassan, and Other Reminiscences of Missionary Life in British Columbia* (London: Society for Promoting Christian Knowledge, 1873) at 105.

107 Begbie reported that he had "asked them what their law was against murderers. They replied 'Death.' I said: 'Our law just the same.'" Quoted in Williams, *supra* note 46 at 115.

108 Transcripts from 2007 BCSC 1700 (*supra* note 19) on 21 April and 3 May 2005.
There may be more references, because the trial record is voluminous: sixty-five
banker's boxes of exhibits and transcripts. But these and a reference to Begbie
by Chief Roger William on 9 January 2004, to the same effect were all the
testimonial examples I could find.

109 On exoneration see, e.g., online: <https://www.macleans.ca/news/canada
/trudeau-was-right-to-exonerate-the-tsilhqotin-who-never-were-defeated/>. The
cultural lens through which colonists saw the Tsilhqot'in and the challenge of
distinguishing war from murder are explored in Loo, "The Road from Bute Inlet,"
supra note 32 and "Colonialism's Insults," *supra* note 44.

110 *Coastal GasLink Pipeline Ltd. v Huson*, 2019 BCSC 2264.

111 For example, Begbie thought that Lhats'as?in suspected Chief Alexis of betraying
him generally and of using his position as interpreter to mislead him and the
others: Begbie to Seymour, 30 Sept. 1864, *supra* note 29. Whether this was so I
cannot say, but Alexis did not join in the attacks. And Chief Anaheim's role was
an ambiguous one at best.

112 See Bruce's letter to the editor of *The Advocate*, Vol. 76, part 5, Sept. 2018, at
769–71. The "Commitment to an Accord of Peace, Respect and Responsibility" is
described in Birchwater, *Chilcotin Chronicles*, *supra* note 31 at 208, where Chinlac
is spelled "Chunlak."

113 Father A.G. Morice, *The History of the Northern Interior of British Columbia*
(Smithers 1978; originally published in 1904) at 16. Morice compiled a six-
thousand-word dictionary of Tsilhqot'in: Moise M. Johnnie & William R. O'Hara,
*The Paper That Relates: Father Morice's Syllabic Newspaper for the Carrier Indians
of British Columbia* (1992) at 3–4.

114 In addition to Morice, sources on the events of 1745 and 1826–7 include Lutz,
Makúk, *supra* note 31 at 128; Joseph McGillivray," Report of Fort Alexandria
Western Caledonia Columbia River District Outfit, 1827" in E.E. Rich, ed, *The
Publications of the Hudson's Bay Record Society: Simpson's 1828 Journey to the
Columbia* (London: The HBRS, 1947), Appendix A at 211–15; and Birchwater,
Chilcotin Chronicles, *supra* note 31 at 206.

115 "Frank Calder and Thomas Berger: A Conversation" in Hamar Foster, Heather
Raven & Jeremy Webber, eds, *Let Right Be Done: Aboriginal Title, the Calder Case,
and the Future of Indigenous Rights* (Vancouver: UBC Press, 2007) at 45.

116 "The writings of many ethnographers, both popular and scholarly, are well supplied
with sentences in the form 'The Haida believe that ...' or 'The Navaho believe
that...' Perhaps not all such sentences are altogether false, but it is certain that no
such sentence is ever entirely true. What people think, and what they believe, from
moment to moment and day to day, is for each of them to say or not to say, as each
of them may choose" (*A Story as Sharp as a Knife*, *supra* note 9, at 66).

117 *Ibid* at 422.

118 "Titanic Disasters, Selective Memories," *Vancouver Sun* (25 April 2012). Tom
    Swanky, in *The True Story of Canada's "War" of Extermination on the Pacific*
    (Burnaby: Dragon Heart Enterprises, 2012) argues that the 1862 smallpox
    epidemic was engineered by the government of Sir James Douglas in order to
    exterminate Indigenous people and take their land. He asserts that historians who
    disagree with him are not worthy of the name – are even "criminally negligent" –
    and he regards any who have anything good to say about Douglas's Indian policy
    as "apologists and collaborators in genocide" (11 and 219). No other secondary
    source is cited as often (three times) as Swanky in the twenty-nine footnotes of
    the advisory committee report relied upon by the Benchers in removing Begbie's
    statue. But that is an issue beyond the scope of the present essay.

119 *A Story as Sharp as a Knife, supra* note 9, at 424.

120 Quoted in the *Globe & Mail*, 9 January 2018.

14 On Getting It Right the First Time: Researching the Constitution Express

EMMA FELTES

One fall morning in 2015, I got on my bike and rode to Commercial Drive. Gwitchin Elder Mildred Poplar was visiting Vancouver, and we had a plan to meet for coffee. This was not our first meeting, though it was pretty close. We had spent the last few days together, kindly ferried around by Secwépemc leader Arthur Manuel, mostly to and from the Union of British Columbia Indian Chiefs' Annual General Assembly, which was taking place in Musqueam. Manuel was deliberate in throwing us together this way, in his truck, where for about eight years most of my political education had taken place. This coffee date would be our first time spent just the two of us, and I was excited, if a bit nervous. I locked up my bike, attempted to smooth out my helmet hair, and found us a table inside.

Upon her arrival, Poplar pulled out of her purse a small stapled booklet, clearly of the typewriter era, titled, "Indian Profile of George Manuel (Shuswap Nation) Neskainlith." Sliding it across the table to me, she explained: it was 1984, and George Manuel had just survived his third heart attack; Arthur's brother, Chief Robert Manuel, asked her to compose a profile of their father and the work he did "on behalf of Indian people in British Columbia, across Canada and throughout the world."[1] The result, this twenty-five-page booklet, narrates the extraordinary career of the Secwépemc leader with a tenderness and grit that only a close friend can achieve.

I was grateful that she would begin our meeting with this gesture, though I wasn't sure of its meaning. At the time, I was three weeks into a PhD I hoped to write about the Constitution Express – a 1980s movement behind which she, her sister Rosalie Tizya, and Grand Chief George Manuel were some of the masterminds. In it, the Union of British Columbia Indian Chiefs (UBCIC) famously chartered two trains from Vancouver to Ottawa and set out to quash Prime Minister Pierre Trudeau's mission to "patriate" the Constitution from the United Kingdom without Indigenous consent. Poplar, I knew, was weighing whether she wanted to engage with my potential research. And I was keen – probably too keen, if I'm being honest – to have her suss me out.

I would like to think that my motivation for the meeting was not just to win her over; rather, that I was relationship building with an honesty and respect that accounted for the possibility of building no research relationship at all. In theory, I am entirely committed to this possibility. I can think of many reasons she might choose not to engage in academic research, be they systemic, historical, or personal. But even so, there is a part of me that questions whether I am ever truly able to remove my ego – wound up tightly in my research – so thoroughly from the equation. In any case, unsure whether the booklet marked the start of our exchange or the end, I was glad for it – the material itself and the gesture, whatever it was.

With the booklet, Poplar gave me something else. It was a small sheet of paper – a note,[2] smartly handwritten – with the heading, "For Emma." A subheading, "Work on Aboriginal Peoples," was followed by a short, numbered list:

1   You have to get it right the first time. The public will depend on your work for reference.
2   Whose original thought is it?
3   Never give credit to one person – the politics are the people in their communities.

Poplar barely remembers giving me this note, of course. But for me at the time, it felt imperative. Maybe I was eager for something to feel imperative. But there is also something about being handed a written page – it makes sense that, in the Western tradition of revering documents, I would I would give it a certain weight. Either way, in three short lines she had articulated some of the most pressing concerns that shoot through the fraught relationship between Indigenous Peoples – their knowledges, stories, political lives and lifeways – and settler scholarship.

I am a settler[3] academic. A white one, and an anthropologist to boot. Sitting there in an important awkwardness, she and I chatted tentatively, though honestly, about the problematic fact that mine would be one of few academic voices to write about the Constitution Express. Tucking her note into the booklet, I knew they were meant to be a pair: research material brings accountability with it. I hadn't won her over per se, but something more important had happened. Together, these documents inaugurated a more nuanced relationality between us that would consist of both engagement and refusal, blurring their binary and my thinking about voice in settler scholarship. More, they marked a kind of material culpability for me, beginning an archive of our exchange.

You Have to Get It Right the First Time

A few years earlier, Arthur Manuel – my mentor and dear friend – asked me to write about the Constitution Express and gather the stories of those involved. Over time, in order to afford this task the depth, breadth, and resources it deserved, dedicating a PhD to it started to look like my most feasible option. After starting my doctorate, however, I found that both the content of this project and the methodological practice of it posed novel challenges that I had not grappled with in the decade I have been working with Arthur and in Secwepemcúĺecw.[4]

During this time, I thought I had figured out the kinds of academic work I was comfortable taking on from my particular subject position as a white settler. This work is different from the non-scholarly work I do that directly supports Indigenous infrastructures of resistance and resurgence (i.e., solidarity activism) in a few key ways. While both share decolonization[5] as the objective of work, and while they may even involve the same kinds of labour,[6] my scholarship is uniquely discursive work in which I set out to confront the structure and operation of the colonial state – namely, its claims to exclusive jurisdiction. In it, my voice is more often positioned in the foreground, and I use it to address settlers and talk about colonialism. I see this as a kind of companion to decentering "the settler gaze,"[7] by recentering the settler gaze upon ourselves. Which is to say, I try not to take on work that hinges on the telling of Indigenous stories, instead framing my work around stories about Indigenous-settler relations. This means telling stories about settler political and legal traditions that are deployed to dispossess Indigenous Peoples of their territories and territorial authority. But it also means telling stories about the refusal of that dispossession, and its alternatives, i.e., decolonial jurisdictional arrangements offered to settlers from within Indigenous political and legal traditions. I approach these particular stories relationally, judiciously, and sparingly: only when initiated by their protagonists and keepers; in accordance with the Indigenous Laws that sustain them;[8] and ever conscious of the political stakes.[9]

The Constitution Express, an unequivocally Indigenous story, messes with these criteria, no matter my framing. More, it revealed to me their fault lines. I guess I had thought that by focusing reflexively on *relations*, I might avoid or even redress some of the more colonial genealogies of settler research, which most overtly appropriate Indigenous story. But in so doing, I found myself drawing mostly arbitrary moralistic lines – for my own comfort, more than anything else – between two types of stories that cannot be so neatly separated. What the Constitution Express makes obvious is that confronting the jurisdictional structures of the settler state and telling stories about its acts of dispossession necessarily mean telling stories about the real experiences and consequences of that dispossession for Indigenous Peoples. Further, telling stories about jurisdictional alternatives to dispossession means engaging with Indigenous Peoples' legal and political traditions in a way that cannot, and should not, focus solely on their relationship to settler peoples and polities.

When Arthur asked me to look into the movement, I was stunned to learn how little had been written about it. This is particularly surprising for a movement so massive in breadth, scale, and consequence – one he frequently described as "the most effective direct action in Canadian history, as it ultimately changed the Constitution."[10] Outside of a vital project by Vicki George – a superb collection of filmed interviews with leaders of the Express[11] – its dearth of scholarship is troubling.[12] Its archive and its canon are predominantly oral, retained by those involved. *People are getting older*, Arthur told me. He worried about the stories not yet recorded and criticized the lack of analytic engagement with them. I thought of his father, his brother Bobby, his sister Vera – all critical to the movement, all departed. I thought about how to build on Vicki George's critically important work. *There should be a book*, he said.

Yet, I felt a tension between the imperative to document the movement with the urgency and rigor that Arthur conveyed and my previous criteria for academic work – particularly my refusal to perform the kind of the "thick description"[13] that characterizes a certain ethnographic tradition of white people writing Indigenous histories. Later, a fellow anthropologist would hit on my unease when she scribbled cheekily in margins of my dissertation proposal: "the inevitable lure of salvage ethnography …" I cringed at this incisive reference to "salvage" – a term invented to lambast any ethnographic enterprise that fashions the presumed disappearance of Indigenous knowledge as its raison d'être.[14] There is a regulatory effect of this kind of ethnographic writing, fixing Indigenous life in the past, against which their present realities and claims are then measured.[15] For all their thick description, there is something audaciously archival about them.

In fact, these accounts often come to stand in for archives in-and-of themselves, taken up as primary sources by courts and academics alike. For example, Antonia Mills's account of giving expert testimony in *Delgamuukw v The Queen* is a compelling reflection on this phenomenon. Both her written testimony and Wet'suwet'en claimants' oral evidence were assessed against early ethnography of Carrier life, taken as historical fact (particularly Julian Steward's claim – in his 1940s work on the neighbouring Stuart Lake Carrier – that the matrilineal descent system was no longer in working order, and thus no basis for title).[16] Certainly Poplar anticipated such pitfalls when she wrote, "You have to get it right the first time. The public will depend on your work for reference." A hefty prospect, as I considered uneasily whether I too was venturing into this tenuous business of writing the archive.

I thought for a long time about the note in the margins of my proposal. *There is truth to this*, I thought. In a way, I am lured. *But*, I also thought, *I will figure this out*. And so, I set out to do just that: to figure out a way to honour Arthur's request and rethink my criteria; to address Poplar's list; to be lured and to push back against this "inevitable" luring.

I quickly encountered two responses to the lure of writing the archive that align more closely with the kind of decolonial jurisdictional arrangements called for by the Constitution Express: Audra Simpson's "ethnographic refusal" and Saidiya Hartman's "narrative restraint."[17]

To start, Simpson's ethnographic refusal resists grand narratives which fetishize tradition and suspend Indigenous stories in some fixed cultural past. It does this by advocating that we refuse the ethnographic drive to divulge "everything."[18] Rather than compromise our rigour, this thinning of thick descriptions strengthens it by encouraging a deep engagement with our research that is attentive to our positionality vis-à-vis the aims, stakes, and jurisdiction of those with whom we work. In this, it is a "positive refusal," prefiguring Indigenous authority.[19] I never planned to write a grand narrative of the Constitution Express, of course. (These days, few anthropologists could get away with such hubris.) Ethnographic refusal provides a kind of "how not to" guide, helping to fend off any such proclivities which might creep up and helping to keep one's hubris in check. For settler academics, I take it as a call to determine, together with our Indigenous interlocutors, which parts of the story are for us to tell, i.e., separating that which we have a responsibility to tell our settler peers and governments from that which we have a responsibility not to, for example, that which appropriates or "disinherits" Indigenous Peoples of their stories[20] or crisis-based narratives which simply chronicle Indigenous pain.[21] Refusal helps to keep a laser focus on the parts of the story that settlers and settler polities need to know in order to dismantle colonialism and forge a pathway out of it.

In a way, figuring out which parts of the story of the Constitution Express might be open to my telling seemed like the easy part. On 24 November 1980, the trains left the station, setting out to intercept Pierre Trudeau's hellbent mission to patriate the Constitution. While one train took the southern route through Calgary, the other headed north through Jasper, converging in Winnipeg. They arrived in Ottawa carrying a thousand people and a transformative vision for Indigenous nationhood. A two-and-a-half-year battle ensued. It was fought in the courts, British Parliament, the United Nations, the *Fourth Russell Tribunal on the Rights of Indians of the Americas*, and, of course, at rallies and protests across Canada and Europe. In each of these forums, the movement argued that Trudeau could not patriate the Constitution without the consenting authority of the Indigenous nations upon whose territories and terms Canada very tenuously sits. They called for an internationally supervised, trilateral, "Imperial Conference" between the United Kingdom, Canada, and Indigenous Peoples to determine what decolonization should look like and their respective jurisdiction within it.[22] Instead, the government added Section 35 to *Constitution Act, 1982*, recognizing and affirming treaty rights along with yet undefined "aboriginal rights." What's more, it domesticated their proposal, morphing their call for an Imperial Conference into four First Ministers' meetings which failed to clarify the rights recognized in Section 35.

Nevertheless, the story of the Constitution Express offers a counternarrative of Canadian constitutionalism which overhauls our federalism, foregrounds Indigenous jurisdiction, and refutes the assertion of state sovereignty in the first place. It questions the legitimacy with which Trudeau might "patriate" the Constitution whatsoever. In this I found a focus that aligns clearly with my old criteria for scholarly work. It is an archive I am keen to write: the movement's novel takedown of Canadian colonialism and its directives for revamping our constitutional architecture today. In close conversation with its leaders, I look to the Constitution Express for instruction as to how we settlers dismantle the current colonial, constitutional order. But I also look to it for blueprints for jurisdictional arrangements rooted in Indigenous Peoples' legal and political formulations.

Which brings me to the harder part: how to contend with the resurgent narratives of Indigenous nationhood that the movement put forth. More than anything, the story of the Constitution Express is a story about the flourishing of Indigenous nationhood in the face of empire. The movement did not just refuse a colonial constitutional future (and past, and present), but put forth a generative alternative. Here the narrative shifts to positive refusal, a "desire-based" narrative, an antidote to the barrage of damage-centred scholarship on Indigenous life.[23] The movement gave rise to a set of conversations among Indigenous Peoples in BC, not just about their relationship to Canadian federalism, but about their own political institutions, and the kinds of confederation they sought to establish (or re-establish) with each other.

As I began to build relationships with participants in the Constitution Express, interview them, and read their submissions, meeting minutes, and position papers, a multitude of nuanced, considered descriptions of Indigenous nationhood began to accrue as it was contemplated in community, on the trains, in the UBCIC offices, in court, and in ceremony. Some are specific, involving a set of pillars on which "Indian government" would be built.[24] Some go on to describe precise areas of Indigenous jurisdiction (UBCIC's 1979 *Aboriginal Rights Position Paper* laid out twenty-four of them). Some align with the language of self-determination as it is invoked in international law.[25] Some with the kind of self-reliance promoted by African anti-colonial nationals, such as Tanzania's Julius Nyerere, with whom George Manuel had fraternized in 1971.[26] Without mimicking its statist institutional form, some nevertheless conjure the kind of autonomous "home rule" that drives Quebecois nationhood,[27] or that of Scotland and Wales.[28] Some invoke a bush economy, seeking to "design an

economy for ourselves, a social, a cultural, a political life" based in "Indian ideology."[29] Many gesture to a land-based relationality, specific to their respective
territorial obligations. Some speak of sovereignty. Some categorically do not.
Many speak of revival.

Descriptions of Indigenous nationhood pour from the archive of the Constitution Express like a "gorgeous generative refusal of colonial recognition."[30]
And yet, in this most important part of the story, my criteria started to get in
the way. For settler scholars, theorizing the shape of and pathway to Indigenous
nationhood is politically dubious business, to say the least. Generally, these stories are not for us to tell. On the other hand, I certainly would not be getting
it right the first time, if *these* were the descriptions thinned as a result of my
ethnographic refusals, particularly when positioned next to a thick description
of settler decolonial futures. Rather, I realized, the refusal lies in declining to
theorize their coherence.

According to Audra Simpson, ethnographic narratives of Indigenous life
risk being deployed as the authoritative benchmark against which Indigenous
Peoples' present realities, goals, and claims are assessed.[31] Such "smooth narrative curves," to use Jodi Byrd's phrase,[32] feed state recognition, by codifying
one version of the story as the authentic one, setting its limits. This is the very
pitfall of Section 35, after all – a section which, in Canada's treatment of it, seeks
certainty by putting definitive bounds around Indigenous Rights. Refusing certainty, Simpson splinters her accounts of Mohawk nationhood into a variety
of narratives which foreground the authority of the collective and "expand the
limits of sovereign knowledge."[33] Following her method, it is not a thin description of Indigenous nationhood which fends off its containment. Rather, it is the
tidying up of disparate descriptions into a neat, bounded container that must
be resisted – a container which could be used, say, to assign Section 35 Rights
to certain Peoples, while denying them to those whose presentations of nationhood fall outside of it, rendering them unrecognizable.

Of course, this means heeding the jurisdiction of my partners in this work
to narrate their own nationhood, filling the gaps of the colonial archive – in
which I have found the Constitution Express exist only in fragments – with
their own dynamic counternarratives. But it also means working carefully with
them to respect the gaps they create in their own archive – their silences and
deviations – taking care not to cross the boundaries they set. If there is a time to
read "along the archival grain," as Ann Stoler advocates, this is not it.[34] Rather,
I learned to refuse my own academic impulse to reconcile a set of narratives
that are already richly diffuse, theorizing along, through, and against their gaps.

Here I began to wonder, what is scholarship – theory, in particular – if not
the pursuit of closure?[35] Of making a "novel" contribution, by filling a supposed
gap? What does it look like to engage in a scholarship that refuses to write
coherence in the face of uncertainty?

Here, Hartman's narrative restraint became a guiding light. If refusal creates gaps in our descriptions, narrative restraint dissuades our closing the gaps already present.[36] It strives to redress the violences that produce fragmented archives in the first place[37] without committing further violence in our own acts of narration,[38] even those borne of an aspiration for justice. In my case, this would include the aspiration to disprove Trudeau's favoured argument that the Constitution Express was fractured or disorganized in its aims – an argument that motivated UBCIC to spell out its demands with ever increasing precision, right down to the kinds of committees it wanted struck.[39] Indeed, the Constitution Express was singly clear in terms of the kind of decolonial process it demanded of Canada. But it was equally clear that the results would be plural – that on the other end, Indigenous nationhood would take many forms. The task, then, for me, would be to the strike the same balance. To fend off tired old, racist charges of disunity, without capitulating to them. To honour the story without making it "useful or instructive"[40] to the state's desire to contain it. And to resist consoling the discursive discomfort this creates.

In her stunning writing on enslaved Black women – women who are emblematic in the archive of Atlantic slavery, yet silent, found only in traces – Hartman leans into discomfort, weaving divergent and incommensurate accounts in an effort "to topple the hierarchy of discourse, and to engulf authorized speech in the clash of voices."[41] She engulfs and yet holds back. She engulfs *by* holding back. She writes: "Narrative restraint, the refusal to fill in the gaps and provide closure, is a requirement of this method, as is the imperative to respect black noise – the shrieks, the moans, the nonsense, and the opacity, which are always in excess of legibility and of the law."[42] In the context of my work,[43] restraint means refusing to sate a settler scholarship – and a settler law – hungry for useful, legible Indigenous nationhood. I came to learn that while getting it right the first time could never mean thinning descriptions of nationhood, it would require resisting my own urge to thicken the threads between them. To respect what we cannot know[44] doesn't mean we can never say anything for certain. Rather, it means engaging with the archive of the Constitution Express in all of its rich cacophony, while letting its silences be.

Whose Original Thought Is It?

With her second question, Poplar asks who claims such a narrative: whose original thought is it? As one of the movement's key strategists, Poplar knows well that the Constitution Express presents not just an archival project, but a theoretically novel one. Alongside the historiographic urgency Arthur conveyed, there is its out-and-out rebuttal of settler sovereignty, and the ever-piling baggage of Section 35 to contend with. These pose an important opportunity to think further about the aims of the Express and its implications today. It is a chance to "restory"[45] Section 35 as a clause about jurisdiction more than rights, swapping its imperial undertones for Indigenous stories that give it a different meaning. For all of these reasons I find myself both rapporteur and analyst, occupying a space common to most anthropological work, though not always made explicit. Also like much anthropological work, I am not alone in this space. Rather, I am a newcomer, joining a league of Indigenous thinkers whose stories of the movement are already thick with theory.

I was struck by this thought as I sat in a packed conference room at the annual meeting of the American Anthropological Association in San Jose in 2018. It was a legacy panel on the work of Sherry Ortner, and Sylvia Yanagisako used her presentation to address the strange heroism of the lone ethnographer, calling for collaboration between anthropologists. This was collaboration in a different sense than I was used to (the methodological one). Pinning analysis as the moment we become lonely – when we return from the field and turn away from our otherwise relational research methods – she called for collaborative theory.

On one hand, I found this refreshing. I have long felt uncomfortable with the institutional relegation of collaboration to methods and methods alone. This goes for all relational considerations, really, including our obligations to lands, stories, and to each other, tidily allocated to the demarcated stage of "data collection." (And to "ethics," which in the Western legal tradition is effectively a liability assessment of methods.)

As a result, on the topic of method in settler scholarship, there is ample social science – decades of anxious anthropology, even – from which to draw. Particularly vital interventions made by Indigenous scholars and those formerly deemed "subjects" of research have changed the game, offering shrewd analyses of the asymmetric structures of academic research and generous proposals for its transformation.[46] While every project will be grounded in its own place-based context, this work means that we settlers need not be so arrogant as to stumble around reinventing the wheel each time we contemplate research that pertains to our relationship to Indigenous Peoples or colonialism. Evidence of the institutional effects of such hard-fought interventions can be found in the reformation of methods syllabi, funding requirements,[47] and within ever-evolving ethical standards[48] for how we conduct ourselves, interpersonally and inter-politically, in "the field."

Which is to say, methods are important, and engaging in Indigenous methodologies that are anchored in their theoretical, political, and epistemological context – i.e., that are centred "in the theoretical home of Indigenous intelligence"[49] – would change "the nature of the academy itself."[50] What is worrisome, then, is the tendency to seek salvation in collaborative methods within an otherwise colonial structure of academic production. Perhaps if we understood method as a "theoretical intervention"[51] this wouldn't be so stifling. But, as things are, the methodological containment[52] of Indigenous interlocutors has a number of consequences. For one, it does not apply equally across disciplines, letting the theory-oriented (and the archive-based!) off the hook. It is stagger- ing that there are no formal accountability structures – within the institutions where I have done work, at least – for scholars whose historical, sociological, political, literary, and even scientific research pertains to Indigenous Peoples but whose disciplinary methods nonetheless do not engage living individuals from those Peoples.[53] Even for those whose methods do involve the participa- tion of others, intellectual accountability is reconstituted as an issue of personal conduct, obscuring its systemic nature. On this point, Eve Tuck and K. Wayne Yang shoot down the misconception that the mere participation of Indigenous Peoples will resolve structural issues related to "representation, voice, con- sumption and voyeurism."[54]

At its very worst, methodological containment smacks of consultation, the much-bedevilled legal process by which the Canadian state demarcates space – with near-impossible restrictions on time and the scope of discussion – into which Indigenous communities might voice opinion on decisions that impact their lands, rights, and heritage. Consultation retains the terms of participation within a settler legal milieu, circumventing Indigenous authority. Like consulta- tion, methods skew towards reforms in "data collection" alone, skirting larger questions about what a knowledge generation process grounded in Indigenous Law and jurisdiction might look like. For those of us whose research pertains to colonialism, these are the very questions provoked by our subject. If juris- diction is the question, are methods the answer? Sitting across from Poplar, scanning and re-scanning her list, the methodological reforms I had to offer felt measly, stingy even.

Like Yanagisako, I also find it strange that anthropology continues to treat theory as a romantically lonesome enterprise. We are meant to have moved on from the days of Malinowski, who saw theory as sourced exclusively in European social science, understanding fieldwork and theoretical work to be mutually exclusive: "in actual research they have to be separated both in time and conditions of work."[55] The idea then was that upon returning to the university from "the field," we turn to a predominantly white, Western, hetero-patriarchal canon to ascribe meaning to the otherwise methodologi- cal experiences we've just had. Nowadays, anthropology professes a "desire to foster ethnographically based theory,"[56] that is, to draw theoretical conclu- sions from the research experience itself, and from within the political, social, and intellectual context of the communities in and with which we work. If our methods are meant to be increasingly collaborative, and our theory is meant to flow from the community-based knowledge these methods gar- ner, it would follow that theory-making itself should be seen as a relational endeavour. And yet, the imperial custom of solitary theory-making persists. It is maintained, in part, by funding and publication structures, which valorize the roles of principal investigator and sole author, individualizing intellectual labour. Loneliness, it seems, is a tenacious institutional habit, and one that's hard to shake.

So, by calling for collaborative theory, I could see that Yanagisako was making a radical point. And yet, by focusing this call on collaboration between anthropologists, I also realized I can't relate. With Constitution Express, analysis is never lonely.

"It is through telling stories that the histories of the peoples, as well as important political, legal, and social values are transmitted,"[57] writes the inimitable Cree lawyer Sharon Venne (masko nohcikwesiw manitokan). Before she went on to become one of the world's leading experts in treaty and international law, Venne was a young articling student working with UBCIC when the Constitution Express was launched. When George Manuel had his second heart attack and couldn't travel to Rotterdam to present the movement's submission at the Fourth Russell Tribunal on the Rights of Indians of the Americas, he sent Venne in his stead (she had written the submission, after all). As a part of the movement's legal team, Venne joined a formidable group of strategists, organizers, and intellects at UBCIC – Poplar included – whose commitment to a grassroots and collective process sustained the two-and-a-half-year movement. Needless to say, when she tells stories about the Constitution Express, they are dense with theory. The accounts she and others relay in our interviews and conversations are those of community leaders and intellectuals who produced the original analysis – of Canada's sovereignty claims, of the legal obligations of the Crown, of decolonization and Indigenous nationhood – which drove the movement's legal and political proposals in the first place. What is more, with four decades of hindsight, our conversations take on a new dimension, restorying Section 35 through a rigorous counterfactual accounting of what could have been had their proposals prevailed. Their archives both remember and theorize the movement at once.

While anthropology was figuring out how to root theory in research material, the proliferation of Indigenous legal theory knit the threads of method and theory – and of story and theory – densely together. Through this literature,[58] and more importantly through the embodied experience of working with leaders of the Constitution Express, I have learned to hear stories differently. Which is to say, when Poplar, Venne, and others share stories of the movement with me, and when we work together to contextualize and understand them, it's not that we make a concerted effort to avoid the old academic detachment of story and theory. Rather, it doesn't come up. That story is an analytic experience is obvious; that it is more than a methodological move need not be discussed. I am the only one for whom this relational, "process-based" mode of "generating intelligence"[59] is relatively new.

Our interviews reflect an engagement in narrating and theorizing together what transpired during the movement and what should happen today as a result. The terms of this engagement are for my interviewees to determine, as are the limits demarcated by their silences and refusals. To be clear, not everyone has the time nor the desire to join researchers like me in an epic, collaborative analytic journey. For some, one short interview is enough. For others, like Venne, our dialogue has extended far beyond the bounds of traditional fieldwork and deep into analysis. For those like Poplar, there has been no formal interview, but a different relational engagement has developed through time spent together and through collaborating on projects which honour the Express in other than academic ways. And for others, I may provide a bit of infrastructure, in the form of funding or forums, and then get out of the way. In each of these engagements, the story of the Constitution Express takes shape, and so too does our analysis of its politics and proposals. It is not, as a consent form or consultation table would have it, an all-or-nothing situation. In intellectual relations such as these, engagement and disengagement (be it pointed or benign) ebb and flow over time. I am constantly learning how to honour both, for while it is one thing to be trusted with someone's stories, it is quite another to be trusted with their silences and refusals.

The suite of materials that emerge from this work – our recorded interviews, transcripts, speeches, and writings – are the outgrowth of these relationships, and are credited as such through scrupulous citational practice, co-authorship, and through editing and supporting each other's work. They are just now starting to be dispersed among Indigenous community archives, in presentations, gatherings, and in publications of both scholarly and non-scholarly types, ready to be taken up in new ways.

As I watch our dialogues and stories multiply, I think about the ongoing "bias in the discipline that urges us to present our ethnographic work as data that happened in the past ... and that is over, now ready for interpretation and analysis."[60] In contrast, our work and analysis are still unfolding. And with it, the story of the Constitution Express – its constitutionalism, its internationalism, and its proposals for Indigenous jurisdiction, still relevant today. In this, it exceeds a salvage project. As anthropologist Arjun Appadurai suggests, archives are not simply the "tomb of the trace," salvaging a fragmented past. Rather, they are "more frequently the product of the anticipation of collective memory ... an aspiration rather than a recollection."[61] The archives that we're creating are both retrospective and aspirational, moving across time, looking forward as much as back.

In so doing, my hope is that we evade the pitfalls of the grand narrative – that singular authoritative voice which fixes Indigenous stories in the past and serves the settler state. Rather than supplant the existing archive of the Constitution Express with one such narrative, the aim is to thicken the archive already there – not with thick description, but with a clamour of stories and voices, among which mine is one. As Nuu-chah-nulth legal scholar Johnny Mack suggests, the best hope of resisting imperialism comes from thickening connections to stories, not from getting the narrative of Section 35 right or "plugging our claims into its proof tests."[62] Rather than delimit the possibility of analysis by theorizing in isolation from each other or by claiming the singly right, most authentic version of the story, I only hope we might build a kind of "storied foundation"[63] of the movement, thickening the possibilities of connection and of analysis. In this we might create, I hope, more than one "first time" for getting it right.

The Politics Are the People in Their Communities

One of the stories that will soon populate the archive is Poplar's. At the Annual General Meeting of UBCIC where we first met, she was implored – to great fanfare by Grand Chief Stewart Phillip – to write a memoir. Originally from the Gwitchin community of Old Crow, she and her siblings were raised on the land before being sent to residential school in the southern Yukon. In 1978, George Manuel offered Poplar the Indian Education Portfolio at UBCIC, initiating a prolific career at the Union that spanned twenty-two years and four UBCIC presidents. In this time, her imprint on Indigenous resistance in BC, in Canada, and transnationally was profound. In retrospect, it is quite astounding that the Constitution Express was one of her first undertakings with the Union. Her memoir is forthcoming.

Nevertheless, in her presentations and written works on the movement, and equally in intimate conversation, Poplar is scrupulously careful to disperse credit for its innovations among the communities and members who participated in it. The Express is a part of her story. But, as she indicated in her note to me, it is a story that belongs to many Indigenous people, and the politics that ground it are rooted in their communities. Indeed, in the five short weeks leading up to the train ride, UBCIC staff, organized by Poplar, visited nearly every reserve in British Columbia – in what must have been one of the most extensive and rapidly organized community engagement campaigns in the history of BC – to discuss the Constitution and what was to be done about it. The delegations that those communities then sent on the trains (and to New York, London, and other parts of Europe) were not comprised of band leadership and administration, but mostly of families, Elders, women, and kids. It is no wonder that the movement's archives are equally dispersed, in stories, oral histories, and anecdotes, as well as in basements, filing cabinets, and photo albums, in homes and band offices across British Columbia.

As a story that belongs to so many polities, the Constitution Express poses a different set of responsibilities than my previous work. When I began to do research in Secwepemcúl'ecw ten years ago, I entered into the legal milieu of the Interior Salish world. I was researching the Laurier Memorial – a 1910 letter written by the Chiefs of the Secwépemc, Syilx, and Nlaka'pamux Nations and presented to Prime Minister Wilfrid Laurier as he was passing through Kamloops on a campaign tour. As a first-hand treatise, it traces the history of colonialism in their territories, which amplified with each wave of newcomers – French-speaking fur traders, American gold miners next, and then British settlers. The first group, however, largely respected Indigenous title and jurisdiction. As with any visitor from another nation, the fur traders were offered security, friendship, the use of certain resources, and trade so long as they respected the economic, legal, and political jurisdiction of the nations who hosted them. Which they were known to do. They would trade or buy salmon from the Secwépemc, knowing that fishing for themselves would violate Secwépemc laws of harvest and resource tenure, and that their weirs would be cut or torn down.[64] If they took up land to use it, they would pay a percentage of what they produced off that land back to the Secwépemc.[65] For these reasons, throughout the Laurier Memorial fur traders are referred to as "the real whites" – a translation of the Secwepemctsin term, *seme7úw'i* – to distinguish them from subsequent waves of colonizers and settlers (*seme7*). The Laurier Memorial goes on to advocate the resurgence of this mode of relationship – one in which their laws, jurisdiction, and knowledge of how to live together on their lands would serve as the basis of their political arrangements with Canada today.[66]

As a white scholar who works in Secwepemcúl'ecw, I have been treated like a seme7úw'i and expected to act like one. Working under the direction of Secwépemc legal, political, and intellectual jurisdiction has brought a rather wonderful synchronicity to my work and life: at the same time that Indigenous-settler (specifically Secwépemc-seme7úw'i) jurisdictional relations are the subject of my work, I get to be guided by those very jurisdictional relations in my own intellectual practice. They appear in all moments of interpersonal and inter-political encounter – moments both quotidian and grand – which produce that work. I made it a goal to become a kind of practitioner of seme7úw'i intelligence,[67] and to promote this intelligence among other settlers through my scholarship, my activism, and all of the frontlines where decolonial knowledge production takes place.

However, while the Laurier Memorial belongs to three Nations, the Constitution Express belongs to many. Whose laws apply? Whose jurisdiction guides the telling of this story?

Before I began the project, I went to UBCIC in search of such guidance. I came away with a couple of posters, a lot of leads, and a request that I help to annotate some of the photos in their archive. I also came away with the understanding that they would not be *signing off* on my work; rather, that I would find the proper authority for this story by seeking out its tellers.

The ubiquitous Chapter Nine of the 2018 *Tri-Council Policy Statement: Ethical Conduct for Research Involving Humans*[68] would call this a "complex authority structure." No kidding. When I interviewed for a large scholarship to fund the project, one of the interviewers – a top-tier, non Indigenous lawyer for a major Indigenous organization – warned me off it, deeming it too complex, too fractured, and too fraught to be feasible. At first, I worried she was right: that the patriation fight had become a kind of sore spot, and that without a distinct authority structure to govern the research, I risked becoming the white arbiter of a now conflictual story. On further thought, I took her warning to be a distressing sign that the tactics of Pierre Trudeau's government to sew factionalism – or the perception of factionalism – in and around Indigenous resistance to patriation had been working to bury stories of the Constitution Express these last forty years. I resolved that I wouldn't let this be the reason I not take it on (though I didn't get that funding).

Strengthening my resolve, I wondered: in colonial Canada, are there any authority structures that *aren't* complex? To shirk complexity is to deny the nested sovereignties[69] within which we already live, relate, and operate. As Shiri Pasternak writes, "jurisdictions are masked when a plurality of legal systems are mapped as a single sovereign space."[70] By looking for exclusive, hermetic models of Indigenous jurisdiction – as I had sought in UBCIC – we risk denying the many nuanced, layered expressions of jurisdiction which do not mimic the state's institutional form. Unfortunately, in hopes of honouring Indigenous authority, research tends to privilege more state-like structures, seeking comfort in their singularity and relative certainty, in order that we might report back to ethics boards with clear documentation of our permissions.

I worried too, though, that without such a structure I was in danger of falling back on the paucity of the consent form. Squarely in the Western legal milieu, I understand consent forms to collapse ethics into "litigation-proof"[71] bilateral relationships which mitigate the rights of the individual and the liability of the research institution. In so doing, they individualize discourse, isolating it from the textured fabric of plural, collective, and relational jurisdictions.

In not giving "credit to one person," as Poplar asked, I was similarly challenged to not individualize authority, for example, by falling back on my relationship with the late Arthur Manuel as the source of my permissions. While my accountability to Manuel may drive this work, I heed the warnings of Lee Maracle that one Elder's request "to write our stories down" does not mean "that it was okay with the rest of us."[72]

With the Constitution Express, I encountered a non-hierarchical jurisdictional structure which can neither be consolidated in a single, aggrandized, permission-granting body, nor whittled down to individual consent. This issue, of course, exceeds research ethics. It hits on the very phenomena that the Constitution Express was trying to prevent, that is: the swapping of complex jurisdictional structures for individual rights; the blanketing of those rights according to a single narrative of Indigenous life; and the arbitration of that narrative by settler state institutions. But, as follows, the alternative also lies with the Express. The movement held within it a structure of Indigenous federalism which dispersed authority across autonomous nations and communities, yet bound those communities in loose yet meaningful political collectives. It interrupted Canadian federalism by prefiguring an alternative: a relational jurisdiction stripped of domination, rooted in the resurgence of Indigenous institutions. In *The Fourth World,* published six years before the moment began, George Manuel repeatedly advocated this kind of cooperative federalism to guide in policy making on everything from education[73] to economic development.[74] He cites the National Indian Brotherhood as an example of such a structure – albeit not a perfect one, but a federation of regional bodies that serve autonomous local lifeways. He writes: "we share that dream with non-Indian North Americans as the one way in which such vast territories can fairly serve their collective and common needs."[75] Such non-authoritative jurisdictional cooperation would make space for the movement's richly diffuse, multiple permutations of Indigenous nationhood, and without collapsing them, link them together in mutually supportive political networks.

When the Express advocated such a jurisdictional framework as an alternative to Trudeau's patriation proposal, it mirrored that framework in its own decision-making structure. Decisions transpired in formal networked settings – UBCIC's general assemblies, community ceremonies, and at least seven "Constitution Express potlatches" – and in intimate, grassroots conversation on the trains, in billets, and in band halls. Accountability, as Poplar's note reminds me, was equally spread out. And here, as with the Laurier Memorial, I found synchronicity again. Decisions around my research transpire in similarly dispersed settings, both formal and quotidian. As I follow the path of the movement across the globe, decisions take shape over time spent with participants in the movement on their territories, in their communities, and in coffee shops on Commercial Drive. Of course, they also arrive carrying with them their own networks of accountability, aspects of which I may or may not see.

Ultimately, without a single body of law or jurisdictional authority to which to defer, I am guided by the Constitution Express itself – its plurality of nationhoods and its nested accountability structures. I interface with multiple legal systems: Canadian, and many Indigenous ones. The individualizing effect of the consent form loses its potency. By interfacing (on a very small scale) with the world of Indigenous federalism that the movement held within it, I too am situated in this archive, and led to resist the gloss of rights in both theory and method. The archive that materializes is generated of and through the very politics the movement deployed.

Conclusion

Poplar and I have shared many coffees since that first one on Commercial Drive. Sometimes she engages with my research, and sometimes she does not. When she does, I have learned, this does not indicate her sign off on the whole story, as a consent form might have it. She shares pieces with me – like the booklet – and I know they are a sample of a much bigger archive, only some of which I'm privy to. I have heard her tell the stories of the Constitution Express to Indigenous leadership, to community, and to students in a class I taught. I have learned from both the openness with which she tells these stories, as well as from her moments of restraint.

I am guided to the parts of the story that are and are not for my telling, almost daily, by Poplar, Venne, and many others. I have learned that getting right the first time means working together to tell it the way that's right for us. And it also means working diligently to open up the possibility of there being many more times – and ways – to get it right.

As the project unfolds, multiple archives amass at once. First, there is the ever-growing pile of historical materials, dug out of boxes and basements. There are the oral histories, stories, memories, and anecdotes – rich with theory – that, once provoked, proliferate like wildfire. There are also subtler archives of the relationships built through this process, made up of things like Poplar's note. And finally, there are the new archives now being written, told, and added to the pile, by Poplar, myself, and others, each clamouring with story.

NOTES

A version of this chapter also appears in my dissertation: Emma Feltes, "We Don't Need Your Constitution": Patriation and Indigenous Self-Determination in British Columbia (PhD diss., University of British Columbia, 2021). Thank you to the participants in the Constitution Express, and especially Mildred Poplar, Sharon Venne, and Vicki Lynne George, for partnering in the research that informed this chapter. Thank you also to Michael Asch, Kent McNeil, Kendra Jewell, and Erin Hanson for their thoughtful comments on early drafts.

1 Mildred C. Poplar, *Indian Profile of George Manuel (Shuswap Nation) Neskainlith* (1984) 25.

2 Shared here with Poplar's permission.

3 A note on terminology: I use "settler" in a few ways. Rarely in reference to the state, though more often as a subject position to refer to people who were subjects of imperial governments and came here with the intention of staying, and their descendants, like myself. I use "settler scholarship," to refer to a certain tradition of research *on* Indigenous Peoples. But, I do not mean to marginalize those that fall

outside of the now prevalent Indigenous-settler binary, nor do I want to gloss the specificities of colonialism across Canada, i.e., the arrangements or guises under which "settlers" came to assume their own permanence in different contexts. I am reminded by Sharon Venne that "people are in our territories at the request of the Crown as per the Royal Proclamation of 1763. They are subjects of the Crown ... Where no treaty exists, then they are squatters" (personal communication, 27 November 2020). So, when I use the term, it is with this qualification. I descend from Irish and British subjects who made treaty territories and non-treaty territories their home. In Vancouver, where I am at the time of writing, I am a squatter.

4   The territory of the Secwépemc Nation in the interior of British Columbia.

5   In the literal, and not the metaphorical, sense: see Eve Tuck & K. Wayne Yang, "Decolonization Is Not a Metaphor" (2012) 1:1 Decolonization: Indigeneity, Education & Society 1.

6   This may include policy and statutory analysis, oral history, archival research, grant-writing, logistical support for frontline organizing, etc. However, in scholarship, most of this is not considered labour but *methods*, and only a fraction of its products are recognized as productive at all. Yet I rely on this to finance the non-scholarly work.

7   Eve Tuck & K. Wayne Yang, "R-Words: Refusing Research" in Django Paris & Maisha T. Winn, eds, *Humanizing Research: Decolonizing Qualitative Inquiry with Youth and Communities* (London: Sage, 2014) 224 [Tuck & Yang].

8   See John Borrows, *Drawing Out Law: A Spirit's Guide* (Toronto: University of Toronto Press, 2010) [Borrows, *Drawing Out Law*]; Val Napoleon & Hadley Friedland, "An Inside Job: Engaging with Indigenous Legal Traditions through Stories" (2016) 61:4 McGill LJ 725.

9   See Noelani Goodyear-Ka'ōpua, "Reproducing the Ropes of Resistance: Hawaiian Studies Methodologies" in Katrina-Ann R Kapā'anaokalāokeola Nākoa Oliveira & Erin Kahunawaika'ala Wright, eds, *Kanaka 'Ōiwi Methodologies: Mo'olelo and Metaphor* (Honolulu: University of Hawai'i Press, 2016) 1.

10 As quoted in Erin Hanson, "Constitution Express," Indigenous Foundations, First Nations and Indigenous Studies, University of British Columbia, online: <https://indigenousfoundations.arts.ubc.ca/constitution_express/>.

11 Vicki Lynne George, *The Constitution Express: A Multimedia History* (UBCIC & University of British Columbia) Constitution Express Digital Collection, UBCIC, 2006, online: <http://constitution.ubcic.bc.ca/node/133>.

12 Notable exceptions include Arthur Manuel & Ronald M. Derrickson, *Unsettling Canada: A National Wake-Up Call* (Toronto: Between the Lines, 2015); Madeline Rose Knickerbocker & Sarah Nickel, "Negotiating Sovereignty: Aboriginal Perspectives on a Settler-Colonial Constitution, 1975–1983" (2016) 190 BC Studies 67; John Borrows, "Indigenous Freedom and Canadian Constitutionalism" in *Freedom and Indigenous Constitutionalism* (Toronto: University of Toronto Press, 2016) 103; Douglas Sanders, "The Indian Lobby" in Keith Banting & Richard

Simeon, ed, *And No One Cheered: Federalism, Democracy, and the Constitution Act* (Toronto: Methuen, 1983) 301; Michael Woodward & Bruce George, "The Canadian Indian Lobby of Westminster, 1979–1982" (1983) 18:3 Journal of Canadian Studies 119; Louise Mandell, "The Union of British Columbia Indian Chiefs Fights Patriation" (1984) 2 Socialist Studies 164; Louise Mandell & Leslie Hall Pinder, "Tracking Justice: The Constitution Express to Section 35 and Beyond" in Lois Harder & Steve Patten, eds, *Patriation and Its Consequences: Constitution Making in Canada* (Vancouver: UBC Press, 2015) 180; Ardith Walkem & Halie Bruce, eds, *Box of Treasures or Empty Box: Twenty Years of Section 35* (Penticton: Theytus Books, 2003) [Walkem & Bruce].

13 Clifford Geertz, "Thick Description: Toward an Interpretive Theory of Culture" in *The Interpretation of Cultures: Selected Essays* (New York: Basic Books, 1973) 3.

14 Jacob W. Gruber, "Ethnographic Salvage and the Shaping of Anthropology" (1970) 72:6 American Anthropologist 1289.

15 See Audra Simpson, *Mohawk Interruptus: Political Life across the Borders of Settler States* (Durham: Duke University Press, 2014) [Simpson, *Mohawk Interruptus*].

16 Antonia Mills, "Problems of Establishing Authority in Testifying on Behalf of the Witsuwit'en" (1996) 19:2 Political and Legal Anthropology Review 39.

17 Thank you to Phanuel Antwi for pointing me in this direction.

18 Simpson, *Mohawk Interruptus*, *supra* note 15 at 105.

19 *Ibid* at 128.

20 Lee Maracle, *My Conversations with Canadians* (Toronto: BookThug, 2017) 99 [Maracle].

21 Leanne Betasamosake Simpson, *As We Have Always Done* (Minneapolis: University of Minnesota Press, 2017) 22 [Simpson, *As We Have Always Done*].

22 "Petition by the Indian People of Canada to Her Majesty Queen Elizabeth II," November 1980, in Walkem & Bruce, *supra* note 12, 29 at 38.

23 Tuck & Yang, *supra* note 7 at 231.

24 Mildred C. Poplar, personal communication, 27 January 2020.

25 Mildred C. Poplar, "We Were Fighting for Nationhood Not Section 35" in Walkem & Bruce, *supra* note 12, 23 at 25.

26 Glen Coulthard, "Introduction: A Fourth World Resurgent" in George Manuel & Michael Posluns, *The Fourth World: An Indian Reality*, second edition (Minneapolis: University of Minnesota Press, 2019): ix–xxxiv [Manuel & Posluns].

27 Manuel & Posluns, *ibid* at 217.

28 Union of British Columbia Indian Chiefs, *Aboriginal Rights Position Paper*, Constitution Express Digital Collection, UBCIC, April 1980, online: <http://constitution.ubcic.bc.ca/node/168> [UBCIC, *Aboriginal Rights*].

29 George Manuel, "Indian Ideology," speech made at *Union of B.C. Indian Chiefs Special General Assembly: Indian Survival State of Emergency*, Constitution Express Digital Collection, UBCIC (14 & 15 May 1981), online: <http://constitution.ubcic.bc.ca/node/148>.

30 Simpson, *As We Have Always Done, supra* note 21 at 9.
31 Simpson, *Mohawk Interruptus, supra* note 15 at 93.
32 Jodi Byrd, *Transit of Empire: Indigenous Critiques of Colonialism* (Minneapolis: University of Minnesota Press, 2011) xxvi.
33 Tuck & Yang, *supra* note 7 at 243.
34 Ann Stoler, *Along the Archival Grain: Epistemic Anxieties and Colonial Common Sense* (Princeton: Princeton University Press, 2009).
35 My small friend Kendra posed such a question at a recent meeting of the American Anthropological Association: Kendra Jewell, "Dissonance, Doubling, and Disregard: Techniques of Climate Change Denial and Evasion," paper presented at the American Anthropological Association Annual Meeting, Vancouver, BC, November 2019.
36 Saidiya Hartman, "Venus in Two Acts" (2008) 12:2 Small Axe 7 at 8 [Hartman].
37 *Ibid* at 3.
38 *Ibid* at 9.
39 UBCIC, *Aboriginal Rights, supra* note 28.
40 Hartman, *supra* note 36 at 14.
41 *Ibid* at 12.
42 *Ibid.*
43 This is an application and not a comparison. I do not want to gloss the vitally important subject of Hartman's work – the lives of enslaved women found in traces in the archive of Atlantic slavery, "extrapolated from an analysis of the ledger or borrowed from the world of her captors and masters and applied to her": *ibid* at 2. I hope my own extrapolation of Hartman's theory of narrative restraint into the context of Canadian colonialism (a different, though structurally related context) pays credit to her breathtaking work and does not in any way trivialize it. As analytic practice, I only hope to demonstrate the kind of care she shows the archive and the lives that exceed it.
44 Hartman, *supra* note 36 at 2.
45 Jessica Wynne Hallenbeck, *The Water We Call Home: Five Generations of Indigenous Women's Persistence along the Salish Sea* (PhD diss., University of British Columbia, 2019).
46 For a sample, see Margaret Kovach, *Indigenous Methodologies: Characteristics, Conversations, and Contexts* (Toronto: University of Toronto Press, 2009) [Kovach]; Sarah Hunt, "Witnessing the Colonialscape: Lighting the Intimate Fires of Indigenous Legal Pluralism" (PhD diss., Simon Fraser University, 2014); Linda Tuhiwai Smith, *Decolonizing Methodologies: Research and Indigenous Peoples* (London: Zed Books, 1999); Shawn Wilson, *Research Is Ceremony: Indigenous Research Methods* (Black Point: Fernwood, 2008).
47 For example, see *Indigenous Research,* Social Sciences and Humanities Research Council, online: <https://www.sshrc-crsh.gc.ca/society-societe/community-communite/indigenous_research-recherche_autochtone/index-eng.aspx>.

48 For example, "TCPS 2 (2018) – Chapter 9: Research Involving the First Nations, Inuit and Métis Peoples of Canada," *Tri-Council Policy Statement: Ethical Conduct for Research Involving Humans*, Panel on Research Ethics, Government of Canada, 2018, online: <https://ethics.gc.ca/eng/tcps2-eptc2_2018_chapter9-chapitre9 .html>.

49 Simpson, *As We Have Always Done, supra* note 21 at 35.

50 Kovach, *supra* note 46 at 12.

51 Simpson, *As We Have Always Done, supra* note 21 at 19.

52 A play on Audra Simpson's "discursive containment": Simpson, *Mohawk Interruptus, supra* note 15 at 105.

53 Here I refer specifically to the lack of institutionalized accountability structures within universities. Of course, scholars may already be made accountable through community-based structures. By the same token, formalizing such structures within universities may not necessarily function to make scholars accountable to Indigenous communities. Nevertheless, the general lack of attention to this issue is staggering.

54 Tuck & Yang, *supra* note 7 at 230.

55 Bronislaw Malinowski, *Argonauts of the Western Pacific* (London: Routledge, 1979) 7.

56 Paige West, "Introduction: From Reciprocity to Relationality" (26 Sept. 2018) Hot Spots, *Fieldsights*, Society for Cultural Anthropology, online: <https://culanth.org /fieldsights/introduction-from-reciprocity-to-relationality-west>.

57 Sharon Venne, "Understanding Treaty 6: An Indigenous Perspective" in Michael Asch, ed, *Aboriginal and Treaty Rights in Canada: Essays on Law, Equality, and Respect for Difference* (Vancouver: UBC Press, 1997) 173 at 174.

58 For example, see Borrows, *Drawing Out Law, supra* note 8; Val Napoleon, "Thinking about Indigenous Legal Orders," Research Paper for the National Centre for First Nations Governance (18 June 2007), online: <http://www.fngovernance .org/ncfng_research/val_napoleon.pdf>; and the entire catalogue of the Indigenous Law Research Unit at the University of Victoria, online: <https://www.uvic.ca/law /about/indigenous/indigenouslawresearchunit/index.php>.

59 Simpson, *As We Have Always Done, supra* note 21 at 23.

60 Paige West, "Holding the Story Forever: The Aesthetics of Ethnographic Labour" (2005) 15:3 Anthropological Forum 273.

61 Arjun Appadurai, "Archive and Aspiration" in Joke Brouwer & Arjen Mulder, eds, *Information Is Alive* (Rotterdam: V2_Publishing/NAI Publishers, 2003) 16.

62 Johnny Mack, "Hoquotist: Reorienting through Storied Practice" in Hester Lessard, Rebecca Johnson, & Jeremy Webber, eds, *Storied Communities; Narratives of Contact and Arrival in Constituting Political Community* (Vancouver: UBC Press, 2011) 301.

63 *Ibid.*

64 Marianne Ignace & Ronald E. Ignace, *Secwépemc People, Land, and Laws: Yerí7 re Stsq'ey's-kucw* (Montreal: McGill-Queen's University Press, 2017) 430.

65 Kukpi7 Ronald Ignace, personal communication, 24 August 2010.

66 Emma Feltes, "Research as Guesthood: The Memorial to Sir Wilfrid Laurier and Resolving Indigenous–Settler Relations in British Columbia" (2015) 57:2 Anthropologica 469–80.

67 Inspired by Leanne Betasamosake Simpson's call for "*practitioners* of Nishnaabeg intelligence" in "Land as Pedagogy: Nishnaabeg Intelligence and Rebellious Transformation" (2014) 3:3 Decolonization: Indigeneity, Education & Society 13 at 13.

68 Canadian Institutes of Health Research, Natural Sciences and Engineering Research Council of Canada, and Social Sciences and Humanities Research Council, TCPS2 (2018) – Chapter 9: Research Involving the First Nations, Inuit and Métis Peoples of Canada, online: <https://ethics.gc.ca/eng/documents/tcps2-2018-en-interactive-final.pdf>.

69 Simpson, *Mohawk Interruptus*, *supra* note 15 at 11.

70 Shiri Pasternak, "Jurisdiction and Settler Colonialism: Where Laws Meet" (2014) 29:2 Canadian Journal of Law and Society 148.

71 Tuck & Yang, *supra* note 7 at 234.

72 Maracle, *supra* note 20 at 99.

73 Manuel & Posluns, *supra* note 26 at 248–52.

74 *Ibid* at 247.

75 *Ibid* at 211.

15 Confronting Dignity Injustices

SA'KE'J HENDERSON

On ne saurait détruire les hommes en respectant mieux les lois de l'humanité.

Alexis de Tocqueville[1]

I have trouble remembering the time when I became aware of and committed to the ideas of justice and dignity. The concept of justice was a gradual, aspirational process with unfolding awareness. However, the belief in dignity was an ancient teaching of Indigenous knowledge systems, yet unrealized for some time. Being born and living in an unjust society, and forced to be educated in a system that justifies and conceals the systemic injustices, has been a personal dilemma for me and every Indigenous person for many generations. This undeserved reality remained a deliberate, sustained, and systematic oppressive legacy for Indigenous Peoples, which might best be thought of as cognitive imperialism or government-sponsored ethnocide or cultural genocide. The premises of these concepts remain fraught with controversy, questions, and doubts. Yet, this situation and dilemma shaped and defined my generation. Our reactions to the power and forces of this situation determine our cognitive life and our actions.

The Rise of the Split-Head Indians

Growing up in the 1950s and '60s in Oklahoma, I was born into a generation facing an endless, pervasive indignity. Our imposed fate was to live in grim, confused hopelessness and profound neglect. State-enforced termination laws and policies resigned us to extinction through a forced assimilative educational system. Like our families, we lived in deep, insidious, and grinding poverty that stemmed from government-sponsored, pervasive, racial discrimination. It was hard-edged oppression, which thrived everywhere and controlled all our activities. Few economic opportunities existed in our communities; employment was rare and confined to physical labour or working in the oppressive system. Our poverty was a manifestation of our bureaucratic "cashtration" or attempting to live without cash. Living conditions generated by governmental policies were lower than those of third-world nations.

The laws and policies of the governments made it difficult to be an Indian in face of the unprecedented power of white supremacy and the racism of European civilization bent on our forced assimilation. The Bureau of Indian Affairs (BIA) in the United States exercised unfathomable degrees of authority over our lives on reservations and our education. As students, they taught us misery. Their mission was to make Indigenous heritage and knowledge vanish and assimilate us, recreating us in their image. We saw the BIA as the source of our misery, impoverishment, forced bad education, and conflicted identities. The bureaucratic legacies of doing a lousy job generated the nihilism that brought our families to the existential abyss. This bureaucratic consciousness was pervasive in all aspects of our life. They took us away from our parents for assimilative education or had us adopted by non-Indigenous parents. We were not allowed to make sense of our inherited world or make necessary human decisions about our families or personal lives.

We lived in a strange, pervasive, incoherent fog. As students, we began to call this fog the "bozone" – a mental atmosphere created by bureaucrats to stop any useful ideas from penetrating consciousness. Instead, the cognitive fog of the bozone trapped many generations in imposed meaninglessness and resignation. Thinking and knowing became inconclusive discussions between the two cognitive strangers that formed our assimilated consciousness. While we had slight conscious relations to the spirits of ancient heritages and knowledge, these spirits nonetheless occupied many of our dreams and feelings. As many Indigenous writers of my generation disclosed, our thinking was ensnared between distinct, incomplete, gagged, and paradoxical knowledge systems searching for meaning.

The federal and state laws on truancy forced us to become educated as "split-headed," thinking and living with at least two distinct knowledge and language systems, which came to reflect the genesis of our genius. We didn't choose to live with Indigenous and Anglo-European consciousnesses – that was our fate determined by these oppressive laws, the consequences of the desire of the settler governments and bureaucracy to assimilate us, to make us fit into and honour their culture. From the ages of six to sixteen, we were legally required to attend assimilation schools. We had to move from Indigenous knowledge and language and learn how to live in an English domain. This language spoke of the elaborate Eurocentric ideology of colonialism, racism, and prejudice. It was a language that we call "anguish" because of our difficulty learning or making sense of it. Learning English was difficult both for those who were raised in our Indigenous knowledge systems and those who were not. It was a language difficult to understand, much less master. It is loaded with categorical biases and has historical connotations against our heritage and knowledge system. Our formal and tacit education involved the experience of many manifestations of colonialism and racism

At different rates and times, we eventually became traumatized high-school or college students in the Eurocentric educational tradition. As I shifted through my formal education, I expressed my feelings and thoughts to my classmates about our situation and our wretched roles. Often, some educated teacher or counsellor would inevitably point out that, in the name of Eurocentric competence, we should be reasonable, put aside our ancient/savage ideas of humanity and tradition, and conclusively accept that nothing can change for the better if we insist on being Indians. As Indians, we were victims of a harsh, unrelenting, and imagined idea of progress, something we had to learn to live with! We were the have-nots. The educators were content with racial, class, and gender divisions and discrimination because they were the "have" people, the treaty takers and breakers. Although they had all the ability to change, they did not want to change because they thought of themselves as superior. They wanted us to melt into them and become like them, a more inferior version of them with a desire to be prosperous. They have written our "race" off as an evolutionary other that was winding down and vanishing, and there was nothing we could do about it. These Eurocentric voices could list many reasons for this position. Keeping silent and being resigned to our predicament were the lessons, unless, of course, you wanted to go to jail or be killed.

Some of us accepted this argument; others did not. Many of us disregarded this enigmatic advice and continued to believe in our traditions. A majority went to jail; others were killed for resisting unjust laws. Most lived with this imposed nihilism, in which nothing much had any meaning at all. The grim situation we were in generated a continuous cycle of deep rage, often called "red rage." This rage was manifested in poverty, bad health, and bad decisions, which resulted in many being sentenced to jail and other forms of imprisonment. The privileged voices of Eurocentric logic and causation would shake their heads uncomprehendingly at our incarceration rates. They would ask what the point was of declaring our culture's value when we couldn't live up to those values, and our actions would only bring more shame and harassment upon our families and ourselves. They refused to understand their forcible role in shaping our behaviour through assimilative educations. The consciousness of these contexts makes us who we are, whether we want them to or not. We could not pretend to float above them. We were marinated in the Eurocentric, colonial context. The spell that the status quo cast on our experience was powerful but never complete. It failed to exhaust our thoughts or desires.

My generation accepted that we were vulnerable and oppressed by a powerful knowledge system based on violence and broken promises, struggling with Indigenous nihilism in our families and ourselves, and living in a never-ending, insignificant realm. We were trapped in despair and resignation under the all-powerful bozone of improvised, jazz-like laws, policies, and whims of Indian agents and a Eurocentric education program of ruthless assimilation that had generated our cognitive prison for many generations. But our acknowledgment of our situation was combined with a continuous, restless willingness to confront, with a tangled, many-sided "red rage," the domination and inequities of distorting and damaging accounts of our diverse heritages, knowledge systems, and languages. We wanted to know where these distortions came from and whose interests they served. We believed that, by reducing and eliminating these harmful humiliations that degraded and dehumanized, we could open a space for dignity to take root and grow.

My split-headed generation sought many ways – inflammatory rhetoric, animosity, red rage, rebellion, and resistance – to struggle against systematic oppression and injustice. Many of these counter-endeavours were assimilated ways of using the violent tools of colonialism we were taught by the schools, of being trapped by them by education rather than subverting them.

All of this forced assimilation was undermined eventually by our summer teachings with our families or on the summer intertribal powwow trail. We sought to renew our Indigenous knowledge systems, languages, and performance laws or ceremonies. In many ways, we began to listen to the ancient voice and rhythms of the territories, the first teachers of ancient life, the creator of sensations being regenerated by the powwow circuit, the Elders and keepers and performers of the powwow songs and dances. Experience on the powwows inspired ancient dreams and dreamed new thoughts of respect for Indigenous Peoples, knowledge, cultures, and lands. The origin of the powwow comes from the core Algonquian language group's concept of "*pauwau*," which is translated as "our dreams," with deeply personal, reverent, spiritual power, or as a gathering or meeting of spiritual or medicine leaders. "*Pawauing*" is translated as a healing or curing ceremony. The drummers' songs and the dancers' moves recreate ancient dreams and themes to celebrate the related heritage and knowledge, and re-inspire our cultural heritage and pride in dark times. The powwows circuit allowed the families to come together for learning, hearing Indigenous languages, and upholding ancient traditions and laws. The powwows' teachings taught us different prismatic comprehensions about honour, respect, dignity, and knowledge sharing.

We learned the ancient teaching: because the environment exists, we do. That everything is interrelated. If one has a learning spirit, any part will unfold the whole regardless of where you begin. In the summers, we found vision quests and knowledge, antidotes for our forced education. The teaching spirits continued to inform our dreams and new thoughts as we returned to our winter schools. They generated learning about who we are and how to make our predicament into a better place through dignity. We made no secret about our visions of a better and just realm. Once we realized that dignity required responsible action and resistance against wretched colonization and the colonizers, we transformed hope into action and restored our voice and consciousness. Our own families and relatives, who were living on the edge, would look at our efforts to confront and change the system with grave concern and alarm. Unable to discern their existence in an unjust situation, they were stuck in the colonial status quo and could not conceive a path for transformation of self, family, or society to generate a better future that did justice to our inherent humanity. They saw our attitude and activism as a terrifying and exceptional risk for them and us. We learned that domination, humiliation, and poverty generate fear in fundamentally different ways. We acknowledged that most would have to endure turmoil to create and live this vision.

We were inspired by the Black people's movement for equal rights in the late 1950s and early 1960s when the federal government threatened our families with the termination of our treaties and federal status. Yet, we did not want equal rights with the non-Indians; we wanted a return to treaty rights, sovereignty, and the greatness of the heritage and traditions of our confederacies that formed the powwow ceremonies.

Regenerating Traditions through the National Indian Youth Council

In a sweltering, hot summer afternoon in 1960 or 1961, those of us who had competed in the boys' warrior dance competition (*helushka* or stealth takers) in Anadarko Indian days were approached by a faculty member from the University of Oklahoma as we were attempting to catch our breath and cool down. He asked us if we wanted to have the honour of becoming the mascot, "Little Red." Young white men had mostly portrayed the Little Red caricature. A student had depicted Little Red in a headdress, silk shirt, and breechcloth bearing the university's name, carrying a baton, dancing, and making war whoops in front of the university's band before thousands of Sooners football fans. Sometime in the 1950s, Little Red became the official mascot of the university, but a fake dancer had existed since the 1930s. I remember the faculty member stated that being the mascot would promote and gain acceptance for our culture and eliminate racism. His offer deeply offended most dancers because we danced for our families and Nations, not for the university. It was not an honour but mocked and debased our Indigenous traditions.

After a quick discussion, the great powwow dancer and artist of the Ponca Nation, Clyde Warrior, spoke for us. He rejected the offer. He told the faculty member that being a mascot for the Sooners would be a disgrace. The university had named themselves to honour the white land grabbers who came to settle before the federal government forced the Indian territory, destined to be the first Indian state of the United States, to be open to settlers. The Sooners had appropriated our name for honourable or courageous Peoples – Oklahoma – for their identity. Clyde Warrior revealed to the faculty member that Oklahoma, wrongly translated from the Chickasaw-Choctaw language as "people who are red," had been taken and debased.

Additionally, he reminded him that the Sooners had taken Indian symbols without permission for the state flag in 1925 to represent their government, created as the forty-sixth state in 1907, while denying our ancestors their treaty governments. The flag of the State of Oklahoma consists of a traditional Plains buffalo-skin shield with seven eagle feathers on a Chickasaw-Choctaw sky-blue field that symbolizes devotion. The shield is covered by two symbols of peace: the Plains-style ceremonial pipe representing Native Americans, and the olive branch representing European Americans, which symbolizes the love of peace. On the shield are golden-brown crosses, with stars representing the Five Civilized Nations.

We agreed that, as a matter of honour and dignity, we had to resist such offers to be mascots of settler universities, colleges, and high schools. Our Elders on the powwow circuit had always cautioned us that our traditions, heritage, and dignity are all we have left. Later in the summer, at the Gallup Powwow, we developed a strategy to reject attempts to use our heritage and language and to create new approaches to attain a more just future. As part of our opposition, we thus began our resistance to the injustices to our dignity.[2]

After the Gallup Powwow, the Indian boarding and residential schools' split-headed youth on the powwow circuit established the National Indian Youth Council (NIYC). We threw our energies into building a grass-roots "activist" network among Indian youth, especially in boarding schools, to protect our heritages and knowledge and promote treaty sovereignty. We elected Clyde Warrior to lead us as president. The NIYC employed non-violent, humorous, and symbolic ridicule of white society and tribal leaders, which would become the split-headed generation's hallmark. Through the NIYC, Clyde spoke honestly, urgently, and justly, with thunder, lightning, and tears against cultural appropriation and the necessity of revitalizing the various Indian heritages and knowledge. He demanded that Indians take pride in being Indian and rejected bowing our heads in humble obedience to the BIA and other "white society" institutions. Clyde demanded respect for our heritage and traditions and condemned the settler society for dehumanizing and alienating treaty nations. He insisted on our right to determine our future and destiny and make decisions about our lives based on our knowledge and traditions. When white student groups advised against trusting anyone over 30, we actively pursued bonds with our Elders, who have a revered status. We looked to them for cultural knowledge and leadership.

Clyde's persuasive speeches and writing inspired the Indigenous youth, but also angered the "old farts" and "suits" (the Indian reorganization politicians).

The NIYC created a new generation of Indians who were young and college-educated split-heads, proud of their Indian heritage and unwilling to accept American paternalism and contemptuous Eurocentric values. Increasingly, the network demanded a return to ancient Indian teaching and languages, re-establishment of a vibrant powwow circuit in North America, re-establishment of treaty governmental systems run by open council and consensus instead of elected officials and the BIA, and replacement of most of the hostile federal laws with new federal laws and tribal-federal compacts. The split-headed network aggressively demanded self-determination, the freedom to choose to return to our ancestors' cultural, political, and economic ways. We attempted to explain the similarities and differences between civil rights and treaty rights, and how the laudable goal of "equal rights" was a catchphrase used against us by treaty-breakers to candy-coat their objective of ending Indian rights and resources.

Searching for Justice in the Settler's Law School

In early July 1968, Clyde Warrior lost his life too soon, at the age of twenty-eight, succumbing to liver failure, leaving our striving network at its fragile beginning without a powerful voice. In word, deed, and spirit, Clyde Warrior inspired the nationalist movement known as Red Power or the American Indian Movement and all its variations, based on a belief in treaty sovereignty, cultural survival, and human dignity.

After the death of Clyde Warrior, my chosen way to continue our campaign was to attend the settler's law school to protect our communities, families, and friends from the law, and restore the tribal governments of the Five Civilized Nations under their treaties. This path captured both my learning spirits and desire for change.

When I told my traditionalist uncle of my choice to go to the white man's law school, he was puzzled and asked: "Do you really think you can change an asshole into an angel by a piece of paper?" My dazed answer was, "For sure, maybe!" His question has been my cognitive companion over all these decades in law. I had started my quest to understand justice by learning the oppressor's laws. And only recently have I realized how profound and crucial this question was.

Many in my generation chose this way of cognitive resistance to create a just transformation in the lives of Indigenous Peoples. The undertaking required us to comprehend the premises of a settler's law of colonization, learn the semiotics and nuisance of legal arguments, master the colonial and "jurispathic" legal system, and seek to transform it. Many became determined, like me, to learn the mysterious power of the law. We were often guided by the ancient teaching that humans have to search for their vision. Some of us had vision quests earlier in life and were trying to work out their implications.

Our law school experience was a distinct vision quest or cry for justice, which was difficult and required many different sacrifices. It was a contemporary form founded on ancient teachings. It sought a vision to change a contaminated environment of colonial laws and oppression, with their arrogant and intolerant doctrines and rules. Like most of the split-headed generation, I became familiar with these ideologies and had to accept them as valid to pass my courses, thus learning to live with an enforced mask of apathy. However, the knowledge learned had tremendous potential for change.

While I was in law school from 1969–74, my efforts were directed to ending the abuse of names, the indignity and commercialization of stereotypes of Indians used to sell products, the settlers using their images of Indians to represent their identities as sport mascots, the legacies of Buffalo Bill Cody, the taking by museums of our material culture, and the plunder of our burial sites. These efforts were a confrontation with Eurocentrism and its asserted superiority.[3] With the assistance of my classmate Russel Barsh and two doctoral anthropology students, Mary Pohl and Joan Lester, we created a protest against misinformation and the use of Indians on commercial labelling. Additionally, we developed an undergraduate course to theorize the need for cultural dignity and integrity of Indians in Eurocentrism. The battleground became the curatorial voice of museums and its savage paradigm. The savage paradigm asserted that that the museums had rescued or taken before they vanished, the pure, uncontaminated Indian culture and artefacts. We began challenging the discourses about the nature of cultural authority and the misrepresentation and undignified takings of Indian cultures, replacing them with a need to restore the dignity of Indigenous heritage and knowledge by collaborating with Indian communities and knowledge-keepers. Without noticing it, we were creating the foundation of a contemporary Indian voice through our challenges to museums and anthropology. These strategies for cultural dignity and integrity became complex and enduring because they were about ideas, forms, images, and imaginings.

Simultaneously, to honour Clyde Warrior the Oklahoma chapter of the NIYC began protesting against Little Red at the University of Oklahoma. They called Little Red the dancing idiot. The university branded them as militants, troublemakers, etc. In an ill-advised attempt to address the NIYC's concerns, the university began choosing Indian students to play the mascot. The university's plan backfired when, in 1969, the talented and courageous Navajo dancer, Ron Benally, honourably refused to perform as Little Red at the university football game on Thanksgiving Day, considering the concerns of NIYC and his fellow Indian students. Ron quickly became the object of the derogatory comments. After the NIYC staged a sit-in at the office of the university president in 1970, he agreed to abolish the Little Red tradition. President J. Herbert Hollomon agreed with the NIYC that the mascot was an abomination to the Indians. He comprehended that being Indian was a certain kind of human and not entertainment for non-Indians. The university's student court agreed and issued a temporary restraining order against the mascot.

After the President's decision, the NIYC began a long series of challenges to Indian-related nicknames and mascots of high schools, colleges, and minor-league franchises. We argued that the mascots and names were inappropriate for educational systems; they represented false stereotypes of aggression and violence. We noted that, at the time these Indian nicknames and mascots were created, due to the spiritual genocide of the Indian Religious Crimes Code or Civilization Regulations,[4] Indians were not permitted to dance. We argued that these stereotypes generated the alarmingly high rates of fear toward and violence against Indian tribes, families, men and women, and the incarceration of Indians in reserves, boarding schools, and prisons. We stressed that the mascots perpetuated negative, mythical cultural stereotypes, and institutional racism generated a less than human view of Indians that hid our heritage and humanity. Playing Indian is not about a profession, like cowboys. It is an appropriation of our identity for their own. These negative images established and affirmed an unfavourable environment for Indians, especially potential or future students. These mascots undermined our cultures, traditions, and spirituality.

The NIYC and the newly formed American Indian Movement united in 1972 to create a coalition against the derogatory Indian images and stereotypes. Winnebago Mary McNeil, Hoopa Lois Risling, and other Indian students at Stanford University convinced the university to change the name of its sport teams from "Indians" to the colour "Cardinal." In the same year, Dickinson College in North Dakota agreed to change the name of its sport teams from "Savages" to "Blue Hawks." In 1974, Mandan-Hidatsa Duane Bird Bear, the spokesman for the network, coined the term "cultural drag" to describe Dartmouth University's version of the Indian mascot, convincing the university to finally agree to change its "Indians" nickname to "Big Green." In 1975, Oren Lyons and Irv Powless Jr. convinced Syracuse University to drop "Saltine Warrior" and replace it with "Orange." St. Bonaventure changed its nickname from "Brown Indians Squaw" to "Bonnies."

Along with relocated Indian activists in urban areas, the split-headed leaders of the NIYC, under the banner of Indians of All Tribes, had refocused on old sites of political resistance and renewal. In 1969–71, guided by Shoshone Bannock LaNada Means and the Indian students at the University of California at Berkeley, they established the occupation of the abandoned prison on Alcatraz Island in San Francisco Bay – based on their claims of discovery. LaNada declared that the purpose of the occupation was to create a cultural centre that included Native American Studies, an American Indian spiritual centre, an ecology centre, and an American Indian Museum. Isani Lakota John Trudell reclaimed the Island as part of the unfulfilled promise in the 1868 Treaty of

Fort Laramie that any abandoned federal property would revert to the Indian Nations. The Alcatraz occupation would cascade into a collective consciousness of an Indian rights movement and many forms of protest and incident, including the 1972 Trail of Broken Treaties led by a former leader of the NIYC, Hank Adams (Assiniboine-Lakota), and the American Indian Movement (AIM). Adams's Twenty Point Proposal demanded restoration and implementation of Treaty Rights, termination of the BIA, and protection of Indians' religious freedom and cultural integrity. When the government ignored the national Trail of Broken Treaties in the nation's capital, this animated Indigenous activists into many protests.

Generating Legislative and Judicial Reforms

Split-head resistance and Indian activists' work led Congress to respond by enacting the *Indian Education Act* (1972)[5] and the *Indian Education Assistance and Self-Determination Act* (1975).[6] In 1976, the NIYC succeeded in *Harjo v Kleepe* in having treaty governance restored to the Five Civilized Nations in Oklahoma.[7]

At the same time, as NIYC struggled against the university and sports nicknames and mascots, a new generation of Eurocentric education Indians joined the effort to assert cultural dignity, integrity, and the sensibilities of the Indian voice. We continued to challenge the museums and their curators for unauthorized takings and to deconstruct the grand narrative of the vanishing or invisibility of Indians, now transformed into identity theft by the use of Indian nicknames and mascots. The Indigenous voice of Indians in confrontations, discussions, debates, published essays, novels, poetry, and museum exhibitions asserted not only their control over and ownership of artefacts and particular sacred objects (and human remains) in museums and beyond. They contended as well that museums must accept responsibility for representing the resiliency, strength, and continuity of contemporary Indian knowledge and culture in their programs and exhibits. We asked museum curators to comprehend or at least accept the existence of Indigenous heritages and knowledges that were distinct from the Eurocentric education in museums, anthropology, and art history.

This confluence of Indigenous voices generated the *American Indian Religious Freedom Act* (1978),[8] which protected the "inherent right of freedom to believe, express, and exercise the traditional religions" and freed Indigenous Peoples to worship through ceremonies and rites at sacred sites. It established the National Museum of the American Indian (1989) to reclaim interpretation and representation.

The network also generated the national legislation of the *Native American Graves Protection and Repatriation Act* (1993)[9] to prevent the unregulated past-taking from our burial sites. The repatriation part required federal agencies and institutions that received federal funding to return Indian and Native Hawaiian cultural items to appropriate descendants, tribes, or organizations. It criminalized the traffic in Native American human remains or cultural objects. And it established complex procedures for the inadvertent discovery or planned excavations of Native American cultural items on federal or tribal lands. Museums were required to inventory their holdings and determine how the acquired artefacts could be returned or repatriated to their rightful owners and keepers. No longer were museums able to maintain the savage paradigm of preserving, researching, exhibiting, and interpreting the silent but sacred objects of the vanishing Indians in their collections.

The Quest to End Disparaging, Racially Hostile Words and Images

After these successes, the united network intensified their challenges against Indian-related nicknames and mascots in professional sports, like the Washington Redskins (hereafter, R**skins), Cleveland Indians, and Milwaukee Braves, and placed the nicknames and mascots of colleges and high schools under siege. Despite various attempts, the professional sports teams and their marketing departments resisted the AIM challenges. In 1992, legendary Cheyenne and Muskogee leader of the NIYC Suzan Harjo and six other prominent, educated Native Americans[10] petitioned the United States Patent and Trade Office (PTO) to cancel the corporations' registrations. They presented evidence and argued that the registered trademarks disparaged the dignity of Native Americans.[11] A three-judge panel of the Trademark Appeal Board (Board), an independent administrative tribunal, held in *Harjo et al. v Pro-Football, Inc* (1999)[12] that, under the anti-disparagement clause in s. 2(a) of the *Lanham Act* 1946[13] that provides for the registration of trademarks, the term "R**skins" was disparaging and held Indians up to contempt and ridicule. The Board admitted the PTO made an error in registering the disparaging trademark in 1967, 1974, 1978, and 1990 for entertainment services. The anti-disparagement clause bars registration of marks that "may disparage" any "persons, living or dead, institutions, beliefs, or national symbols, or bring them into contempt, or disrepute."[14]

Susan Harjo and the Indian petitioners had to spend another decade defending the Board's ruling in the federal courts as Pro-Football, Inc[15] (Corporation) appealed the Board's decision. In 2003, the United States District Court for the District of Columbia, on a summary motion brought by the Corporation, reversed the Board.[16] The District Court gave two reasons: (1) it found the Board's finding of disparagement was not supported by substantial evidence and must be reversed; (2) it found the decision should also be reversed because the doctrine of laches (unreasonable delay in bringing the action) precluded consideration of the petitioner's case.[17] On appeal, the United States Court of Appeals held that the District Court applied the wrong standard in evaluating laches to at least one of the petitioners. It retained jurisdiction over the case but remanded the record back to the District Court to assess whether laches barred one petitioner's claim. The District Court's re-evaluation found the remaining petitioner's lawsuit was barred by laches; he did not demonstrate due diligence and a decision in his favour would result in economic prejudice to Corporation.[18]

In 2009, Susan Harjo and the petitioners appealed back to the Court of Appeals, which affirmed the District Court decision to bar the petition by the equitable defence of the laches doctrine. It did not address the District Court finding of a lack of evidence of disparagement. The Indians lost to the Corporation because they did not file their lawsuit soon enough after they reached the legal age of majority of 18, regardless of the fact that they were still considered wards of the federal government at that time, nor were their poverty or level of legal education taken into account. In this case, equity aided the corporate appropriators, not the appropriated.

A new wave of educated Indians returned to the issue of the mascots' names and symbols. Because of our initial successes, we thought the universities and colleges were composed of educated people who would understand the wrongs of the nicknames and mascots. Instead, the small number of Indians admitted to university and college encountered threatening pushback and resistance to their criticism from administrators, professors, staff, sororities and fraternities, students, fans, and the press. They became targets of endless hostility, bigotry, and discrimination that verged on hate crimes. Still, they convinced fifteen universities and colleges to switch nicknames that were secured by trademark protection away from Indian-related terms.[19]

The Native American protests continued against the National Collegiate Athletic Association (NCAA), the governing body for college athletics, concerning the nicknames and mascots in their association. Finally, in 2005, the NCAA condemned the use of these disparaging references. It banned the use of "Native" names, logos, and mascots by universities and colleges in its championship tournaments.[20]

In 2008, while the *Harjo* case was pending, a new generations of young Native Americans, under eighteen years of age and led by Amanda Blackhorse,[21] a Navajo psychological worker, resumed the challenges against the trademark of "R**skins." In *Blackhorse et al. v Pro-Football, Inc*,[22] they renewed the petition with the United States Patent and Trademark Office's Trademark Trial and Appeal Board through a notice of reliance to cancel the registration of over six trademarks using the term "R**skins." The Blackhorse petition noted that article 1708(14) of the *North American Free Trade Agreement* requires the parties, including the United States, to refuse to register trademarks that "may disparage ... persons, living or dead ... or bring them contempt or disrepute."[23] In the *Blackhorse* decision (2014),[24] the Board affirmed the petition.

They determined, based on the evidentiary record in the proceeding before it and on applicable law, that the petitioners met the burden of establishing that the term "R**skins" was disparaging of Native Americans when used concerning professional football services at the times the various registrations of the trademarks were issued.[25] The Board looked at the trademarks from the view of the disparaged group, i.e., the Indians, and not the American public, from 1967 to 1990.[26] It held that federal registrations for the "R**skins" trademarks should be cancelled.

One Board member dissented. He concluded that the "evidence submitted by [the individual respondents] can most charitably be characterized as a 'database dump'"; that the individual respondents did not "introduce any evidence or argument as to what comprises a substantial composite of [the Native American] population"; and that they failed to show that the term "R**skins" was disparaging in 1967, 1974, 1978, or 1990.[27]

The Board's decision to cancel the federal trademarks' legal benefits included cancellation of the legal presumptions of ownership of the trademarks and the nationwide scope of commercial rights in them. The Board did not have jurisdiction in a cancellation proceeding to require that a party cease using a trademark, but only to determine whether it may continue to be registered. A federal court can review the Board's decision to cancel registration of the trademark.

The Corporation challenged the Board's decision on constitutional and statutory grounds. They argued that the cancellation of the trademarks' registration violated the First Amendment's free speech clause. In 2015, the federal District Court entered summary judgment for the *Blackhorse* petitioners and denied the Corporation's motion.[28] It held that the First Amendment is irrelevant because the cancellation of registration of a trademark does not involve any burden or restriction, or prohibit speech.[29] It held that trademarks are government speech and exempt for First Amendment scrutiny.[30] It affirmed the Board's cancellations, rejecting the Corporation's arguments that s. 2(a) of the *Lanham Act* violates the First Amendment, is unconstitutionally vague,[31] and violates procedural due process.[32] It concluded that trademarks were disparaging and the public interest barred the laches defence.[33] It held that trademark registration was different from trademarks themselves, thus the Corporation remained free to use their nickname and trademarks in commerce without registration.[34]

The Corporation appealed the District Court's decision to the US Court of Appeals, asking that the Board's decision be vacated. Two months after the Corporation filed its opening brief in the Fourth Circuit Court of Appeals, an en banc Fourth Circuit held in the *Tam* case that s. 2(a)'s anti-disparagement clause facially violates the First Amendment by overbreadth or vagueness and amounts to an unconstitutional viewpoint discrimination.[35] Simon Shiao Tam was the Asian lead singer of the Asian American band "The Slants" who had attempted to reappropriate this disparaging slur to make the term a positive statement about East Asians identity. He attempted to register the band's name as a trademark even though it was considered offensive to Asian Americans. The Board said the anti-disparagement clause prohibited the registration.[36] The Circuit Court reasoned that the First Amendment protects even hurtful speech that often harms members of stigmatized communities.

The United States sought certiorari of the *Tam* decision in the US Supreme Court. The Pro-Football Corporation asked the Supreme Court for permission to join the petition for certiorari as a companion case. In 2016, their request was denied.[37] While an East Asian seeking to reappropriate a slur is distinct from Native Americans preventing corporate use of a disparaging term for a mascot regardless of the harm to Native Americans, the Blackhorse legal team was obliged to wait until after the *Tam* decision for their case to be heard.

In 2017, the Supreme Court ruled unanimously in *Matal v Tam*[38] that the anti-disparagement clause in the *Lanham Act* violates the free speech clause in the First Amendment, even if the speech expresses ideas that offend or are offensive.[39] Speech may be hateful, but it is still protected by the First Amendment. The *Lanham Act* unlawfully allowed the government to engage in viewpoint discrimination and impose on the permissibility of speech.[40] The Court also held that registration of trademarks is not protected government speech, which allows the government to communicate its own viewpoints without violating the First Amendment.[41] It avoided deciding that trademarks are commercial speech,[42] a category that allow governments to serve important interests related to commerce that might be an incidental burden on speech. After the Supreme Court decision, the PTO stated that, although a trademark may "disparage … or bring … into contempt or disrepute," that is no longer a valid reason for refusing to register it or for cancelling a registration.[43] The Supreme Court's ruling does create a harmful side effect: protection for those corporate entities that wish to trademark names that demean and caricature Indigenous and other peoples.

In 2018, the US Court of Appeals reversed the District Court judgment in *Blackhorse* and remanded the case with instructions to reinstate the Corporation's federal trademark registrations.[44] This decision ended the judicial quest on the Indian-related trademarks. It protected the unauthorized use of Native American images as a form of cultural production or artistic appropriation that permeates the entertainment industry in the United States. It required the network to consider other ways to protect Native American names and symbols and terminate deceptive or misleading trademarks and cultural production by focusing on the funders of the abusers of our identity.

As an enduring legacy of the wisdom of Clyde Warrior and the NIYC, subsequent research in the United States has affirmed that American Indian mascots in high schools, colleges, and professional sports have predictable and adverse effects on Indigenous people. Research has shown that dignity matters. Studies have found that mascots and symbols reinforce negative stereotypes, undermining the inherent dignity of Native Americans, divesting them of Treaty Rights, and creating collective humiliation and individual harms. A study has found that these mascots and symbols are an enduring and contemporary form of racialized, colonial violence that embodies numerous forms of the colonialism that is created, perpetuated, and protected by white settler surveillance and control.[45] Another study revealed that exposure to American Indian mascots created negative and positive implicit stereotypes about contemporary American Indians.[46] Another study found that students who agreed to use Indian mascots were more likely to engage in racial prejudice and discrimination against American Indian students than students who disagreed with American Indian mascots.[47] The harsh statistics surrounding Native Americans in dropout rates and youth suicide, and disparities in education and public health, confirm the harm of racialized stereotyping. Social science and humanities research on this theme has revealed the negative psychological consequences for American Indians,[48] positive psychological consequences for European Americans,[49] and adverse effects on race relations and equality.[50] Many times, the negative impacts to dignity decrease self-esteem and increase the level of anxiety and depression of Indian high school and college students.[51]

Beyond explicit (conscious) attitudes and stereotypes, American Indian mascots and symbols may also elicit unconscious attitudes, biases, and stereotypes.[52] They not only promote the development, endorsement, and activation of negative attitudes and behaviours toward contemporary American Indians, but also reinforce inequality and, in so doing, undermine race relations in the United States. Moreover, these misappropriations of Indigenous heritage and knowledge systems and the commodifications of their identities are wrongful takings of Indigenous Peoples' inherent dignity.[53] While the generation of stereotypical images of long-dead Indians as mascots and cultural production are tolerated by Americans, it sustains implicit and false biases and prejudices about Native Americans.[54] They create overt hostility and racism as well as covertly deny the inclusion of Native Americans in political institutions, law firms, and corporations.[55]

In a legal age where the constitutional right of freedom of expression allows citizens and corporations to use Native American cultural imagery, identities, and cultural production as an expression of freedom and liberty, Dakota scholar Vine Deloria Jr. declared: "[w]hat we need is a cultural leave-us-alone agreement, in spirit and fact."[56] A new generation of Indigenous legal scholars has had to face the painful legacies of an era that used racialized images of Indians in the appropriation of Indian languages and images for their states, counties, and public schools. The Native American lawyers began to ask who owned the images of the Indians and for what purpose, and why Eurocentric knowledge and law almost exclusively defined their identity. Indigenous (Yaqui) law professor Rebecca Tsosie became the legal voice of the Native American lawyers.[57]

They began to reconceptualize the harms of cultural appropriation[58] to inherent dignity and equality.[59] They are establishing the beginnings of a systematic examination and analysis of cultural appropriation. They have argued against the commodification of racially derogatory terms or images that in the past has been used to justify genocides. Some have suggested using stewardship or the fiduciary model of property law to protect cultural heritages and properties.[60] They have gradually turned to innovative approaches and to tribal legislation and defamation suits to restore traditional knowledge systems, creative arts, cultural expressions, and genetic resources.[61] Some Native American scholars have argued that Indian mascots harm the civil rights of Native Americans as well as undermine tribal sovereignty.[62] Most have argued that, as an act of tribal sovereignty, tribal governments should licence the use of their names for commercial purposes. In the 1990s, appropriation of Aboriginal cultural heritage entered Canadian consciousness and similar creative approaches have been developed among the Indigenous Peoples in Canada toward protecting their traditions.[63]

The coalition has achieved moderate successes.[64] The existing intellectual property law in the United States does not protect Native American expressions, symbols, and ideas because they are collective, intergenerational, religious, and spiritual properties.[65] In this situation, tribal governments have stepped up to protect these collective expressions by litigation and enactment of codes to ensure preservation of knowledge systems, language, and cultural identities.[66] Tribal governments have sought trademark rights in tribal symbols, the return of Indian burial and ceremonial objects from museums, and easements in sacred sites.[67]

Politicians and public educators have become sensitive about caricatures and representations that are racially derogatory. In 2017, Native Americans generated successful efforts by using civil rights approaches to have California and Oregon prohibit any public school from using the term "R**skins" for "school or athletic team names, mascots, or nicknames."[68] Similar attempts in Michigan,[69] Wisconsin,[70] and Colorado[71] failed. In 2019, Maine banned the use of all "Native themed" mascots and imagery in public schools, colleges, and universities.[72] More than 2100 sports teams in the United States maintain a reference to Indian identities.[73] Gradually the movement against this use of Indian identities is travelling to Canada, with Bedford Road Collegiate High School in Saskatchewan changing its athletic name and mascot from Redmen to Redhawks[74] and the Edmonton football team recently dropping "Eskimos" as the team name, replacing it with "Elks."[75] In the United States, under a new alliance with Native Americans and Black Lives Matter, the Washington football corporation agreed to terminate its use of "R**skins," rebranding as the "Commanders" after a two seasons without a name.[76] The controversy is flourishing. The ethical case against racialized representation and the underlying legal issues of cultural appropriation are complicated and will likely be discussed and litigated for years to come.

Reclaiming Inherent Dignity

At the same time as attempting to end the disparaging words and images in the United States, another Native American coalition led by Elder and Medicine person Phillips Deere turned in the late 1970s to the multifaceted United Nations system to reclaim our humanity and dignity that was being trapped and denied in the United States and beyond.[77] We were guided by the Indigenous teaching of inherent human dignity and integrity. We found that the ideal of inherent human rights held a prominent and canonical position in United Nations laws.[78] It is the starting-point, the "shaping principle," and the "overarching principle" of the law of human rights.[79]

The split-headed Indigenous Peoples and their allies in the United States, Canada, and beyond have transformed the network into an emerging global Indigenous renaissance or, as John Ralston Saul has called it, "the comeback."[80] This global renaissance breached the principle of confinement. Eurocentric knowledge systems are no longer able to control the minds of Indigenous Peoples. The renaissance argues that Eurocentric knowledge is not universal, the pinnacle of human achievement, or complete within its disciplines, sub-disciplines, and interdisciplinary approaches. Instead, Eurocentrism is viewed as the unconcealed triumphalism of European supremacy, as vindictive and discriminatory to other knowledge systems, and as false exceptionality. The renaissance argues that no knowledge system is compete in itself if it excludes and ignores others. The educated split-head movement argues that knowledge systems and education systems need to learn from and validate each other. A new transsystemic dialogue among knowledge systems must generate an ethical space where innovative language can arise to balance or replace Eurocentrism and its categories. This dialogue privileges the reanimation of the dignity of ancestral knowledges, languages, and cultures that generate Indigenous potentiality in balancing Eurocentrism. It argues that the knowledge of the future must be born outside of Eurocentrism and from a blending of all knowledges systems. It acknowledges that Eurocentric education and its related cultures cannot adequately restore that which it has dismantled and denied.

The interconnection of the visions of the global Indigenous renaissance was realized by their decades-long advocacy and sustained diplomacy in the United Nations through the *International Labour Organization Indigenous and Tribal Peoples Convention* (No. 169)[81] and the *Declaration on the Rights of Indigenous Peoples* (2007).[82] The *Convention* contains a number of rights relating to the cultural heritage of Indigenous Peoples and requires governments to promote and safeguard their cultural heritage. The *Declaration*, in its seventh preambular paragraph, confirms that the rights and standards are "inherent" or pre-existing; they are not new rights. It reflects the existing global consensus that Indigenous Peoples are the bearers of inherent and inalienable human rights not given by any governmental authority. The *Declaration* has established corroborating, constitutive principles and rules concerning the constitutionally affirmed Aboriginal and Treaty Rights in Canada's Constitution. The United States in 2010 and Canada in 2016 announced their full support of the *Declaration*, without qualification.[83] British Columbia and Canada have implemented the *Declaration* into provincial and federal law to bring national law in line with their international commitments.[84] The United States has not. The provincial and federal Acts in Canada protect the inherent rights of Indigenous Peoples and provide a framework for the governments and Indigenous Peoples to protect and reconcile Indigenous Peoples' knowledge systems, cultures, and identities.

These inherent rights affirm the NIYC's beliefs in cultural dignity, integrity, and self-determination. Article 1 of the *Declaration* directly incorporates the international treaties on human rights law so they apply to Indigenous Peoples. Article 11 affirms the inherent human rights of Indigenous Peoples to practice and revitalize cultural traditions and customs and to redress their religious and spiritual property taken without their free, prior, and informed consent and in violation of their laws, traditions, and customs. Article 12 affirms the right to "manifest, practice, develop and teach their spiritual and religious traditions, customs, and ceremonies" and "the right to maintain, protect, and have access in privacy to their religious and cultural sites," as well as "the right to the repatriation of their human remains." Article 13 affirms the right to "revitalize, use, develop and transmit to future generations their histories, languages, oral traditions, philosophies, writing systems and literatures." Article 31 affirms the right to "maintain, control, protect and develop their cultural heritage, traditional knowledge and traditional cultural expressions." These rights affirm the distinct Indigenous domain separate from the global or public domain of Eurocentrism. They eliminate the Eurocentric epistemicide of Indigenous knowledge systems and ensure cognitive and cultural justice.

Concurrent with the drafting of the *Convention* and *Declaration*, in the 1990s the UN Educational, Scientific, and Cultural Organization (UNESCO) was the drafting and establishing the principles and guidelines for the protection of heritages of Indigenous Peoples.[85] UNESCO defined cultural heritage as "the totality of tradition-based creations of a cultural community, expressed by a group or individuals and recognized as reflecting the expectations of a community in so far as they reflect its cultural and social identity."[86] Heritage is collective, representing intangible or tangible property and expressions that shape a way of life and thought.

In 2015, the Expert Mechanism on the Rights of Indigenous Peoples returned to the issue in the report entitled *Promotion and Protection of the Rights of Indigenous Peoples with Respect to Their Cultural Heritage.*[87] The Expert Mechanism emphasized that many misappropriations and misinterpretations of Indigenous Peoples' knowledge and culture exist in many forms. It proposed at paragraph 7:

> Indigenous peoples' cultures include tangible and intangible manifestations of their ways of life, achievements and creativity, and are an expression of their self-determination and of their spiritual and physical relationships with their lands, territories and resources. Indigenous culture is a holistic concept based on common material and spiritual values and includes distinctive manifestations in language, spirituality, membership, arts, literature, traditional knowledge, customs, rituals, ceremonies, methods of production, festive events, music, sports and traditional games, behaviour, habits, tools, shelter, clothing, economic activities, morals, value systems, cosmovisions, laws, and activities such as hunting, fishing, trapping and gathering.

The World Intellectual Property Organization (WIPO) has remained the UN specialized agency responsible for treaties and agreements involving copyright, patent, and trademark laws that fail to recognize the Indigenous domain – containing Indigenous knowledge, cultural expression, genetic resources, and rights – in the global forum for intellectual rights. The existing international intellectual property system does not protect traditional knowledge, traditional cultural expressions, or genetic resources since they are characterized as part of the audacious metaphor of global domain, the "common heritage" or "public domain" of Eurocentrism.[88] Indigenous knowledge, expressions, and genetic resources have been free for European appropriation. The Indigenous renaissance turned its attention to intellectual property rights within the WIPO.[89] The WIPO defines traditional knowledge of an Indigenous People as "a living body of knowledge passed on from generation to generation within a community ... [that] often forms part of a people's cultural and spiritual identity."[90] Since 2000, the Indigenous Peoples and the WIPO's Intergovernmental Committee on Intellectual Property and Genetic Resources, Traditional Knowledge, and Folklore have ventured to eliminate this insidious and fundamentally unjust situation in formal, text-based negotiations and finalize international, legal, working instruments providing *sui generis* protection for Indigenous Rights.[91]

Unconcluded Future

The journey of my generation for protecting the inherent dignity and cultural integrity of our nations has been a long, tricky journey into the Eurocentric heart of darkness in North America. We have extended the journey to Indigenous

Peoples around the Earth and created unique forms of Indigenous diplomacy. We have continually asked, in many ways, how the Eurocentric knowledge systems can appropriate and destroy Indigenous knowledge, identities, and cultures while asserting the notion of universal humanity. We have unfolded its systems of injustices built around its civilized humanity and its legal defences and justifications. We have exposed the social imaginaries in the United States and Canada[92] constructed by the mythical binary of natural versus artificial, savage versus civilized, us and them.[93] We have had to endure insults to our inherent dignity and disparagements of our cultures.

These Indigenous struggles with Eurocentrism – its negative stereotypes, disparagements, and cultural appropriation – establish a pattern of systemic injustice to our humanity and dignity that perpetuates inequalities and harm.[94] The trans-systemic struggles reveal that the resilient power of the different knowledge systems, experiences, determination, and creativity of the Indigenous Peoples has never been exhausted by the oppressive situations into which they happen to have been born. Indigenous knowledge, languages, humanity, and ecological sensibilities have allowed the first generation of split-headed lawyers, scholars, educators, and activists to generate a good road to justice.

The Indigenous renaissance continues to develop many manifestations of the growing capacity to change in people's consciousness and transform the colonial imperatives in intellectual property laws. Its resistance and reconciliation have forged a unique predicament in North American thought, as revealed by Cherokee writer Thomas King: "North America loves the dead Indian and ignores live Indians, North America *hates* Legal Indians. Savagely."[95]

The knowledge and dignity takings in these epic, excruciating legal and cultural confrontations continue. Like systemic racism itself, these dignity injustices know no bounds. Cultural appropriation remains an overarching and undergirding ethos in American and Canadian society as well as globally. It can overwhelm the self-image of youth and even adults. The appropriators have gotten used to controlling and using the laws, and it remains difficult for them to see or accept the injustices associated with the taking. They cling to their appropriations that forge their colonial and postcolonial identities, imaginary or not.

Like ancient teaching about visions, my split-headed generation has stealthfully unleashed the Indigenous renaissance and imperative to protect Indigenous knowledge systems, heritages, and cultures. Our performance of our emerging visions of inherent dignity, integrity, and humanity has empowered national and global transformations in consciousness and thought. However, a better, trans-systemic future is still waiting for the next generations of split-headed scholars, lawyers, and activists to envision and create a better United States, Canada, and world.

NOTES

1 *De la démocratie en Amérique* (*Democracy in America*), Henry Reeves trans. (Pennsylvania State Univ Classic Series Publication, 2002), at 390 ("It would be impossible to destroy men with more respect for the laws of humanity").

2 As my Chickasaw Elders taught: *Himmaka' nittakookano hattak yokasht toksalicha 'nikat ki 'yo* (all humans are born free and equal in dignity and rights). In retrospect, this was a classic situation of epistemic injustice, a concept that covers experiences and harms that we struggled to make sense of because the educational system and American society have not made them intelligible. See Franziska Dübgen, ed, "Epistemic Injustice in Practice" (2016) 15:1 Wag a du: J Transnat'l Women's & Gender Stud; Miranda Flicker, *Epistemic Injustice: Power and the Ethics of Knowing* (Oxford, UK: Oxford Univ Press, 2007).

3 James (Sa'ke'j) Youngblood Henderson, "Postcolonial Ghost Dancing: Diagnosing European Colonialism" in Marie Battiste, ed, *Reclaiming Indigenous Voice and Vision* (Vancouver: UBC Press, 2000) 57.

4 The Department of Interior's 1883 *Code of Indian Offenses* punished the "old heathenish" Indian dances and feasts by imprisonment or withholding food (treaty rations) for up to thirty days. Any Medicine Man convicted of encouraging others to follow traditional practices was to be confined in the agency prison for not less than ten days or until he could provide evidence that he had abandoned his beliefs. The *Dawes Act* of 1887 outright prohibited and made illegal Indian religious ceremonies and practices. In 1933, the code removed the ban on dances and other customary cultural practices. See online: <https://en.wikisource.org/wiki/Code_of_Indian _Offenses>; Francis Purcha, *Documents of United States Indian Policy*, 2nd ed (Lincoln, NB: Univ of Nebraska Press, 1990) at 160–1, 187–8; Steve Talbot, "Spiritual Genocide: The Denial of American Indian Religious Freedom, from Conquest to 1934" (2006) 21:2 Wicazo Sa Rev 7. In Canada in 1884, similar prohibitions were included in the *Indian Act* by An Act further to amend "The Indian Act, 1880," S.C. 1884, c. 27, s. 3.

5 *Indian Education Act of 1972,* Pub. L. No. 92-318, also known as Title VII of ESEA.

6 *Indian Self-Determination and Education Assistance Act of 1975*, Pub. L. No. 93-638, 88 Stat. 2203 (1975).

7 420 F. Supp. 1110 (D.D.C. 1976), *Harjo v Andrus*, aff'd, 581 F.2d 949 (D.C. Cir. 1978). District Court Judge William B. Bryant held that "the tribe has the right to determine its own destiny" and the "right to democratic self-government": *ibid* at 1143. He concluded that "the re-creation of the constitutional Creek government should be accomplished by the Creeks themselves": *ibid* at 1144.

8 *American Indian Religious Freedom Act*, 1978 42 USC § 1996.

9 *Native American Graves Protection and Repatriation Act* 1993, Pub. L. No. 101-601, 25 USC 3001 et seq., 104 Stat. 3048.

10 The other Indian petitioners were Raymond D. Apodaca (Ysleta del Sur Pueblo), Manley A. Begay Jr., Ed.D. (Navajo), Vine Deloria Jr., Esq. (Standing Rock Sioux),

Norbert S. Hill Jr. (Oneida), William A. Means Jr. (Oglala Lakota), and Mateo
Romero (Cochiti Pueblo).

11 The PTO has to weigh three categories of evidence to determine whether a
term "may disparage": (1) dictionary definitions and accompanying editorial
designations; (2) scholarly, literary, and media references; and (3) statements of
individuals or group leaders of the referenced group regarding the term.

12 *Harjo, et al v Pro-Football, Inc*, 50 USPQ 2nd 1705,1749 (TTP 1999) [*Harjo*];
reversed in *Pro Football, Inc. v Harjo*, 284 F. Supp. 2nd 96, (DDC 2003), reversed in
Pro Football Inc v Harjo, 415 F. 3rd 44 (D.C. Cir. 2005); *Pro-Football, Inc v Harjo*,
464 F. 3d 800 (D.C. Cir. 2009), cert denied 130 S. Ct. 631 (2009) 96.

13 15 USC 1051–72.

14 *Ibid* at 1052(1).

15 Pro-Football, Inc. is a Maryland corporation with its principal place of business in
Virginia. Pro-Football is the owner of the Washington Commanders, formerly the
Washington R**skins, a professional football franchise located in the Washington,
D.C. area, and one of the thirty-two member clubs of the National Football League.

16 *Pro-Football, Inc. v Harjo, supra* note 12, 284 F Supp 2nd 96.

17 *Harjo, supra* note 12, 68 USPQ2d at 1263.

18 *Harjo, supra* note 12, 87 USPQ2 1903.

19 These institutions were: Siena College, from Indians to Saints (1988); Eastern
Michigan University, from Huron to Eagles (1991); Simpson College (Iowa),
from Redmen to Storm (1992); Hartwick College (NY), from Warriors to Hawks
(1994); Marquette University, from Warriors to Golden Eagles (1994); St. John's
University (NY), from Redmen to Red Storm (1994); Adams State University
(Colo.), from Indians to Grizzlies (1996); Miami (Ohio), from R**skins to
RedHawks (1997); Southern Nazarene University, from R**skins to Crimson Storm
(1998); Morningside University (Iowa), from Maroon Chiefs to Mustangs (1998);
Oklahoma City University, from Chiefs to Stars (1999); Seattle University, from
Chieftains to Redhawks (2000); Southwestern College (Calif.), from Apaches to
Jaguars (2000); Quinnipiac University (Conn), from Braves to Bobcats (2002); and
Massachusetts College of Liberal Arts, from Mohawks to TrailBlazers (2002).

20 NCAA Executive Committee Issues Guidelines for Use of Native American
Mascots at Championship Events (2005), online: <http://fs.ncaa.org/Docs
/PressArchive/2005/Announcements/NCAA%2BExecutive%2BCommittee
%2BIssues%2BGuidelines%2Bfor%2BUse%2Bof%2BNative%2BAmerican%2
BMascots%2Bat%2BChampionship%2BEvents.html>.The policy caused the
University of Louisiana at Monroe to change from Indians to Warhawks (2006),
Arkansas State University from Indians to Red Wolves (2008), and University
North Dakota University from Fighting Sioux to Fighting Hawks (2012). Other
universities and colleges have partially eliminated the nicknames or logos,
such as the University of Illinois, which removed Chief Illiniwek as the official
mascot in 2007 but retained the nickname "Fighting Illini." Bradley University

(Illinois) and Alcorn State University stopped using Native American mascots but kept their "Braves" nicknames. To comply with the NCAA decision, William and Mary University adjusted the team's Tribe logo to remove feathers because it could be offensive; however, their athletics teams are still called "Tribe." A few universities and colleges successfully appealed to the NCAA that their nicknames are not "hostile or offensive" because of partnership or consent with particular tribes, i.e., Utah (Utes), Central Michigan (Chippewas), Florida State (Seminoles), and Mississippi College (Choctaws). See andré douglas pond cummings & Seth E. Harper, "Wide Right: Why the NCAA's Policy on the American Indian Mascot Issue Misses the Mark" (2009) 9 U Md LJ Race, Religion, Gender & Class 135.

21 The others were Marcus Briggs (Muscogee), Phillip Gover (Paiute), Shquanebin Lone-Bentley (Tonawanda Seneca), Jillian Pappan (Omaha), and Courtney Tsotigh (Kiowa).

22 *Blackhorse v Pro–Football, Inc.*, 111 USPQ 2d (BNA) 1080, 111–12, 114 (TTAB 2014); 2014 WL 2757516 (T.T.A.B.2014), aff'd 112 F Supp 3d 439 (ED Va 2015 [*Blackhorse*].

23 *North American Free Trade Agreement*, 1992, 32 I.L.M. 289 (1993), Art. 1708(14), online: <http://www.sice.oas.org/trade/nafta/chap-171.asp#A1708>.

24 *Blackhorse, supra* note 22.

25 *Ibid* at 178.

26 *Ibid* at 101.

27 *Ibid* at 190.

28 *Blackhorse, supra* note 22, Memorandum Opinion and Order of District Judge Lee.

29 *Ibid* at 447–8, 453–64.

30 *Ibid* at 457–62.

31 *Ibid* at 464–7.

32 *Ibid* at 467.

33 *Ibid* at 467–89. The record contains eleven dictionaries, expert linguists' opinions, scholarly, literary, and media references, and statements of Native American leaders and individuals defining "r**skins" as a term referring to North American Indians and characterizing "r**skins" as offensive or contemptuous and an ethnophaulism (ethnic slur in hate speech).

34 *Ibid* at 453–4.

35 *In re Simon Shiao Tam*, 808 F.3d 1321, 1328, 1337 (Fed. Cir. 2015) (*en* banc). Initially, the Federal Circuit Court affirmed the Board denial, *In re Tam*, 785 F. 3d 567, 568, 571 (Fed Cir. 2015).

36 The Board found the name to be disparaging to other Asian people and refused to register the trademark. The majority rejected the disparagement clause as viewpoint-based discrimination: *ibid* at 1334. The majority held that it was subject to and failed the strict scrutiny test for commercial speech because the clause regulates the expressive component of trademarks.

37 *Pro-Football, Inc v Blackhorse*, 137 S Ct 44 (2016) (Petition No. 15 13311), petition for certiorari denied October 3, 2016; Order Placing Case in Abeyance, *Pro-Football, Inc. v Blackhorse*, No. 15-1874 (4th Cir. Nov. 15, 2016), ECF No. 121.

38 *Matal, Interim Director, United States Patent and Trademark Office v Tam*, 137 SCt 1744 (2017) [*Matal v Tam*]. The Court in *Iancu v Brunetti*, 139 SCt 2294 (2019), held that the immoral or/and scandalous clause is also facially unconstitutional under the First Amendment.

39 *Matal v Tam, supra* note 38, at 1751.

40 *Ibid* at 1763–4.

41 *Ibid* at 1758. The United States tried to argue that trademarks are government speech because the government registers them and provides benefits to the owners of such federally registered marks: *ibid* at 1757. The Supreme Court rejected the government's argument, reasoning that trademarks are created by individuals and not the government, and registration of a trademark does not represent approval by the government: *ibid* at 1758.

42 *Ibid* at 1749.

43 U.S. Patent & Trademark Office, Examination Guide 01–17, Examination Guidance for Section 2(a)'s Disparagement Provision after *Matal v Tam* and Examination for Compliance with Section 2(a)'s Scandalousness Provision while Constitutionality Remains in Question (2017), online: <https://perma.cc/AHL5 -X2HZ>.

44 Unpublished per curiam opinion, *Pro-Football v Blackhorse*, No. 15-1874 (4th Fed. Cir. 2018). Unpublished opinions are not binding precedents in the 4th Circuit.

45 Dakota historian Phillip J. Deloria, *Playing Indians* (New Haven, CT: Yale Univ Press, 1998), and Lumbee Law professor Robert A. Williams Jr., *Savages Anxieties: The Invention of Western Civilization* (New York, NY: Palgrave Macmillan, 2012) note that Western European peoples have, for centuries, employed negative cultural imagery of Indigenous Peoples to construct them as "savage" as a means to divest them of natural resources, equal rights, and status. See also Native American Studies professor Shari M. Huhndorf, *Going Native: Indians in the American Cultural Imagination* (Ithaca, NY: Cornell Univ Press, 2001); B. Farnell, "The Fancy Dance of Racializing Discourse" (2004) 28:1 J of Sport & Soc Issues 30; E.J. Staurowsky, "You Know, We Are All Indian: Exploring White Power and Privilege in Reactions to the NCAA Native American Mascot Policy" (2007) 31:1 J Sport & Soc Issues 61; National Congress of American Indians, *Ending the Legacy of Racism in Sports and the Era of Harmful "Indian" Sports Mascots* (October 2013), online: <http://www.ncai.org/attachments/PolicyPaper _mijApMoUWDbjqFtjAYzQWlqLdrwZvsYfakBwTHpMATcOroYolpN_NCAI _Harmful_Mascots_Report_Ending_the_Legacy_of_Racism_10_2013.pdf>.

46 J. Stone, E. Focella, S. Fryberg & R. Covarrubias, "Native American Sports Mascots Activate Stereotypes about Contemporary Native Americans," manuscript, Univ of Arizona, 2011.

47 J. Gonzales, "In-Group, Out/Group Dynamics of Native American Mascot Endorsement" (unpublished PhD diss., Univ of South Dakota, 2005).

48 S.A. Fryberg, H.R. Markus, D. Oyserman, J.M. Stone, "Of Warrior Chiefs and Indian Princesses: The Psychological Consequences of American Indian Mascots" (2008) 30:3 BASP 208.

49 S.A. Fryberg & D. Osyserman, "Feeling Good about Chief Wahoo: Basking in the Reflected Glory of American Indians," unpublished manuscript, Univ of Arizona, 2001.

50 T. Nelson, *Handbook of Prejudice, Stereotyping, and Discrimination* (Philadelphia: Psychology Press, 2009); S.A. Fryberg & A. Watts, "We're Honoring You Dude: Myths, Mascots and American Indians" in H.R. Markus & P.M. Moya, eds, *Doing Race: 21 Essays for the 21st Century* (New York, NY: W.W. Norton & Co, 2010); J.A. Steinfeldt, B.D. Foltz, J.K. Kaladow, T. Carlson, L. Pagano, E. Benton & M.C. Steinfedt, "Racism in the Electronic Age: Role of Online Forums in Expressing Racial Attitudes about American Indians" (2009) 16 Cult Divers Ethn Minor Psychol 362.

51 A. LaRocque, "Psychological Distress between American Indians and Majority Culture College Students Regarding the Use of the Fighting Sioux Nickname and Logo" (unpublished PhD diss., Univ of North Dakota, 2004).

52 B.A. Nosek, F.L. Smyth, J.J. Hansen, T. Devos, N.M. Linder, K.A. Ranganath, C.T. Smith, K.R. Olson, D. Chugh, A.G. Greenwald & M.R. Banaji, "Pervasiveness and Correlates of Implicit Attitudes and Stereotypes" (2007) 18 Euro Rev Soc Psychol 36.

53 Victoria F. Phillips, "Beyond Trademark: The Washington Redskins Case and the Search for Dignity" (2018) 92 Chi-Kent L Rev 1061.

54 Anita Cernstein, "What's Wrong with Stereotyping?" (2013) 55 Ariz L Rev 655.

55 US Commission on Civil Rights on the Use of Native American Images and Nicknames as Sports Symbols (2001), online: <https://www.usccr.gov/press/archives/2001/041601st.htm>; American Psychological Association Resolution Recommending the Immediate Retirement of American Indian Mascots, Symbols, Images and Personalities by Schools, Colleges, Universities, Athletic Teams, and Organizations (2005), online: <https://www.apa.org/about/policy/mascots.pdf>; Statement by the Council of the American Sociological Association on Discontinuing the Use of Native American Nicknames, Logos and Mascots in Sport (2007), online: < https://www.asanet.org/sites/default/files/use_of_native_american_nicknames_logos_and_mascots.pdf>; Erik Stegman & Victoria Phillips, *Missing the Point: The Real Impact of Native American Mascots and Team Names on Native American and Alaska Native Youth* (2014), online: <https://www.americanprogress.org/issues/race/reports/2014/07/22/94214/missing-the-point/>.

56 Vine Deloria Jr., *Custer Died for Your Sins: An Indian Manifesto* (Norman, OK: Univ of Oklahoma Press, 1998) at 27.

57 Rebecca E. Tsosie, "Indigenous Peoples' Claims to Cultural Property: A Legal Perspective" (1997) 21 Mus Anthropol at 5; "Reclaiming Native Stories: An Essay on Cultural Appropriation and Cultural Rights" (2002) 34 Ariz St L J 299; "Cultural

Challenges to Biotechnology: Native American Genetic Resources and the Concept of Cultural Harm" (2007) 35 JL Med & Ethics 396; "Native Nations and Museums: Developing an Institutional Framework for Cultural Sovereignty" (2009) 45:1 Tulsa LJ 3; "Indigenous Peoples and Epistemic Injustices: Science, Ethics, and Human Rights" (2012) 87 Wash L Rev 1113; "Just Governance or Just War? Native Artists, Cultural Production, and the Challenge of Super-Diversity" (2015) 6 Cybaris: An Intell Prop L Rev 61; "Indigenous Identity, Cultural Harm, and the Politics of Cultural Production: A Commentary on Riley and Carpenter's 'Owning Red'" (2016) 94 Texas L Rev 250.

58   Cultural appropriation occurs when settlers or corporations use Native American names, imagery, representations, iconography, and other symbols for commercial purposes and without tribal government or individual consent. In 2017, the *Oxford English Dictionary* finally characterized our resistance as opposition to "cultural appropriation." However, the term is deeply contested.

59   Law professor Bernadett Atuahene, in *We Want What's Ours: Learning from South Africa's Land Restitution Program* (Oxford: Oxford Univ Press, 2014) and "Dignity Takings and Dignity Restoration: Creating a New Theoretical Framework for Understanding Involuntary Property Loss and the Remedies Required" (2016) 41 L & Soc Inquiry 796, has developed the concept of "dignity taking" and "community dignity taking" which is an involuntary property confiscation that involves the dehumanizing or infantilization of the dispossessed and community destruction. Atuahene argues that the appropriate remedy for dignity taking is "dignity restoration, the material compensation that affirms their humanity and reinforces their agency." Justin B. Richland applied the concept to separation of the Hopi People from their sacred lands in "Dignity as (Self-) Determination: Hopi Sovereignty in the Face of US Dispossessions" (2016) 41 L & Soc Inquiry 917. Victoria Phillips, *supra* note 53, has extend the theory to the taking of intangible property and the misappropriation of cultural identity and imagery.

60   Kristen A. Carpenter, Sonia Katyal & Angela Riley, "In Defense of Property" (2009) Yale LJ 118 [Carpenter et al, "Property"].

61   Kristen A. Carpenter, "Considering Individual Religious Freedoms under Tribal Constitutional Law" (2005) 14 Kan JL & and Pub Pol'y 561; Kristen A. Carpenter, Sonia A. Katyal & Angela R. Riley, "Clarifying Cultural Property" (2010) 17 Int'l J of Cult Prop 581; Angela R. Riley & Kristen A. Carpenter, "Owning *Red*: A Theory of Indian (Cultural) Appropriation" (2016) 94:5 Texas L Rev 859 [Riley & Carpenter, "Owning *Red*"]; D.B. Shabalala, "Intellectual Property, Traditional Knowledge, and Traditional Cultural Expressions in Native American Tribal Codes" (2017) 51:4 Akron L Rev 1125 [Shabalala, "Tribal Codes"].

62   Riley & Carpenter, "Owning *Red*," *ibid*.

63   See generally Rosemary J. Coombe, "The Properties of Culture and the Politics of Possessing Identity: Native Claims in the Cultural Appropriation Controversy" (1993) 6 Canadian JL & Juris 249; Bruce Ziff & Pratima V. Rao, eds, *Borrowed*

Power: Essays on Cultural Appropriation (New Brunswick, NJ: Rutgers Univ Press, 1997); Marie Battiste & J.Y. Henderson, *Protecting Indigenous Heritage and Knowledge: The Global Challenge* (Saskatoon: Purich Publication, 2000); Intellectual Property Issues in Cultural Heritage (IPinCH), *Indigenous Peoples, Cultural Heritage, and the Law,* online: <https://www.sfu.ca/ipinch/project -components/working-groups/customary-conventional-and-vernacular-legal -forms-working-group/>; Assembly of First Nations, Resolution No. 60/2019, The Protection of First Nations Intellectual Property Rights and Traditional Knowledge, Cultural Expression and Genetic Resources; Canada, Standing Committee on Industry, Science and Technology, 2019, Statutory Review of the *Copyright Act,* online: <https://www.ourcommons.ca/Content/Committee/421/INDU/Reports /RP10537003/indurp16/indurp16-e.pdf> at 87 #15.

64 Failed attempts were *Lyng v Nw. Indian Cemetery Protective Ass'n*, 485 U.S. 439, 451–53 (1988) (stating that the traditional ceremony sites used for Indian religious ceremonies could not be protected from government development on the basis of a First Amendment claim); *McBride v Motor Vehicle Div. of Utah State Tax Comm'n,* 977 P 2d 467 (Utah 1999) (R**skins on license plates permitted).

65 Potawatomi law professor Angela R. Riley, "Recovering Collectivity: Group Rights to Intellectual Property in Indigenous Communities" (2000) 18 Cardozo Arts & Ent LJ 175.

66 Riley & Carpenter, "Owing *Red,*" *supra* note 61 at 927–30; Shabalala, "Tribal Codes," *supra* note 61.

67 Carpenter et al, "Property," *supra* note 60 at 1024–5, 1060–5.

68 *Racial Mascot Act,* 2017 Cal. Edu. Code, Chapter 2, Article 3.5, s. 221.1–221.3; Oregon State Board of Education 2017 Or. Admin R. 581-02100045.

69 State of Michigan State Board of Education Resolution Use of American Indians Mascots, Nicknames, and Logos (2003), online: <https://www.michigan.gov /documents/mascots_69612_7.res.pdf>. The Michigan Department of Civil Rights attempted to halt the use of American Indian mascots and racialized imagery in thirty-five schools in Michigan that created a hostile environment and denied equal rights, which failed when the U.S. Department of Education Office of Civil Rights dismissed the complaint for lack of specific, identifiable harm to individual students. The Michigan Department of Civil Rights, in an effort to protect American Indian students from a possible backlash at their schools, had offered only empirical studies that supported the psychological harm experienced by American Indian students in lieu of specific examples of race-based incidents and the identity of students and individuals who suffered specific harm because of the alleged discrimination. The Education Office concluded that these omissions rendered the complaint insufficient to support an inference that racial discrimination had occurred or was occurring.

70 *2009 Wisconsin Act 250* (2010), online: <http://www.indianmascots.com /act_250_-_web.pdf>.

71 Governor's Commission to Study American Indian Representations in Public
    Schools, Report 2016, online: <https://www.denvergov.org/content/dam
    /denvergov/Portals/643/documents/Commissions/DAIC/2018/CSAIRPS
    -Report-2016.pdf> (recommending the elimination of American Indian mascots,
    imagery, and names).

72 *An Act to Ban Native American Mascots in All Public Schools*, MRSA s. 4013.

73 See C.R. King, *The Native American Mascot Controversy: A Handbook* (Lanham,
    MD: Scarecrow Press, 2010); <https://www.mascotdb.com/teams/team-name
    /indians>; <http://www.ncai.org/NCAI_School_Mascot_Tracking_Database
    _-_Overview_and_Numbers.pdf>. It is ironic that states from which Indians were
    forcefully removed have the highest concentration of public schools using the term
    R**skins. The sport teams of public schools maintain the names Braves, Chiefs,
    Indians, Redmen, Reds, R**skins, Savages, Squaws, Tribe, and Warriors, as well
    as names of Nations such as Apaches, Arapahoe, Aztecs, Cherokees, Chickasaws,
    Chinooks, Chippewas, Choctaws, Comanches, Eskimos, Mohawks, Mohicans,
    Seminoles, Sioux, and Utes. However, not all teams with the name "Warriors" are
    referencing Native Americans. It has remained difficult to resolve these issues
    without proper respect and dignity, and without relationships with the tribes and
    their consent and partnership in the first place.

74 Sheelah McLean, Cree Alex Wilson & Erica Lee, *The Whiteness of Redmen:
    Indigenous Mascots, Social Media and an Antiracist Intervention* (2017) 21
    Australasian J Infor Sys, online: <https://journal.acs.org.au/index.php/ajis/article
    /view/1590/780>.

75 See Alex Boyd & Omar Mosleh, "Edmonton Eskimos Name Change Is Praised by a
    National Inuit Group, Seen as a Step toward Dismantling Racism," *Toronto Star* (21
    July 2020), online: <https://www.thestar.com/news/canada/2020/07/16/edmonton
    -eskimos-to-make-major-announcement-amid-name-change-speculation.html>.

76 Online: <https://www.sbnation.com/nfl/2020/7/13/21322508/washington-nfl
    -football-team-nickname-change>.

77 See James [Sa'ke'j] Youngblood Henderson, *Indigenous Diplomacy and the Rights of
    Peoples: Achieving UN Recognition* (Saskatoon: Purich Publishing, 2008); Kristen A.
    Carpenter & Angela R. Riley, "Indigenous Peoples and the Jurisgenerative Moment
    in Human Rights" (2014) 102 Calif L Rev 173.

78 The first preambular text of the United Nations, *Universal Declaration of Human
    Rights* (1949) declares: "Whereas recognition of the inherent dignity and of the
    equal and inalienable rights of all members of the human family is the foundation
    of freedom, justice and peace in the world" (in Chickasaw translation: "*Hattakat
    yaakni ' áyya 'shakat mómakat ittíllawwi bíyyi 'ka . Naalhpisa 'at hattak mómakat
    immi '. Alhínchikma hattak mómakat ishtayoppa 'ni*"), online: <https://www.un.org
    /en/universal-declaration-human-rights/>.

79 See, Patrick Capps, *Human Dignity and the Foundations of International Law*
    (Oxford: Hart Publishing, 2009); Roberto Andorno, "Human Dignity and

Human Rights as a Common Ground for a Global Bioethics" (2009) 24:3 J Med
& Philosophy 223; Samuel Moyn, *The Last Utopia: Human Rights in History*
(Cambridge, MA: Harvard Univ Press, 2012).

80 John Ralston Saul, *The Comeback: How Aboriginals Are Reclaiming Power and
Influence* (Toronto, ON: Penguin Canada, 2014).

81 *Convention on Indigenous and Tribal Peoples in Independent Countries*, 1989, No.
169, 28 I.L.M.1382, online: <https://www.ilo.org/dyn/normlex/en/f?p=NORMLEX
PUB:12100:0::NO::P12100_ILO_CODE:C169>.

82 *Declaration on the Rights of Indigenous Peoples*, G.A. Res. 61/295, arts. 13–14, U.N.
Doc. A/61/L.67 (add.1, 12 Sept. 2007), online: <https://www.un.org/development
/desa/indigenouspeoples/wp-content/uploads/sites/19/2018/11/UNDRIP_E_web
.pdf>.

83 In December 2010, the United States withdrew opposition and "fully endorsed" the
Declaration, online: <https://2009-2017.state.gov/documents/organization/154782
.pdf>. For Canada's endorsement, see Address of The Honourable Carolyn Bennett,
Minister of Indigenous and Northern Affairs, to United Nations, 10 May 2016,
online: <https://www.canada.ca/en/indigenous-northern-affairs/news/2016/05
/speech-delivered-at-the-united-nations-permanent-forum-on-indigenous-issues
-new-york-may-10-.html>; Address by The Honourable Jody Wilson-Raybould,
Minister of Justice and Attorney General of Canada, to Assembly of First Nations,
Annual General Assembly, 12 July 2016, online: < https://www.canada.ca/en
/department-justice/news/2016/07/assembly-of-first-nations-annual-general
-assembly.html>.

84 In 2019, a private member's bill (C-262) by MP Romeo Saganash to make federal
law consistent with the *Declaration* passed the House of Commons but died in the
Senate after being blocked by Conservative senators. In 2019, the Government of
British Columbia enacted the *Declaration on the Rights of Indigenous Peoples Act*,
S.B.C. 2019, c. 44. The federal government of Canada implemented the *Declaration*
in the *United Nations Declaration on the Rights of Indigenous Peoples Act*, S.C. 2021,
c. 14. Canada has had a dismal record of implementing human rights covenants
that it has ratified: see Report of the Standing Senate Committee on Human Rights,
Promises to Keep: Implementing Canada's Human Rights Obligations (2001), online:
<http://www.parl.gc.ca/Content/SEN/Committee/371/huma/rep/rep02dec01
-e.htm>.

85 See Erica-Irene Daes, *DISCRIMINATION AGAINST INDIGENOUS PEOPLES
Study on the Protection of the Cultural and Intellectual Property of Indigenous
Peoples*, E/CN.4/Sub. 2/1993/28 (1993), Sub-Commission on Prevention of
Discrimination and Protection of Minorities, Commission on Human Rights,
UNESCO; Erica-Irene Daes, *Preliminary Report of the Special Rapporteur:
Protection of the Heritage of Indigenous Peoples*, E/CN.4/Sub.2/1994/31 (1994);
Erica-Irene Daes, *Final Report of the Special Rapporteur: Protection of the
Heritage of Indigenous Peoples*. E/CN.4/Sub.2/1995/26. (1995); Erica-Irene Daes,

Supplementary Report on the Protection of the Heritage of Indigenous Peoples, E/CN.4/Sub.2/1996/22 (1996); Erica-Irene Daes, *Protection of the Heritage of Indigenous Peoples*, UN Doc e/CN.4/Sub. 2/2000/26 (2000). See Siegfried Wiessner & Marie Battiste, "The 2000 Revision of the United Nations Draft Principles and Guidelines on the Protection of the Heritage of Indigenous People" (2000) 13:1 St. Thomas L Rev 383; Catherine Bell & Robert Patterson, eds, *Protection of First Nations' Cultural Heritage: Laws, Policy and Reform* (Vancouver, BC: University of British Columbia Press, 2009).

86 *Recommendations on the Safeguarding of Traditional Culture and Folklore*, UNESCO, 25th Sess., Vol. 1, Annex I, (1990) at 231.

87 *Promotion and Protection of the Rights of Indigenous Peoples with Respect to Their Cultural Heritage*, 2015, A/HRC/30/53 ENG.

88 Ruth Okediji, "Traditional Knowledge and the Public Domain in Intellectual Property" in Carlos Correa & Xavier Seuba, eds, *Intellectual Property and Development: Understanding the Interfaces* (Singapore: Springer, 2019) at 249.

89 Cree scholar Gregory Younging, "Traditional Knowledge Exists; Intellectual Property Is Invented or Created" (2015) 36:4 U Pa J of Int'l L 1077 at 1083–5. Greg Younging was one of the leaders of the Aboriginal Peoples in the WIPO Intergovernmental Committee of Intellectual Property and Genetic Resources, Traditional Knowledge and Folklore.

90 World Intellectual Property Organization, Traditional Knowledge, online: <https://www.wipo.int/tk/en/>.

91 World Intellectual Property Organization, Intergovernmental Committee on Intellectual Property and Genetic Resources, Traditional Knowledge and Folklore (2019), online: <https://www.wipo.int/meetings/en/details.jsp?meeting_id=50424>.

92 Charles Taylor, *Modern Social Imaginaries* (Durham, NC: Duke Univ Press, 1994).

93 Edward W. Said, *Culture and Imperialism* (New York, NY: Alfred A. Knopf, 1993); Stephanie Martins, *The Americas in Early Modern Political Theory: States of Nature and Aboriginality* (New York, NY: Palgrave Macmillan, 2016).

94 For an exploration of human dignity and how, when it is violated, the response is often aggression, violence, hatred, and vengeance, see Dona Hicks, *Dignity: Its Essential Role in Resolving Conflict* (New Haven, CT: Yale Univ Press, 2011), and *Leading with Dignity: How to Create a Culture That Brings Out the Best in People* (New Haven, CT: Yale Univ Press, 2019).

95 Thomas King, *The Inconvenient Indian: A Curious Account of Native People in North America* (Toronto, ON: Doubleday Canada, 2012) at 69.

Contributors

A. Christian Airhart was born and raised in Ontario on Anishinaabe Lands and is descended from settlers of English and German origin. His research has included a focus on the influence of political liberalism on Canadian law and its implications for Indigenous Peoples. Christian received his JD from Osgoode Hall Law School and is an associate at Paul, Weiss, Rifkind, Wharton & Garrison LLP in New York.

Michael Asch was born in New York City and is the child of progressive Jewish parents. He studied anthropology at the University of Chicago and Columbia University, and became a faculty member at the University of Alberta, after spending a year with Margaret, his partner, in a Dene community in the NWT. He subsequently went to the University of Victoria, where he is now a professor (limited term) in anthropology. Michael has devoted his work to advancing a just political relationship between Indigenous Peoples and the settler state. He has written and edited a number of books, including *Home and Native Land: Aboriginal Rights and the Constitution* (1984), *Aboriginal and Treaty Rights in Canada: Essays on Law, Equality and Respect for Difference* (1997), and *On Being Here to Stay: Treaties and Aboriginal Rights in Canada* (2014). He was an expert witness at the Mackenzie Valley Pipeline Inquiry, served as Research Director with the Dene-Métis negotiations secretariat between 1979 and 1990, and was a Senior Research Associate for Anthropology at the Royal Commission on Aboriginal Peoples. Dr. Asch received the 2001 Weaver-Tremblay Award in Canadian applied anthropology, was elected a Fellow of the Royal Society of Canada in 2002, and received a DLitt from Memorial University in 2010. His book, *On Being Here to Stay,* received the 2015 Canada Prize for the Social Sciences (English) from the Federation for the Humanities and Social Sciences.

Hannah Askew is an environmental lawyer and is currently the executive director of Sierra Club BC, a not-for-profit environmental advocacy organization.

She was born on Anishinaabe territory into a family of English and Scottish descent. When invited in, she is passionate about learning from Indigenous communities about their systems of law and governance. She previously worked as a researcher on Anishinaabe and Coast Salish legal orders for the Indigenous Law Research Unit at the University of Victoria and also worked with Tsilhqot'in and Ktunaxa Law as part of the RELAW project (Revitalizing Indigenous Law for Land, Air, and Water) at West Coast Environmental Law. She loves mountains, rivers, lakes, trees, plants, fish, birds, insects, and animals (including humans), and is always learning how to be a better relative.

John Borrows, BA, MA, JD, LLM (Toronto), PhD (Osgoode Hall Law School), LLD (Hons, Dalhousie, York, SFU, Queen's & Law Society of Ontario), DHL (Toronto), OC, FRSC, is the Canada Research Chair in Indigenous Law at the University of Victoria Law School in British Columbia, and Loveland Chair in Indigenous Law at the University of Toronto Law School. His publications include *Recovering Canada: The Resurgence of Indigenous Law* (Donald Smiley Award for the best book in Canadian Political Science, 2002), *Canada's Indigenous Constitution* (Canadian Law and Society Best Book Award 2011), *Drawing Out Law: A Spirit's Guide* (2010), *Freedom and Indigenous Constitutionalism* (Donald Smiley Award for the best book in Canadian Political Science, 2016), *The Right Relationship* (with Michael Coyle, ed.), *Resurgence and Reconciliation* (with Michael Asch, Jim Tully, eds.), *Law's Indigenous Ethics* (2020 Best Subsequent Book Award from Native American and Indigenous Studies Association, 2020 W. Wes Pue Best Book Award from the Canadian Law and Society Association). He is the winner of the 2017 Killam Prize in Social Sciences, the 2019 Molson Prize from the Canada Council for the Arts, the 2020 Governor General's Innovation Award, and the 2021 Canadian Bar Association President's Award. He was appointed as an Officer of the Order of Canada in 2020. John is a member of the Chippewa of the Nawash First Nation in Ontario, Canada.

Lindsay Keegitah Borrows has ancestral roots spread across western Europe: some ancestors came to Turtle Island/North America as early settlers, and others arrived as more recent immigrants. She is also of Anishinaabe descent and is a member of the Chippewas of Nawash First Nation. She draws strength and meaning from her family and territorial relationships with the rocks and forests of the Niagara Escarpment and sparkling waters of Georgian Bay. Her work focuses on the revitalization of Indigenous legal traditions for application in contemporary contexts. She has worked as a lawyer and researcher for the Indigenous Law Research Unit at the University of Victoria Faculty of Law, and for West Coast Environmental Law as part of the RELAW (Revitalizing Indigenous Laws for Land, Air, and Water) Project. Lindsay received her LLM from the University of Alberta Faculty of Law, her JD from the University of Victoria Faculty of Law, and her BA from Dartmouth College. She is a current

PhD candidate in law (U of A) and an assistant professor at Queen's University Faculty of Law.

Keith Thor Carlson was hired by the Stó:lō Tribal Council to be their staff historian in 1992 and has been has been working with Coast Salish Knowledge Keepers ever since. He currently holds the Canada Research Chair in Indigenous and Community-engaged History at the University of the Fraser Valley, where he has additionally been appointed Director of the new Peace and Reconciliation Centre. Individually or with partners Carlson has authored or edited eight books and over fifty articles. His scholarship has been translated into three languages, transformed into video documentaries and works of public art, and found expression in expert witness legal reports. Carlson was made an honorary member of the Stó:lō Nation in 2001 and was appointed a member of the Royal Society of Canada's College of New Scholars in 2017.

Aimée Craft is an award-winning teacher and researcher, recognized internationally as a leader in the area of Indigenous Laws, treaties, and water. She is an Indigenous lawyer (Anishinaabe-Métis), an associate professor at the Faculty of Common Law at the University of Ottawa, and an adjunct professor in law at the University of Manitoba. Her expertise is in Anishinaabe Law and Canadian Aboriginal law. She holds a University Research Chair entitled Nibi miinawaa aki inaakonigewin: Indigenous Governance in Relationship with Land and Water. Aimée prioritizes Indigenous-led, interdisciplinary, and collaborative research, including through visual arts and film. She co-leads a series of major research grants on Decolonizing Water Governance and works with many Indigenous Nations and communities on Indigenous relationships with, and responsibilities to, nibi (water). She also plays an active role in international collaborations relating to transformative memory in colonial contexts and to the reclamation of Indigenous birthing practices as expressions of territorial sovereignty. *Breathing Life into the Stone Fort Treaty*, her award-winning book, focuses on understanding and interpreting treaties from an Anishinaabe inaakonigewin (legal) perspective. *Treaty Words*, her critically acclaimed children's book, explains treaty philosophy and relationships.

Karen Drake is a member of the Wabigoon Lake Ojibway Nation and an associate professor and Associate Dean (Students) at Osgoode Hall Law School at York University. She researches and teaches in the areas of Canadian law as it affects Indigenous Peoples, Anishinaabe constitutionalism, Indigenous pedagogy within legal education, property law, and dispute resolution including civil procedure and Indigenous dispute resolution. She is a member of the legal advisory panel for RAVEN and previously served as a Commissioner of the Ontario

Human Rights Commission, on the Board of Directors of the Indigenous Bar Association, and on the Board of Directors of the Human Rights Legal Support Centre.

Emma Feltes is a settler of Irish, British, and German ancestry. She grew up in Toronto, on the traditional and ancestral territory of the Huron-Wendat, Haudenosaunee, and Anishinaabe Peoples. Her lineage includes working-class settlers in rural Quebec and suburban Ontario, middle-class Marxists from the United States, and upper-class colonialists during the British Raj in India. Each of these lines informs her understanding of whiteness and colonialism, and her place within it. Most of her formal education on colonialism in Canada has come through years of working with the Secwépemc and Tŝilhqot'in Peoples in the British Columbia Interior. Emma is currently a postdoctoral visiting scholar in anthropology at Columbia University. Her PhD dissertation, completed at the University of British Columbia, focused on the Constitution Express, seeking to draw attention to this historic movement and examine its political and legal implications today. She currently lives in Toronto with her partner Graeme, toddler Andie, and infant twins Max and Mabel.

Hamar Foster is a settler whose grandparents and great-uncles scattered over what was then the British Empire over a century ago in search of a better life, with those who came to Canada ending up in Manitoba, British Columbia, and the Yukon. Hamar was born in Alberta and began life in Fort Vermillion, where his father was an RCMP constable, before the family moved to BC. He and his partner have two adult daughters and two young grandchildren who are members of the Heiltsuk First Nation. Hamar practised law before joining the law faculty at the University of Victoria in 1978, where he is professor emeritus and taught until retiring in 2015. His main research focus has been on legal history and Aboriginal/Indigenous Law, especially with respect to BC. He has volunteered with organizations such as Project North and UVic's Speakers' Bureau to increase public awareness of the history of the struggle for Indigenous Land Rights and was an expert witness in *Tsilhqot'in Nation v British Columbia*. He was appointed a QC in 2010, and in 2019 the Canadian Historical Association awarded him their Clio Lifetime Achievement Prize (for BC). His most recent publication is an article on Gitanyow resistance to reserve surveys in 1927, in the *Manitoba Law Journal* (2020), vol. 43, issue 1, at 1–58. He is also a coeditor of, and contributor to, *To Share, Not Surrender: Indigenous and Settler Visions of Treaty Making in the Colonies of Vancouver Island and British Columbia*, published by UBC Press in December of 2021.

Hadley Friedland is an associate professor at the University of Alberta Faculty of Law. She is of non-Indigenous descent, with Jewish and Irish ancestors, and was taken in as an adolescent by a large family in the small Cree community of Aseniwuche Winewak Nation. She has been a married-in member for over twenty-five years and is a proud mother of two amazing children and aunty of over seventy amazing nieces, nephews, and now great-nieces and nephews. Dr. Friedland holds a Child and Youth Care diploma, an LLB from the University of Victoria, and an LLM and PhD from the University of Alberta. Her research focuses on Indigenous law, Aboriginal law, Family law and Child Welfare law, Criminal Justice, Therapeutic jurisprudence, and Community-led research. She helped establish and was first Research Director of the Indigenous Law Research Unit [ILRU] at the University of Victoria Faculty of Law and has had the honour of working extensively with Indigenous communities across Canada to identify and articulate their own laws. She has published numerous articles but is most passionate about collaboratively producing accessible Indigenous legal resources for Indigenous communities, legal professionals, and the general public. She is author of the book *The Wetiko (Windigo) Legal Principles: Cree and Anishinabek Responses to Violence and Victimization*. Dr. Friedland is Academic Director and Co-founder of the Wahkohtowin Indigenous Law and Governance Lodge, a dedicated research initiative developed to uphold Indigenous law through supporting community-led research.

Robert Hamilton was born and raised in Fredericton, New Brunswick, in Peace and Friendship Treaty lands and the unceded territory of the Wolastoqey Robert is an associate professor at the University of Calgary Faculty of Law, where he lives with his partner and two children. He holds a PhD from the University of Victoria Faculty of Law, a BA (Hons) in Philosophy from St. Thomas University, a JD from University of New Brunswick Law School, and an LLM from Osgoode Hall Law School. Robert has published on a range of legal issues concerning Indigenous Peoples and the state and the contemporary doctrine of Aboriginal Rights. He has also worked closely with First Nations on treaty rights, title, and governance issues.

Sa'ke'j Henderson. Born between the bear clan prophets of the red road and heir to the ruined past of the Chickasaw and Cheyenne Nations, I reluctantly found the mysterious, anguishing, and unraveling law road of the intruders toward restoring old ceremonies and awarenesses with new knowledge. I found love with Marie Battiste and our three children, served the Mi'kmaw Nation as constitutional advisor, and engaged in international Indigenous diplomacy. I have attempted to explain the lived law road to future generations in many books and articles.

Felix Hoehn is an associate professor at the College of Law, University of Saskatchewan. He is a first-generation immigrant, having been born in Darmstadt,

Germany, and coming to Canada at the age of seven. He studied at the University of Saskatchewan and the University of Toronto, and practiced law for about seventeen years before making academia his principal focus. He is the author of *Reconciling Sovereignties: Aboriginal Nations and Canada*, winner of the scholarly writing award at the Saskatchewan Book Awards in 2013. He also wrote *Municipalities and Canadian Law: Defining the Authority of Local Governments*. He has taught Aboriginal law, administrative law, property law, municipal law, and legal research and writing. He is a contributing editor of the *Canadian Native Law Reporter* and a part-time member of the Saskatchewan Municipal Board.

Charlene George ~ kQwa'st'not, M.A. Interdisciplinary Studies. A very good new day I am making this introduction following our oral tradition … My UYhwulmuhwSNÁis kQwa'ste'not … English name is Charlene George … I am from t'souke (a community that is Coast Salish~NuuChaNulth) & am honored to carry a second heritage English/French…. This blending of heritages speaks much of what my life & gifts have been … being a bridge to both heritages by finding the gifts … strengths & joy each brings … following that strong mind given by my grandparents … As an artist & scholar … weaving inspirations from culture … history … stories & the interconnected world into bridges to facilitate change…. With the goal … to make this world a better place for our children & many generations to follow … honoring past & blending future …

Kent McNeil is mainly of Scottish heritage. Besides McNeils, there are Hamiltons, Harrises, Lairds, and McDonalds in his family tree. He grew up in the relatively small prairie city of Regina in the 1950s when young kids were still free to explore. That vagabond spirit must have gotten into his blood because he spent his twenties wandering around the Americas and Europe. Upon turning thirty he realized he needed a career, so he returned to the law school in Saskatoon that he had dropped out of in 1969. It was just by chance that he was drawn to Indigenous Rights when Roger Carter offered him a job as a research associate at the University of Saskatchewan Native Law Centre. When he learned how Euro-Canadian law has facilitated colonialism, he decided to do what he could to turn the tables and use law to promote rather than undermine Indigenous Rights. For the past forty years, his research and publications have all been designed for this purpose. He retired from Osgoode Hall Law School in 2016 but is still actively engaged in supporting Indigenous Rights. The highest honour he has received was being made an honorary member of the Indigenous Bar Association in 2018.

Sarah Morales (*Su-taxwiye*), JD (University of Victoria), LLM (University of Arizona), PhD (University of Victoria), postdoc (University of Illinois), is Coast

Salish and a member of Cowichan Tribes. She is an associate professor at the University of Victoria Faculty of Law, where she teaches torts, transsystemic torts, Coast Salish Law and languages, legal research and writing, and field schools. Prior to joining the faculty at the University of Victoria, she taught Aboriginal law, Indigenous legal traditions, and international human rights with a focus on Indigenous People at the University of Ottawa Faculty of Law. Sarah's research centres on Indigenous legal traditions (specifically the traditions of the Coast Salish people), Aboriginal law, and human rights. She has been active with Indigenous nations and NGOs across Canada in nation building, inherent rights recognition, and international human rights law.

Joshua Ben David Nichols is originally from Treaty 8 Territory in Northeastern British Columbia and has mixed Métis-Anishinaabe roots. He is an assistant professor in the Faculty of Law at McGill University. He completed his PhD in law from the University of Victoria in 2017, where his research focused on the meaning of reconciliation, Aboriginal self-government, and the future of federalism in Canada. Prior to that, Joshua obtained a JD from the University of British Columbia, a PhD in philosophy from the University of Toronto, and a MA in sociology and BA (Hons) in political science from the University of Alberta. Joshua's work has been published in several leading journals, including the *University of Toronto Law Journal, Osgoode Hall Law Journal, UBC Law Review, Alberta Law Review*, and the *Journal of Historical Sociology*. His latest book is entitled *A Reconciliation without Recollection? An Investigation of the Foundations of Aboriginal Law in Canada*. He is a research fellow at the Wahkohtowin Law and Governance Lodge at the University of Alberta and a member of the Law Society of British Columbia.

Index